THE

# Royal Treasury

OF

# ENGLAND:

OR, AN

## HISTORICAL ACCOUNT

OF ALL

# TAXES,

UNDER

What DENOMINATION foever,

FROM THE

CONQUEST to this prefent YEAR.

Collected from the beft Hiftorians, as well Antient as Modern ; likewife from many valuable Manvfcripts in the COTTON, and feveral other choice Libraries, and fome peculiar Offices in this Kingdom.

Containing a confiderable Number of Particulars, not to be found in printed Books.

Shewing when the Crown was fupply'd, and Impofitions laid on the People, only by Virtue of the King's Prerogative, at what Times the Houfe of Lords alone has done the fame, and when reduc'd to the Parliamentary Method now Eftablifh'd.

Intermixt with fome other remarkable Occurrences.

THE LAWBOOK EXCHANGE, LTD.
Clark, New Jersey

ISBN 978-1-58477-400-6

Lawbook Exchange edition 2004, 2017

*The quality of this reprint is equivalent to the quality of the original work.*
*The irregular pagination is reproduced as it was found in the original work.*

THE LAWBOOK EXCHANGE, LTD.
33 Terminal Avenue
Clark, New Jersey 07066-1321

*Please see our website for a selection of our other publications*
*and fine facsimile reprints of classic works of legal history:*
www.lawbookexchange.com

**Library of Congress Cataloging-in-Publication Data**

Stevens, John, d. 1726.
    The royal treasury of England, or, An historical account of all taxes,
under what denomination soever from the conquest to this present year.
        p. cm.
    Originally published: London: Printed for T. Tebb and J. Wilcox, 1725.
    ISBN 1-58477-400-2 (cloth: alk. paper)
    1. Taxation—England—History. 2. Taxation—Law and legislation—
England—History. I.
    Title: Royal treasury of England. II. Title: Historical account of all
taxes. III. Title.

    HJ2603.S78 2004
    336.2'00942'0902—dc22                                        2003058949

*Printed in the United States of America on acid-free paper*

# THE

# 𝕽𝖔𝖞𝖆𝖑 𝕿𝖗𝖊𝖆𝖘𝖚𝖗𝖞

OF

# ENGLAND:

OR, AN

## *HISTORICAL ACCOUNT*

OF ALL

# TAXES,

UNDER

What DENOMINATION foever,

FROM THE

CONQUEST to this prefent YEAR.

Collected from the beft Hiftorians, as well Antient as Modern; likewife from many valuable Manufcripts in the COTTON, and feveral other choice Libraries, and fome peculiar Offices in this Kingdom.

Containing a confiderable Number of Particulars, not to be found in printed Books.

Shewing when the Crown was fupply'd, and Impofitions laid on the People, only by Virtue of the King's Preroga- tive, at what Times the Houfe of Lords alone has done the fame, and when reduc'd to the Parliamentary Method now Eftablifh'd.

Intermixt with fome other remarkable Occurrences.

*LONDON:* Printed for T. TEBB, and J. WILCOX, in *Little-Britain.* MDCCXXV.

# THE

# PREFACE.

HE Revenues of the Crown being a Contribution from which very few are exempted, and having, of Consequence, in many Reigns, given Occasion, or at least a Pretence, to the Clamours of the People, are a proper Subject to raise the Curiosity of most Men; and as yet I know not of any one that has undertaken to satisfy them fully in this Particular. Mr. Madox, in his History of the Exchequer, has exerted himself, and met with universal Approbation; informing the World of all the Proceedings and Management in that Ocean, into which all the Rivers of the various Branches of the said Revenues do continually flow. However, that Work is of another Nature, and not calculated to mention all that every King receiv'd, which is the only Design of this small Volume; wherein all the several Taxes rais'd upon the Subjects in every Reign are exactly collected, under their several Denominations; by which it will appear, what Princes were most plentifully supply'd, and what Use was made of the Generosity of their Subjects. All that shall be said in Favour of this Undertaking, is, that it has been collected

a                                                                          from

*from moſt of the Authors, who have written the Hiſ-
tory of this Nation ſince the Conqueſt; for before that
Time little or nothing can be ſaid of this Matter. We
will therefore proceed, in the firſt Place, to explain all the
ſeveral Denominations, under which the Royal Treaſury
has been ſupply'd; which cannot be better done than from
the above-mention'd Author, who is ſo knowing in thoſe
Affairs, and deſcribes them in the following Manner.*

### Notable Branches of the Crown Revenue.

Mr. Madox's *Hiſtory of the* Exchequer, p. 202.

The Demeaneland of the Crown, at the Time of
the Conqueſt, and during ſome Reigns after, was
very conſiderable, as appears by *Doomſday-Book,*
&c. *p.* 202.

*Eſcheats* were another Part of the Crown Revenue, comprehending not only thoſe Lands which
were moſt properly call'd *Eſcheats,* but alſo thoſe
which at ſundry times after the Conqueſt became
veſted in the Crown, either by Devolution, Forfei-
ture, Seizure, or perhaps ſome other Title.

Vacancies of Biſhopricks, and ſuch Monaſteries
as were of Royal Foundation and Patronage, yielded ſome Revenue to the Crown, the Kings uſing
to ſeize and enjoy their Temporalities till the Vacancy was fill'd. *p.* 207.

Treſpaſſes and Miſdemeanors likewiſe were
made uſe of to add to the Royal Revenue, Seizures being made on thoſe Accounts, and the Parties, whoſe Lands had been ſo ſeiz'd, making Fine
to the King for Reſtitution of the ſame. *p.* 215.

Feudal and other Profits, *viz.* Reliefs, Ward-
ſhips, Marriages, &c. *p.* 216.

Ferms of the Counties of the Realm (when they
were letten to Ferm) or the Iſſues of the Cuſtody
of

of them (in cafe they were put into Cuftody). *p.* 223.

Ferms of Towns, Burghs, and Gilds of Merchants. *p.* 226.

Fines, *Oblata* and Amerciaments made another Part of the Crown Revenue, which was very confiderable, efpecially during the Reigns of the firft Kings after the Conqueft. Thefe may be reduc'd to two Claffes; Fines and Amerciaments for the Foreft, and Fines and Amerciaments in Civil and Criminal Cafes. *p.* 272.

Manifold Fines were paid for Grants and Confirmations of Liberties and Franchifes of fundry Kinds; as, *p.* 272.

1. Fines to have Juftice and Right.

2. Fines for Writs, Pleas, Tryals, and Judgment.

3. For Expedition, or Difpatch of Pleas, Tryals, and Judgment.

4. For Surceafement, or Delay thereof.

5. Fines payable out of Debts to be recover'd. *p.* 293.

6. Fines for Leave either to hold, or to quit certain Offices, or Bailywicks. *p.* 315.

7. Fines for Licences to marry, or that they might not be compell'd to marry, by Tenants *in Capite. p.* 320.

8. Fines relating to Trade and Merchandize. *p.* 323.

9. Mifcellaneous Fines, that cannot be reduc'd under particular Heads. *p.* 325.

10. Fines for the King's Favour, or good Will, and that the King would remit his Anger and Difpleafure. *p.* 327.

11. Fines for the King's Protection and Aid. *p.* 329.

12. Fines to obtain the King's Mediation, or Interpofal in Men's Affairs. *p.* 332.

a 2      13. Fines

13. Fines to have Seisin, or Restitution of their Lands, or Chattels; and that they might not be disseis'd. *p. 333.*

14. Fines that Men might be discharg'd out of Prison, and replevy'd or bail'd to the Custody of lawful Men. *p. 341.*

15. Fines for Persons accused to be acquitted in certain Cases. *p. 344.*

16. Fines about holding of Lands, and several other Cases too long to be here mention'd.

17. Concurrent Fines, when both Parties fined to obtain the same Thing.

18. Counter-Fines, when two Parties fined, one for a Thing, the other against it.

*Note,* That all these sorts of Fines were generally very inconsiderable, and not so numerous as to amount to a Sum worth speaking of in any one King's Reign. *p. 347.*

Amerciaments are so much of the Nature of Fines, that it is not worth Time to speak of them apart; for indeed very little Difference will appear between them. Such as desire to be further satisfy'd as to that Point, may have recourse to *Madox's History of the* Exchequer. *p. 365.*

## Of the Revenue arising by Aids.

The Aid payable out of Baronies and Military Fees was an honourable kind of Service, or Duty, render'd by a free Vassal to his Lord. It has been observ'd by Writers, that in *England* there were in ancient Time three Sorts of Aid due to the Lords from their immediate Tenants, of common Right, or by reason of Seigniory; to wit, Aid to make his eldest Son a Knight, to marry his eldest Daughter, and to ransom his Person, when taken in War. These Aids were paid by those who held of the

King

King *in Capite,* which was to hold of him immediately, *sine Medio.* Towns and Manors also, which the King held in Demeane, paid Aid to him. *p.* 396.

In Procefs of Time, the Word Aid came to be us'd in a large indefinite Senfe.

Next fucceeded a new Word, *Subsidy,* not much us'd in ancienter Times. *p.* 421.

Efcuage, or Scutage, was a Duty or Service arifing of Fees holden of the King *in Capite,* as Baronies and Knights Fees. It denoted *Servitium Scuti,* the Service of the Shield; and was wont to be render'd thus, to wit; for every Knight's Fee the Service of one Knight; for every half a Fee the Service of half a Knight; and fo in proportion. Baronies were charg'd with Efcuage after the like manner; to wit, according to the Number of Knights Fees (whether they were more, or fewer) whereof the Barony by its original Enfeofment did confift. This Service of Scutage was perform'd two ways, either perfonally in the King's Army, or elfe by pecuniary Commutation. It is true that the Word *Scutagium,* when us'd in an extenfive Senfe, did anciently fignify any Payment affefs'd upon Knights Fees, whether fuch Payment was for the Army or not. Thus the Aid arifing out of Knights Fees for ranfoming of King *Richard* I. is call'd *Scutagium ad Redemptionem Regis*; and other Aids fet upon Knights Fees were alfo fometimes call'd Scutages. *p.* 431.

Scutage was alfo render'd for Fees holden of Honours and Efcheats, which were in the King's Hands; and for Fees holden of Lands purchafed by the King; and for Fees holden of the King's Wards during the Wardfhip. For the Tenants holding of the King's Wardfhips and Efcheats, were immediate Tenants to the King, whilft the Wardfhips and Efcheats refted in him. *p.* 447.

There

There were alfo fome Serjeanties that paid Efcuage. *p.* 452.

Efcuage was not chargeable upon Lands holden
in Frankalmoigne of Royal Foundation, or in So-
cage. *p.* 466.

As the Lord who held of the King *in Capite* by
Knight's Service paid Efcuage to the King for his
Knights Fees ; fo the Tenants of fuch Lord, who
held of him the fame Fees by Knight's Service,
paid Efcuage for the fame to their Lord, according
to the Quantity of their Tenure ; and then the Lord
was faid *habere Scutagia fua*, to have his Efcuage,
to wit, of his Tenants. The Tenants paid Efcuage to their Lord, to enable him to pay his Efcuage
to the King, or to reimburfe him when he had paid
it. When the Lord holding *in Capite* did perfonal
Service in the King's Army, or paid or became duly charg'd with his Efcuage to the King, he was
entitled to have Efcuage of his Tenants, for the
Fees which they held of him, and which he held of
the King *in Capite*. In this Cafe, the Lord might
*jufticiare Tenentes fuos*, compel them by Diftrefs to
pay him Efcuage ; or if he could not himfelf *jufticiare Tenentes fuos*, he often had a Writ of Aid directed to the Sheriff to affift him. *p.* 469.

Danegeld was different from either Aid, Efcuage,
or Tallage. It was firft fet on foot in the *Anglo-Sax-
on* Times. However, it continu'd for many Years after the *Norman* Conqueft. It is not certain whether
it was a fettled yearly Revenue. The Author of
the Dialogue concerning the *Exchequer* feems to have
thought it was a yearly Revenue in the Times before the Conqueft, but not afterwards. *p.* 475.

Tallage was of two Sorts, one paid to the King,
the other to a fubordinate Lord, of which latter it
is not of our Purpofe here to fpeak. The Tallage
render'd to the King (excluding the Tallage of the
*Jews*)

*Jews*) was rais'd upon his Demeanes, Efcheats and Wardfhips, and upon the Burghs and Towns of the Realm. In the elder Times it was ufually call'd *Donum* and *Affifa*. *Donum* was a general Word, and us'd with great Latitude. When it was paid for or out of Lands which were not of a Military Tenure, it fignify'd Hidage ; when it was paid out of Knight's Fees, it was Scutage ; and when it was paid by Towns and Burghs, it was Tallage. Thofe Manors and Lands were properly talliable to the King, which the King had in his own Hands, and under the fame were comprehended the King's Efcheats and Wardfhips. Moreover, fome Serjeanties were wont to be tallag'd together with the King's Demeanes ; that is (I fuppofe) certain Petit Serjeanties of an ignoble and inferior Kind, and fuch as had no Military Service annex'd to them. If Men were not the King's immediate Tenants, they were not tallageable to the King, but to their immediate Lord. The Tallages affefs'd upon the King's ancient Demeanes were more heavy than the Tallages upon other Perfons living in the Counties at large. When a Town was tallag'd, the Tallage was rais'd upon the Men of the Town ; and they were properly the Men of the Town, who belong'd to the Gild, and made Merchandize in the Town. *p.* 480, 497, 498, 499, and 500.

Carucage was alfo a Duty paid to the King in ancient Time; to wit, fo much for each Carue of Land holden by bafe or inferior Tenure. Of this Duty we find but little Account. *p.* 502.

*None, Difme, Quinzieme, Vintifme, Trentifme,* were fo call'd from the Quantity and Proportion of their Payment, as the feveral Names do import. *p.* 503.

Tallage was wont to be affefs'd upon the Men of the Demeanes and Towns, fometimes *in communi* ; fometimes by the Poll, *per Capita,* or *per fingulos* ;

at

at other times, partly one of thefe ways, and partly the other. Tallage was not demandable of
Lands held in Frankalmoine. *p.* 506.

Cuftom paid to the King was anciently wont to
be call'd in *Latin,* *Confuetudo* and *Cuftuma.* *Confue-*
*tudo* was us'd in an extenfive Senfe, for Payments
or Duties of many Kinds.

There was a Cuftom or Duty paid to the King
for Wines, which was call'd *Prifa* and *Recta Prifa* ;
the Proportion of which was one *Dolium* before the
Maft, and another behind the Maft. 'Tis true,

*Prifa* is a Word of equivocal Meaning: Properly
it fignify'd *Capture,* and was fometimes us'd for
Captures taken in War ; fometimes for Purveyance,
Impoft, or Capture of other Kinds. *p.* 525.

*Difme, Quinzime,* &c. were alfo taken of Merchants trafficking along the *Thames* ; and this Duty,
or at leaft one Part of it, was call'd *Avalagium*
*Thamifiæ. p.* 529.

To thefe Duties may be added thofe paid to the
King's Chamberlains of *London* for his Ufe ; the
Duties arifing at *Billingsgate,* and by Tronage. *p.* 531.

In Procefs of Time, the King's Cuftoms came
to be moft generally call'd *Cuftuma,* and were wont
to be laid on Wool, Pelts, or Skins with the Wool
or Hair on, and Leathers. *p.* 535.

*Having faid thus much concerning the Duties in gene-*
*ral, it will not be improper to fee from the fame Gentle-*
*man, how the Payments were made ; with a Word of old*
*Coins and Mints,*

In the Time near the Conqueft there was in *Eng-*
*land* very little Money in *Specie* ; the general Payments were by Services, by Work, and Provifions.
Till the Reign of K. *Henry* I. the Rents and Ferms
due to the Crown were render'd in Provifions and
Neceffaries for his Houfhold ; but in K. *Henry* the
Firft's Reign the fame were chang'd into Money ; and

in fucceeding Times were chiefly anfwer'd in Gold and Silver, and Horfes, Dogs, and Hawks, &c. *Hift. Excheq. p.* 186.

Payments *ad Scalam* and *ad Penfum* were by Weight. Twenty Shillings was then a Pound, and the Officers took Six Pence over, called Vantage-Money. This kind of Payment was very ancient. When Payment was made *ad Penfum,* the Payer was to make good the Weight, tho' he had allow'd the 6 *d.* over. To prevent Fraud in the Finenefs, as well as Weight, part of the Money was melted down, called Combuftion. There were two Sorts of Payments by Combuftion, real and nominal; real, when a Sample of the Money was put into the Furnace; nominal, when a 20th Part of a Pound was taken and accepted in lieu of actual Combuftion.

When Money paid in was melted down, or the Supplement made by adding one Shilling to each twenty, the Ferme was faid to be dealbated or blanched. So 100 *l.* thus paid into the *Exchequer,* after Combuftion, was faid to be 100 *l.* Blank. Payments made *Numero,* or by *Tale,* is our modern Way. *Ibid. p.* 187.

Payments, or at leaft Computations, were made by Pounds, by Marks, half Marks, Shillings, Pence, &c. Silver Marks, and half Marks; Ounces, and half Ounces of Gold. The Mark of Gold was equivalent to fix Pounds of Silver, or fix fcore Shillings of Silver. The Ounce of Gold was equivalent to 15 *s.* Silver. The Pound of Silver was 20 *s.* The Mark of Silver 13 *s.* 4 *d.* The Shilling 12 *d. Ibid. p.* 189.

In King *Stephen's* Time there was a Coin call'd *Denarius.*

A Bezant was of the Value of two Shillings, and that was anfwer'd in lieu of a Talent.

About the Year 1175 (22 *Hen.* II.) new Money was made in *England. p.* 190.                    In

In or about 1207 (9 K. *John*) there were feve-ral Mints in *England*; as at *Winchefter*, *Exeter*, *Chi-chefter*, *Canterbury*, *Rochefter*, *Ipfwich*, *Norwich*, *Lynn*, *Lincoln*, *York*, *Carlile*, *Northampton*, *Oxford*, *Bury*, *Durham*.

About the Year 1318, (12 *Edw.* II.) at *London* and *Canterbury* was minted, between the 11th of *June* and 19th of *November*, being the 11th Year of his Reign, and to the 21ft of *April* in his 12th Year, 40730 *l. p.* 198.

*Having explain'd all the feveral Denominations of Taxes and Contributions, and how the Payments were made, with fomething of Coins and Mints from the Hif-tory of the Exchequer, the next fhall be a* M·S. *in the Cotton Library, fhowing by whom firft, and how often afterwards, thofe Duties were levy'd, with the many Con-tefts about Purveyors,* &c.

### Cotton Library, Cleopatra, F. VI. Fol. 60.

## Money rais'd by Impofitions for Defence of the State.

For fuppreffing Incurfions and Piracy upon the Coaft by the *French* (as formerly Danegelt was among the *Saxons*) Tonnage and Poundage was granted by Parliament in the forty-fifth Year of *Edward* III. and was rais'd of every Tun of Wine 2 *s.* and of every Pounds worth of Merchandize 6 *d.* And two Fifteenths, with the like Poundage, in the forty-feventh Year. The Tonnage, with the laft, being renew'd in the fecond Year of *Richard* II. for eleven Months only. And both of them granted in the feventh of the fame King for one Year. And in the tenth of the fame King, for Guard of the Sea, half a Tenth and Fifteenth granted. And
the

the Tonnage improv'd to 3 *s.* and the Poundage to
1 *s.* was granted for one Year to him; and, by feveral Admittats, fo continued until the twentieth
of his Reign.

Two Shillings Tonnage and eight Pence Poundage were impos'd the fecond of *Henry* IV. and fo
continued, with one Year's Intermiffion, unto his
Death. *Henry* V. held them, as his Father did, all
his Life. And fo did *Henry* VI. but with two
Years Intermiffion. And *Edward* IV. his firft Year;
and, after his third, held them both, at the laft
Rate, for Term of Life. To *Henry* VII. they were
advanc'd, the one to 3 *s.* and the other to 12 *d.*
and continued the moft part of his Reign without
Interruption. Thus, what in the firft Nature was
not invefted perpetual in the Crown, but permiffive and reftrictive, as pleafed the Affent and Occafion of the general State, is now become no conditional Gratuity, but a prerogative Duty.

## *Money rais'd for Conclufion of Peace.*

King *William* II. to procure and buy Peace at
the Hand of his elder Brother, was inforc'd to
borrow of his Subjects 1000 *l.* And in the Time
of *Richard* II. in the Year 1395, the Clergy and
Commons grant the King a Moiety of a Tenth
and a Fifteenth for Conclufion of a Peace with
*France.*

## *For fuppreffing of Herefies and Defence of the Church.*

To *Henry* II. 1166, was given from the Value of
every Man's Eftate 12 *d.* in the Pound, for Defence of the Church. And in the Year 1290, the
Clergy grant a tenth, and the Laity a fifteenth
Penny

Penny of all their Goods, to work the King for
expelling all the *Jews.* And the 4th of *Richard* II.
there is granted by the Clergy a Tenth, and by the
Commons a Fifteenth, for that the King fhould
put his helping Hand to the Subverfion of the
*Wickliffian* Herefy.

## *For advancing the King's Children.*

*Henry* I. rais'd the Portion of his Daughter
*Mawd,* the Wife of the Emperor *Otho,* by impofing of 6 *s.* upon every Hide of Land. And at the
Marriage of *Henry* IId's. Daughter to the Duke of
*Saxony,* there was a Contribution laid upon the Subjects of *Danegelt.* An Impofition, call'd *Carucage,*
which is two Marks upon every Plough Land,
was taken by the third *Henry* for the Marriage of
his Sifter *Ifabell* to the Emperor. And the fame
King had 20 *s.* *Scutage* for the Marriage of his
eldeft Daughter. And *Edward* III. levied his Sifter's Dowry by Collection from Spiritual Men, as
appeareth *Rot. Clauf. Anno* 7 *Edward* III. 1 *pars.*
And to produce Precedents of Record for Allowance due to the King's eldeft Son, and his Knighting, there needeth fmall Labour.

## *Money rais'd for paying of the King's Debts.*

*Richard* I. to reduce the Debt his Ranfom had
laid upon him, took not only of all the Rents in
*England* the 4th Part, but all the Wools of the
*Ciftercian* Monks; and further tax'd the Clergy fo
heavily, that they were conftrain'd to fell the
Church Ornaments, as Pope *Clement* VII. did, when
the Army of the Emperor *Charles* befieged *Rome,*
who melted all the holy Veffels to pay the Soldiers.
The Debts King *John* was grown into to *Philip* of
*France,*

*France,* he paid with the Impofition of 3 *s.* upon
every Plough Land.    And to difcharge the Sums
due to the Earl of *Britain* from *Henry* III. 1232, a
40th Part of all Mens Goods, Spiritual and Temporal, was granted the King.    The Debts of this
King are fumm'd up by *Matthew Paris* to 950000
Marks, the daily Intereft amounting to 100 *l.* fo
that he was inforced to take the Tenth of the
Clergy for five Years, befides a Benevolence from
the Prelacy of 42000 Marks, and 40 *s. Scutage* of
the common People            is the Leventh he
receiv'd.    *Edward* II. being in Debt, fent his
Writs *de Pecunia mutuanda* to all the Bifhops and
Abbats of the Kingdom.    For relieving the great
Neceffities of *Edward* III. in the 43d Year of his
Reign, by reafon of Debts, the State gave freely
40 *s.* Subfidy of every Sack of Wool.    And when
*Richard* II. to fupply his Wants, was inforc'd to
pawn his Jewels, the Parliament did rate the Head
of every Man and Woman at 12 *d.* Payment, befides the Subfides of Wool, as in former Times.

## *For increafing of the Treafure.*

The Ways, that either Record or Story hath
publifh'd the Kings of this Realm to have us'd for
the enriching their Coffers, befides fome Parcimony,
hath been in daily taking of Benefits, or dearly
felling their Favours : And the firft are either by
Impofitions ancient, ufual, or thofe more late and
burdenous. In the firft Rank will be thefe of *Danegueldt, Scutage,* and others.

*Danegueldt* was, as is before mention'd, levied by
the Hide-Land, upon which was rated fometimes
12 *d.* fometimes 4 *s.* as the Hiftory of *Henry* of
*Huntingdon* teftifieth, at 6 *s.* by the Conqueror.

*Scutage*

*Scutage* is an Impofition not mention'd before the Reign of *Henry* I· who by it raifed in that Time, at one Taxation entire, as *Gervafius Dorober- nienfis* faith, 124000 *l.* This continued until *Richard* II. where, in the 9th of his Reign, there is a Petition in Parliament, it may be pardoned.

*Carucage*, an Impofition of 2 *s.* by King *John* upon a Plough Land.

*Tenementale*, as the *Carucage* afore, a Duty by *Richard* I· fet upon every Plough Land, as *Rogerus Hoveden* teftifieth; who likewife took 5 *s.* of the fame, as appeareth by *Walter* the Monk of *Coventry.*

*Tallagium.* It was by the Commiffioners of *Edward* II. in the 6th of his Reign, gathered of all his Boroughs, Cities and Demaynes, and was 15ᵉ *de Mobilibus* and 15ᵈ *de Redditibus.*

Many more ancient Duties there are, that be lo- cal, as that of 1000 Marks yearly Penfion from *Lincoln* to the King for his Mantle of Sables; which may be overpaffed.

The Collections, that are next offer'd, are either fuch as are permiffive and by Leave, or fuch as Princes have in their Will or Neceffity done. Of the firft, they are either from Gift, or Loan; if from the firft and publick, they are Subfidies, Tenths, Fifteenths, or the like. The feveral Numbers, as by Record, I can refer them to their particular Mafters. *Henry* III. received, as appeareth by the Stories of his Time, twelve; *Edward* I. feven- teen; his Son, three; and *Edward* III.
*Richard* II. twenty-two; *Henry* IV. ten; his Son, fix; *Henry* VI. feventeen; and *Edward* IV. fix. *Richard* III. one; *Henry* VII.          *Henry* VIII·
           *Edward* VI.                  *Mary*
       *Elizabeth*

Amongft the Gifts that Sovereigns have exacted from their Subjects, that mention'd by *Matthew*
                                              *Paris*

*Paris* of *Henry* III. deferveth Note, who, in the Year 1249, demanded of the wealthieft Citizens New-Years Gifts, and refted not until they had given him 2000 *l.*

The next Courfe in colleﬔing Money, which is by Loans, hath been ancient, as appeareth by the Stories of our Nation; remembring in King *Henry* the IId's Time, and his Sons, fometimes 5000 *l.* and 8000 *l.* wrefted from the *Londoners* in that Kind. And that hath been in this Sort frequent lately, and fometimes, for Neceﬃty, with our Neighbour Nations; as with the Merchants of *Frankfort, Antwerp,* and *Aufpurg,* in the Times of both the laﬔ Princes.

Another Kind of gathering fome Kings of this Realm have faﬃhioned, out of their Will and Power; as in pulling from the Church, as the Conqueror did, the Treafure laid up in Religious Houfes; or, as *Edward* I. the Colleﬔion made for the Pope; or the Lands of the Friers Aliens, allotting them to flender Stipends; or, as a Sovereign of the State lately did, all. But Error in fuch taking is of more Blame than that of *Edward* II. who in the 5th Year of his Reign, under Pretence of being mifled and deceiv'd, refum'd moft of his Grants of Penfions and Offices; and, in the 8th Year, thofe of his Manors and Seigniories, according to an Ordinance by himfelf made, with the Advice of the Prelates, Earls and Barons only; and, in the 10th of his Reign,recalleth *omnes Donationes faﬔas ad Damnum & Diminutionem Regis & Coronæ fuæ.* And the Commons made Petition in a Parliament 1 *Richard* II. to which the King yielded, that the Grants of *Edward* III. to unworthy Perfons might be recall'd. The like Petition in Parliament was in 1 *Henry* IV. who in the 6th of his Reign recalled all Patents for Life, or Years, granted fince the 40th of *Edward* III. as
likewife

likewife all Hereditaments, Liberties and Cuftoms, that fince that time were in the Crown.

The like Refumption did *Henry* VI. make in the 28th of his Reign, reaching to all Grants made fince his Coronation. That by *Edward* IV. in *Anno* 3, was the like, looking back to the firft of his Reign. And fuch another there is in the 12th of the fame King, revoking all to that Day. And one in the 3d of *Henry* VII. refuming divers Offices made by *Edward* IV. or *Richard* III.

The later Means, wherewith fome of the Kings have much (although with Blemifh) enhanced their Wealth, hath been by Sales, even often of common Juftice. So did *Henry* VII. his Letters to Judges for Expedition of Suits; and in bargaining with Creditors, his Name to advantage them in recovering of their Debts; for Liberties and Immunities conferring or confirming, as well to Places Corporate, as Societies, he made a Benefit, tho' not as *Richard* I. who feigning, as *Radolphus de Coggefhall* faith, to have loft his Seal, caus'd all that claim'd by former Grants, to fine a-new at his Pleafure. The like did *Henry* III. at his full Age, rating his Fines by the Judgment of his own Chief Juftice. By Sale of Offices did *Henry* VII. attain much Money. Neither was it the Blemifh of thefe Times only; for King *John* was not afhamed to leave 5000 Marks, his Price of the higheft Chancellor's Place to *Graye*, upon Record. As for the Bar of free Trade by referv'd Patents, fome Parliaments of elder Days have admitted Monopolies; as that of the 29th of *Henry* the VI.th, in which, for Fine of 8000 *l.* the only Trade of Allome was confirmed to certain Merchants of *Southampton.* Of Grants in this Nature, and Licences of tranfporting Commodities by Law forbidden, and Difpenfations with Penal Statutes, King *Henry* the VIIth did raife, for divers Years, the Sum of 116000 *l.*

*Provifion*

*Provision for the King's Houshold by Purveyors.*

Of this laſt Branch touching Purveyors, I only can, my Lord, obſerve unto your Honour, ſuch Fragments of Records as I have collected ; wherein perchance ſomewhat your Lordſhip may obſerve, whereof your Judgment can make far better Application than any bold Direction of mine.

*William* Biſhop of *Ely* and Chancellor, 1190, took for Proviſion of *Richard* I, of every City two Palfreys and two Sumpter Horſes, and of every Abbey one Palfrey and one Sumpter Horſe.

Ordinations were made in 18 *Edward* I. in Parliament, *de Priſis pro Rege capiendis.*

And 8 *Edward* II. an Ordination was made *per Regem & Concilium de pretio victualium particulatim limitato.* Dors. Pat. *Anno* 8 *Edward* II. Part 2. *m. n.* and this is alſo recall'd by Proclamation, *Anno* 9 *Edward* II.

And 9 *Edward* II. the Sheriff of *Lincoln* is commanded to bring Wood for the King's Fuel, from *Sherewood* Foreſt to *Lincoln,* by the Country Carriage.

And the ſame Year an Ordination *de ferculis Eſculentorum* &c. *ad menſas Nobilium & aliorum moderandas,* and a Proclamation *contra Proviſores Victualium pro Hoſpitio Regis.*

The 10 *Edward* II. There is a Reward *de inquirendo de Miniſtris Regis Victualia & Blada capientes ad opus Regis & ad commodum ſuum convertentes.*

And for the Price of Corn for the King's Proviſion, there is a Record the ſame Year of that King's Reign.

And the 11th of the ſame King, upon Complaint that divers following the Court *Bona Subditorum nomine Regis & Hoſpitia capiunt,* the King

appointeth

appointeth certain to overfee that no fuch Fault be committed.

And the fame Year an Order is fet down, that no Man fhall take *Victualia aut alia mercimonia contra voluntatem poffefforum nifi foluto pretio.*

And there is further an Order made, that they which fhall take Victuals *nomine Regis contra voluntatem poffefforum tanquam Felones puniend'.*

And in *Anno* 16 *Edward* II. a Commiffion is granted to punifh fuch as fhall, contrary to certain Ordinances made by the King and his Council, take any Victuals.

And in the 2d Part *Pat. Anno* 17 *Edward* II. there is one *William de Northwell* appointed to overfee all the Purveyors, that they do their Duties without Exaction of the People.

And in the 18th Year of the fame King, there is an Order fet down for the Queen's Houfhold, wherein moft of the Officers have their particular Limitations.

And there is alfo an Inquifition of the Prices, and of Exactions ufed by the Officers of the King's Houfhold, contrary to the Ordination made by *Edward* I.

In the 5th of *Edward* III. there is a Decree made that no Purveyors but for the King, Queen and his Children, by good Warrant and ready Money, be made.

And 8 *Edward* III. enacted, no Purvey to be, but for the King.

And 13 *Edward* III. the Commons defire the Purveyors, tho' with Commiffion, may be arrefted if they pay not.

And 17 *Edward* III. the Commons defire Remedy againft the outragious taking of the Purveyors. The King anfwer'd, the Statute fhall be obferv'd.

And

And 18 *Edward* III. there is a Statute about Purveyors printed.

And the same Year the Commons defire that thofe
Purveyors that take not with them the Conftable,
according to the Statute of *Weftminfter*, may be
taken as Thieves; but to this there is no Anfwer by
the King.

The Commons defire *Anno* 22 *Edward* III. that
Purveyors by Indenture may take the Victual. The
King anfwereth, the Laws heretofore fhall fuffice.

The Commons 25 *Edward* III. defire no Purveyors to be made for Hay or Oates. The King anfwereth the Statute fhall be obferv'd.

*Anno* 25 *Edward* III. There is another Statute
touching Purveyors.

The Commons defire the fame Year, that the
Subject may be paid for Victual taken up. The
King faith it fhall be with Opportunity.

And in the 28 *Edward* III. a Petition is made
by the Commons, that Purveyors may make prefent Payment under 20 s. and of greater in a
quarter of the Year. The King's Anfwer is, that it
is good to pay according to the firft Payment, and
to redrefs the fecond.

In the 36th Year of *Edward* III. there is a printed Statute of Purveyors.

And 47 *Edward* III. the King's Anfwer in Parliament is, that no Man fhall be impeach'd for re-
fifting the Purveyors, if they deny ready Payment.

And 50 *Edward* III. the Commons by Petition
defire, that the King's Carriages for himfelf and
Houfhold, may be by his own Horfes. To which
the King anfwereth, that he knoweth no Means to
work it.

The Commons by Petition *Anno* 51 *Edward* III.
defire the Execution of the Statute of Purveyors,
all which the King alloweth.

And 1 *Richard* II. there is a Statute printed of Purveyors ; and another printed Statute *Anno* 7 of the fame King ; and another in the 2 *Henry* IV.

*Anno* 4 *Henry* IV. the Commons by Petition, defire that the Statute made 36 *Edward* III. touching Purveyors may be obferved; which the King granteth.

In the 5th of *Henry* IV. two Fifteens are granted, upon Condition, that Purveyors fhould not take their Goods or Carriages againft their Wills.

And 8 *Henry* IV. the Commons praying Payment for Victuals due by the Purveyors, taken fince the time of the King's Coronation, which the King granteth.

The Speaker in Parliament *Anno* 9 complaining againft the Abufe in Purveyors, the Steward and Treafurer of the King's Houfe do promife Remedy.

And 11 *Henry* IV. the King promifeth convenient Payment for Victuals taken by Purveyors.

And 3 *Henry* V. that Purveyors take no Provifion in Markets without the good Will of the Party. The King anfwereth the Statutes fhall be obferv'd.

And 1 *Henry* VI. there is a printed Statute of Purveyors, and one other touching the Affize againft Purveyors, *Anno* 11 *Henry* VI. And another 23 of the fame King. And thefe be all I can haftily ob-obferve for your Honour ; and in thefe thus much out of the hard Succefs in all the Contentions againft them by the Commons ; that were they not requifite for the King's Service, and a Minifter raifed out of his Prerogative, they could never have ftood.

And therefore if it be a Prerogative, then it is clear, by Opinion in Parliament, 21 *Richard* II. that whatfoever Law fhall contradict the Prerogatives given the King in his Coronation is void and
revo-

revocable by the Law ; and there be divers Laws in Parliament, that do confirm the fame ; and therefore, if in M A G N A   C H A R T A there is any thing to impair it, paffed, it may be feared to be in fuch Regard avoidable.

*The next fhows what the Power of Kings once was, and how they were wont to fupply their own Wants.*

*Cotton Library,* Cleopatra, F. VI. *Fol.* 80. *in Sir* Robert Cotton's *own Hand.*

**M**oney raifed by the King without Parliament from the Conqueft until this Day, either by Impofition or free Gift, taken out of Records or ancient Regifters.

*William* I. to furnifh his Wars in the fourth Year of his Reign, took all the Money, Jewels, and Plate out of Religious Houfes. He reduc'd the Land of the Church into Knights Fees, expelling fuch as oppos'd that Work. He rais'd out of every Plough Land Hidage and Danegelt divers times, fometimes at 2 s. fometimes at 6 s. the Hide or Plough Land.

*William* II. his Son that fucceeded, raifed of the Bifhops and Religious Perfons, great Sums ; of fome, as *Lincoln,* 500 Marks, in the fifth Year of his Reign. In the 7th Year, of 20000 Footmen to go for *Normandy,* he took 20 s. a Man, and fo difcharg'd them. To furnifh his Brother *Robert,* upon the Pawn of *Normandy,* for the holy Voyage, much Money he got from the Abbots, Nobles and wealthieft Subjects, in the 9th of his Reign ; and Danegelt of all his People, long keeping, to encreafe his Treafury, the Revenues of the Religious Houfes in Vacancy.

*Henry* I. (the laft of the Firft *William's* Sons) in his 10th Year, took 5 s. Danegelt ; and often after the like.            **b 3**                          His

His grand Child, *H.* II. in the firſt 5 Years levied once Scutage, and in the 6th thorough all *England* ; which amounted to 102004 *l.* the Standard of Silver being then not the third to ours. In his 7th Year the like, at 2 Marks every Knight's Fee, for the Charge of his Siège before *Toloſe.* The fourth for the ſame Service he levied in his 8th Year, aſſeſt at one Mark each Fee. An Aid he had in 11th *pro ſervientibus inveniendis in exercitu Walliæ.* And the 14th of his Reign, for Marriage of his Daughter, Scutage, rated at a Mark of all that held in Knight Service ; and of thoſe in Soccage, Danegelt, being by the Hide or Plough-Land, having the Year before taxed the Church and Laity, at 12 *d.* in the Pound for one, and a Penny in the Pound for four Years after, all Perſons to anſwer their juſt Eſtates upon Oath. The 18th he took his ſixth Scutage for his Army in *Ireland,* at 20 *s.* the Fee. The ſeventh and his laſt was the 33d of his Reign, 20 *s.* the Scute, for his Forces in *Galloway* ; and dying, left 900000 *l.* in Bullion, beſides his Jewells and Regal Ornaments.

*Richard* his Son ſucceeding, commanded his firſt Year a large Benevolence from all his Subjects, under the Title of Almes, becauſe he pretended it for the Holy Land. In the ſecond, his Chancellor Biſhop of *Ely,* impoſed upon every City and good Town, two Horſes of Service, and two Hackneys : And of every Abbey and rich religious Houſe, one of either. In his fifth Year, his Juſtices by that Ordinance, levied in his Abſence, the 4th Part of the Clergy and Nobilities Goods, and of the *Ciſterciaſ* Monks, the Woolls. Hidage under a new Name *Tenementale* he impos'd at 2 *s.* every Plough, the 3d Part of Scutage ; and forced the White Monks again for Money to redeem their Wools. His ſixth Year, having in this time by account of

his

his Treafury fpent *undecies centena millia Marcarum.* In the tenth he took again of every Plough Land 5 *s.* and faining to have loft his old Seal, whilft he was Prifoner in *Almayne,* inforc'd all that would enjoy their Lands or Liberties, to fine for Confirmation under his new.

*John* fucceeded his Brother, and took of every Knight's Fee two Marks his firft Year, and twice the fecond three Shillings of every Plough Land. A Tenth he impos'd the third for the Holy Land. Of the next five there is no mention in Record or Story. In the ninth he took of all Goods the tenth Part; and in the twelfth 100000 *l.* of the Clergy. In the thirteenth he taxed every Knight's Fee that attended not his Wars in *Wales,* at two Marks, and affeffed on the *Ciftercian* Monks in the fourteenth 22000 *l.*

*Henry* III. his Son, his fecond Year, impos'd two Marks on every Fee; and the third a Talliage on the *Jews* 2 *s.* in every 5 of every Plough Land, to fupport his Eftate; and the Year following twice Scutage, once at 10 *s.* then at two Marks the Knight's Fee. In the eighth on every Plough Land of the Clergy half a Mark, of others 2 *s.* which the Record calleth *Subfidium voluntarium.* In the ninth 2 *s.* Carucage of every Plough Land, two Marks of every Knight's Fee, and the fifteenth *de mobilibus & redditibus* of all Boroughs. In the tenth a fifteenth Part of all Goods of the Church and Laity. And for confirming the great Charter, he impos'd a fifteenth in the eleventh Year. The next he took 5000 Marks of the *Londoners,* befides their fifteenth. Relief of divers Boroughs, as of *Northampton* 1200 *l.* and changing his Seal, inforc'd all to renew their Patents under a Fine. In the fourteenth, this King took two Marks of every Knight's Fee, and the Pope's Legate a tenth of the Clergy. In the next

b 4 he

he impos'd large Sums upon the Churchmen and Jews. The 17th 40 *s.* of every Fee, and of Moveables the 40th Part. *Everfden,* in his Regifter, writes down how it was collected. In the 18th 20 *s.* Scutage, and in the 20th two Marks of every Plough Land by the Name of Carrucage.

Twice in the 22d Year he took of all Moveables the 30th Part, and the Year following 40 *s.* of every Knight's Fee. In the 24th he took the third Part of all Debts due to the Jews; a fifteenth of all Subjects Goods affefs'd by the Juftices itinerant, and the Pope the fame Year a thirteenth of all the Clergy, rated by his Legat. Of fuch as went not in this King's Service into *Gafcoine* and ferved *in capite,* he took 20 *s.* The Compofition that divers then made, remains yet on the File Rolls; and impos'd an Aid upon the *Premonftraten-fes* and *Ciftercian* Monks for thofe Wars, in the 26th of his Reign. Forty Shillings of every Knight's Fee he took the Year following, rating the Jews at 20000 Marks; and levied Victual in *England* upon the publick Charge, to maintain his Army in *France.*

In 28, *Edward* his Son, for maintenance of the Wars in Foreign Parts, impofed upon the *Irifh* a Subfidy, with *provifo quod non trahetur in Confequentiam.* The Father in *England* commanding, that all Merchant's Money put to Ufury fhould be feiz'd to his Ufe, and their Bodies imprifon'd ; raifing a Tallage thro' *Wales,* and impofing great Sums upon the *Jews* and *Londoners :* Taxing the next Year that City at 1500 Marks, and all that ferved in Knights Service, at 20 *s.* the Fee, for marrying of his Daughter. In the 30th 40 *s.* Scutage for the Siege of *Gaunvell* Caftle ; and exacteth in the 34th great Sums of Money of the *Londoners* and others, under the Name of New Years Gifts. A Tallage by the

the Name of *Cornagium* he impofeth to be yearly
after levied by his Itinerant Juftices, in 36. Of
the *Londoners*, he affefleth 5000 Marks, in his 38th
Year; and the next keepeth the Lands of all vacant religious Houfes, to pay his Debts. Again
of the *Londoners* in 40 he levieth 3000 Marks, and
of the *Jews* 1000, binding the Houfes of Religion
to pay his Debts unto the Pope, the Sum being
250000 *l.* the Intereft amounting to 100 *l.* a Day.
The Citizens of *London* are once more, the fucceeding Year, taxed at 5000 Marks; and in the 42
40 *s.* Scutage impofed, being the eleventh in this
King's time; befides an Aid of all his Subjects, for
which he promifeth to fettle the State of the King-
dome with fpeed, in Order. The 44th he taketh
the 30th Part of the Clergy's Goods, and 300000
Marks of the *French* King, for the Releafe of *Normandy*. He affefs'd on the Clergy a 10th for fix
Years, and took the 20th Penny of the Laity in 51.
to furnifh the Prince in his holy Journey, he tax-
eth all his Subjects with the 15th Part of their
Goods; and Tallage of all the Demain Lands of
the Crown.

*Edward* his Son fucceeding, impofed the firft
Year Tallage *per capita*, appointing Commiffioners
to fee it levied. The next Year he took a 10th
from the Clergy, exiling all Ufurers under Confifcation of Goods and Bodies Prifonment; and of
the *Jews* he levied for Tallage 5000 Marks the
Year fucceeding. In the 4th Year he taxed his
Subjects at a 15th, and the *Jews* at 5 *d.* a Head.
A Tallage through *Wales* he affefs'd the 6th Year,
and 40 *s.* Scutage the next; 40 *s.* he took of every
Knight's Fee. In the 13th and the 15th on the
*Jews* he impos'd 12000 Marks for Redemption of
the Ufury. The next Year he fearched one Day all
the religious Houfes, and took to his Ufe, the Money

ney and Plate. The Lords by themfelves without the Commons, afſeſs'd for the King the 18th Year, ſuch a Levy as *Henry* III. rais'd for Marriage of his Daughter. And in the 12th the King chargeth the Clergy with a 10th for ſix ſucceeding Years. The Abbeys are again ſearched in 22. And the Lands of the Priors Aliens ſeized into the Kings Hands.

The Times ſucceeding this Princes Reign, afford Examples in this Kind, of Sovereign Power, more rarely than before; for Parliaments becoming more frequent, and almoſt annual ſupply'd their Sovereign at all Occaſions.

*Edward* II. impos'd 2 *s. ultra antiquam conſuetudinem* upon all the Goods of Merchants Strangers, in his 2d Year, no other Exerciſe of Royal Power falling within my Obſervation in his Time.

*Edward* III. impos'd Tallage thro' all his Domains, in his 6th Year.

Of *Richard* II. I find no Preſident of Regal Power in this Sort uſed.

*Henry* IV. levied ſo great a Sum by Contribution upon his People, in the 8th of his Reign, that he deſired *ut Evidentia poſt datum Compotum cremaretur.* A Contribution he took to defray his Voyage into *France* in his laſt Year.

*Henry* VI commanded in his 15th Year, two of each Pariſh to appear before Commiſſioners to ſerve in Perſon in his Wars, or allow in Money the Rate of two Days Expence, according to their Degree and Quality. And in the 32d he chargeth the Lords Spiritual and Temporal with a Benevolence for Defence of *Calice,* and hath it willingly, according to the Proportion of his Demand that there is rated.

*Edward* IV. in his firſt Year, hath of the Clergy a Benevolence, which in the Record is call'd a voluntary Subſidy. And in the 12th, led on by the

Advice

'Advice of Parliament, of the three Estates, to undertake the Recovery of his            for which they
grant him Supply by Subsidies, which falling short
of his Occasions, he taketh of his People a Benevolence.

*Henry* VII. had of all his Subjects for a Voyage
into *France*, a voluntary Gift in his 7th Year; and
to aid the *Christians* against the Incursions of the
*Turks*, he impos'd an Aid upon his People, at the
Popes Request, in the 17th of his Reign.

*Henry* VIII. levying an Army to invade *France*
and assist the Duke of *Bourbon*, demandeth of his
People a Contribution, which he calleth an Annual Grant, which tho' with some Distraction and Dis-
taste, was yet collected in his 14th Year. A Benevolence was paid in the 21st into the *Exchequer*,
where Priors and Clergymen of like Ability, are rated
at 40 *l.* Knights at 40 Marks, Esquires at 10 *l.* and
Persons of inferior Quality, at 5 Marks. He gathered in 37 and 38 of his Reign, for urgent Occasions touching his Person and State, (for such are
the Words of the Instructions) two several Grants
of free Gifts from his Subjects; the last being stiled
*Devolution Money* was most collected in the first of
*Edward* VI.

A Project was drawn in the late Queen's time,
1598, by Advice of her Council, for a Benevolence,
and the like is in the Lord *Burleigh*'s Hands, in the
Book.

*To these I will add one more Manuscript out of the
same Library and Volume, showing to what Extremities
some Kings have been reduc'd, and what Methods they
have taken, to ease themselves in some Measure of the
Pressures they lay under.*

*Cotton*

*Cotton Library,* Cleopatra, F. VI.

### Extremity *beyond Exactions of the People occa-*
### *sion'd by War.*

Having thus far with as light a Hand as I could
drawn down the many and mighty Burdens of the
Common-Wealth, if but with a touch of the Princes
Extremity beyond the Eafe of thefe former Helps
I heighten up this Draught, it will with much more
Life and Luftre, exprefs the Figure of Wars Mife-
ry. The Credit of our Kings it hath brought to fo
low an Ebb, that when by force of Neceffity they
borrow'd Money, they could not take it up by col-
lateral Security and extreme Intereft, as *Edward* III.
in the Patent to *William de la Poole* confeffeth, that
*propter defectum Pecuniæ negocia sua periculofiffima fue-*
*runt retardata,* (they are the Words of the Record)
and the Honour of him and his Royal Army, *mag-*
*næ fuiffet depreffioni patenter expofitus & progreffus non*
*fine suo dedecore perpetuo impeditus,* if *De la Poole* had
not as well fupply'd him with the Credit of his Security, as with the beft Ability of his own Purfe;
for which Service he honoured him and his Pofterity with the Degree of Baronets, and 500 *l.* Land
of Inheritance.

The Intereft of *Henry* III. *ad plus quam centum quo-*
*tidie Libras afcenderat; ita ut immineret tam Clericis*
*quam populo Angliæ defolatio & ruina.* The late
Queen was enforc'd to the like thrice with Strangers upon the City of *London*'s Infurance, as before,
and with her own Subjects after, upon Mortgage
of Land; a Courfe more moderate than either that
of the firft *William,* that took out of Churches fuch
Money as feveral Men had committed thither for
more Security; or that of *Charles* the Firft, that to
repair

repair the Wafte of his *Italian* Wars, went in Perfon to *Barcelona* to feize into his Hands a Maffe of
Money call'd *Depofitum Tabulæ*, which as well Strangers as Subje  ̆s had there laid up in San  ̆uary.
But thefe are not the Condition of Princes of our
time only, for in the Lives of *Caligula, Nero* and
*Vefpafian, Suetonius* of them feverally writeth, *Extrac-
tus & egens calumniis rapinifque intendit animum* : For
*perniciofa res eft in Imperatore tenuitas* ; and as *Theodo-
ricus* faid *Periculofiffimum animal eft Rex pauper:*
  It hath abated the Regalties of Houfe, as, 3 *Edward* II. 36 *Edward* III. 1, 4 and 6 *Richard* II. 4, 7
and 11 *Henry* IV. 12, 18 and 31 *Henry* VI. when
as well for want of Means as the Subje  ̆s Petitions
in Parliament; for *expeditiffima eft ratio augendi Cenfus,
detrahere fumptibus,* they have much leffen'd their
Hofpitality, their Tables being either defrayed by
their Subje  ̆s, as 18 *Henry* VI. or as *Henry* III. con-
*fueta Regalis Menfæ hofpitalitas abbreviata fuit, poftpo-
fita folita verecundia, cum abbatibus Clericis & Viris fa-
tis humilibus hofpitia quæfivit & prandia.*
  It hath caus'd our Kings to fell and alienate the
Poffeffions of their Crown, as *Henry* III. who gave
to *Edward* his Son *Licentiam impignorandi terram Vaf-
coniæ,* to pawn a Dutchy ; and himfelf not long after, by the like Occafions, releas'd for 300000 *l.*
(except fome Pitances referv'd) the entire Seigniory
of *Normandy.*
  What our late Miftrefs and her Father did, is
frefh in Memory, but this Mifchief hath trenched
deep into the Fortunes and Afflictions of the Sub-
jeds, when Princes to repair the Breach of their
own Revenues, have receiv'd the Poffeffions of their
People, as 6 *Henry* III. 5, 8 and 10 *Edward* II. *omnes donationes per Regem factas ad damnum & diminutionem Regis & Coronæ fuæ.* 5 *Richard* II. did the
like of all Grants made to unworthy Perfons by
                                                    his

his Grandfather, and recall'd all Patents dated since the 40 *Edward* III. Thus 1, 2, 6 and 8 *Henry* IV. 1 *Henry* V. and 28 *Henry* VI. the 3 and 12 *Edward* IV. and 3 *Henry* VII. with all Offices of his Crown granted either by the Usurper or his Brother. Neither is this in itself unjust, since as well by Reasons of State, as Rules of the best Government, the Revenues and Profits *quæ ad sacrum Patrimonium Principis pertinent* should remain firm and unbroken; and therefore many of our best Princes, to avoid as well the Effect as Importunity of Suitors have secretly wrought forward their Commons in Parliament to petition Redress in this Point, not by Restraint of the Sovereign's Bounty, but the Subjects Capacity, putting such impudent Suitors out of the King's Protection, as, ⸺⸺⸺

But when neither Credit, Frugality, nor Sale of Lands would stop the Gulph of Want, our Princes have been so near beset, as with *Nero* and *Anthonius* (the Emperors) to sell and pawn their Jewels. The Archbishop of *York* had Power from *Henry* III. (*An.* 26 in Wars beyond Sea) *impignorandi Jocalia Regis ubicunque in Anglia pro Pecunia perquirenda.* *Edward* I. sendeth *Egidius Andever ad Jocalia sua impignoranda.* *Edward* II. pawneth his Jewels to pay the Ld. *Beaumond* and other Strangers their Wages in War. The Black Prince was constrain'd to break his Plate into Money to pay his Soldiers. *Richard* II. pawned *Vasa aurea & diversa Jocalia* to Sir *Robert Knowles.* 3 *Henry* IV. to a Merchant for Money *invadiavit Tabellam & Frisellas suas Argenteas de Hispania.* *Henry* VI. gageth and selleth to the Cardinal of *Winchester* and others, in the 10th, 12th and 29th Years, many Parcels of his rich Jewels. And the late Queen in the end of her Days, to ease her Subjects, did the like with much in the *Tower.*

But

But Extremity hath yet ſtretch'd ſome of our Kings to ſo high a ſtrain of Shift, that *Edward* III. *invadiavit magnam Coronam Angliæ,* pawn'd the Imperial Crown three ſeveral times, *Anno* 17. *in partibus tranſmarinis,* and twice to Sir *John Weſenham* his Merchant, firſt in the 24th and after *Anno* 30, in whoſe Cuſtody it remained eight Years. To *Henry* Biſhop of *Wincheſter, Henry* V. *invadiavit magnam Coronam auream* in the 5th of his Reign. And when *Henry* III. had laid to gage *omnia inſignia regalia,* all his Robes and Kingly Ornaments, and upon Aſſurance of Re-delivery or Satisfaction, had pawn'd *Aurum & Jocalia feretri Sancti Edwardi Confeſſoris* (a Courſe more moderate, than by Force to have taken as *William* the Conqueror did, the Challices and Shrines of their Churches; or as *Clement* the VIIth who to pay the Soldiers of *Charles* V. melted the Conſecrated Veſſels) was in the end, when he had neither Means of his own left, nor Reputation with others, forc'd to beg Relief of his Subjects in this low Strein; *Pauper ſum omni deſtitutus Theſauro Neceſſe habeo ut me juvetis, nec aliquid exigo niſi per gratiam.* And turning to the Abbot of *Ramſey,* ſaid, *Amice obnixe ſupplico quatenus me juves, mihi centum Libras conferendo,* adding withal, *majorem Elemoſinam fore ſibi juvamen conferre pecuniare quam alicui oſtiatim mendicanti.* So that of the Waſte of theſe Times, and Want of theſe Princes, I may truly with the Satyriſt ſay,

*Oſſa vides Regum vacuis exuta medullis.*

*Theſe Manuſcripts are Curioſities which it is thought will be acceptable to moſt Readers, and to give them any further Account of this Work, ſeems ſuperfluous, the Deſign and Uſe of it being ſo obvious to all Perſons.*

# THE
# ROYAL TREASURY
## OF
# *ENGLAND.*

## K. WILLIAM I.

AVING fubdu'd *England* by Force of Arms, behav'd himfelf accordingly like an abfolute Monarch, difpofing of all Things at his Pleafure, as having none to queftion his Actions. His Will was a Law, and all the Land and Treafure of the Nation he look'd upon as his own. He ftood not in need of Parliaments to fupply his Wants ; nor could he want, who had it in his Power to take all that his Subjects poffefs'd. Having therefore reduc'd all the Kingdom to his Obedience, he diftributed the greateft Part of the Lands among his *Normans*, and others, who had help'd him to gain them ; by which means he fecur'd their Affections, and fo deprefs'd the Natives, that they were in no Condition to do him Harm. The Lands he had fo difpos'd of he divided into Baronies, and Knights Fees, obliging every Baron and

B                                    Knight,

Knight, on account of thoſe Eſtates, to ſerve him at his own Coſt, in his Wars, with a certain Number of Men, proportionable to what he had conferr'd on him. Thus the Wars were then maintain'd with much leſs Expence to the Crown, the Army being compos'd of Soldiers and Officers, who receiv'd no Pay, as being before paid by the Tenure of their Poſſeſſions.

Beſides this, he had Lands of his own in every County throughout the Kingdom, and reſerv'd to himſelf Quit-rents and Chief-rents upon all other Eſtates. The Lands being all held of the Crown, upon moſt capital Offences became again forfeited to it, which was ſtill a great Addition to the King's Revenue.

The *Norman* Army had pretty well rifled the People of the little Treaſure that was in their Poſſeſſion; but ſome of the wealthier Sort had taken care to conceal what they could in Mona-ſteries; upon Information whereof made to the King, he caus'd all thoſe Depoſits to be brought into his Treaſury, as properly appertaining to him. Some Authors, who can ſpeak well of no Kings, have ſaid, that with the aforeſaid Treaſure he alſo took to himſelf all the Plate belonging to thoſe religious Houſes, and even the ſacred Veſſels de-dicated to the Uſe of Churches, a ſacrilegious Violence not to be ſo ſlightly fix'd upon that Mo-narch, whoſe Character is much fairer with thoſe who had moſt Reaſon to know him beſt. Among theſe *Gulielmus Pictavienſis*, or *William* of *Poictiers*, whom Biſhop *Nicholſon*, in his Hiſtorical Library, has been pleas'd to repreſent as an Hiſtorian of good Credit, and whoſe Reputation is certainly great with moſt Lovers of Truth, liv'd at the ſame Time with King *William* the Conqueror, and left us his Life in writing. This Author juſtifies
the

the said Conqueror, and his single Testimony is sufficient to weigh down that of many others, in regard that he deliver'd what he saw and knew, whereas the others afterwards impos'd upon Posterity the uncertain Stories handed about among the *English*, who for some Ages bore an implacable Hatred to the *Normans*, that then kept them under, of whom they could not speak with any Charity. This *William* of *Poictiers* assures us, that *William* the Conqueror was a religious Prince, that he was not in the least tainted with Avarice, and that he never opprefs'd his Subjects with unjust Exactions; much less would he rob the Churches of their Plate, as some have maliciously suggested, and among them *Matthew Paris*, an Historian much esteemed by some for his railing Temper.

Besides, in the last Page of Dr. *Gale's* first Vol of *Historiæ Britannicæ & Anglicanæ Scriptores XX,* where he speaks of *Doomfday Book*, we have the following Account of that Monarch, as I translate it into *English*. Of how great Authority *Doomfday Book*, made by *William* the *Norman*, is in deciding Controversies relating to the *Ancient Defmefne*, can scarce be unknown to any Man. This I put them in mind of, which has been observ'd by few, that *William* himself was often cast by the Authority of this Book, and submitted to what was in it decreed against his Will and unjust Possession. *For he being Conqueror subdu'd Harald and his Party; yet did not abolish the Rights, Laws and Customs of the* Englifh *People, but submitted himself to them; and would allow himself no Privilege more than others. Neither did he take any thing from any* Englifh *Man, but what the Laws adjudg'd to him.* This is the Character there given of him; let any Man judge how different it is from what some peevifh Writers have falfly suggested of him.

This, however, the Conqueror did, that whereas before his Time the Bishopricks and Abbies were exempt from all secular Service, he brought them under the Obligation of Knights Service, on account of the Baronies they possess'd, appointing what Number of Soldiers each of them should furnish him, and his Successors with, in their Wars; which seem'd to him most reasonable, in regard that the Possessions of the Church being very large, if they had been altogether exempt from contributing to the necessary Defence of the Kingdom, the Burden must have fallen very heavy upon the Laity, and perhaps have prov'd deficient in Times of great Danger.

Next he caus'd an exact Survey of the whole Kingdom to be taken, dividing every County, Hundred, Wapentach, and greater District into Hides, and Plow-Lands; by which means he knew how many Acres of Land there were in the Nation, not taken in the gross, but distinctly how much Arable, Meadow, Pasture, Common, Wood, Marsh, or any other Sort whatsoever, and tax'd the same according to its Value. He also caus'd all Cities, Towns, Boroughs and Villages to be rated in like manner. This Survey was fairly enter'd upon Vellum, and is preserv'd to this Day in the *Exchequer*, by the Name of *Doomsday-Book*, so call'd, because an universal Discovery, and no Person exempted.

What all these Incomes of the Conqueror might amount to is not possible to be known, there being no Estimates extant even of those Sums which he rais'd by way of Tax; nor can there be any of all the other Profits he made by the several Ways above mention'd. The same Obscurity will remain under some ensuing Reigns, till those Matters begin to come into a clearer Light.

For

For the better illuftrating of this Matter, Recourfe has been had to the feveral curious Pieces written by learned Men, whofe original Manufcripts are preferv'd in the *Cotton Library,* under feveral Heads, but relating to the fame Subject, which fhall be here inferted under each King. The firft of thefe by the following Title,

*Impofitions and Taxes on the State, gather'd out of Monkish Regifters, and Stories, from the Conqueft to* Henry *the 7th.*

This Tract is of the Hand of the famous Antiquary *Leland, Cleopatra, F. 6. Fo.* 145. What relates to King *William* the Conqueror is thus, as tranflated from the *Latin :*

The Duty of *Danegeld* was firft eftablifh'd on account of the Pirates ; for they infefting the Country did their utmoft to lay it wafte. In order to check their Infolence, it was decreed that *Danegeld* fhould be paid yearly, *viz.* 12 *d.* for every Hide of Land throughout the County, for the Maintenance of thofe that fhould oppofe the Irruptions of the Pirates. All the Church was exempted from this *Danegeld* ; as alfo all the Land that was in the proper Demefne of the Church, wherefoever it lay; fo that it contributed nothing towards this Payment ; becaufe they had more Confidence in the Prayers of the Church, than in the Defence by Force of Arms. This Immunity the *Englifh* Church preferv'd, till the Days of King *William* the younger. See King *Edward's* Laws, Fol. 128. of *Danegeld.*

In the Year of our Lord 1070, King *William* the Conqueror, having difpos'd of the Cities, and Caftles, and plac'd Officers of his own in them, fail'd over into *Normandy* with the *Englifh* Hoftages, and immenfe Treafure. *Mat. Paris. p. 6. lin.* 11.

*Ab.*

*An. Dom.* 1070, the 4th of his Reign, King *William*, in *Lent*, caus'd all the Monasteries in *England* to be search'd, and order'd the Money which the richest of the *English* had deposited there, on account of his Severity and Rapine , to be taken away. *Gualt. Gisborn.* And spar'd not the Chalices and Shrines, *Mat. Paris. p. 8. l. 29.*

He also brought under military Servitude all the Bishopricks and Abbies that held Baronies, and till then had been exempt from all secular Service, enrolling each Bishoprick and Abby according to his Pleasure, every one of them to furnish him and his Successors in time of War with as many Soldiers as he thought fit : And laying up the Rolls of this ecclesiastical Servitude in his Treasury, banish'd out of the Kingdom many religious Men who oppos'd this Decree. *Mat. Paris. p. 8. l. 30.*

*An. Dom.* 1075 , *Walter*, Bishop of *Durham*, purchas'd the Earldom of *Northumberland* of King *William*, and extorted an immense Sum of Money from all the Inhabitants of that Province, as well Nobles as Vassals. *Mat. Paris. p. 12. l. 40.*

At length the People being reduc'd to extream Poverty by the continual Exactions of the Bishop and his Ministers, were much provok'd, for that they were oblig'd to such exorbitant Contributions, without any Intermission. Hereupon all the People rose up in Arms against the Bishop, and slew him. *Mat. Paris. p. 12. l. 43.*

*An. Dom.* 1083, the 17th of this Reign, King *William* sent his Justices to all the Counties of *England* in particular, to enquire how many Acres of Land were sufficient for one Plough every Year, in each Township, and what Number of Cattle might suffice for tilling one Hide. *Mat. Paris. p. 14. l. 39.*

He alſo caus'd Inquiſition to be made, what
Aſſeſſment the Cities, Caſtles, Towns, Villages,
Marſhes and Woods paid yearly, and how many
Knights there were in each County throughout the
Kingdom. *Ibid.*

All theſe Particulars being reduc'd into Writing, and brought to *Weſtminſter,* are preſerv'd to
this Day in the King's *Exchequer.* The great
Book, wherein all theſe Things are contain'd, is
called *Doomſday;* becauſe it ſpares no Man, as will
happen on that great Day. *Mat. Paris.* in his ſhort
Hiſtory.

Afterwards he took ſix Shillings in Silver of each
Plough-Land, or Hide, throughout the Kingdom.
*Mat. Paris. p.* 14. *l.* 45. and *H. Huntington.*

*An. Dom.* 1084, the 18th of his Reign, *William,*
King of *England,* receiv'd the Homage of all Men
throughout *England,* and an Oath of Allegiance,
whatſoever Fees, or Tenements they held ; and
having right or wrong extorted great Sums of
Money from all People promiſcuouſly, ſail'd over
into *Normandy. Mat. Paris. p.* 15. *l.* 9.

*An. Dom.* 1085, the 19th of the Reign, unjuſt
Taxes, and wicked Cuſtoms ſwarm'd in *England;*
and the more the *Engliſh* exclaim'd, the more they
were oppreſs'd. *Mat. Paris. p.* 15. *l.* 18.

Another MS. of the Hand of Sir *Robert Cotton,*
in the ſame Volume above quoted, (entitled,
*Money rais'd by the King without Parliament from the
   Conqueſt untill this Day, either by Impoſition, or free
   Gift, taken out of Records, or ancient Regiſters* )
In a few Words ſums up all the Exactions of this
ſame King, without taking notice of all thoſe Re-
proaches caſt upon him, as above, by *Matthew
Paris.* It runs thus :

*William* I. to furniſh his Wars, in the 4th Year
of his Reign, took all the Money, Jewels, and

Plate

Plate out of religious Houfes, to furnifh him in
his Wars. He reduc'd the Land of the Church
into Knights Fees, expelling fuch as oppos'd that
Work. He rais'd out of every Plough-Land Hide-
age and *Danegeld* divers times; fometimes at 2 *s.*
fometimes at 6 *s.* the Hide, or Plough-Land. *Walt.*
*Gisborn*, *Mat. Paris*. *Hen. Huntingdon*.

Much the fame is again repeated of King *Wil-*
*liam* the Conqueror , in another MS. in the fame
Vol. above quoted, fol. 9. which is therefore here
omitted. So alfo in another Tract ftill in the fame
Volume, fol. 6. entitled, *The Courfes by the Kings*
*of* England *ufed in raifing Money for Defence of the*
*Realm, by Power of Prerogative ,* what follows is
faid of the fame King's Reign, *viz.*

The Kings of *England*, both before and fince
the Conqueft, ever took, as an ufual Duty ( to
fupply fuch Charge, as either the fecuring of the
Land from Invaders Spoil, or the Sea from Rovers
Piracy, fhould enforce them to) *Danegeld*, or *Gelda*
*Regis*, fefs'd by the Hide Land, but by no Rate
definite ; for fometimes it was 12 *d.* as by *William*
the Conqueror, *&c.* Next we proceed to

# K. WILLIAM RUFUS,

SON and Succeffor to the Conqueror, who govern'd, as his Father had done, in a defpotick
manner, as inheriting all his Rights, and confequently had the fame Property in all Lands. As
for other Ways of raifing Money, he fpar'd no
manner of Rapine or Simony ; for as foon as
Bifhopricks and Abbies became vacant, he feiz'd
all their Temporalities, and farm'd them out to
his Favourites, or to fuch as giving moft for them
did not fpare to rack thofe Poffeffions for their
own

own Profit ; and after all, he conferr'd not those, or other ecclesiastical Dignities, on Persons of Merit, but sold them to the highest Bidder, by which means he rais'd very considerable Sums upon the Church. As for the Laity, he opprefs'd them without Mercy, laying the most unreasonable Impositions on their Lands, Houses and Goods, insomuch that no Man could call any thing his own ; and in this manner he reign'd, or rag'd, for the Space of thirteen Years, at the End whereof he was accidentally kill'd by a random Shot as he was hunting, in the Year of *Christ* 1100. By what has been said, it appears that no Estimate can be made of the Treasure he receiv'd.

The Particulars of his Exactions in the above quoted MS. Account of *Leland*, *Cleopatra*, *F. 6. fol.* 145. are these :

*An. Dom.* 1089, the 2d of the Reign of *William Rufus*, Archbishop *Laufrank* being dead, King *William*, holding in his own Hands almost all the Churches and Monasteries throughout *England*, their Pastors being deceas'd, wasted them all with heavy Impositions, and committed them to Lay Persons by way of Farms. *Mat. Paris. p.* 20. *l.* 33.

*An. Dom.* 1091, the 4th of his Reign, King *William Rufus* being very sick, promis'd he would establish good Laws, and preserve Peace with the Church ; but when recover'd, he repented him of his Promise, and opprefs'd both the Church and Kingdom more grievously than he had been wont to do ; so that upon some feign'd Pretence he extorted from one only Church, which was that of *Lincoln*, five thousand Marks. *Mat. Weston.* and *Hist. Roffen.*

*Anno Dom.* 1092, the 5th of his Reign, King *William* grievously opprefs'd both the Kingdom and Clergy with sundry Exactions, and reduc'd them

them into Servitude, on which account he drew
on himſelf the Curſe of many oppreſs'd Perſons.
*Mat. Weſtm.*

*Anno Dom.* 1093, the 6th of his Reign, the King
cauſed 20000 Foot to be liſted in *England,* to rendezvous in *Normandy;* but when they were come to
the Sea Coaſt, in order to be tranſported, he ſent
them all home again, after exacting 10 *s.* from each
of them for their Diet. *Mat. Paris. p. 23. l. 23.*

That ſame Year, the King returning out of
*Normandy,* oppreſs'd all the Churches and Monaſteries throughout the Kingdom. *Mat. Paris. p. 23.
l. 29.*

Still the ſame Year, *Paul* the Abbat of St. *Albans* dying, the King kept that Monaſtery four
Years without a Paſtor, cut down its Woods, oppreſs'd and rob'd it. *Mat. Paris.* in his ſhort Hiſtory.

*Anno Dom.* 1094, the 7th of his Reign, King
*William* ſent his Brother *Henry* into *Northumberland,*
with a great Sum of Money, for him every where
to waſte that Country with plundering. *Mat. Paris.
p. 20. l. 33.*

The ſame Year, the King demanded a thouſand
Pounds in Money of *Anſelm* Archbiſhop of *Canterbury,* on account that he had readily granted his
Conſent to his Promotion; but the Archbiſhop refuſing to give that whole Sum, and deſigning to
paſs over to the Pope of *Rome,* the King immediately ſeized all his and his Churches Effects to his
own Uſe. *Mat. Paris. p. 24. and 25.*

*Anno Dom.* 1095, the 8th of his Reign, *Robert*
Duke of *Normandy* ſent Meſſengers to his Brother
King *William,* deſiring he would lend him 1000
Marks in Money, promiſing to mortgage *Normandy*
to him for the ſame. The King being willing to
comply with his Requeſt, perſwaded the prime
Men of *England,* each of them to lend him as much
as they could immediately. Whereupon the Abbats,

bats, Priors, Bifhops and Abbeffes, melted down
the Gold and Silver Veffels of the Church, turning
them into Money. The Earls, Barons, and other
great Men of the Country pillag'd their Men and
Vaffals, and bringing in a vaft Sum of Money
pleas'd the King with their Prefents. He fail'd
over into *Normandy* in *September,* and having concluded a Peace with his Brother, paid him down
6666 *l.* for which he had *Normandy* mortgag'd to
him. *Walter Gifburn, cap.* 22.

The King demanded of all the Barons in *England*
the Aid which is called *Danegeld,* to fecure *Normandy* from his Brother Duke *Robert,* who was going to *Jerufalem.* Accordingly it was granted to
him, not eftablifh'd or fettled by Law; but to fupply his Neceffity he had 4 *s.* of every Hide of Land,
not excepting the Church. Whilft the fame was
collecting, the Church oppos'd, claiming its Exemption; but could not prevail. Thus in King
*Edward's* Laws, *fol.* 128, *law* 11.

*Anno Dom.* 1097, the 10th of his Reign, King
*William,* who was by many call'd the Red Dra-
gon, divers ways impoverifh'd the *Englifh* Churches,
and efpecially thofe that were vacant. He quite
crufh'd the Poor of the Archbifhoprick of *Canterbury*
and of the Monaftery of St. *Alban.* He cut down
the Woods, and drew the Wealth of the Church
into his own Treafury; befides all which, he moft
wrongfully prefs'd the Inhabitants to build *Weft-
minfter-Hall,* and his Caftles. *Mat. Paris.* in his fhort
Hiftory.

*Anno Dom.* 1098, the 11th of his Reign, the
Bifhop of *Winchefter* died, when King *William* immediately laying his ravenous Hands on that
Bifhoprick, drew from it as much Money as he
could. *Mat. Paris.* in his fhort Hiftory.

That

That ſame Year the King was in *Normandy,* intent upon warlike Affairs, during that time rather fleaing than ſhaving the People of *England* with Taxes and Exactions, being burdenſome and an Enemy to all Men. *Mat. Paris. p.* 59. *l.* 25.

*Anno* 1100, the 13th of his Reign, and the firſt of King *Henry* the firſt, King *William* in the Height of his Injuſtice was ſnatch'd away by a violent Death, having ruin'd all his Subjects with continual Impoſitions and Taxes, and provok'd his Neighbours with frequent Wars and Depredations; ſo that *England* being oppreſs'd, could not breath under him. *Mat. Paris. p.* 73. *l.* 27.

At the time of his Death, this King held in his own Hands the Archbiſhoprick of *Canterbury,* the Biſhopricks of *Wincheſter* and *Salisbury,* and twelve Abbies, which he was wont either to ſell, or let out to farm, or keep them to himſelf. *Mat. Paris. p.* 73. *l.*34. and *Mat. Weſtm. p.* 21. *l.* 33.

The other Tracts in the *Cotton Library,* before mention'd in the Reign of King *William* the Conqueror, only briefly hinting the ſame that has been here ſaid more fully of King *William Rufus,* it will be needleſs to take farther Notice of them. Only it is proper to obſerve, that whereas it is above ſaid, that he extorted 5000 Marks from the Biſhop of *Lincoln,* another MS. makes it but 500, which is moſt likely; for at that time, when all *England* was heavily tax'd to raiſe 10000 Marks to be lent to the Duke of *Normandy,* it is not likely, that any one Biſhop could raiſe 5000 Marks, much leſs 5000 *l.* as *Holingſhed* has made it; but in him Errors are ſo numerous, that it would be a tedious Work to take notice of them. We will therefore go on to

HENRY

# K. HENRY I.

HE succeeded his Brother *William* in the Fullness of the Sovereign Prerogative, but was naturally a much better temper'd Prince; besides that apprehending the Danger he was in from his eldest Brother *Robert*, Duke of *Normandy*, who claim'd the Crown, to oblige the People, at his Coronation he promis'd to govern in a more legal manner than his Father and his Brother had done. The first Imposition we read of laid by him on his Subjects, was of three Shillings on every Hide of Land throughout *England*, for marrying his Daughter *Maud* to the Emperor *Henry*; a Custom then us'd by all Kings to have an Aid of their People towards disposing of their Daughters, and this rais'd of their own Authority, without any Acts of Parliament, which were not then in being. Notwithstanding his other good Qualities, he is also said to have rais'd much Money by keeping of Church Dignities vacant, and enjoying their Revenues all the time they were so ; as particularly, the Archbishoprick of *Canterbury* for the Term of five Years; and by selling of some Bishopricks, and among them that of *Durham* for a thousand Pounds. These are all the Sums we can find he any way exacted from the People, tho' he reign'd 35 Years and 4 Months, dying on the first of *December* 1135. Thus his long Reign appears to have been much less burdensome to the Nation than those of his two Predecessors had been. The above quoted *Latin* MS. in the *Cotton Library*, continues this King's Behaviour as to Impositions, to this Effect, as render'd into *English*,

*Anno*

*Anno Dom.* 1100, the firſt of King *Henry* the firſt, the ſaid King *Henry* at his Coronation granted certain Liberties:

1. In regard (ſaid he) that the Kingdom has been oppreſs'd with unjuſt Exactions, I, in reſpect to God, and for the Love I bear to you all, do make the Holy Church free, ſo that I will neither ſell, nor ſet it to farm; nor will I, when an Arch-biſhop, or a Biſhop, or an Abbat dies, take any thing of the Demeſne of the Church, or of its Men, till a Succeſſor be in Poſſeſſion thereof.

2. I ſuppreſs all the ill Cuſtoms with which the Kingdom of *England* was unjuſtly oppreſs'd, the which evil Cuſtoms I partly here mention.

1. If any one of my Barons, Earls, or others, holding of me, ſhall happen to die, his Heir ſhall not redeem his Lands, as was wont to be done in my Father's time, but ſhall relieve them by a juſt and legal Relief. In like manner my Barons Men ſhall relieve their Lands of their Lords by a juſt Relief.

2. If any of my Barons, or other Men, ſhall think fit to diſpoſe of his Daughter, Siſter, Niece, or Kinſwoman in Marriage, he ſhall not be oblig'd to conſult me; nor will I take any thing of him for ſuch Licence; nor will I obſtruct his diſpoſing of her, unleſs he ſhall deſign to give her to my Enemy.

3. If at the Death of a Baron, or any one of my Men, his Daughter ſhall be left Heireſs, I will beſtow her, by the Advice of my Barons, with her Land. And if, the Husband dying, his Wife ſhall ſurvive, and have no Children, ſhe ſhall have her Dower and Jointure, and I will not give her to any Husband without her own Conſent. But if the Wife ſhall be left with Children, ſhe ſhall have her Dower and Jointure, as long as ſhe legally preſerves her Body; nor will I give her without
her

her own Confent, and fhe fhall be Guardian of the Land and Children ; or elfe fome other near Relation, to whom it belongs to be fo. And I ordain that my Men do in like manner behave themfelves towards the Sons and Daughters and Wives of their Men.

4. The Mintage, or Coinage, which was wont to be taken throughout Cities and Counties, and which was not in the Days of King *Edward,* I abfolutely forbid being taken.

5. If any of my Barons or Men fhall happen to forfeit, he fhall not be fin'd in Money at Pleafure, as was done in the time of my Father and Brother, but according to the Meafure of the Offence ; nor fhall he make amends, as he would have done formerly in the Days of my Father and Brother.

6. I have, with the Advice of my Barons, kept the Forefts in my Hands, as my Father had them.

7. I grant to the Knights, who defend their Lands by Knights Service, the Lands of their Demefne Carucates quit from all Gelds (or Duties) fo that they may furnifh themfelves with Horfes and Arms fufficiently, that they may be fit and ready for my Service, and for the Defence of the Kingdom. All this is faid by *Richard* of *Hagulftad,* or *Hexam,* who flourifh'd at that time.

As many Charters of thefe Liberties were made as there are Counties in *England,* and a Seal being immediately made by the King's Order, they were feal'd, and plac'd among the Records of each County, for a perpetual Monument and Teftimony. However, afterwards when the King began to repent of what he had done, they were taken away by feveral Artifices, only three remaining, viz. at *Canterbury, St. Albans,* and *York. Mat. Paris. in brevi Hiftoria.*

King

King *Henry*, after he was crown'd, gave the Biſhop-rick of *Wincheſter* to *William Giffard*; and then, ac-ting like his Father and his Brother, contrary to the aforeſaid Statutes of his new Council, inveſted him in the Lands of the ſame, after having receiv'd a Reward for ſo doing. *Mat. Paris. in magna Hiſto-ria, p. 74. l. 40. Item in brevi Hiſtoria.*

*Anno Dom.* 1101, Reg. 2. In like manner the King gave the Biſhoprick of *Hereford* to one *Reinel-mus*, without any canonical Election, and, contrary to the Decrees of the new Council, publickly inveſted him in the ſame ; for then he ſeem'd to be ſecurely poſſeſs'd of the Kingdom. *Mat. Paris. p. 78. l. 24. Et in brevi Hiſtoria.*

*Anno Dom.* 1104, Reg. 5. King *Henry* exacted a great Sum of Money of his Kingdom, and the Land lay under many Oppreſſions; for the former Diſcord was reviv'd between the King and his Brother *Robert* Earl of *Normandy*; whereupon the King having rais'd an Army, ſail'd over into *Nor-mandy*, with an immenſe Sum of Money. *Walter Giſ-born, cap.* 30.

*Anno Dom.* 1105, Reg. 6. *William de Warewaſt*, the King of *England's* Lieutenant, in the King's Name, prohibited *Ameline* Archbiſhop of *Canter-bury*, then returning from *Rome*, to come into *Eng-land*, unleſs he would ſolemnly engage to maintain to him all his Father's and his Brother's Cuſtoms. And King *Henry*, when he perceiv'd that both the Pope and the Archbiſhop oppos'd him, immediately ſeiz'd the Archbiſhoprick into his own Hands, and ſtripp'd *Ameline* of all his Poſſeſſions, ſparing neither the Woods, nor the Men. *Mat. Paris. p.* 80. *l.* 47. *Idem in brevi Hiſtoria.*

*Anno Dom.* 1106, Reg. 7. King *Henry*, being at War with his Brother *Robert*, that he might gain the Affections of all Men, promis'd again that he
would

would keep the Liberties before granted, and alfo willingly enlarge them, if there were any Defect. By thefe Promifes, which neverthelefs he afterwards boldly broke through, he fo far reconcil'd all People to him, that they took his Part againft his Brother. *Mat. Paris. p.* 83. *l.* 16. and 25.

*Anno Dom.* 1107, Reg. 8. King *Henry* having fubdu'd his Enemies to his own Heart's Defire, and béing deliver'd from all Danger of War, refus'd to fulfil thofe Things he had promis'd to his great Men, adding Threats upon Threats; whereupon they all laid their Complaints before God, begging Revenge. *Matth. Paris. p.* 84. *l.* 40.

*Anno Dom.* 1109, Reg. 10. King *Henry* gave his Daughter *Maud* in Marriage to the Emperor *Henry,* whofe Wedding was kept at *Munfter.* At that time *Danegeld* was paid throughout *England.* Thus *Radulphus Niger.*

This *Danegelt* is better explain'd by *Matthew Paris,* who writes thus: The King's Daughter was given to the Emperor, as was behoveful. To fay it briefly, the King took fix Shillings of every Hide of Land, as it is in the fhort Hiftory, and in *Henry Huntingdon;* three Shillings, as it is in the great Hiftory. *Mat. Paris. p.* 85. *l.* 35.

*Anno Dom.* 1113, Reg. 14. King *Henry* gave the Archbifhoprick of *Canterbury* to *Ralph London,* and invefted him with a Ring and a Crofier; for he was grown bold as well againft the Church, as againft the Generality of the Nation; having fubdu'd his Brother *Robert,* and others; whereupon he broke his Original Seal, and made void the Charter he had fo often fworn to; and now, by flat Refufal, broke through all thofe things he had before granted out of artful Diffimulation. *Mat. Paris. in brevi Hiftoria.*

*Anno Dom.* 1116, Reg. 17. *England* labour'd under feveral forts of Exactions, and was, not without

C

Sin,

Sin, many ways ftript of its Wealth, to fupply the King's Wants; becaufe there was much Difcord between him and the King of *France.* *Mat. Paris.* 85. *l.* 22. and *Mat. Weftm.* p. 28. *l.* 38. *England* was this Year opprefs'd with many Gelds (or Impofitions) to fupply the King's Wants, fays *Henry Huntingdon.*

*Anno Dom.* 1131, Reg. 32. In the 32d Year of King *Henry's* Reign he decreed that no *Dane* Tax, that is *Danegeld,* fhould be demanded for feven Years. *The Continuator of Florence of Worcefter.*

*Anno Dom.* 1135, Reg. 36. or the firft of King *Stephen,* King *Henry* died, in whom two Vices were over prevalent, *viz.* Luxury, and the Love of Money; fo that many were corrupted by his Example. *Ric. Haguftaldenfis,* or *Richard* of *Hexam.*

At his Death he left an hundred thoufand Pounds, which he had hoarded up, befides Veffels of Gold and Silver, and Imperial Jewels, all which King *Stephen* feiz'd upon. *Mat. Weftm.* p. 35. *l.* 4.

Upon his Death, immediately Peace and Juftice, which had long reign'd with him in *England,* and *Normandy,* both vanifh'd together. So fays *Richard* of *Hexam,* with much more to the fame purpofe concerning his upright Government, and the Calamities which afterwards enfu'd, which I here omit, as to be taken notice of under King *Stephen.* But here it is worth obferving, how this agrees with the dreadful Complaints of Perjuries, Extortions, and other horrid Grievances abovemention'd, chiefly from *Matthew Paris,* an Author, who, as has been obferv'd, very lavifhly beftows the worft of Characters on whom he pleafes; for if Peace and Juftice reign'd with him, and ceas'd as foon as he expir'd, how could he be guilty of fo many Enormities as are charg'd upon him? It is impoffible to reconcile fuch Actions with fuch a Character. It will be therefore reafonable to affign fome Part of what fuch Men write to their

Spleen,

Spleen, and Disaffection to their Monarchs, without wholly excufing them, who, as Men, and in Power, need not be fuppos'd to have been without their Faults. But it is the Talent of fome Men to reprefent all Superiors as Devils, and of others to make them Saints; two Extremes, which difcredit all Hiftory, and give a Difguft to fuch as defire to be inform'd of the Truth of what paft in former Ages. That he was not fo covetous as reprefented, appears by the Treafure left at his Death, being an hundred thoufand Pounds, which if we fhould allow to be of ten times the Value that Money is now, amounts but to one Million; and what is a Million in our Days? He had much occafion for Money in his Wars, which might raife a Clamour againft him; and if after thofe were concluded, he laid up fome Treafure for the next Emergency, that feems to have been rather Forefight than Avarice; and had he left the *Exchequer* quite empty, the fame Men, that charg'd him with Covetoufnefs, would not have fail'd affirming he had been a moft profufe and extravagant Prince. Monarchs have the Misfortune of being expos'd to publick View, being as it were rais'd upon a Stage to be obferv'd by all their Subjects, who all take the Liberty to cenfure their Behaviour, not as they would be judg'd themfelves, but as their Inclination dictates.

It is urg'd that this King beftow'd fome Bifhopricks of his own Authority, without allowing the Liberty of Election. If fo, it was an Incroachment, yet no more than what had been done by his Predeceffors, and many other Monarchs, being a Point much controverted at that time; nor is that to be thought criminal at this time, when the fame Practice has univerfally prevail'd. The Inveftiture by a Ring and a Crofier was indeed carrying it too far; but whether it be done with Ring and Crofier, or without them, the Matter is not much. To return to the Point of the Revenues; it does not appear but that this King was as good to his Subjects as moſt have been. He took, being then abſolute, ſuch Duties as were requiſite to ſupport the Dignity of the Crown, and to defend the Nation, which is due to all Monarchs; and not only to them, but to all that have the Government of every State, whether it be Monarchy, Ariſtocracy, or Democracy. Thoſe that govern muſt be ſupported, and yet thoſe out of whoſe Pockets it comes are always apt to complain, tho' the Burden be ever ſo eaſy. There muſt always be an Allowance for the preſent Humours of the People; for thoſe who will pleaſe to obſerve it, may hereafter, in the Sequel of this Account, find leſs muttering at much heavier Impoſitions. But let us proceed.

# K. STEPHEN.

KING *Henry* (the firſt) who was the Peace of his Country, and Father of the Nation, dying, a dreadful Calamity overſpread the Kingdom, and fill'd it with Confuſion. *England,* which before had been the Seat of Juſtice, the Habitation of Peace, the Manſion of Piety, the Mirror of Religion, ſoon after became the Place of Wickedneſs, the Receſs of Diſcord, the Pattern of Confuſion, and the Miſtreſs of Rebellion. The Laws, which curb the unruly Multitude, being neglected, or rather diſſolv'd, Men, being under no Reſtraint, acted whatſoever Villanies came into their Thoughts. Thus writes the nameleſs, but contemporary Author of the Life of King *Stephen,* in *du Cheſne's Hiſtoriæ Normannorum Scriptores antiqui, p.* 927.

And

And again, *p.* 961, he gives us a difmal Defcription of this King *Stephen's* Reign, reprefenting the State of the Nation to be fo miferable, that many forfook their native Soil to fhun the difmal Calamities then prevailing; many, who had before liv'd well, were reduc'd to dwell in miferable Cottages, feeding on Dogs and Horfes, Herbs and Roots, for Want, Famine enfuing upon the general Defolation; many Towns of Note entirely depopulated, all the Inhabitants being either deftroy'd, or fled; and the Fields lay fallow for want of Tillers. To add to all thefe Miferies, a Multitude of Foreigners, brought over to fupport the Barons, without any Senfe of Humanity, committed the utmoft Barbarities. Nor did they fpare the Churches, or other facred Places, or the Perfons of the Clergy, or Religious Men.

Much more may be feen in the above-quoted Author, expreffing the wonderful Calamity of this Nation at that Time; all which evidently appears to have been the Confequence of his Ufurpation; for he being Son to *Adela*, Daughter to King *William* the Conqueror, by the rebellious Confent of the prime Clergy and Nobility, wrongfully poffefs'd himfelf of the Throne, which of Right belonged to *Maud*, the Daughter of King *Henry* the firft, and to her Son, who was afterwards King *Henry* the fecond. The Barons incroaching upon him they had traiteroufly rais'd, and the rightful Heir claiming his Due, the whole time that *Stephen* held the Crown was one continu'd Scene of Blood and Devaftation; the Government being quite unhing'd, and, as has been briefly fhown above, all brought into Confufion, the Sword decided all Controverfies, and Taxes were rais'd by plundering and robbing; for we do not find that this intruding King laid any ufual or regular Impofitions or Duties; all

Historians are silent as to this Particular. His Forces liv'd upon the Country ; he and they took all they found ; so that he stood not in need of Parliaments, or any usual and regular Prerogative; whatsoever he met with was his own, the Sword made it so ; and such is generally the Behaviour of Usurpers.

There is no doubt but that during those Civil Wars the Expence must be prodigious, and the Demands being at Will, there was much Profuseness ; all which was seiz'd without regard either to Clergy or Laity, both of them suffering alike; or if any Difference were, the greater Burden always fell upon the Possessions of the Church. This Usurpation lasted almost 19 Years, and was a continual Course of Exactions and Depredations; of which no Account can possibly be given. However, we will here insert what we find in the above-quoted MS. Bib. Cot. *Cleopatra.* F. VI. *fol.* 145.

*Anno Dom.* 1135, Reg. 1. King *Stephen* on his Coronation-day granted, 1. that he would never keep the Churches of Bishops deceas'd in his own Hands, but would immediately invest Bishops in them.

2. That he would not keep the Woods of any Person in his Hands, as King *Henry* had done, impleading them yearly, if they took any Game in their own Woods, or if they, to supply their own Wants, destroy'd, or diminish'd them.

3. That he for ever remitted to the People the Duty of *Danegeld,* that is, two Shillings of every Hide of Land, which his Ancestors had us'd to receive to defray the Expence of the Wars against the *Danes,* and had never quitted them of in time of Peace. This and more he promis'd ; but he perform'd no part of it. *Mat. Paris. p. 99. l. 38. and Rad. Niger.*

King

King *Stephen* having once eftablifh'd and fecur'd himfelf, feiz'd upon all the Treafure which his Uncle King *Henry* had laid up, being an hundred thoufand Pounds, befides Gold and Silver Veffels, and Jewels.

King *Stephen*, who now reigns, by his Royal Decree promis'd, that he would never demand *Danegeld*; but by a Perjury hateful to God, the faid Tax is again rais'd throughout *England*, as we are inform'd. So *Florence of Worcefter*, who flou-rifh'd in the Reign of King *Stephen*.

*Anno Dom.* 1137, Reg. 2. *Roger* Bifhop of *Salif-bury* falling fick out of Grief and Sorrow, and being reduc'd to Extremity, paid the laft Debt to Nature at his Epifcopal See, on the 2d of the *Nones* of *December*, leaving an immenfe Sum of Money in his Caftles; which did not fall to the Service of God, but to the Ufe of King *Stephen*. Some fay there were above forty thoufand Marks in Silver, be-fides much Gold, and Variety of Ornaments. The Continuator of *Florence* of *Worcefter*.

*Anno Dom.* 1139, Reg. 4. King *Stephen* came with his Court to *Salifbury*, there to keep the Feaft of the Nativity of our Lord. The Canons repair-ing to him there, offer'd him two thoufand Pounds, to whom he granted Exemption from all Gelds or Taxes of all their Lands. *Idem.*

After the fixth Year of this King's Reign, there was no Peace in the Kingdom; all was deftroy'd with Fire and Rapine, a very great Treafure was fquander'd, violent Depredation rag'd every where, and in all Parts. *Walter Gifborn.*

*Matthew Paris* entring upon this King's Reign fays, he invaded the Crown, tempting God, tho' he had taken an Oath of Allegiance to *Maud* the Emprefs; and yet afterwards fpeaking of his Death calls him moft pious, as if Piety were confiftent

with

with his Perjury, and with all the horrid Effuſion of Blood and Deſolation, which enſu'd on account of his Uſurpation during the whole Courſe of his Reign.

*Holinſhed* tells us, that tho' he continu'd all his time in a manner in the Maintenance of Wars, yet he levy'd but few Tributes, or none at all. That he levy'd *Danegeld* contrary to his Oath, has been ſeen above; and it muſt be granted, that beſides it we do not find any regular Taxes he impos'd, in lieu whereof, he and his Army took whatſoever they found: As to which Point having ſpoken above, the ſame ſhall not be here repeated. The ſame *Holinſhed* proceeds in relation to him thus: Indeed he put divers Biſhops to grievous Fines, and that not without the juſt Judgment of Almighty God, that they might be puniſh'd duly for their Perjury committed in helping him to the Crown. Thus he, and it may well be imagin'd that the whole Nation ſuffer'd for the ſame Perjury, the Laity as well as the Clergy having taken that Oath; and accordingly greater Deſolation ſcarce ever came upon the Kingdom; yet very often People think, that becauſe Vengeance is delay'd, it will never come.

# K. HENRY II.

THE rightful Heir to the Crown, as being Son to *Maud* the Empreſs, Daughter to King *Henry* the firſt, was advanc'd to it after the Death of the aforeſaid Uſurper *Stephen*.

The firſt Tax we find this Monarch impos'd on his Subjects, was that which they then call'd Eſcuage, being a Duty payable by thoſe who held Lands by Military Services, when they went not
themſelves

themfelves to the Wars, nor provided another in their Place; fo that it was not an arbitrary or tyrannical Impofition, but juftly due from the People. This Duty at that time yielded to the King no more than twelve thoufand four hundred Pounds. What he rais'd in his other Dominions beyond the Seas does not appertain to us, and is therefore not taken notice of here; but it is to be obferv'd, that this was the great Burden he impos'd on his Subjects for the carrying on a War. Mr. *Madox,* in his Hiftory of the *Exchequer, p.* 436, fays this was in the fecond Year of his Reign, and that it was rais'd only upon thofe Prelates who were bound to military Services, the Quota being 20 *s.* for every Knight's Fee.

*P.* 436, the fame Author informs us, that in the fifth Year of his Reign another *Scutage* was affefs'd at two Marks for each Knight's Fee, and this not only upon Prelates, but alfo upon other Perfons, and their Knights, who held of the King *in Capite,* according to the Number of their Fees. It was affefs'd alfo upon the reft of the Knights of each County in common.

The fame Year the *Jews* paid to the Crown a Tallage or *Donum.* The Sheriff of *Lincoln* paid into the *Exchequer* 40 *l.* which he had levy'd of the *Jews* in his County; the Sheriff of *Oxfordſhire,* 20 Marks; the Sheriff of *Cambridgeſhire,* 50 Marks. *Ibid. p.* 441. What the whole Sum amounted to is not there mention'd.

In his feventh Year there was another *Scutage. Ibid. p.* 437.

In the 12th Year of this King, an Impofition was laid towards the Holy Wars, being two Pence in the Pound upon all arable Lands and Vines, deducting the Charges; and upon Goods, Houfes, and Employments, for one Year; and one Penny

in

in the Pound for four Years after. For the better underſtanding of the Value of Money at this Time, it is to be obſerv'd, that a Meaſure of Wheat, which would make Bread for an hundred Men, was then worth twelve Pence ; the Carcaſe of a fat Ox twelve Pence; a fat Sheep four Pence, and Provender for twenty Horſes four Pence. The Reaſon of it does not appear ; but it is remarkable, that the Prices above, of a fat Ox, and a fat Sheep, are not at all proportionable, the Ox being valu'd but as three Sheep, whereas at preſent it is worth much more. It may well be imagin'd that there muſt be ſome Error in it ; but ſo I find it.

Mr. *Madox,* p. 398, gives us an Account of an Aid rais'd by this King (but the Year he omits, and I have not found it elſewhere) for marrying his Daughter *Maud* to the Duke of *Saxony.* This Aid was of one Mark for each Knight's Fee throughout *England,* and by the Payments appears how many Knights Fees each Biſhop, Abbat, or religious Houſe was poſſeſs'd of.

The Biſhop of *Norwich* paid 40 Marks for the Knights Fees which he acknowledg'd he held of the King *in Capite,* and was charg'd with c x v i s. v i i i d. for the Fees which he did not acknowledge. Thus it appears that he own'd himſelf poſſeſs'd of 40 Knights Fees, and was charg'd with holding nine Knights Fees more ; for ſo many Marks 116 s. 8 d. amount to, and 5 s. over, the which Crown I cannot aſſign how it was charg'd, being under half a Knight's Fee.

The Abbat of St. *Edmund* paid 40 Marks for 40 Fees, which he acknowledg'd, and was charg'd with 12 Marks and an half for the Fees which he did not acknowledge.

In *Northamptonſhire,* the Abbat of *Peterburgh* ren-dred 60 Marks for 60 Knights Fees.

In

In the fame King's Reign, the Bifhop of *Chi-chefter* paid only for four Knights Fees, which he own'd, and was in Debt for the other Fees, which he did not own. It appear'd by a Particular of the faid Fees, that the faid Bifhop held nine Fees and an half, and a ninth Part of a Fee.

The Archbifhop of *York* paid 20 Marks for 20 Fees.

The Bifhop of *Durham* paid 10 Marks for 10 Fees.

The Bifhop of *Worcefter*, 32 *l.* 17 *s.* 4 *d.* for his Fees, which Sum makes fifty Marks for as many Fees, and 7 *s.* 6 *d.* over.

Much more may be feen of thefe Fees paid by the Laity in the aforefaid Author; but as neither thofe of the Clergy, nor the Laity, are perfect to make up the whole Sum throughout the Kingdom, it is needlefs to add more Particulars here. But fince we are enter'd upon that Gentleman's excellent Hiftory of the *Exchequer*, we will here fubjoin what he has farther of this King's Reign.

P. 476, he fays, in the Beginning of King *Henry* the 2d's Reign *Danegeld* was ftill paid. The *Danegeld* of *Middlefex* was in the whole 81 *l.* 1 *s.* 6 *d.*

P. 438. In his 18th Year another Scutage for the Service of *Ireland*.

In his 33d Year another Scutage for the Army of *Galway*.

The fame Year he took of the *Jews* a fourth Part of their Chattels by way of Tallage.

P. 441. In the 34th Year he levied a Tenth throughout all his Dominions.

Having done with Mr. *Madox*, we next come to the MS. in the *Cotton* Library, *Cleopatra. F.* VI. *fol. 9*, which fays thus :

*Henry*

*Henry* II. alluding not unlike to the *Feoda* given the *Emeriti* in the Decline of the Empire, as Salaries, by which they stood bound to defend the Frontiers against the Incursions of the barbarous Nations, continu'd the Policy of his Progenitors, who allotted the Land into such, and so many equal Portions, as might seem competent for Supportation of a Knight, or a Man at Arms, from whom, as Occasion requir'd, they receiv'd either Service, or Contribution; and to understand the better his own Strength, by publick Command set forth, each Prelate and Baron was to declare by their solemn Instruments, how many Knights held of him in *Capite*. By this Rule of *Scutage*, constant in the Number, he levied always his Subsidies, and Relief, tho' divers in the Rate. Of the first, which was near the Beginning of his Reign, there is no Record. The 2d *Scutage*, which was in the 5th Year, amounted to one hundred twenty four thousand Pounds of Silver, which, reduc'd to the Standard of our Money, 5 *s.* the Ounce, will amount to near 400000 *l.*

In the 7th Year, the *Scutage* was assess'd at two Marks for the Army of *Tholouse.* The like in the next Year.

In the 11th Year there was an Aid for Men to serve in the Army in *Wales.*

The following Year a Subsidy of 2 *d.* in the Pound, and the four following Years one Penny in the Pound, was taken of all Men, the State of Men's Fortunes being deliver'd upon their Oaths. *Gervasius Dorobernensis.*

In the 14th Year, a *Scutage* was assess'd at one Mark of each Fee. And the 18th Year, for the Army in *Ireland*, it was assess'd at 20 *s.* for each Fee. *The red Book in the Exchequer.*

In

In the 35th Year, a Tenth of all Moveables; in which Year dying he left 100000 *l.* in Gold and Silver, besides Plate and Jewels. *Matth. Paris. Hift. major.*

In the same MS. Vol. above-quoted, fol. 80, is a Summary of the Taxes of this King's Reign, of the Hand of Sir *Robert Cotton*; which being to the same Effect as that above, needs not to be here inserted. Only this Difference between them is to be noted, that whereas that here above makes the Sum rais'd by the *Scutage* in the 2d Year of this King's Reign to amount to 124000 *l.* this of Sir *Robert Cotton* makes it no more than 102004 *l.* which is a confiderable Difference, being no lefs than 21996 *l.* But I am apt to believe there is an Error in this MS.

The MS. fol 145, mentions the *Scutage* of this King's 2d Year, and refers to the *Red Book in the Exchequer* for the 7th and 11th Years; all which being mention'd above, we proceed to the 12th Year, 1166, which is here much more full and particular, thus:

*Anno Dom.* 1166, Reg. 12. King *Henry* made a Collection of Money throughout all his Lands, for the Defence and Support of the Eaftern Church and Countries; *viz.* that all Perfons for their Lands, all Moveables, whether Gold or Silver, excepting precious Stones, or Cattle, or Coin, or any other Thing, except wearing Apparel, and of all Incomes in like manner, do pay this Year, 1166, two Pence in the Pound, and one Penny in the Pound the four following Years. The fame for Tillage, and Vineyards, fo that the Expence thereof be not included: As alfo of the Debts which there is a Certainty will be paid. The fame to be done by the Archbifhops, Bifhops, and Abbats, who have Royalties; and by the Clergy, Earls, Barons,

Barons, Vavafors, Knights, Citizens, Burgeffes, Peafants, and all Men having an Houfe to the Value of one Pound, to pay a Penny. A Man who has not the Worth of one Pound, but yet has fome Office, to give one Penny. And there fhall be a Cheft in all Cities, and in the Cathedral Church, and in every Town in the feveral Churches, into which every Man, after having fworn and juftly fumm'd up his Effects, fhall juftly put in whatfoever can be collected of them in the Manner aforefaid, fo truly that he may not break his Oath, nor incur the Excommunication which is denounc'd againft thofe who act fraudulently therein. The aforefaid Cheft is to have three Keys, one of which fhall be kept by the Prieft, and the other two by the moft creditable Men of the Parifh. On the Feaft of *All Saints*, the Money gather'd in the Towns fhall be carried to the Bifhop by thofe that collected it, and other legal Witneffes. Afterwards it fhall be brought into one Place, where I fhall appoint, by the Archbifhops and Bifhops. The third Part of their Penance is remitted to all thofe who fhall juftly pay this Charity of all their Goods. So *Gervafe of Canterbury*.

*Anno Dom.* 1167, Reg. 13. King *Henry* gave his Daughter in Marriage to *Henry* Duke of *Saxony*, with incredible Wealth, as well in Cloaths, and rich Goods, as in Gold and Silver; for then was paid that Tribute in *England* which is call'd *Danegeld. Radulphus Niger and the Red Book.*

The fame Year of CHRIST, and the 14th of the King, died *Robert* Bifhop of *Lincoln*, and his Bifhoprick being return'd into the *Exchequer*, that Church was 17 Years without a Paftor, that is, till the King's Death. *Gul. Neubrigenfis, & Gualt. Gifborn.*

For

For the 18th Year this MS· refers to the *Red Book;* but the Tax then was, as has been mention'd before, a *Scutage* for the Service in *Ire-land.*

*Anno Dom.* 1173, Reg. 19. the following Bishopricks were vacant, *viz.* *Canterbury, Winchester, Ely, Lincoln, Bath, Hereford* and *Chichester. Mat. Paris. p.* 17. *lin.* 22. For he was wont to keep the Arch-bishopricks, Bishopricks, and Abbies that were vacant upon the Death of their Pastors, and the Ecclesiastical Revenues, many Years to his own Use. *Ralph Cogshall, who liv'd at that Time, and Walter Gisborn.*

*Anno Dom.* 1175, Reg. 21. Twelve Abbies were vacant in *England,* in the Province of *Canterbury,* as also the Bishoprick of *Norwich.* The Names of them were, *Abingdon, Grimesby, Crowland, Thorney, Holm, Westminster, St. Augustin Canterbury, Battle, Hyde, Abbotsbury, Michenney,* and *Shrewsbury. Rad. de Deceto, & Gualt. Covent.*

*Anno Dom.* 1177, Reg. 23. *Hugh* Bishop of *Durham* having been slack and defective in his Service to the King during the War, when the Peace ensu'd, gave the King 1000 Marks in Silver, to gain his Favour. *Gualt. Covent. & Rog. Hoveden.*

*Anno Dom.* 1181, Reg. 27. died *Roger* Archbishop of *York.* Upon his Death, the King, by his Officers, seiz'd all that could be found, and extorted such Things as were alienated from those they had been given to; alledging, that Treasures, by whomsoever laid up till Death, belong'd only to the King. The Archbishoprick also being return'd into the *Exchequer,* the See continu'd vacant ten Years. *Will. Neubrigensis, & Gualt. Gisborn, cap.* 101.

*Anno Dom.* 1182, Reg. 28. King *Henry* generously assign'd 42000 Marks in Silver, and 100

Marks

Marks in Gold, for the Relief of the Holy Land, in the Prefence of the Nobility of the Kingdom, at *Waltham. Gervafius, & Hift. Roffenfis.*

*Anno Dom.* 1185, the King promis'd 50000 Marks in Silver for the Defence of the Holy Land.

For the Year 33 the MS. again refers to the *Red Book,* where that Year's Tax appears to have been a *Scutage* for the Army of *Galway,* as above.

*Anno Dom.* 1189, Reg. 35, which was alfo the firft of King *Richard* the firft, a Tenth of all Moveables was granted and collected throughout all *England* for the Relief of the Holy Land, then in great Danger. *Hift. Roff.*

After *Philip* King of *France,* and *Henry* King of *England,* and their Princes, and Earls, Archbifhops, and Bifhops, had violently tithed the Poffeffions of the Clergy and Laity, and the Ecclefiaftical Revenues, and the Money of all Perfons whatfoever, in order to an Expedition into *Jerufalem,* by the juft Judgment of God, who abhors to receive Rapine in Sacrifice, there broke out much Difcord between the faid Kings and Princes; whereupon all that Money fo extorted was fpent in Donatives to Commanders, and the Pay of Soldiers. *Rad. Coggefhale.*

The King of *England* paid the King of *France* 20000 Marks, on account of the Expence he had been at about *Ralph's Caftle,* to eftablifh the Peace. *Tho. Walfingham.*

King *Henry* having loaded great Men with Difgrace, and eas'd them of every thing elfe, took away their Eftates, or elfe brought them to nothing by crafty pilling and paring them, confifcated the Poffeffions of the Church, and audacioufly revok'd thofe he had indifcreetly given. He permitted

mitted Biſhops to make Wills, but ſubtilly with-
drew what they left to the Church, and took away
by Violence what was given to private Perſons.
He permitted none that liv'd within the Liberties
of any Foreſt to cut Oziers in their own Woods,
or to grub up and manure any Waſte, without the
Conſent of his Foreſters. He plac'd Foreſters
over the Countries, and made an unheard-of
Foreſt Law, by which many who had no hand
in the Offences of others were put to Fine, tho'
no way ally'd to thoſe that were dead. Being
never ſatisfy'd at any Rate, he aboliſh'd the ancient Laws, and every Year made new ones, which
he call'd Affizes. He reviv'd the ancient *Danegeld* ; he preferr'd the *Jewiſh* Law before Chriſti-
anity, and accordingly took much Uſury. He
drew Gold and Silver into his Cheſts under Pretence of his Vow, extorting two Pence out of
every Shilling. Being ill advis'd by Archbiſhop
*Richard,* he ſuffer'd the Coin to be debas'd, but
at length hang'd the Debaſers of it. To Foreigners he became tributary, but rob'd his own People. He oppreſs'd moſt Men with *Scutages,* Re-
cogniſances, and divers other Burthens. Being
wholly intent on Gold, he hunger'd, thirſted and
gap'd after it, and his Avarice ſtill roſe above
his increaſing Heap of Gold. He long obſtructed
Elections to vacant Biſhopricks, that he might
the longer abuſe their Revenues. *Rad. Niger.*
*I have given this ſhameful Charge as I found it, yet
cannot in Juſtice but warn the Reader to be cautious in
crediting all he meets with in Hiſtorians of this ſort ;
they have very often private Grudges, or natural Preju-
dices, which prevail upon them to inveigh bitterly
againſt the beſt of Princes, and to magnify their moſt
inconſiderable Failings, much more ſuch as are heinous
enough in themſelves.*

D                                    An-

*An.* 1189, King *Henry* dying left 900000 *l.* in Gold and Silver, besides Plate, Jewels and precious Stones. *Mat. Paris. p.* 204. *lin.* 41.

This indeed was immense Treasure in those Days, yet in my Opinion no Proof of the King's Avarice, as some Writers endeavour to insinuate, but rather a Vindication of him from those Slanders rais'd to sully his Memory; as, that he rais'd much Money on Pretence of the Holy War, and then squander'd it at his own Will; for this seems to have been a Treasure laid up to carry on that pious Enterprize, either by himself, or by his Son, who performing that Journey, found it all too little for the Undertaking, and therefore still added to it by such Ways and Means as we are now to see in his Life.

These were the Impositions we find of this sort during his Reign of 34 Years and an half; his other Revenues being such as have been mention'd above in the Reign of King *William* the Conqueror; besides which there were several other sorts of occasional Taxes, which may properly be taken notice of. There was frequently a Demand upon the Subject towards building, or repairing of Cities, Towns or Castles, and that was call'd *Burgbote*; for building and repairing of Bridges, by the Name of *Brigbote*; for an Expedition to be undertaken, and the Support of the Army, entitled *Herefare* and *Heregelt*. *Danegeld*, being a Tax impos'd by the *Saxon* Kings to prevent the Incursions of the cruel *Danes*, or rather a Tribute paid to them; the which Duty impos'd on the People, continu'd for many Years after it had ceas'd to be paid to that Nation. 5thly, *Horngeld*, being an Imposition upon all Sorts of Cattle. By these and other Denominations the Kings then supply'd their Wants, having full Power to do it of themselves, felves, or at the moft by the Advice of their Councils; the which Prerogative of theirs was afterwards circumfcrib'd, as will foon be fhown.

## K. RICHARD I.

SUrnam'd *Cœur de Lion*, or *Lyon's Heart*, for his undaunted Courage, afcended the Throne on the 6th of *July*, in the Year 1189. He is tax'd by Hiftorians with the three Vices of Pride, Avarice and Luft, but with very little Proof to make out fo black a Charge; for they give us not one Inftance of his Pride, but on the contrary, that he was magnanimous, and at the fame time affable. For his Avarice, there is as little to make it out; becaufe tho' great Sums of Money were rais'd in his Time, they were firft for the Holy Wars, next for his Ranfom when taken, and laftly for his other Wars, and neceffary Expences, having never been known to have hoarded up much Treafure. And then as to his Luft, tho' he was guilty of fome Failings with Women, it is certain he might be reckon'd innocent, if compar'd with many other Monarchs, and even private Men. The greateft Fault he evidently appears to have been guilty of, was fome Undutifulnefs to his Father, wherein his elder Brother much exceeded, as did both his younger: However, that is no Excufe to him. Let us now come to his Revenue, or what he receiv'd from his Subjects whilft he govern'd them.

In the firft Year of his Reign, being refolv'd to perform the Vow he had made to make War againft the Infidels in the Holy Land, he apply'd himfelf diligently to provide Money for that Expence; and in order to it levy'd a Tax, pawn'd, fold and let to farm his Lands, Tolls, Cuftoms, and other Reve-

nues,

nues, with certain Counties and Offices, all which
amounted to a vaſt Sum.

One Method he took to raiſe Money was by
Fines, and accordingly *Ranulf de Glanvill*, Lord
Chief Juſtice, ſeveral other great Officers, and almoſt all the Sheriffs and their Deputies throughout
*England,* having been convicted of much Corruption in the Adminiſtration of their ſeveral Employments, were not only diſcarded, but ſeverely
fin'd. So ſays *Matthew Paris.* But *William Parvus*
excludes the aforeſaid *Ranulf de Glanvill* from that
Number, and ſays, he laid down that Employment voluntarily, to attend the King into the Holy Land , being a wiſe and good Man.

*Hugh Pudſey,* Biſhop of *Durham,* being very
wealthy , the King ſold to him the Manor of *Seg-
gefield,* with the Wapentake belonging to it, as alſo
the whole County of *Durham* , for an immenſe
Sum, making him Earl as well as Biſhop of *Durham.*

The ſame Biſhop gave the King a thouſand
Marks to be made Chief Juſtice of *England.*

The Citizens of *London* preſented the King with
a conſiderable Sum, or perhaps bought with it
their Liberties, which he granted them at that
Time.

All other Things that then came in his Way he
alſo ſet to Sale, as Jewels, Moveables, and whatſoever would yield Money; inſomuch that many
thought he had never intended to return, and ſome
took the Liberty to tell him, that what he did
was diſhonourable to himſelf, and prejudicial to
his Succeſſor. To which he anſwer'd, that it was
neither diſhonourable to himſelf, nor any Wrong
to his Succeſſor to make uſe of his own in time
of need; and he thought that Neceſſity ſo urgent,
that he would ſell the City of *London,* if he could
meet

meet with one that was able to purchafe it. No doubt but that it proceeded from a good Difpofi-tion, that he chofe rather to fell all he had of his own, than to overburthen his People, on whom at that time he might have laid what Impofitions he pleas'd.

Another Way he found to increafe his Stock, was the obtaining a Licence from Pope *Innocent* the third, to difpenfe with as many of his Subjects as he thought fit, who had made Vows to go into the Holy Land, or taken the Crofs upon them. The Number of thefe being confiderable , and many of them wealthy, the Treafure rais'd after this manner was very great.

The laft Shift at this Time, and moft grievous , was the making of a new Great Seal , and then proclaiming throughout all *England*, that all who had any Grants from the Crown under the for-mer, fhould come in and have them confirm'd un-der this new Seal; which, as may well be ima-gin'd, muft needs turn to great Account, none daring to hazard what might afterwards follow, in cafe they did not thus renew.

What Sum was rais'd by all thefe feveral Ways and Means is impoffible to be afcertain'd, nor is there any gueffing at it. Whatfoever it was, fuch an Expedition as he then undertook demanded no lefs, and the Event fhow'd that all was rather too little. In his Return home , being taken Prifoner by the Duke of *Auftria*, and fold to the Emperor, that Monarch, contrary to all Right and Equity, demanded an exorbitant Ranfom to reftore him to his Liberty. It was agreed that the King fhould pay an hundred and forty thou-fand Marks, befides all Expences, before he was difcharg'd. *Matth. Paris.*

Fo

For defraying of that Expence a Tax was laid, being the fourth Part of the Revenues of all Persons, as well ecclesiastical as secular, for one Year; likewise the fourth Part of all their Moveables, and twenty Shillings of every Knight's Fee. Besides, the Religious Orders of the *Cistercians*, and of *Sempringham*, which had never before been liable to Impositions, were oblig'd to give all their Wools for that Year. The Clergy gave their Gold Chalices, and much other Plate belonging to their Churches. *John* Bishop of *Norwich* gave the one half of the Value of the Plate in all the Churches of his Diocese, and of whatsoever else belong'd to the Clergy. By this it appears how hard so small a Sum as 140000 Marks was then to raise, whereas Millions are now look'd upon as Trifles.

In the 6th Year of his Reign, of our Lord 1194, the King being return'd from his Expedition, and Captivity, and quite bare of Money to support his Wants, reassum'd all the Grants he had made before his Voyage to the Holy Land; persuaded the *Cistercians* to give so much of their Wool as would discharge a great Debt he had contracted with foreign Merchants; and, after all, levy'd a Tax of two Shillings of every Hide of Land throughout the Realm. *Ibid.*

The same sixth Year, the Justices Itinerants in their Circuits caus'd Inquisitions to be taken by Juries of Pleas of the Crown, both old and new, of Recognisances, Escheats, Wards, Marriages, and all manner of Offenders against the Laws and Ordinances of the Realm, of all Transgressors, Falsifiers, Murderers of *Jews*; of the Pledges, Goods, Lands, Debts, and Writings of *Jews* that had been slain: Likewise Accounts of Sheriffs, and of the Lands of Earl *John*, the King's Brother, of his Abettors, he being then in Rebellion; of Usurers,

rers, of Wines fold contrary to the Affize, of falfe Meafures. The *Jews* were alfo appointed to enroll their Debts, Pledges, Lands, Houfes, Rents and Poffeffions. Inquifition was taken of Juftices, Bailiffs, Conftables, Forefters, and other Officers belonging to the King, to know how they had behav'd themfelves in their feveral Trufts. Next, the great Seal having been loft with the Chancellor, who was caft away, a new one was made, and all Perfons whatfoever, who had any Grants from the Crown, commanded to have the fame confirm'd by the fame; otherwife they fhould be of no Effect. *Idem.*

Befides all that has been faid, it was ordain'd, that there fhould be Jufts and Tournaments throughout *England*, for the better exercifing of Men in Martial Affairs; yet fo that all Perfons fhould pay for their Licence, to bear a Part in thofe Exercifes, after the following Rates, *viz.* every Earl twenty Marks, every Baron ten Marks, every Knight having Lands four Marks, and fuch as had no Lands two Marks.

Much Treafure was rais'd by thefe feveral Means, all that were faulty being fin'd; all who had Grants for the new Seal, and all that exercis'd themfelves in warlike manner for their Licences; but no Computation can be made of thefe extraordinary Levies.

In his tenth Year, the King rais'd five Shillings of every Hide of Land. *Hoveden.*

I find nothing more, than the fame as is above mention'd, in Mr. *Madox's* Hiftory of the *Exchequer*, relating to this King; but only that in the firft Year of his Reign, *Ifaac*, the Son of *Rabbi* a *Jew*, fin'd in 200 *l.* that he might be quit of his Part of the Tallage impos'd upon the *Jews* by King *Henry* II.

In

In the third Year of the fame King, *Joffe*, the Son of *Lic*, paid 100 *s.* towards the fecond *Donum* of 1000 Marks charg'd upon the *Jews*.

In this King's Time, the Scutage of *Wales* was affefs'd at 100 *s. per* Fee.

Sir *Robert Cotton*'s MS. in his own Hand, before quoted, fums up all the Impofitions under this King thus : *Richard* his (*Henry* the fecond's) Son , fucceeding, commanded his firft Year a large Benevolence from all his Subjects, under the Title of Alms, becaufe he pretended it for the Holy Land. In the 2d, his Chancellor, Bifhop of *Ely*, impos'd upon every City and good Town two Horfes of Service, and two Hackneys ; and of every Abbey, and other Religious Houfe, one of either. *Mat. Paris.* In his 5th Year, his Juftices by that Ordinance levy'd in his Abfence the fourth Part of all the Clergy and Nobility's Goods, and of the *Ciftercian* Monks the Wools. *Rad. Cogfhall. Hidage*, under a new Name *Tenementale*, he impos'd at two Shillings every Plow, the third Part of *Scutage* ; and forc'd the White Monks again for Money to redeem their Wools. *Walt. Covent. Rog. Hoved.* His 6th Year, having in this Time, by Account of his Treafury, fpent eleven hundred thoufand Marks. *John Everfden. Walt. Coventry.* In the 10th, he took again of every Plow Land 5 *s.* and feigning to have loft his old Seal, whilft he was Prifoner in *Almaign*, inforc'd all that would enjoy their Lands or Liberties to fine for Confirmation under his new. *Rad. Cogfhall. Mat. Paris.*

Thefe Things are here repeated, as containing fome Additions to what was faid before : And it is worth obferving, that the great Sum fpent in fix Years, including the Expences of the holy War, and the King's Ranfom, amounts but to 1100000 Marks, being 753332 *l.* another notable Inftance of of the Difference between Money rais'd then and fince that Time. It may alfo be noted, that Sir *Robert* fays, the King pretended for the Holy Land, tho' he knew he actually went; and again, that he feign'd to have loft his Seal, whereas it has been fhown above that it was caft away with the Chancellor. Thefe are two Calumnies upon this King, and therefore deferve to be taken notice of.

The other Tract in the above often quoted MS. Vol. p. 9. to what has been already faid adds, that, *An Dom.* 1194, *Reg.* 5. King *Richard* held a Council at *Nottingham*; wherein he ordain'd that every Carucate of Land throughout all *England* fhould pay to him 2 *s.* which is by the Ancients call'd *Tenementale.* Afterwards he commanded that every one fhould do him the third Part of military Service, as he fhould impofe on each Fee, to go over with him into *Normandy. Rog. Hoveden. Walt. Covent.*

Next he exacted of all the *Ciftercian* Monks all their Wool of that Year; but in regard it was grievous, and intolerable to them to do fo, they compounded with him for a Fine in Money. *Walt. Covent. Rog. Hoveden.*

*An. Dom.* 1195, *Reg.* 6. *Hugh* Bifhop of *Lincoln* gave the King for a Sables Mantle a thoufand Marks, which had been yearly allow'd him by his Predeceffors. *John Everefden.*

*An. Dom.* 1196, *Reg.* 7. *Hubert* Archbifhop of *Canterbury,* Chief Juftice of *England,* by his Meffengers made Suit to the King to difcharge him of the Government of the Kingdom, fhewing that he was not capable of governing both the Church and Kingdom; and having infpected the Records, and examin'd the Accounts, made it appear to the King, that he had within two Years laft paft

procur'd

procur'd 1100000 Marks for his Service of the *English* Nation. *Walt. Covent.* and *Rog. Hoveden.*

This is the only positive Sum we hear of rais'd in this King's Reign, all the others being no where expres'd. The 1100000 Marks amount to 753332 *l.* for the two Years, that is, 376666 *l.* a Year ; a Sum then thought very grievous ; now ten times that is look'd upon as very moderate, especially considering the Wars, and other immense Expences that King had always upon him during his short Reign.

# K. JOHN.

UPON the Death of King *Richard*, his Brother *John*, who had before been in Rebellion against him and his Father, hasted over into *England* out of *Normandy* ; and having corrupted the Arch-bishop of *Canterbury*, and others both of the Clergy and Laity, with their Assistance easily usurp'd the Crown from his Nephew *Arthur*, Son to his elder Brother *Jeffry*, whom it is believ'd he also afterwards murder'd ; for having seiz'd, and imprison'd him in the Castle of *Roan*, he was never after heard of. His Reign prov'd suitable to the wicked Methods by which he ascended the Throne, and endeavour'd to secure himself in it, *viz.* Usurpation and Murder. He liv'd a restless Life, and made a wretched End ; and the Nation, which had so unjustly set him up, to the disinheriting and Destruction of the rightful Heir, groan'd under his Oppressions during the whole Course of his Reign, being a continual Scene of Rapine and Slaughter. Being soon after his Coronation in *Normandy*, he never offer'd to oppose the *French*, who

who invaded and took from him the greateſt Part of that Province; whereupon moſt of his Nobility forſook him, and he finding himſelf ſo abandon'd fled over into *England.* Hereupon picking a Quarrel with the great ones, pretending that all his Loſſes had happen'd through their Fault, he took from them the ſeventh Part of all their Moveables; nor did he forbear exerciſing the ſame Rapine in all the Conventual and Parochial Churches, being furniſh'd with proper Inſtruments to put the ſame in Execution, *viz. Hubert,* Archbiſhop of *Canterbury,* who had baſely rais'd him to the Throne, among the Spirituality; and *Geffry,* the Son of *Peter,* Chief Juſtice of *England,* who both ſpar'd no Man in the Practice of that Extortion. This was in the Year 1203.

In the Year of our Lord 1204, being the ſixth of his Reign, on the Day after the Circumciſion of our Lord, the King and the Nobility aſſembled at *Oxford,* where military Supplies were granted to him, *viz.* two Marks and a half of each Knight's Fee; nor did the Biſhops, and Abbats, or other Eccleſiaſtical Prelates go off without conſenting to the ſame.

Thus *Mat. Paris,* where it is to be noted, that he only ſays, the *Magnates,* that is, the Prime Men, or Nobility met the King; whereas *Holinſhed,* quoting this ſame Author on account of this Scutage, calls this Aſſembly a Parliament; which ſhows that he tranſlates and quotes as pleaſes his Fancy, there being no Parliament in thoſe Days; ſo that there is no relying on his Quotations, as may be ſeen in many other Inſtances.

*Anno Dom.* 1208, *England* being put under an Interdict, the King took that Occaſion to ſeize into his own Hands all the Temporalities of the Clergy throughout the Kingdom, committing moſt horrid

Rapine

Rapine on all the Possessions of the Church, and carrying away the Corn, and other Effects belonging to the Clergy.

*Anno* 1210, by the King's Command all the *Jews* in *England* of both Sexes were seiz'd, imprison'd, and tortur'd; whereupon they gave the King all they had. One of them refusing to comply, was order'd to have a Tooth beaten out every Day, till he paid ten thousand Marks. Seven of his Teeth were accordingly struck out in seven Days, and at length the eighth Day, to save the rest, he paid the Sum at first demanded. So says *Mat. Paris* ; Mr. *Madox* says, the whole taken from them amounted to 66000 Marks.

To what is above taken from *Mat. Paris*, I have this to subjoin from Mr. *Madox, p.* 444.

In the first Year of King *John* there was an Escuage of two Marks *per* Fee.

*P.* 421, In his fifth Year he had an Aid from the Prelates, under the Name of *Donum Prelatorum.*

In the 9th Year, the Citizens of *London* stood charg'd 1000 *l.* for a Fine towards the King's Voyage.

In the 12th Year, at *Bristol,* on the Feast of All Saints, a Tallage was assess'd upon the *Jews.* To this Tallage *Isaac* the Chirographer fin'd in 5100 Marks, for himself, his Wife, and Children ; and other *Jews* in their respective Sums.

The *Cotton* MS. *fol.* 9, sums up this King's Exactions thus: He took in the first Year of his Reign a Scutage assess'd at 2 Marks. In the 2d Year, 3 *s.* of every Plow. In the Year following, besides a Scutage as before, the 40th Part of the Revenues of the Clergy and Laity. In the 4th Year he took the like Scutage, and the 7th Part of the moveable Goods of the Baronage and Clergy. In the 5th Year, a Scutage assess'd at 2 Marks. The like in
the

the 6th and 7th Years. In the following Year, twenty
Shillings *Scutage,* and the 30th Part of Moveables,
as well of the Church as Laity. In the 9th Year
he exacted by Redemptions of the Concubines of
the Clergy a great Sum. In the 11th he extorted
a grievous Tax, *viz.* 140000 *l.* from the Clergy.
In the 12th, a *Scutage,* affefs'd at two Marks, befide
an Exaction of 22000 *l.* from the *Ciftercian* Monks.
In the 13th he took a *Scutage,* affefs'd at 20 *s.*
for the Army of *Scotland,* and another at 2 Marks,
for the Army of *Wales.* In the Year following, he
exacted from the Minifters of the Church 400000
Marks. And in the 16th, the *Scutage* was affefs'd
for the Army of *Poictou* at 3 Marks. Thus in
the Space of 17 Years the State was deliver'd but
three from Impofitions.

The MS. at *fol.* 145, in *Leland's* Hand, tells us
as follows of this King's Reign. King *John* daily
more and more ravag'd not only Ecclefiaftical Perfons, but alfo his Barons, Knights, Citizens, and
Burgeffes, ftripping them of what they had feveral
Ways. Hence enfu'd a War between the King and
the Barons, which only ended with the Death of
King *John. Mat. Paris. in his fhort Hiftory.*

*Anno Dom.* 1210, Reg. 11. King *John* returning
out of *Ireland,* caus'd all the Prelates, Abbats, Priors, Abbeffes, Templars, Hofpitallers, Wardens of
Townfhips of the Order of *Cluni,* and other foreign
Orders, of what Rank or Dignity foever, to af-
femble before him at *London,* who were all compell'd to fo grievous a Ranfom, and Dilapidation of
the Poffeffions of the Church, that the Sum of
Money fo extorted is faid to have amounted to
100000 *l.* Sterling. *Mat. Paris.*

The White *Ciftercian* Monks in *England,* befides
all others, contrary to their Privileges, paid 40000 *l.*
in this Tallage to the King, whether they would
or no. *Mat. Paris.* The

The *Jews* likewife were oblig'd to a moft heavy Ranfom. *Idem.*

*Anno Dom.* 1211, Reg. 12. King *John* exacted two Marks of Silver of each Fee of every Knight that had not been in the Army in *Wales. Idem.*

All the Servants of Abbats and Priors, of what Profeffion foever, were by the King's Command regifter'd. *Rad. Coggefhale.*

The fame Year the King again feiz'd the Barns of the Clergy. *Idem.*

*Anno Dom.* 1212, Reg. 13. The King again accus'd the *Ciftercians,* that the Earl of *Tholoufe,* who had marry'd his Sifter *Jone,* had been ruin'd by their Council and Affiftance; in Reparation of which Damage he exacted 22000 *l. Idem.*

The fame Year of our Lord, the Archdeacon of *Huntingdon,* being imprifon'd, gave the King 22000 Marks to be releas'd. *Jo. Everefden.*

The fame Year ftill, King *John* extorted Certificates from all Religious Houfes, and Clergymen, wherein they by Force teftify'd, that they had voluntarily given him all that he had by Violence forc'd from them. *Mat. Paris.*

*Anno Dom.* 1213, Reg. 14. During the time of the Pope's Interdict, King *John* by his Officers damnify'd the Churches to the Value of 400000 Marks. *Mat. Paris. in his fhort Hiftory.*

*Anno Dom.* 1215, Reg. 16. the Citizens of *London* conceiv'd much Hatred againft King *John,* on account of many unjuft Exactions with which he had continually harrafs'd them. *Mat. Weftmonaft.*

At the fame time the noble *William d' Aubigny* was releas'd out of Prifon, after having ranfom'd himfelf for a Fine of 6000 Marks. *Mat. Weftmonaft.*

*Anno Dom.* 1216, Reg. 17. *Walo,* the Pope's Legate, gather'd Procurations throughout all *England,* without any Compaffion for the Church and Clergy,

Clergy, which had been impoverish'd and brought to Desolation in all Parts; and he extorted 50 *s.* for each Procuration from the Cathedral Churches, and Religious Houses. *Mat. Paris. in his short History, and in the great.*

He also sequester'd all the Possessions of the Clergy and Religious Men, who had aided, abetted, or supported the Barons against their King, and converted the same to his own, and the Use of his Chaplains. *Mat. Paris.*

This same Year, the Barons being idle, and doing nothing, the King ceas'd not daily to bring into his own Hands their Castles, Towns, Men and Possessions, whilst his Officers in several Parts quite ruin'd all the Possessions of the Barons. *Mat. Westmonast.*

King *John* render'd himself odious to many, on account of the Tribute by which he held the Kingdom in continual Servitude. *Mat. Westmonast.*

# K. HENRY III.

SUcceeded his Father King *John*, as rightful Heir of the Crown, in the Year 1216; for tho' his Father usurp'd the Crown from his Nephew *Arthur*, when the said *Arthur* was dead, he was the next lawful Heir, and so his Son after him. He reign'd 56 Years, and odd Months.

The *Cotton* MS. quoted in every Reign, *fol. 9.* sums up the Taxes rais'd by this King in the following manner, *viz.* In the time of H. III. upon the Clergy, Nobility and Gentry there were assess'd 15 *Scutages*; one at 10 *s.* two at 20 *s.* eight at 2 Marks, and four at 40 *s.* the Knights Fee. The Land of the inferior twice tax'd, first at 2 *s.* after at two Marks the Plow, and two Tallages

upon

upon the Lands of the Crown. From out of the Subjects moveable Goods hath been taken five times; as, the 40th, the 30th, the 20th, and the 15th Parts, and once the 16th of the Clergy for the King. A Tenth he nine times impos'd upon the Church, ſix times for a Year only, and by itſelf, once accompany'd with the firſt Fruits, once for three Years, and once for five; beſides two Aids, the one moderate, the other call'd an heavy Exaction, and worthily, if to the 800 Marks impos'd upon *St. Edmund's* all the other Abbeys were rated accordingly; and by the Account made of his Impoſitions on the *Jews*, he receiv'd in the time of his Government of them 402000 Marks. And as in all the 56 Years of his Reign, excepting five, either the Church, or Commonwealth, were charg'd with Contribution Money to relieve the Expence of War, ſo were they griev'd with other Exactions, either for Carriages, Victuals, or perſonal Attendance. In his 26th Year, the Inhabitants of *Winchelſey* were enjoin'd to furniſh ten good Ships, and large, to go over to *Poictou* upon the King's Service; and at another time for twenty. *Dunwich*, and *Ipſwich* five apiece, and the other Ports proportionably, all at their own Charge: For the ſame Year, and for the ſame Service, there were tranſported 100000 (*Quarters I ſuppoſe*) of Wheat, 5000 of Oats, and many Bacons. The Church not forborn in thoſe Charges; for from *Wincheſter* 2000 Quarters of Wheat and Oats, and one thouſand of Beans were taken, the other Biſhops and Clergy bearing their Parts of Victuals in the like Exactions; as one Wave follows upon the Back of another, ſo *England* appear'd like an inexhauſtible Well.

In the 12th and 14th Years the King levy'd Soldiers for his Wars beyond Sea, collecting for his Army of every two Hides or Plow Land two

Men

Men with a good Ax (*I suppose a Battle-Ax*) and to bring Victuals with them; and those for whose Services the King dispens'd, whom the King would have stay in their own Countries, to contribute to the Victuals of those that went for 40 Days; commanding the Sheriffs to swear all that remain'd behind him in *England* under Arms, in the same manner as they had been sworn in the Days of his Father King *John.* By which Ordinance of King *John,* all able Subjects, from Youth to decrepit Age, were bound to arm themselves, and be in continual Readiness, from Night till Morning, for so the Record is, to attend the King's Pleasure.

In the 14th Year of his Reign he sent Orders to the Sheriffs, that they should cause the Men so sworn to come to the King's Army, bringing with them Coats of Male, Head-pieces, &c. and to such as neglected this Service, he sent his Writs, reprehending them at first in a severe manner, and afterwards fining them to their Abilities or Tenures. *Anno* 26, he took of *William de Umfrevil* to quit him from passing over into *Gascony* 100 Marks, and so in Proportion of many others.

The MS. *fol.* 80, of Sir *Robert Cotton's* own Hand. King *Henry* his 2d Year impos'd two Marks on every Fee, *Red Book*; and the 3d a Tallage on the *Jews,* *Jo. Eversden; Rot. Clauf. an.* 3 *H.* 3. 2 *s.* in the 5th of every Plow Land to support his Estate; and the Year following twice Scutage, once at 10 *s.* then at two Marks the Knight's Fee. *Tho. Walfingham,* *Jo. Eversden.* In the 8th, of every Plow Land of the Clergy half a Mark, of others 2 *s.* which the Record calls a Voluntary Subsidy. *Rot. Pat.* 8 *Hen.* 3. *Mat. Westm.* In the 9th, 2 *s.* Carucage of every Plow Land, two Marks of every Knight's Fee, and the 15th of all the Moveables and Revenues of all Boroughs. *Rot. Pat. an.* 9 *H.* 3. *Mat. Westm.* In the

E                                                      10th,

10th, a 15th Part of all the Goods of the Church and Laity; and for confirming the great Charter, he took a fifteenth in the 11th Year. *Rad. Cogſhall.* The next he took 5000 Marks of the *Londoners*, beſides their 15th; ſo of divers Boroughs, as of *Northampton* 1200 *l. Mat. Weſtm.* Then changing his Seal, he inforc'd all to renew their Patents, under a Fine. In the 14th, this King took two Marks of every Knight's Fee, and the Pope's Legate a Tenth of the Clergy. In the next, he impos'd large Sums upon the Churchmen, and *Jews. Mat. Weſtm.* The 17th, 40 *s.* of every Knight's Fee, and of Moveables the 40th Part. *Everſden* in his *Regiſter* writes down the manner how it was collected. In the 18th, 20 *s.* Scutage; and in the 20th, two Marks of every Plow Land, by the Name of *Carucage*.

Twice in the 22d Year he took of all Moveables the 30th Part, and the Year following 40 *s.* of every Knight's Fee. In the 24th he took the third Part of all Debts due to the *Jews*, a fifteenth of all his Subjects Goods aſſeſs'd by the Juſtices Itinerant. *Jo. Everſden.* The Pope the ſame Year a 13th of all the Clergy, rated by his Legate. Of ſuch as went not in this King's Service into *Gaſcony*, and held *in Capite*, he took 20 *s.* The Compoſition that divers then made remains yet on the File Rolls. *Rot. Clauſ. an.* 26 *H.* 3. He impos'd an Aid upon the *Premonſtratercian* and *Ciſtercian* Monks in the 26th Year of his Reign for theſe Wars, and 40 *s.* of every Knight's Fee. The following Year he tax'd the *Jews* at 20000 Marks, and levy'd Victuals in *England* upon the publick Charge to maintain his Army in *France. Jo. Everſden.* In the 28th his Son *Edward*, for Maintainance of the Wars in Foreign Parts, impos'd upon the *Iriſh* a Subſidy, with Proviſo that it ſhould not be made a Precedent. The Father in *England* commanding that all Merchants
Money

Money put to Ufury fhould be feiz'd to his Ufe,
and their Bodies imprifon'd, raifing a Tallage
through *Wales*, and impofing great Sums upon the
*Jews*,and *Londoners*,taxing the City the next Year at
1500 Marks, and all that ferv'd in Knights Fees
at 20 *s.* the Fee, for marrying his Daughter. *Jo.
Everfden.* In the 30th, 40 *s.* Scutage for the Siege of
*Glaunvell* Caftle ; and in the 34th he exacted great
Sums of Money of the *Londoners*, and others, under
the Name of New Years Gifts. A Tallage, by the
Name of *Cornagium*, he impos'd to be yearly levy'd
by his Itinerant Juftices in the 36th Year. *Communia
in Scac. H.* 3. *Rot.* 15. On the *Londoners* he affefs'd 5000
Marks in his 38th Year; and the next kept all the
Lands of all vacant Religious Houfes, to pay his
Debts. Again of the *Londoners*, in the 40th Year,
he took 3000 Marks, and of the *Jews* 1000, binding the Houfes of Religion to pay his Debts unto
the Pope, the Sum being 250000 *l.* the Intereft
amounting to 100 *l.* a Day. The Citizens of *London* were once more the fucceeding Year tax'd at
5000 Marks; and in the 42d, 40 *s.* Scutage impos'd,
being the eleventh in this King's Time. *Mat.
Weft. Jo. Everfden.* Befides an Aid of all his Subjects, for which he promis'd to fettle the State of
the Kingdom with Speed in Order. *Pat. an.* 42 *H.*
3. 2 *Maii.* The 44th he took the 30th Part of
the Clergy's Goods, and 3000000 Marks of the
King of *France* for the Releafe of *Normandy. Tho.
Walfingham.* He affefs'd on the Clergy a 10th for
6 Years, and took the 20th Penny of the Laity in
the 51ft. *Jo. Everfden, Ran. Ceftrenfis.* To furnifh the
Prince in his holy Journey, he tax'd all his Subjects
with the 15th Part of their Goods; and Tallage
of all the Demefne Lands of the Crown. *Walt. Gifborne. Clauf. an.* 55 *H.* 3. *in fchedula.*

*Anno Dom.* 1225, King *Henry* at *Christmas* held his Court at *Westminster*, the Clergy and People, with the great Men of the Country, being present. When the Solemnity was over, *Hubert de Burg*, the King's Justice, in his Name acquainted the Archbishops, Bishops, Earls, Barons, and all others, with the Losses and Wrongs the King had sustain'd in the Parts beyond the Sea, whereby not only the King, but also many Earls and Barons were outed of their Inheritances; and whereas many were concern'd, the Assistance of many was necessary. He therefore ask'd of them all both Advice and Aid for recovering the Rights of the Crown of *England.* For performing hereof he thought it would be sufficient, if the 15th Part of all Moveables of the Clergy, as well as the Laity, were granted to the King. This Proposal being made, the Archbishop, and Bishops, Earls, Barons, Abbats, and Priors, having taken it into Consideration, answer'd, That they would readily comply with the King's Request, provided he would grant the Liberties so long demanded. The King desiring the Money, consented to what the Nobility ask'd, and Charters being accordingly writ and seal'd were sent into all the Counties of *England*; and to those Liberties which are within the Forests two Charters were sent, the one of the general Liberties, and the other of the Liberties of the Forest. These Liberties were the same we now call *Magna Charta*, and *Charta de Foresta*, both which this King two Years after, *viz. Anno* 1227, made void, alledging, that having been granted when he was under Age they were not binding.

At the same time the King made a new great Seal, and order'd that all the Clergy and Laity should bring their Grants, or whatsoever Muniments they had from the Crown, to be seal'd therewith,

with, or elfe they fhould be of no Effect. By this Practice he rais'd a confiderable Sum of Money; all which was thought to be done by the Advice of *Hubert de Burg,* his Juftice, and great Favourite.

*Anno Dom.* 1231, King *Henry* kept his *Chriftmas* at *Lambeth.* After which, on the 7th of the Calends of *February,* the King met the Prelates and Nobility of the Kingdom at *Weftminfter,* where he demanded a Scutage of three Marks *per* Fee of all that held Baronies, as well Clergy as Laity. *Richard* Archbifhop of *Canterbury,* and fome Bifhops oppofing, the Matter in relation to the Prelates was put off till a Fortnight after *Eafter.* All the reft, as well Laity as Clergy and Prelates, were for the King.

*Anno* 1232, The Bifhops and other Prelates, with the Nobility of the Kingdom, met the King at *Lambeth,* at the Exaltation of the Holy Crofs, where they granted to him, to difcharge the Debt he had contracted with the Earl of *Britany,* the 40th Part of the Moveables of the Laity and Clergy, as the fame had been after the Harveft in the faid King's 14th Year; for the better underftanding whereof we will here infert the King's Letters directed to the Collectors for levying of the faid Duty.

" *Henry,* by the Grace of God King of *England,*
" to *Peter de Thaney, William de Culewurthe,* and
" *Adam Fitz-William,* Collectors of the 40th Penny,
" Greeting. Know ye, that the Archbifhops, Bi-
" fhops, Abbats, Priors, and Clergy, having Lands
" which do not belong to their Churches; the
" Earls, Barons, Knights, Freemen, and Villains
" of our Kingdom, have granted to us, as an Aid,
" the fortieth Part of all their vifible Moveables,
" as they had them on the Morrow after the Feaft
" of St. *Matthew* in the 14th Year of our Reign;

" *viz.*

" *viz.* of Corn, Plows, Sheep, Cows, Swine,
" Breeds of Horses, Cart Horses, and such as are
" appointed for Wainage in Manors; excepting
" such Goods as the Archbishops, Bishops, and
" other Ecclesiastical Persons have of Parish Chur-
" ches, and of other Prebendary Churches, and
" Prebends, and the Lands belonging to Prebends,
" and to Parish Churches. It is provided in gene-
" ral by our aforesaid Lieges, that the aforesaid
" fortieth Part be thus assess'd and collected, *viz.*
" that there be chosen of every Township four of
" the best and most legal Men, together with the
" Chiefs of each Township, by whose Oath the
" fortieth Part of all the aforesaid Moveables be
" rated, and assess'd upon every one, in the Pre-
" sence of the Knights Assessors appointed to this
" Effect; and afterwards upon the Oath of two
" legal Men of the same Towns, the 4th Part of
" all the Moveables, the aforesaid four Men, and
" Chiefs have, shall be enquir'd into and assess'd;
" and it shall be exactly and plainly regifter'd in
" whose Barony or Baronies each Town ftands,
" either in part, or in the whole. And when the
" 4qth Part shall be assess'd, and reduc'd into wri-
" ting, a Roll of all the Particulars of each Town,
" and every County, shall be deliver'd to the Ste-
" ward of every Baron, or the Steward's Attorney,
" or the Bailiff of the Liberty, where any has a
" Liberty, *viz.* that the Baron, or the Lord of
" the Liberty may, and be entitled to collect the
" said 40th Part, and distrain to recover it; but
" if he will not, or cannot, the Sheriffs shall make
" the said Diftrefs, so that they receive nothing
" from it, but that all the aforesaid 40th Part be
" deliver'd to the aforesaid Knights Assessors in
" the greateft and safeft Town of each County.
" And of each Town, Sum, or Total, Tally shall
　　　　　　　　　　　　　　　　　　" be

" be ſtruck between the Baron's Steward, or his
" Attorney, or the Stewards of the Lord of the
" Liberty, and the aforeſaid Aſſeſſors. And the
" Money ſhall be depoſited by the ſame Aſſeſſors
" in ſome ſafe Place of that Town; ſo that the
" Aſſeſſors have their Seals, and their Locks and
" Keys on the aforeſaid Money; and the Sheriffs
" in like manner their Seals, and Locks and Keys.
" And the Aſſeſſors ſhall ſend Rolls of the Aſſeſs-
" ment of the 40th Part by them, of all their Pro-
" greſs. And in like manner, when the ſaid Money
" ſhall be collected by them, they ſhall ſend their
" Rolls to the *Exchequer* of their Receipt, and the
" aforeſaid Money ſhall be kept in the Places where
" depoſited, till by our Command it ſhall be
" brought to the *New Temple* of *London.* But no-
" thing ſhall be taken by the way of the 40th
" Part from any Man, who has not the Value of
" 40 *d.* at leaſt of ſuch moveable Goods. We
" have appointed you to aſſeſs the aforeſaid 40th
" Part in the County of *Hertford,* and we have
" order'd our Sheriff of *Hertford* to cauſe to come
" before you by our Command all the People of
" the Towns in his County, upon certain Days, and
" in ſuch Places as you ſhall ſignify to him; and
" that they be aſſiſting and obedient to you in all
" Things that appertain to the ſaid Buſineſs.
" Farewel.

About this ſame time, the King being inform'd,
that *Hubert,* his late Chief Juſtice, had ſecur'd much
Treaſure in the Hands of the *Knights Templars,*
demanded the ſame of them, which they refus'd to
deliver without the Owner's Conſent; whereupon
the King ſent to him, and he readily order'd the
ſame to be deliver'd. The ſame being brought into the Royal Treaſure, there was found an immenſe Quantity of Silver and Gold Plate, beſides
much Money, and abundance of precious Stones,

the

the real Particulars whereof, if related, would feem incredible. There wanted not fome then who were Enemies to *Hubert*, and took the Liberty to perfwade the King to put him to Death, as a Robber of the Publick; but the King being better temper'd anfwer'd, he would rather chufe to be reputed foolifh and remifs, than cruel and tyrannical, with much more in Favour of him, and fo order'd all the Lands his Father had given him, or which he had purchas'd, to be reftor'd to him.

*Anno Dom.* 1237, Reg. 22, The King kept his *Chriftmas* at *Winchefter*, from whence he fent his Writs of Summons to all the Archbifhops, Bifhops, Abbats, and Priors inftall'd, as alfo Earls and Barons, to meet on the Octave of the *Epiphany* at *London*, about the weighty Affairs of the Kingdom. In this Affembly the King demanded a thirtieth Part of all Moveables throughout all *England*, which, after much Altercation, upon the King's confirming of *Magna Charta*, and all other Privileges, was granted, excluding from it every Man's Gold and Silver, Arms and Horfes. Yet this Condition was annex'd, that the Money collected fhould be for fome time depofited in Abbies, and other Places of Safety, that in cafe the King fhould recede from his Promife, it might be reftor'd to the Owners.

*Anno Dom.* 1240, The King fent his Juftices Itinerants, who taking their Progrefs through all Counties belonging to the King, and correcting the Offences of many, under Colour of doing Juftice, collected a very great Sum of Money for the lavifh King's Ufe.

*Anno Dom.* 1241, The *Jews* were compell'd to pay 20000 Marks, under Pain of being banifh'd, or to fuffer perpetual Imprifonment.

*Anno Dom.* 1243, The Citizens of *London* were compell'd to pay a large Contribution to the King.

The

The fame Year, the wretched *Jews* were again put to a very heavy Ranfom; infomuch that, to omit others, *Aaron* of *York* alone paid four Marks of Gold, and 4000 Marks of Silver. The King receiv'd the Gold of every *Jew*, whether Man or Woman, with his own Hands; the Silver was receiv'd by others. He alfo extorted Gifts from the Abbats and Priors, in fuch manner, that if what they offer'd did not pleafe him, he rejected it, and they were oblig'd to enhance their Offering rather than incur his Difpleafure.

*Anno Dom.* 1244, The Lords Spiritual and Temporal (*for no Mention is yet found of any Commons*) granted to the King, for marrying of his eldeft Daughter, 20 *s*. Scutage of all that held of the King *in Capite*, to be paid the one half at *Eafter*, and the other at *Michaelmas*.

The fame Year, the King of his own Authority extorted from the *Londoners* 15000 Marks.

Still this fame Year, the King rais'd very great Sums of Money, by fining all that had any way encroach'd upon his Forefts, or otherwife offended in that fort. *Robert Paffeleve* was the Advifer and Carrier on of this Extortion, by which he rais'd many thoufand Marks, and grew greatly into the Royal Favour.

*Anno Dom.* 1246, Reg. 30, The *Londoners* were again compell'd to pay 1000 Marks by the Name of a Tallage.

*Anno Dom.* 1249, Reg. 33, The King demanded New Years Gifts of all the wealthy Citizens of *London*, and by that means receiv'd fome Supply. Yet afterwards the fame Year he compell'd them to pay 2000 *l*. as another Contribution. Befides this, fome fmall Sum he gather'd by downright begging of the Nobility and Prelates.

*Anno Dom.* 1250, Reg. 34, *Walter Clifford,* one of the greateſt of the *Engliſh* Barons, was fin'd 1000 Marks, for his Inſolence in ſeizing a Meſſenger of the King's, and compelling him to eat the Letters he was carrying, with all the Wax that was at the Seals. The ſame Year the *Jews,* being convicted of many abominable Crimes, were alſo fin'd to the utmoſt of what they had; inſomuch that *Aaron* the *Jew,* of *York,* paid 14000 Marks, beſides a Preſent of Gold to the Queen; and the ſame *Aaron* proteſted to *Matthew Paris,* the Author of this Hiſtory, that ſince the King's Return out of *France,* he had paid to him 30000 Marks Silver, and 200 Marks of Gold to the Queen. Yet none pity'd thoſe People; becauſe, beſides all other their enormous Villainies, they were very frequently prov'd to be falſe Coiners, and Forgers of Seals and Writings.

*Anno Dom.* 1253, The *Londoners* again compell'd to pay 1000 Marks.

The ſame Year the Clergy granted to the King the Tenth of all the Revenues of the Church for three Years, towards his intended Journey to the Holy Land; the Nobility then giving him a Scutage, at the Rate of three Marks *per* Fee. For which Grant he moſt ſolemnly ſwore to obſerve the great Charter of Liberties before aſſented to by King *John* his Father.

*Anno Dom.* 1257, Reg. 41, *Matthew Paris* having all along bitterly inveigh'd againſt this King's Profuſeneſs, and Extortions, tells us that his whole Expence during the ſaid 41 Years, or, as he terms it, from the time he began to be the Dilapidator of the Kingdom, being ſumm'd up by knowing Men, amounted to *octies centum Millia Marcarum, & centum & quinquaginta Millia Marcarum, quod eſt horribile cogitatu;* that is, eight hundred thouſand

Marks,

Marks, and an hundred and fifty thoufand Marks, which is horrible to think. So he expreffes it, but why in two Sums I know not; yet reducing them into one, the whole is but 950000 Marks, 50000 fhort of a Million of Marks in 41 Years. Obferve now, that in the End of the Reign of King *Richard* it was faid that *Hubert*, Archbifhop of *Canterbury*, fhow'd that King, that in the Space of two Years he had rais'd for his Service 1100000 Marks. If fo, it follows that King *Henry* had 150000 Marks lefs in the faid forty one Years than King *Richard* had in two Years; and then all this Clamour againft King *Henry* muft be prepofterous. If by the Expreffion, from the Time he began to be the Dilapidator of the Kingdom, he means a fhorter Time, ftill that muft be fuppos'd to be above two Years, and fo the Account will again fall much fhort of that under King *Richard.* It is true, he adds that the Kingdom of *England* never receiv'd any Benefit by that Expence, but rather fuftain'd Lofs ; and Dr. *Watts* in the Margin calls this the Sum of the King's ufelefs Expences; whence muft be inferr'd, that this Money was all lavifh'd and fquander'd, in the Judgment of *Matthew Paris*, who being a private Monk was not a proper Perfon to decide what became the Dignity of fuch a Monarch, as may be feen by his bitter inveighing againft him for his Generofity to his Brothers by the fame Mother, as if it were a moft heinous Crime for fuch a Prince to raife Perfons fo near to him in Blood above the other Nobility. But enough of this.

*Anno Dom.* 1257, the Clergy granted the King 42000 Marks upon certain Conditions ; but whether thofe Conditions were perform'd, or the faid Sum paid, does not appear.

*Anno Dom.* 1258, the Citizens of *London*, being charg'd with several Enormities, were fin'd and otherwise punish'd.

*Anno Dom.* 1259, Reg. 43, The King being reduc'd to extream Want, and accordingly disabled from recovering the Lands taken from him and his Father by the King of *France*, sold his Right to the Dutchy of *Normandy* and the Earldom of *Anjou* to him for the Sum of 300000 Livres *Turnois* in ready Money , and Lands in *Gascony* to be restor'd of the yearly Value of 20000 Livres of the same Money. Upon this Contract he resign'd all Claim to those Provinces, and accordingly in his Titles left out those of Duke of *Normandy*, and Earl of *Anjou*. This being no Money rais'd upon the Subjects might have been pass'd by in this Place; but it is fit to be taken notice of to shew how low that Prince was brought, since he stripp'd himself of the Claim to such Dominions to procure a necessary Support for his Family. Whether all the Fault were on his Side, as *Matthew Paris* inculcates, is much to be doubted; there being much Reason to believe, that the Subjects, who had always Money enough to squander in supporting their Rebellions, and other Extravagances, might as well have contributed towards keeping him out of such Streights. That they were not innocent plainly appears, in that both the King and the Barons having referr'd all their Differences to the Arbitration of the King of *France*, and solemnly engag'd to stand to his Award, when that was given, and found to be in Favour of the King, the Barons immediately flew from it, and actually rose in Rebellion. The Pope also then espous'd the King's Quarrel ; so that the Barons were adjudg'd to be in the wrong by those two Judges, chosen by themselves,

and

and as Foreigners, and no way concern'd in the Controverfy, the more impartial ; and yet thofe Men would ftand to no Judgment but their own. Thus much from *Mat. Paris,* who is apt to mention Sums given the King in feveral Places in fuch manner, that it is doubtful whether they were the fame, or repeated Grants. He alfo is particular in the Demands made by the King, and the Aids conditionally promis'd, but will not determine whether they were ever rais'd.

Having done with that Author, the next fhort Account of Taxes impos'd by this King is from Mr. *Madox*'s Hiftory of the *Exchequer,* being all I find in him.

About the third Year of King *Henry* the third a Tallage was impos'd on the Community of the *Jews.*

In or about his thirteenth Year, he had a Grant of *Scutage,* at the Rate of three Marks for each Knight's Fee. *p.* 422.

In or about his 20th Year, the Archbifhops, Bifhops, Abbats, and other Ecclefiaftical Perfons granted him an Aid of two Marks out of each Knight's Fee belonging to them. *Ib.*

*Aaron* the *Jew,* of *York,* gave 60 Marks to be quit of a Tallage affefs'd in the twenty firft Year of the King's Reign. *p.* 152.

The twenty fifth Year of his Reign a Precept was fent to certain *Jews* of *Exeter,* to take care, at their Peril, about levying and anfwering to the Crown their Contingent of the Tallage of 20000 Marks affefs'd on them, at the Terms appointed for that Purpofe ; and the like Precepts were fent to the *Jews* in other Parts. *p.* 152.

In or about his twenty fixth Year the Bifhops granted him another Aid of 40 *s. per* Fee. *p.* 423.

In

In or about his twenty eighth Year, the *Jews* made Fine with the Crown in 20000 Marks, *p.* 152.

About the same Time was also impos'd upon the *Jews* a Tallage of 60000 Marks. *Ib.*

(*In the twenty ninth Year of his Reign*) An Aid was rais'd for marrying his eldest Daughter. *p.* 412. (*This was* 20 *s.* Scutage *of all that held of him* in Capite.)

The Bishop of *Hereford* paid 15 *l.* for 15 Fees, which he acknowledg'd.

In *Hampshire*, the Bishop of *Winchester* paid 60 *l.* for sixty Fees, which he admitted, and stood charg'd with 14 *l.* 10 *s.* for fourteen Fees and an half, which he disown'd.

The Abbat of *Winchcumb* in *Gloucestershire*, 40 *s.* for two Knights Fees.

The Prior of *Coventry* was charg'd 10 *l.* for ten Knights Fees.

The thirty first Year of his Reign he had an Aid for his Voyage to *Gascoigne. p.* 423.

The thirty fifth Year, the whole Body of the *Jews* in *England* stood charg'd with 5000 Marks of Silver and 40 Marks of Gold for a Fine. *p.* 154.

In his thirty seventh Year, an Aid or *Vintisme* was granted him, the Total whereof was 31488 *l.* 17 *s.* 10 *d. ob.* This is the first I here meet with that has the Amount of it set down. *p.* 424.

King *Henry* had also an Aid to marry his Sister *Elizabeth* to the Emperor, being then two Marks out of every Knight's Fee. *p.* 412.

Likewise an Aid, to make his eldest Son a Knight, of every Knight's Fee 40 *s.* *p.* 414.

The Scutage of *Biham* in his Reign was assess'd at 10 *s. per* Fee.                                    The

The Scutage of *Poictou* at 40 *s. per* Fee.

The Scutage for the King's firſt Voyage to *Britany* at three Marks *per* Fee.

This is all I find in Mr. *Madox* during this King's Reign, wherein are ſome Particulars worth obſerving, as the Sums paid by certain Biſhops and Abbats for their Knights Fees, and the Amount of the *Vintiſme*, or twentieth Part, in the thirty ſeventh Year of the Reign.

*Leland's* MS. in the *Cotton* Library, *Cleopatra. F.* VI. Fol. 145, comes next.

*Anno Dom.* 1217, Reg. 1, Upon the withdrawing of *Lewis* the King of *France's* Son out of *England*, the King had a Scutage granted him of two Marks on each Knight's Fee. *Jo. Everſden.*

*Lewis*, having borrow'd of the Citizens of *London* 5000 Marks, by reaſon of his great Poverty, return'd into *France. Mat. Paris.*

The Biſhops, Abbats, Priors, ſecular Canons, and many of the Clergy, who had been aiding and adviſing to *Lewis*, being depriv'd of all their Benefices by *Gualo* the Legate, were oblig'd to go to *Rome. Mat. Paris.*

*Hugh* Biſhop of *Lincoln* returning into *England* was oblig'd to pay to the Pope 1000 Marks, and 100 to the Legate, to be ſettled in his Biſhoprick. *Ib.* The ſame was done by other Biſhops and many of the Clergy. ( *Note, that theſe were Sin Offerings for their being in Rebellion.*)

*Anno Dom.* 1220, Reg. 4, The King had 2 *s.* of every Carucate in *England*, for the Support of his State. *Tho. Walſingham.*

*Anno Dom.* 1221, Reg 5, The King beſieg'd the Caſtle of *Biam*, at which Time he took 10 *s.* Scutage of every Knight's Fee. *Jo. Everſden.* The

The fame Year, after the building of the Caftle of *Montgomery* in *Wales*, the Nobility granted
the King two Marks Silver of every Knight's
Fee. *Mat. Paris. Jo. Everſden.*

*Humphry Bohun*, Earl of *Hereford* and *Eſſex*, paid
196 Pounds and one Mark, of the Scutage of
*Wales* in the aforeſaid fifth Year of the King, for
*Eſſex*; and 52 *l.* and half a Mark for *Hereford* ; and
23 *l.* for *Gloucefter*; and paid as much of the ſecond Scutage of *Wales*, in the tenth Year of the
ſame King, for his Lands in the ſame Counties ; as
likewiſe in the Scutage of *Wales* in the 16th Year
of the King. *Out of moſt ancient Rolls.*

*Maud* Counteſs of *Eſſex*, towards the Aid for
marrying King *Henry*'s Daughter, 51 *l.* 11 *s.* 3 *d.*
as is expreſs'd in *Rot.* 50.

*Anno. Dom.* 1223, Reg. 7, The King of *Jeru-
ſalem* arriv'd in *England*, to treat with King *Henry*
and the Nobility about the Relief of the Holy
Land. The King, with the Advice of his Council, publiſh'd a general Order throughout all *England*,
of what each Earl, Baron, Knight, and others
were to give. *Rad. Coggeſhale.* But the ſame is more
expreſsly in *Walt. Covent.* as follows : Proviſion
was made by the general Council of the Kingdom
for Relief of the Holy Land, that every Earl
ſhould give three Marks, each Baron one Mark,
each Knight 12 *d.* and every Houſekeeper one
Penny. *Walt. Covent.*

*An. Dom.* 1224, Reg. 8, There was granted to
the King, as well by the Prelates as Laity, in
Conſideration of his great Trouble and Expence,
*Carucage* throughout all *England*, viz. 2 *s.* of every
Carucate. *Mat. Paris.* and *Mat. Weſtm.*

Scutage was alſo granted to the King at the
ſame time, that is, after the taking of the Caſtle

of

of *Bedford, viz.* two Marks for each Knight's Fee. *Jo. Everfden.*

*Anno Dom.* 1225, Reg 9, There was a general Tax of the fifteenth Part of all Moveables, and Chattels, throughout *England,* as well on Clergy and Religious Men as on the Laity. *Mat. Weftm.*

*Anno Dom.* 1226, Reg. 10, The Barons of *England* granted to King *Henry* the fifteenth Part of all Moveables, and Chattels, in *England,* for Confirmation of the Liberties which his Father King *John* had before granted, and confirm'd by his Charter, at *Runenrede. Rad. Coggefhale.*

*Anno Dom.* 1227, Reg. 11, The Citizens of *London* were compell'd to pay to the King 5000 Marks, not without much muttering, and many Curfes. *Mat. Weftm.*

He alfo took of them the fifteenth Part of all their Moveables, and of all their Subftance, as had been before granted him by all *England. Mat. Weftm.*

From the Burgeffes of *Northampton* he took an Aid of 1000 *l.* befides the fifteenth paid by all the Kingdom to no purpofe. *Matthew Weftm.*

The Religious Men and benefic'd Clergy were alfo compell'd to pay this fifteenth of all their Goods, as well Ecclefiaftical as Secular, nor did their appealing to the Pope avail them. *Idem.*

The fame Year, the King being then come to Age, he made a new Seal. Then was it fignify'd to religious Men, and others, who were willing to enjoy their Liberties, that they muft renew their Charters under the King's new Seal, for that the King look'd upon their former Charters as of no Effect. For the which renewing, they were not rated according to their feveral Abilities, but

F oblig'd

oblig'd to pay whatfoever the Juftice thought fit. *Idem.*

*Anno Dom.* 1229, Reg. 13, *Stephen*, the Pope's Chaplain, and Nuncio, for retrieving of the Treafure the Pope had loft, *&c.* exacted all the Tenths of the Churches, without deducting Charges, throughout *England, Ireland*, and *Wales*, and by the King's Permiffion recover'd the fame. *Mat. Weftm. & alij.*

The fame Year the King receiv'd Scutage, two Marks of every Knight's Fee. *Jo. Everfden.*

*Anno Dom.* 1230, Reg. 14, The Archbifhops, Bifhops, Abbats and Priors throughout all *England*, at the King's Demand, gave no fmall Sum of Money, towards recovering of his Rights in the Parts beyond the Seas. *Mat. Weftm. &c.*

The Citizens of *London* were oblig'd to contribute very largely towards that Affair. *Idem.*

The *Jews* alfo very fpeedily paid the third Part of what they had. *Idem.*

*Anno Dom.* 1231, Reg. 15, The King exacted Scutage, two Marks of every Knight's Fee, from all that held Baronies, as well the Laity, as the Prelates; *Richard*, Archbifhop of *Canterbury*, and fome other Bifhops, in vain oppofing it. *Jo. Everfden, &c.*

*Anno Dom.* 1232, Reg. 16, The King again took Scutage, 40 *s.* of each Knight's Fee. *Idem.*

The fame Year, there was granted to him, for Payment of the Debts he had contracted on account of the Affair in *Britany*, and due to the Earl of *Britany*, the fortieth Part of the Moveables of the Bifhops, Abbats, Priors, Clergy, and Laity. *Mat. Weftm. &c. (See the manner of collecting this* fortieth *Part above.)*

*Anno*

*Anno Dom.* 1233, Reg. 17, The King laid a Scutage on the *English*, at 20 *s.* the Knight's Fee. *Jo. Everſden.*

*Anno Dom.* 1235, Reg. 19, The King took Carucage, at two Marks the Carucate, to marry his Siſter *Elizabeth* to the Emperor, upon whoſe Wedding the King paid down 30000 Marks.

*Anno Dom.* 1237, Reg. 21, The King exacted the thirtieth Part of all the Moveables in the whole Kingdom. *Mat. Weſtm. &c.*

The ſame Year again the thirtieth Part of Moveables was granted to the King. *Mat. Paris.* ( *Theſe two Taxes are doubtleſs only* one *and the ſame, repeated over again by that Author, there being no likelihood that the ſame Impoſition ſhould happen twice in the ſame Year ; and, as I have before obſerv'd, the ſaid Writer is often guilty of ſuch Repetitions.*)

*Anno Dom.* 1238, Reg. 22, The King took Scutage, 40 *s.* of every Knight's Fee. *Jo. Everſden.*

*Anno Dom.* 1239, Reg. 23, The wretched *Jews,* to their great Oppreſſion and Confuſion, paid to the King the third Part of all they had, as well in Debts as in Chattels, that they might for ſome time enjoy their Lives and Peace. *Matth. Paris.*

*Anno Dom.* 1240, Reg. 24, The Biſhops, and the Nobility, in the Preſence of the Legate, complain'd of ſundry Oppreſſions, and daily Deſolations brought upon the Church by the King's evil Council ; and blam'd the King, for extorting the Goods of the Church by ſeveral Arguments, and detaining them many Years in his own Hands. *Idem.*

F 2 The

The King sent his Justices Itinerants throughout *England*, who, under Colour of Justice, collected a vast Sum of Money for the King. *Idem.*

*Anno Dom.* 1241, Reg. 25, The *Jews* were compell'd to ransom themselves at a most grievous Rate, paying 20000 Marks, at two Terms within the Year, under Pain of being banish'd, or suffering perpetual Imprisonment. *Idem.*

*Anno Dom.* 1242, Reg. 26, The Barons told the King, that they had often granted him Aids since he had been their Lord, *viz.* a thirteenth of their Moveables, then a fifteenth, a sixteenth, and a fortieth, *Carucage, Hidage,* and divers Scutages, and afterwards one great Scutage to marry his Sister, the Empress. Afterwards, before four Years were elaps'd, or thereabouts, he again ask'd an Aid of them, and at length, with many Intreaties, obtain'd of them a thirtieth Part. Besides, they well knew that since then, he had so many Escheats, *viz.* the Archbishoprick of *Canterbury*, and several of the richest Bishopricks in *England*, and the Lands of Earls, Barons, and Knights that held of him, and were dead, that if it had been carefully laid up, he must have a very considerable Sum of Money by him from only those Escheats. And yet farther, from the Time of the aforesaid thirtieth Part given, the Itinerant Justices had not ceas'd to take their Progresses into all Parts of *England*, as well upon Forest Pleas, as all others; so that almost all the Counties in *England*, all the Hundreds, Cities and Boroughs, and almost all the Towns had been amerced; so that what by those Amerciaments, and what by other Aids before given, all the People of the Kingdom were so oppress'd and impoverish'd, that they had little or nothing left them. *Mat. Paris.*

The

The fame Year the King impos'd a Scutage, at 40 s. the Knight's Fee. *Jo. Everfden.*

Provifions were alfo fent the King out of *England* into *France, viz.* 10000 Loads of Wheat, and 5000 of Oats, with as many Bacons, and no fmall Sum of Money, as if *England* had been an inexhauftible Pit. *Mat. Paris.*

The King fell into fuch Poverty, that having extorted a Scutage, and mifpent all the Treafures and Donatives beftow'd on him, and invented Extortions, Tallages, and other Collections, he contracted great Debts in *Gafcony* at this Time, notwithftanding he had in the aforefaid Scutage exacted three Marks of every Knight's Fee, to the great Grief of the *Englifh* People.

*Anno Dom.* 1243, Reg. 27, More Money was drein'd from the Citizens of *London.* *Matth. Paris.*

The fame Year the King forc'd from the moft miferable *Jews* a very great Ranfom in Gold and Silver, infomuch that he had from only *Aaron,* the *Jew* of *York,* four Marks in Gold, and 4000 in Silver. He alfo had rich Gifts from the Abbats and Priors. *Idem.*

The Nobility of *England* agreed to grant the King an Aid to marry his eldeft Daughter, *viz.* 20 s. for every Knight's Fee, of all that held of the King *in Capite,* the one half to be paid at *Eafter,* and the other half at *Michaelmas. Idem.*

The King again extorted from the Citizens of *London* 1500 Marks.

*Anno Dom.* 1245, Reg. 29, A Scutage of 4 s. of every Knight's Fee was given the King, on account of the Siege of the Caftle of *Gannon* in *Wales. Jo. Everfden.*

*Anno*

_Anno Dom._ 1248, Reg. 33, A Parliament was held at _London_, wherein the King asking an Aid was reprov'd; and endeavour'd to qualify the Nation with fair Promises; but being deny'd any Supply, he fold his Furniture to the _Londoners._ From the Abbat of St. _Edmund's-bury_ 1200 Marks.

_Anno Dom._ 1249, Reg. 33, The King demanded new Years Gifts of all the wealthiest Citizens of _London_. The City being much oppress'd gave him 2000 _l._ and at the same time such Things as were expos'd to Sale, especially all that belong'd to eating and drinking were taken up for his Use.

_Anno Dom._ 1250, Reg. 34, The _Jews_ were again tax'd, and Justices sent all over _England_ to discover what Money they had.

The King extorted Money on all Hands, as well from his own Christian Subjects as from _Jews_, insomuch that one only _Jew_, whose Name was _Aaron_, paid 14000 Marks, and 10000 Pieces of Gold for the Queen. It appear'd that the said _Aaron_ had given the King, since his Return from beyond the Seas, 30000 Marks of Silver, and 200 Marks of Gold to the Queen. (_Note, that all this is taken from_ Matthew Paris, _and no other Author mention'd; whereas if all had been true, they would not certainly have omitted Matters of such Moment; and it seems incredible that the said_ Jew _should have been able to pay so great a Sum as_ 30000 _Marks. Besides, in the Total he adds_ 200 _Marks to the Queen, after having just above said he gave_ 10000 _Pieces of Gold to the Queen; so that we are at a great Loss to find what those_ 10000 _could be, when the whole then, and at other times, amounted only to_ 200 _Marks. Thus either the_ MSS. _must be very erroneous, or else_ Matthew Paris _did not much regard what he writ, provided it were in-_
_jurious_

*jurious to the King; for indeed he seems to have been intent upon nothing more than vilifying of him.* For a *farther Demonstration of his Way of writing, after he has sufficiently inveigh'd against the Papal Extortions, which as not belonging to the Subject in Hand are here omitted, he tells us, that the Revenues of the Alien Clergy in* England *amounted to above* 70000 *Marks, whereas the King's real Revenue did not rise to the* 3d *Part of that Sum.* Accordingly, *that Monarch's Revenue could scarce arrive to* 23333 *Marks, or* 15554 l. *a miserable Pittance for such a Monarch, and plainly evincing that his Wars and other necessary Expences must needs require very large extraordinary Contributions to enable him any way to subsist.*

*Anno Dom.* 1253, Reg. 37, The *Londoners* compell'd to give the King 1000 Marks.

The Sheriffs, and other Officers of the King, pillag'd all they could upon any Occasion; and so many were attending the King's Rapines in *England*, that I think it dangerous to name them; for they seiz'd of poor People, and especially of Traders from one Place to another, Horses, Carts, Wines, Provisions, Cloth, Wax, and other Necessaries. *Still the same Mat. Paris.*

There was granted to the King the tenth of Ecclesiastical Revenues for three Years (or, as *John Eversden* has it, for five) as it were for the Relief of the Holy Land; but it was rather that the King might make his Son *Edmund* King of *Sicily* and *Apulia. Mat. Westm.* and *Jo. Eversden.*

*Anno Dom.* 1254, Reg. 38, The small Substance, that had been before left the miserable *Jews,* was taken from them.

The King paid his Debts, and the Use growing upon them, out of the Revenues of Bishopricks and Abbies, which he had caus'd to be brought into the *Exchequer.*

*Anno Dom.* 1255, Reg. 39, The King caus'd the *Londoners* to pay 3000 Marks upon some slight Occasion.

He exacted 8000 Marks of the *Jews*, under the Penalty of being hang'd. (*These two Exactions being the same Year, from the same People, and only spoken of by the same* Mat. Paris, *seem again to be a Mistake, or a Repetition of the same, under two several Denominations.*)

The King swore that the Sum he stood indebted for amounted to 200000 Marks; and if he should say 300000, he should not exceed the Truth.

A Computation being made, the yearly Revenue of *Edward*, the King's Son, amounted to above 15000 Marks. (*Observe the great Sum of* 10000 *l. a year for a King's eldest Son: And again, how could he afford his Son* 10000 *l. a year, when, as is said above, his own whole Revenue was but* 15554 *l. a year ?*)

The King forcibly took away the Money deposited at *Durham*.

This Year died the noble Baron, the noblest and the wisest of all the *English* Nobility, *Warin de Munchensy*, whose Will is said to have amounted to 200000 Marks. (*This Baron was worth such an immense Sum, at the same time that the King was deny'd the least Aid, by reason, as was pretended, of the great Poverty of the Barons.*)

*Peter* Bishop of *Hereford*, at the King's Instigation, bound almost all the Religious Houses in *England*, whether exempt or not exempt, to the Merchants of *Sens* and *Florence*, the lesser from 100 *l.* to 200 Marks, the greater from 300 *l.* to 400 Marks, and some to 500; and the Church of St. *Edmunds-bury* in 700. *Jo. Eversden*.

*Anno Dom.* 1256, Reg. 40, The Citizens of *London* again paid a Tallage of 500 Marks.

All

All the Sheriffs in *England* were amerc'd to pay five Marks each.

*Anno Dom.* 1257, Reg. 41, The Treafure of Earl *Richard* (*the King's Brother*) was computed to amount to fo great a Sum, that he might fpend 100 Marks a day, for the Space of ten Years, without reckoning the Revenues accruing to him daily from *Germany* and *England.* (*By this he muft be worth* 365000 *Marks, that is,* 243332 *l. which again fhows how rich the great ones then were, notwithftanding all the Clamours of Extortions from the Crown, and of their being reduc'd to Poverty by them.*)

The Poffeffions of the Bifhop of *Ely* were pillag'd by the King's Officers.

The King asks an Aid for his Son *Edmund;* and when they granted and offer'd him 52000 Marks, he would not accept of that confiderable Gift.

The King affirm'd, that with the Advice and Affiftance of the Pope, and Church of *England*, he had oblig'd himfelf towards gaining of the Kingdom of *Sicily*, under the Penalty of forfeiting his own Kingdom, in the Sum of 140000 Marks, befides the Intereft, which daily ran on.

He alfo obtain'd the Tenths of all the Clergy for five Years; as alfo the firft Year's Income of all vacant Churches, for five Years. (*This muft be the fame Grant before mention'd, and now again repeated.*)

The Prelates of *England* granted the King 42000 Marks, to the great Lofs and Detriment of the Church (*in the Judgment of Mat. Paris.*)

The King at this time caus'd *Scutage* to be collected throughout *England*, taking 40 s. of every Knight's Fee. *Mat. Weftm.* and *Jo. Everfden.* This was the 11th *Scutage* fince the beginning of his Reign.

*Anno Dom.* 1258, Reg. 42, The King, to appeafe the Pope, paid to him 500 Marks.

*Anno*

*Anno Dom.* 1259, Reg. 43, A general Collection of Money was made upon all the Clergy of *England*, as well exempt as not exempt; *viz.* the thirtieth of all Ecclefiaftical Revenues, and the Arrears of Tenths, and other things contain'd in the Writings of the Bifhops, in order to pay on the Quindene of *St. Michael* next enfuing to the three Bifhops of *Bath, Ely* and *Rochefter*, who had bound themfelves at the Court of *Rome* in the Sum of 5500 Marks for the King, to ftop the Sentence of Excommunication. *Mat. Weftm.*

The fame Year, the King of *France* having paid to the King of *England* 300000 *l.* and promis'd to reftore Lands to the Value of 20000 Livres a year, King *Henry* made an abfolute Refignation to him of all the Lands then in the King of *France's* Hands. *Tho. Walfingham.*

*Anno Dom.* 1264, Reg. 48, The Bifhops, to fupport the Earl of *Leicefter* againft Aliens, rais'd a Tenth of Spirituals from Religious Houfes, and Rectors of Parifhes. *Mat. Weftm.* (*This was not for, but againft their King, for they had ftill Money to carry on Rebellion.*)

*Anno Dom.* 1265, Reg. 49, The King having fummon'd the Parliament to meet on the *Nativity* of the Bleffed Virgin at *Winchefter*, he and his Son, and other Courtiers, extorted much Money from almoft all the *Englifh* Prelates; fo that they had near 800 Marks from the Church of *St. Edmund's-bury.*

The *Londoners*, having taken Part with Earl *Simon* againft the King, were fain to purchafe their Peace at the Price of 20000 Marks. *Jo. Everfden.*

*Anno Dom.* 1266, Reg. 50, The Pope granted the King the Tenth of all the Ecclefiaftical Revenues in *England*, according to their real Value, for three Years. *Jo. Everfden.*

*Walter*

*Walter Gifborne* fays thefe Tenths were granted for fix Years. Of the Laity the 20th Penny was given to the King at this fame time. *Ran. Ceftrenf.*

*Anno Dom.* 1269, Reg. 53, The King receiv'd the 20th Part of all the Goods in *England.* Thus it is in an ancient Hiftory in the Hands of *John Savil.*

*Anno Dom.* 1270, Reg. 54, Prince *Edward* went away to *Acon,* with a great Number of Soldiers. He fet out in Summer that Year, and a thirtieth Penny was given throughout all *England* upon this pious Occafion. *Walt. Gifborne.*

Thus ends *Leland's* MS. and with it we will conclude this King's long Reign, whofe greateft Misfortune it is that *Mat. Paris* was his contemporary, and writ his Life at large, which has much fully'd that Prince's Reputation, moft Men having a great Veneration for that Author for the fake of his continual railing, which is generally very acceptable; notwithftanding that, as has been hinted before, if they would give themfelves the Trouble to examine him impartially, they would eafily find many grofs Errors in him.

For the better underftanding what the Value of Money was in thofe Days, which is very neceffary towards judging of the Value of what was then receiv'd by the King, no better Recourfe can be had than to the Statute of the 51ft Year of King *Henry* the Third for the Affife of Bread and Beer. There the Weight of the feveral Sorts of Bread is afcertain'd in Proportion to the Price of the Corn; but as that Proportion is not to the Purpofe in Hand, it will be fufficient to note the Price of Wheat, which is there fet down from 1 *s.* the Quarter to 12 *s.* By which it appears, that Wheat at the cheapeft was actually fold for 1 *s.* the Quarter, and the deareft Price then known was 12 *s.* the Quarter.

Quarter. So great a Difproportion between that Time and this would almoft feem incredible, were not the Authority of the Statute, ftill preferv'd entire, an undeniable Teftimony of the Truth of it. At this Time, if Wheat happens to fall to 20 *s.* the Quarter, the Farmers, and even the Gentry, think themfelves all undone; and the loweft they will allow to be a living Price, as they call it, is 40 *s.* the Quarter. Every Man may fee the vaft Difference.

Again, the fame Act directs, that when a Quarter of Wheat is fold for 3 *s.* or 3 *s. 6d.* and a Quarter of Barley for 20 *d.* or 2 *s.* and a Quarter of Oats for 14 *d.* then Brewers in Cities ought and may well afford to fell two Gallons of Beer, or Ale, for a Penny; and out of Cities, to fell 3, or 4 Gallons for a Penny.

Farther, By the Confent of the whole Realm of *England*, the Meafure of our Lord the King was made, that is to fay, that an *Englifh* Penny, call'd a Sterling, round and without any clipping, fhall weigh 32 Wheat Corns in the midft of the Ear, and 20 Pence do make an Ounce, and 12 Ounces a Pound, and 8 Pounds do make a Gallon of Wine, and 8 Gallons of Wine do make a *London* Bufhel, which is the 8th Part of a Quarter.

Here we fee there was clipping in thofe Days, as well as the Defcription of the Coin, the Weights, and Meafures, all of them Particulars well worth remarking, and whatfoever appertains to the three laft of thofe things very pertinent for the Readers of this Treatife, as leading them into the more perfect Knowledge of thofe Times, and accordingly of the Difference between then and now.

K.

# K. EDWARD I.

KING *Henry* the Third departing this Life in the Year 1273, his Son *Edward*, the first of the Name, was proclaim'd King; but being then absent in the Holy Land, the Nobility, with the Queen's Approbation, appointed Justices to govern the Nation till his Return, and other proper Officers under them. He was in the 34th Year of his Age when he ascended the Throne : And, as to his Character, *Walsingham* says, he was discreet in the Management of Affairs from his Youth, addicted to martial Exercises, by which he gain'd greater Renown abroad than any Christian Prince of his Time; of a great Soul, impatient of Wrong, regarding no Danger when he sought Revenge, and yet easy to be appeas'd by Submission. Advice being sent to him into the Holy Land of his Father's Death, he hasted home, and was crown'd the next Year.

We will begin, as to the Taxes rais'd by this King, with Sir *Robert Cotton*'s MS. above quoted, and so proceed to the others. His Words are :

*Edward* his Son (*Henry the Third's*) succeeding, impos'd the first Year a *Tallage per Capita*, appointing Commissioners to see it levy'd. *Pat. an.* 1 *E.* 1. *Jo. Eversden.* The next, he took a Tenth from the Clergy, exiling all Usurers, under Confiscation of Goods, and Bodies Imprisonment. *Clauf. an.* 2 *E.* 1. And of the *Jews* he levy'd for *Tallage* 5000 Marks the Year succeeding. *Clauf. an.* 3 *E.* 1. In the 4th Year he tax'd his Subjects at a fifteenth, and the *Jews* at 5 *d.* a Head. A Tallage. *Jo. Eversden.* A Tallage through *Wales* he assess'd the 6th Year. *Pat.* 6 *E.* 1. And 40 *s.* Scutage the next. *Commu-*

*nia*

*nia* 7 *E.* 1. 40 *s.* he took of every Knight's Fee the 13th and the 15th. *Rot.* 4. *de Term. Paschæ.* On the *Jews* he impos'd 12000 Marks for Redemption of their Ufury. *John Everfden, Thorne.* The next Year he fearch'd one Day all the Religious Houfes, and took to his Ufe the Money and Plate. *Rad. Ceftrenfis.* The Lords by themfelves, without the Commons, affefs'd for the King, the 18th Year, fuch a Levy as King *H.* III. rais'd for Marriage of his Daughter. *Jo. Everfden.* And in the 12th, the King charges the Clergy with a Tenth for fix fucceeding Years. *Rad. Ceftrenfis.* The Abbeys are again fearch'd in the 22d, and the Lands of the Priors Aliens feiz'd into the King's Hands. *Jo. Everfden.*

The Times fucceeding this Prince's Reign afford Examples of this kind of Sovereign Power more rarely than before. For Parliaments becoming more frequent, almoft annually fupply'd the King.

This is all Sir *Robert Cotton* fays of this Reign. The next is the MS. *fol.* 64.

The firft *Edward, an.* 1274, for Maintenance of *Welfh* Wars, took of every Knight's Fee 50 Marks, and large Sums of all his Cities and Boroughs by way of Loan; the Proportion of *London* being then 8000 Marks. And in the Year 1283, to fupply all Wants of his *Welfh* Wars, he took by Force all the Pope's Treafures here away. And for his laft Wars in *Wales,* 1285, took 40 *s.* Scutage; and after, in the Year 1294, feiz'd all the Revenue of the Priors Aliens, to help out that Charge of War, leaving the Monks to a Stipend of 18 *d.* by the Week.

The firft of Subjects Contribution by Parliament, towards the Nation's Defence, I obferve not before the Year 1283, when the Commons gave to *Edward* I. the 30th Part of all their Moveables; and that the Clergy of *Canterbury* Diocefe, for two Years, gave

gave the 20th Part of their Revenues; and for his Wars in *Gafcony, an.* 1289, the Clergy gave half, the fixth the Boroughs, and the tenth the Commons of all their Goods, to that Purpofe. *Jo. Everfden. An.* 1294, half of the Clergy the King obtain'd, which by the Rate of the laft Tenths amounted to 100000 *l.* and after, for the like Occafion, 1295, the Boroughs granted the feventh, the Commons the eleventh, and the Clergy the tenth of all their Moveables. To fupprefs an Inroad of the *Scots,* 1298, the Clergy beftow'd the tenth of their Goods. And 1306, for the Wars againft the *Scots,* the 30th Part of all Goods, and the 20th of all Merchandize is beftow'd. *Hift. Roffen.*

Next from *Leland's* MS. p. 145.

*Anno Dom.* 1273, Reg. 1, The Clergy granted to King *Edward* the Tenth of all Ecclefiaftical Revenues, as well Temporal as Spiritual, for one Year; and the fame to his Brother for another, as a Recompence for their Expences in the Holy Land. Whereupon the Convent of St. *Edmund's-bury* compounded for the Tenth of all Goods of one Year, in common with the Abbat's of one Year, for 100 *l.* and the like for the fecond, the Abbat paying 50 Marks of the Money, and the Convent 100 Marks. *Jo. Everfden.*

*Anno Dom.* 1275, Reg. 3, The Nobility of *England* granted the King the 15th Penny. *John Everfden.*

The *Jews* throughout the Kingdom of *England* were forbid for the future putting out their Money to Ufe to any Perfon, but to live upon Trade; enjoying the fame Law as the Chriftian Merchants in buying and felling. And it was ordain'd that every one of them, of what Age, Condition, or Sex foever, fhould yearly pay to the King 3 *d.* Pole-money. *John Everfden.*

*Anno*

*Anno Dom.* 1276, The half of the fifteenth granted to the King the Year before was collected. *Jo. Everfden.* and *Hift. Roffen.*

*Anno Dom.* 1277, The Abbat and Convent of *St. Edmund's-bury* compounded for the fifteenth of their Goods for 90 *l.* the Abbat paying 30, and the Convent 60 *l. Jo. Everfden.*

The Abbat and Convent alfo compounded for the Townfhip of *St. Edmund's* at 100 *l.* to be levy'd on the fame Town, and to be paid to the King by the aforefaid Convent, for preferving the Liberty of the Town.

The fame Year, a Tenth was granted throughout *England* for the Relief of the Holy Land, and continu'd full fix Years; and the Collectors of the fame for four Years, in the Diocefe of *Canterbury,* were the Brothers *William Wilmington,* Prior of that Place, and *John Bellam.* And it appear'd that the Total of all the Receipts for the whole third Year by the faid Prior, was 804 *l.* 2 *s.* 2 *d.* The Receipt of the 4th Year, 1704 *l.* 10 *s.* 7 *d.* The Receipt of the 5th Year, 828 *l.* 14 *s.* 5 *d. ob.* And the Receipt of the 6th Year, 1027 *l.* 4 *s.* And the Receipt of the Arrears of the two firft Years, during which they were not Collectors, 126 *l.* 1 *s.* 2 *d. ob.* And the Receipt of the firft Collectors depofited 1264 *l.* 7 *s.* 11 *d. ob.* The Sum of all the Receipts by them in the Diocefe of *Canterbury,* 5125 *l.* 0 *s.* 5 *d. ob. Chron. Will. Thorne.*

King *Edward,* becaufe *Leolin* Prince of *Wales* had refus'd to come to the Parliament of *England,* enter'd *Wales,* built the Caftles of *Flint* and *Rutland;* and then *Leolin* came to him, fubmitting himfelf to the King's Mercy; and to purchafe his Peace gave 50000 *l.* in Silver, and for the Ifle of *Anglefey* 1000 Marks yearly. *Ran. Ceftrenfis.*

*Anno*

*Anno Dom.* 1278, Another Moiety of the fifteenth granted to the King was collected, for which the Abbat and Convent of *St. Edmund's-bury* compounded with the King at 90 *l.* the Abbat paying 30 *l.* for his Part, and the Convent 60 *l.* *Jo. Everſden.*

*Anno Dom.* 1279, The King took *Scutage* for the Expedition into *Wales,* impoſing 40 *s.* upon each Fee.

*Simon* Abbat of *St. Edmund's-bury* dying, the King ſeiz'd both the Abbat's Portion, and the Barony, which was till then a thing never heard of; which Portion of the Convent could not be reſcu'd out of his Poſſeſſion either by Intreaty or Money; but all things were diſpos'd of by the Direction of *John* of *Berwick,* the King's Attorney, making a ſufficient Exhibition to the Convent, and the Homages of the Manors of the Convent, as well within the Town of *St. Edmund's,* as without it, being tally'd.

The Parliament of the Kingdom of *France* being aſſembled at *Ambois,* there met the Kings of *France* and *England,* as alſo many great Men of both Nations, and there the King of *England* quitted all Claim to *Normandy* to the King of *France* for ever, for which he was to receive out of the *Exchequer* of *Roan* 30 *Pariſian* Livres yearly for ever. He alſo receiv'd, for the ſaid quitting of Claim, *Agenois,* *Limoſin,* *Perigort* and *Saintonge.* This done he return'd into *England.* *Jo. Everſden.*

The Coin was alter'd in *England,* the triangular Farthing being made round; but yet ſuch old Money as was reaſonable was not forbid paſſing among the new. But yet contrary to what had been us'd, the Half-pence being quite laid aſide, one great Piece was coin'd equivalent to 4 *d.* of the common Sort. *Jo. Everſden.*

G

*Anno*

*Anno Dom.* 1280, A fifteenth of Spiritual Goods was granted to the King by the Clergy of *England,* according to the Taxation of *Walter* Bifhop of *Norwich,* and this for three Years. *Jo. Everfden.*

*Anno Dom.* 1281, There was at length obtain'd of the King a Separation between the Portions of the Abbat and the Convent of *St. Edmund's-bury,* paying to the King 1000 *l.* befides the Queen's Gold proportionable to fo great a Sum of Money, and other Expences collaterally accruing, which amounted to a vaft Sum. *Jo. Everfden.*

*Anno Dom.* 1282, The King, for maintaining of his War againft the *Welfh,* took up Money by way of Loan from all his own Cities and Boroughs, as alfo of the Cities and Boroughs of the Clergy. From the *Londoners* he had a Contribution of 8000 Marks; after the fame manner, from *Yarmouth,* 1000 Marks; and from *Norwich,* 500 *l.* The Burgeffes of *St. Edmund's-bury* were tax'd at 500 Marks. There was alfo a taxing of thofe that belong'd to the Monks Court, which had never been before, and it amounted to 260 Marks. Likewife the Brotherhood of the twelfth Town of St. *Edmund* was tax'd at 12 Marks. But from the Abbat and Convent of *St. Edmund's* he extorted 100 Marks, under the fame Colour. *Jo. Everfden.*

In the aforefaid Expedition the King took for each Knight's Service 50 Marks, yet dealt more favourably with the Abbat of *St. Edmund's,* taking 300 *l.* for his Service. *Jo. Everfden.*

*Anno Dom.* 1283, The People of *England* granted to the King, for maintaining of his Wars, the 30th Penny of all their Moveables, Horfes, Armour, Treafure, and Apparel excepted. On the Contribution of which Money, the King caus'd all the Money receiv'd the Year before in any Place whatfoever, under Colour or Pretence of a Loan,

to

to be plac'd to Account. *Jo. Everſden,* and *Walt. Gisborn.*

On Mid-Lent *Sunday*, the King, breaking the Locks, took away all the Treaſure of the Pope's Tenths, granted for the Relief of the Holy Land, and depoſited in ſeveral Parts of *England,* and diſpos'd of it according to his own Will. *Jo: Everſden.*

The twentieth of all Eccleſiaſtical Profits was granted to the King, for the Charge of his Wars, by the Clergy of the Province of *Canterbury,* for two Years, according to the Taxation of *Walter* late Biſhop of *Norwich. Jo. Everſden,* and *Gisborn.*

*Anno Dom.* 1284, *Thomas Tidon,* Abbat of St. *Auguſtin's,* perform'd the Service of one Knight in the King's Army in *Wales,* and for his Expedition there, by the Perſon of the Lord *Henry de Cobham,* for 20 *l. Will. Thorne.*

*Anno Dom.* 1285, The King took 40 *s.* Scutage of every Knight's Fee for the Army in *Wales. Jo. Everſden, Will. Thorne.* And it is to be obſerv'd that Scutage is ſometimes more, and ſometimes leſs, according to the King's Pleaſure. *Will. Thorne.*

*Anno Dom.* 1287, The *Jews* throughout all *England,* of all Ages, and both Sexes, were on *Friday,* the Day after the Feaſt of the Apoſtles *Philip* and *Jacob,* committed to ſafe Cuſtody; till at length having given the King Security to pay him 12000 *l.* they return'd to their own Houſes. *Jo. Evereſden.*

*Anno Dom.* 1288, Reg. 16, King *Edward* caus'd all the Monaſteries in *England* to be ſearch'd much about the ſame time of the Day, and took all the Money depoſited in them to his own Uſe. King *William* the Conqueror had made the like Search, as has been mention'd before. *Rand. Ceſtrenſis.*

*Anno Dom.* 1289, There was granted to *Edward* King of *England* an Aid for his Wars in *Gaſcony,* being one half of the Clergy, a ſixth of the

Citizens,

Citizens, and of the rest of the People a tenth of their Goods. *Thus in the History in the Hands of Mr.* Savill.

The Churches in *England* were tax'd according to the real Value, by Order of Pope *Nicholas,* and from that time the *Norwich* Taxation made by Pope *Innocent* IV. ceas'd. *Ran. Cestrensis.*

*Anno Dom.* 1290, There was granted to the King a Tenth of all Spiritual Profits, for one Year; yet so that the said Tenth should not be collected before the Feast of St. *Michael* of the ensuing Year. There was taken a fifteenth of all the People of *England. Jo. Eversden.*

The Laity gave the King the 15th Penny, and all the Clergy a tenth, for expelling the *Jews* out of the Land. *Walt. Gisborne.*

Both the Clergy and Laity granted the King a fifteenth of all their Goods, as well Spiritual as Temporal, for the Relief of the Holy Land, and that tax'd before to the utmost was at this time exacted together with the tenth of the Goods of the Clergy assign'd him in the Court of *Rome* for six Years. *Hist. Roffen.*

The Pope also bestow'd on the King the tenth of all the Product in Temporals of all Religious Persons, excepting only the *Templars* and *Hospitallers;* for taxing whereof Persons were appointed throughout all *England, Scotland,* and *Ireland.*

*Anno Dom.* 1291, The fifteenth above granted to the King was collected; but the Abbat and Convent of *St. Edmund's-bury* compounded with the King for 1000 Marks, in lieu of the fifteenth of their own Goods, those of the Burgesses of their Town of St. *Edmund,* and their Natives, or Vassals. *Jo. Eversden.*

*Anno Dom.* 1292, The Pope granted the King the Tenth of all the Product of the Clergy, as

also

also of the Goods of all Religious Men whatfoever, for fix Years, excepting only the *Templars* and
the *Hofpitallers*, and this for the Relief of the Holy
Land; and a new Taxation was made of our Spiritual Goods, and of others: and the annual Tenth
of the Spiritual Goods of the Cellarer, the Sacrift, the Chamberlain, and the Almoner was 32
Marks, 5 *s.* 4 *d.* of the Sum of the whole Taxation, which was 324 Marks, for the Spirituals; of
the Hofpital of St. *Saviour*, 6 *l.* 5 *s.* 10 *d.* of the
Temporal, out of the Sum of 29 *l.* 11 *s.* 11 *d.* of
Spirituals of the fame Hofpital, 58 *s.* 8 *d. ob.* The
Tenth of the Temporals of the Convent of *St.
Edmund's-bury*, computed by the Bifhops of *Winchefter* and *Lincoln*, was firft of the Goods of the
Cellarer in *Suffolk* and *Norfolk*, 70 *l.* 7 *s.* 8 *d.* in
other Counties —— of the Goods of the Sacrift in
*Suffolk* and *Norfolk*, 16 *l.* 6 *s.* 1 *d. ob.* and moreover
1 *d. q.* of the Temporal Goods of the Chamber-
lain in *Suffolk* and *Norfolk*, 12 *l.* 5 *s.* 2 *d. ob.* of the
Goods of the Pitancer, 23 *s.* 8 *d. ob.* of the Almoner, 25 *l.* 11 *s.* 6 *d.* of the Infirmarian, 14 *s.* 3 *d.
ob. q.* of the leffer Obedientiaries in the Town of
*St. Edmund's-bury*, 20 *s.* 10 *d. q.* and moreover 1 *d.
ob.* of Obventions at the Tomb of St. *Edmund*,
the tenth 4 *l.* of the Goods of the Precentor——
of the Goods of the Hofpital, 50 *s.* 10 *d.* ——The
Sum of the Taxation of all the Temporal Goods
of all the Obedientiaries in *Suffolk* and *Norfolk*,
1098 *l.* 8 *s.* 8 *d.* The Tenth of this Sum 109 *l.*
16 *s.* 10 *d. ob. q.* and moreover 1 *d. Jo. Everfden.*

The fifteenth of all Temporals and Spirituals
throughout *England* was granted to the King about
the Feaft of St. *Andrew* the Apoftle. Of this the
fifteenth appertaining to the Abby of St. *Auguftin* of
their moveable Goods, according to the true Taxation of them in all their Manors, was 137 *l.* 15 *s.*
11 *d. q. Will. Thorne.*　　　G 3　　　*Anno*

*Anno Dom.* 1294, King *Edward* caus'd all the Monasteries in *England* to be search'd, and the Money found therein to be brought to *London.* He also caus'd Wool and Leather to be seiz'd, and there ensued a great Dearth of Wheat and Wine. *Ran. Ceftrenfis.*

The King feiz'd into his Hands all Religious Houfes throughout all *England,* that were fubordinate to foreign Chapters, with all their Profits, whatfoever Way accruing. The Charge of them was given to his Officers and Wardens, and a certain Allowance given to the Religious Men dwelling in the faid Houfes, *viz.* 18 *d.* a Week to each Monk. The Overplus he apply'd to the Charges of his Wars. However, he did not touch the *Ciftercians* in this Cafe; but he fpar'd not the *Cluniacks,* or the *Premonftratenfes,* or any other whatfoever; but having confifcated all they had, oblig'd them to live in Sorrow, Poverty, and Dejection. Moreover, he order'd all the yearly Penfions due to their principal Houfes to be brought into his Treafury. *Jo. Everfden.*

Likewife, the King holding a Parliament at *Weftminfter,* on the Day after the Feaft of St. *Michael,* fparing neither for Intreaties, Perfwafions, or Threats, compell'd, and forcibly induc'd all and fingular the Prelates of *England,* with their Clergy, as alfo the Religious who had any Poffeffions, and had been fummon'd to the faid Parliament, to grant and to pay to him at three Terms within the fame Year the one half of all their Spiritualities and Temporalities, according to the Rate of the Taxation of the Tenth juft before had. The Total of which Gift is faid to have amounted to 101000 *l.* Our Part of the Contribution was 655 *l.* 11 *s.* o *d.* *ob. q. Jo. Everfden.*

On

On the Day after the Feaſt of St. *Martin*, there was granted to the King by the Laity, at *Weſtminſter*, a Tenth of all their Goods, as an Aid for his Wars, as well in *France* as in *Wales*. But the Inhabitants of Cities, Boroughs, and other Places of the King's Demeſnes were rated at a ſixth, and other Traders living elſewhere at a ſeventh, the reſt of the Commonalty at the tenth Penny. *Everſden*, and *Walt. Giſborne.*

The Sum of the Moiety of the Goods granted to the King by the Clergy was ſixty hundred thouſand Pounds. *Almoſt at the End of* Adam Merimuth's *Hiſtory. Here is certainly a great Miſtake in the Sum, which could never amount to any thing near it, and I am inclin'd to believe it ſhould be* 60000 *l.* The very Town of *St. Edmund's-bury*, in which no Officer of the King's had ever preſum'd to exerciſe any Juriſdiction ever ſince the time our Liberties were firſt granted us, was now tax'd by the common Aſſeſſors of the Country, ſitting in the publick *Toll-houſe*, or Hall of the Town, and delivering the Articles to the Burgeſſes put to their Oaths; from which Aſſembly, to our great Grief, we could no way, either by Intreaties, or Money, exempt our own Servants. However, the King comply'd ſo far, as to grant that for the future this ſhould not be a Precedent ever after to do us any Prejudice in relation to theſe and other Liberties of ours till then enjoy'd and practis'd, and a ſpecial Charter was paſs'd for us to this Effect. *Jo. Everſden.*

*Anno Dom.* 1295, *William* Biſhop of *Bath* and *Wells*, the King's High Treaſurer in the *Exchequer*, having grievouſly offended the King and thoſe about him, was diſgracefully turn'd out of that great Poſt, and oblig'd to make his Peace by paying down 2000 *l. Jo. Everſden.*

About

About the Feaft of St. *Andrew* the King held his Parliament at *Weftminfter*, where he order'd it fo as to receive the feventh Penny of his Boroughs and Demefnes for carrying on of his Wars. Of others the eleventh Penny was granted him. The Collectors in *Suffolk* were *P. de Melles* Kt. and *R. Bomund* Clerk. But when he came to the Spiritualities, it was anfwer'd him by the Clergy, that by his Statutes he had lately ordain'd many things deteftable to God and the Church, contrary to the State, and in Prejudice of the faid Church. Whereupon, in that Affembly, there was granted to him by the Clergy a Tenth of all their Temporalities and Spiritualities, upon Condition he fhould correct paft Errors, repeal thofe cruel Statutes, and reftore the Holy Church to its former Condition ; and befides, that the Taxation and Collection fhould be made by Clergymen, and not by the King's Officers. As for him, tho' he accepted of the Gift at any Rate, yet he did not prefently perform what he had promis'd. *John Everfden.*

*Anno Dom.* 1296, The King held his Parliament at *St. Edmund's-bury*, the Day after the Commemoration of *All Souls*, defigning efpecially to ask an Aid of the Clergy and People of his Land. The common fort of the Laity, after a fhort Confultation, granted him the twelfth Penny of all their Eftates, and the Burgeffes the feventh Penny. The Archbifhop held his Council with the Clergy at *St. Edmund's-bury*, where he publifh'd the new Papal Conftitution ; which exprefly forbids all Ecclefiaftical Perfons whatfoever contributing any thing to the fecular Power, after any manner, or under what Pretence foever, without confulting the Pope. Having therefore debated among themfelves about the aforefaid Conftitution, to enquire by what means they might comply with the King's Defire, without

without running any Hazard, they found none ; whereupon the Archbishop, in his own and in the Name of all the Clergy, made the same known to the King ; who being thus inform'd of it, resolv'd from that Day to opprefs and moleft the Archbishop , the other Bishops, and all the Clergy of *England* ; appointing the Clergy a farther Day, *viz.* the Octave of St. *Hilary* at *London* . Till then the King granted Peace to the Church. *John Everfden.*

A general Convocation of the Clergy was held at *London* on the Octave of St. *Hilary,* to consult about the Peace of the Church of *England,* the King's Threats, and for avoiding of voluntary Oppreffion. Thus, by the unanimous Confent of them all, as ftanding more in Awe of the eternal King than of him that was momentary, and rather fearing the Lofs of their Souls than that of temporal Things, it was refolv'd, that the holy Decrees of the fupreme Paftor of the univerfal Church ought to be with a fervent Conftancy obferv'd by them all entire, and untainted. This Refolution, together with the Dangers of tranfgreffing the Papal Conftitution, was fignify'd to the King by fpecial Meffengers of the Clergy. The King being therewith provok'd, refolv'd to practife unheard-of Severity towards the Church, and withdrawing the Shelter of his due Defence from the Lady and Queen of the World, leaving her expos'd to the Rage of impious Men and Plunderers, for his private Conveniency depriv'd her of all Protection, or rather feem'd mifchievoufly to fpur on fuch as were willing to infeft her. Befides, as it is faid by fome, an Order was put out, that no Court of Juftice fhould reftrain Lay Men, who were averfe to the Clergy, and took from them any Horfes they rode on that were above the
Value

Value of 40 *s*. The very Day on which the King pronounc'd this wretched Sentence againſt the Clergy, very many of the prime Men of his Army in *Gaſcony* were by the *French* ſlain in Battle, and ſome taken, among whom was the Lord *John St. John*, not long before the King's Seneſcal in *Gaſcony*. Several of the Clergy, not regarding their own Salvation, and being altogether addicted to the World, wavering in their Minds like Women, as if they had been in the King's Secrets, and his Councellors, at firſt made their Peace with the King ; and nothing regarding the Papal Decrees, granted him a Sum amounting to the fifth Part of all their Poſſeſſions as well ſpiritual as temporal. The King on his Part caus'd to be ſeiz'd into his Hands all the Lay Fees of the Archbiſhops, Biſhops, Religious Men, and others of the Clergy, of what Degree or Condition ſoever, who had not taken his Protection, as alſo all other Things belonging to them that could be found without the Eccleſiaſtical Encloſures; and the ſaid Goods ſo ſeiz'd by diſmal plundering were confiſcated. Then our Lord the King held his Parliament at *Sarum* on *Aſh-Wedneſday*, calling none but the Laity to it, there to treat of his Expedition for the Wars againſt the King of *France*.

*Memorandum*, that on *Aſh-Wedneſday* all the Goods of the Abbat and Convent of *St. Edmund's-bury* were confiſcated, and all their Manors ſeiz'd, together with the Borough of *St. Edmund's-bury*.

A third Time all the Clergy were aſſembled at *London*, about *Mid-Lent*, to conſult ſeriouſly about innumerable Exactions, Injuries, and unjuſt Damages daily put upon the Church and Clergy. When they had ſpent eight Days in canvaſſing the
Point,

Point, they could not poſſibly find any Way to comply with the Regal Power without Danger. In that Council, a certain Frier of the Order of Preachers publickly aſſerted before all the Aſſembly, that the King's Requeſt was juſt, and boldly proteſted that he would maintain his Right before the Pope. The King alſo ſet a Day, about which all the Moveables of the Clergy, who had no Protections, found in their Manors were to be condemn'd, and to have no farther Service of the Laity ; but the King ſhould diſpoſe of their Poſ-ſeſſions at his Pleaſure ; and if ever they were found without the Defence of the Council, they ſhould be puniſh'd by Impriſonment, as publick Enemies. *Jo. Evereſden.*

The ſame Year, the Abbat of St. *Auguſtin's* acknowledg'd the doing the Lord the King the Service of one Knight in *Gaſcony,* and compoun-ded the ſame for 100 Marks ; but nothing was at that time perform'd, nor paid of that Service. *W. Thorne.*

*Anno Dom.* 1297, The King ſummon'd the Par-liament to meet at *Lincoln* on the Octave of St. *John Baptiſt;* at which Diſcord aroſe between him, and certain Earls, and Barons of the Kingdom, on account that he endeavour'd to oppreſs both the Clergy and the People with intolerable Bur-thens. For he again ask'd of the Clergy the Moi-ety of all their Goods, and of the Laity the ſixth Penny, but of the Boroughs the third. The Earls and Barons hereupon anſwer'd, that they would by no means undergo ſo grievous and in-ſupportable an Exaction, without the Conſent of the Archbiſhop of *Canterbury,* and of all the Clergy. On the contrary they earneſtly preſs'd that the Goods of the holy Church, and all that had been wrongfully taken in general by the King's

Officers,

Officers, fhould immediately be reftor'd, as alfo that all the Articles and Points contain'd in *Magna Charta* fhould for the future be obferv'd. The King did not comply with their rightful Demands, but put off that Affair, gaining Time by Diffimulation. However, at length coming to himfelf, and being actuated by a more gentle Spirit, he voluntarily by his Letters reconcil'd to his Peace and Protection all Perfons belonging to the Bofom of the Church, who had kept the Pope's Decrees, and had not been afraid of the Regal tranfitory Tyranny.

The Archbifhop held a general Council of the Clergy at *London,* on the *Sunday* next after the Feaft of St. *Laurence,* to debate again about the Contribution to be made, which the King had fo often demanded; but ftill they diffented, alledging the Offence to their Confcience.

On St. *Giles's* Day a general Sentence was pronounc'd by all and fingular the Archbifhops, and Bifhops of *England,* in their feveral Diocefes, by Apoftolical Authority, againft thofe who had lately by Violence, and contrary to the Ecclefiaftical Liberties, broke in upon the Churches, and the Ecclefiaftical Immunities, and made Search in facred Places, and againft all others who had been any Way confenting to them.

The Earls and Barons held their Parliament at *Northampton* on St. *Matthew's* Day, about the Difcord broke out between the King and them. *Edward,* the King's Son, held his Parliament at *London,* on the Feaft of St. *Michael,* to treat of Peace between the King his Father and the Barons. There, by the univerfal Confent of the King's Council refiding in *England,* Archbifhops, Bifhops, Earls and Barons, the great Charter of *England* was return'd, and fome Additions made

to

to it; and the same being confirm'd with the King's Seal of the *Exchequer*, and those of all the prime Men of the King's Council, was with all speed transmitted to their Lord the King, being then beyond the Sea. The King having receiv'd it, and having advis'd with his great Men there present, he approv'd of what was done, and ratify'd the same for ever, affixing to it his great Seal. That done, it was immediately sent back into *England* to the Barons by special Messengers.

*Anno Dom.* 1298, which according to *Walsingham* is the 25th of the King's Reign, but the 26th according to *Rand. Cestrensis,* the King caus'd all the Temporalities of the Clergy to be seiz'd, excluding them his Protection, for that they would not the Year before give him any Supply against the *Scots. Rand. Cest.*

In order to repress the Boldness of the *Scots,* who had enter'd the *English* Borders, the Earls *Marshal* and of *Hereford* were taken into Pay by the King's Son, towards whose Expedition the Clergy gave the tenth of all their Spiritualities and Temporalities; Command being given them, on the Penalty of the Papal Statute, by the Archbishop, that they should not at the Expence of that Money pursue the Enemy beyond the *English* Borders. This Grant of the Clergy occasion'd a Muttering among some Persons; because they this Year voluntarily gave what they had refus'd the Year before. *Jo. Eversden.*

The same Year, the Parliament being summon'd to meet at *York,* on the Day after *Trinity Sunday,* being the 4th of the *Nones* of *June,* there the King, and the Barons, laying aside all Grudges of intestine and unlawful Quarrels, join'd themselves in mutual Bonds of Friendship. The King also

alſo promis'd that he would in all Things obſerve the Form of the Great Charter. *John Everſ-den.*

The Archbiſhop held a Council at *London* on the Day after the Feaſt of St. *John Baptiſt,* to which came the King's Son, in his Father's Name, to ask among other Things of the Clergy, that it would pleaſe them to give him the Remainder of the Money granted to the Earls; as alſo, if there ſhould be urgent Neceſſity, that it would pleaſe the ſame Clergy to afford the King ſome Supply of Money. There came alſo ſome of the Court Clergy-men, attempting in a bold Manner to thruſt themſelves into their private Debates; whom the Archbiſhop turn'd out of the Synod, threatning to excommunicate them. *John Everſ-den.*

The King ſummon'd his Parliament to meet at *London ,* and went away privately from it, becauſe he would not confirm the Great Charter. Nevertheleſs, Sentence paſs'd againſt all the Infringers thereof, as had been before ordain'd in the Archbiſhop's Council; and it was decreed that the ſame ſhould be done twice a year. *Joh. Everſ-den.*

*Anno Dom.* 1299, The King held his Parliament at *London,* at *Mid-Lent,* where, after long and tedious Delays, great and grievous Expences, and ſundry dangerous Reproaches between the King, and the Earls and Barons, they were at length reconcil'd, the Great Charter was ſeal'd, and ſent all about to the Cathedral Churches; for which Favour the fifteenth Penny was granted to the King by the Laity. *Joh. Everſden.*

*Anno Dom.* 1300, The King aſſembled his Army towards *Scotland,* and ſummon'd all the Earls and Barons to be ready with their Services on
the

the Feaſt of St. *John Baptiſt* , to attend him; but ſome Oppoſition was made for a time in the Parliament held at *York*, after *Pentecoſt*, becauſe certain Barons alledg'd, that they were not oblig'd to perform any Service there. However, in regard that it was prov'd in the ancient Acts of Kings that ſeveral Expeditions had been made, their Plea was adjudg'd to be vain, and of no Force ; which is made out by the Chronicles of *Malmſbury*, *Marianus Scotus*, Maſter *Henry Huntingdon*, and *Hoveden*. All above written from the Year of our Lord 1272-3 to this Time is taken from *Joh. Everſden*, Cellarer of the Abby of *St. Edmund's-bury.*

The ſame Year, to obtain a Confirmation of the Liberties contain'd in *Magna Charta*, the Earls and Barons of the Kingdom granted a fifteenth of all their Moveables on the Feaſt of St. *Michael* then next enſuing ; but the Archbiſhop would grant nothing for the Clergy, either of the Spiritualities, or of the Temporalities annex'd to the Church, without ſpecial Licence from the Pope. *Hiſt. Roff.*

*Anno Dom.* 1301, The Pope uſurp'd the Tenth of all Eccleſiaſtical Poſſeſſions throughout all *England* for three Years. *Hiſt. Roff.*

*Anno Dom.* 1306, Pope *Clement* granted the King of *England* for two Years the Tenth of the Profits of Churches, towards the Affairs of the Holy Land ; but it was put to other Uſes. But the Pope himſelf perceiving the inſatiable Avarice of certain *Engliſh* Biſhops, importunely begging that the firſt Churches becoming vacant within a Year might be granted to them ; and conſidering that the Superior might take what the Inferior crav'd, appropriated to himſelf all the Profits of the firſt vacant Churches in *England* for three Years;

Years; *viz*. the firft Fruits of the firft Year, as well of Bifhopricks, Abbies, Priories, Prebends, Parfonages, Vicarages, as of other fmaller Bene-fices. *Hift. Roff.*

The fame Year, the thirtieth Penny was gran-ted to the King by the Clergy and Laity; but the Merchants gave the twentieth for the King's Son's carrying on the War againft the *Scots*. *Hift. Roff.*

This is all *Leland's* MS. above quoted contains as to this King's Reign; but *Walfingham* in his Life adds feveral Particulars by the other omit-ted, *viz*.

*Anno Dom*. 1280, A Subfidy of a Twentieth was granted to the King for his Wars in *Wales*.

*Anno Dom*. 1284, a Thirtieth granted to the King by the Laity for the Expence of his Wars, and a Twentieth by the Clergy.

*Anno Dom*. 1290, All the *Jews* in *England* were banifh'd, and their Effects feiz'd, allowing them only fo much as would carry them over into *France*. At the fame time Complaint being brought againft the Juftices, they were all convicted of many Corruptions, and thereupon put to great Fines.

*Anno Dom*. 1295. Here *Malmsbury*, and *Everfden*, quoted by *Leland*, differ very much. The latter fays the King this Year had a feventh of his Boroughs and Demefnes, an eleventh from the reft of the Laity, and a tenth of the Clergy; whereas the former tells us, it was a Moiety of the Clergy, a fixth of the Citizens, and a tenth of the other People. Which of them to believe is left to the Reader.

*Anno Dom*. 1298, *Walfingham* fays the King rais'd the Duty upon Wool, taking 40 *s.* of every Sack, whereas only half a Mark was paid before.

The fame Year, the Barons being in Rebellion, a Peace was concluded between the King and them,

them, upon Condition that he fhould confirm *Magna Charta,* and the Foreft Charter; and that for the future neither he, nor his Succeffors, fhould impofe any Tallage, or Aid, either on the Clergy or Laity, without the Confent of the Archbifhops, Bifhops, Abbats, and other Prelates, and of the Earls, Barons, Knights, Burgeffes, and other Free-Men. For this Conceffion the People of *England* granted the King the ninth Penny, the Clergy of the Province of *Canterbury* the tenth, and thofe of *York* the fifth, becaufe they were nearer to receive Damage.

The Difference between this and the Account above from *Everfden* every one may obferve, and fo of many more, which it would be endlefs here to take notice of. All that can be faid is, that Authors vary much, either having been mifinform'd, or elfe writing with more Prejudice, and to reconcile them is impoffible; nor is the Difficulty lefs to decide who was in the right.

Befides the Aids and Subfidies which he levy'd of his People, King *Edward* I. receiv'd fome Advantage from certain Silver Mines found in his Time in *Devonfhire*, as appears by the Records ftill preferv'd in the *Exchequer*, and are as follows.

The Accounts of *William de Wimondham*, who had the Infpection of thofe Mines, after the firft Difcovery of them, inform us, that from the 12th of *Auguft* to the laft of *October*, in the 22d Year of this King's Reign, there was try'd and fin'd at *Mortineftow* in *Devonfhire*, at feveral times, 370 Pounds Weight of Silver, whereof, when brought to *London*, Plate was made for the Lady *Elenor* Dutchefs of *Bar*, Daughter to this King *Edward*.

In the 23d Year of his Reign, there was fin'd at the fame Place 521 Pounds ten Shillings Weight.

In the 24th Year, 704 Pounds 3 Shillings one Penny Weight.

In the 25th Year, more Miners were added, and so in the 27th Year; but what the Product was I have not found.

It has been seen that the Kings of *England* took Tallages and Aids by their Royal Prerogative; to prevent which for the future, in the 34th Year of King *Edward* I. it was enacted, that no Tallage or Aid shall be taken or levied by us, or our Heirs, in our Realm, without the good Will and Assent of Archbishops, Bishops, Earls, Barons, Knights, Burgesses, and other Freemen of the Land. The same had before passed in the 25th Year of this King. It was also now enacted, that no Officer of ours, or of our Heirs, shall take Corn, Leather, Cattle, or any other Goods of any manner of Person, without the good Will and Assent of the Party to whom the Goods belong'd. Likewise, nothing from henceforth shall be taken of Sacks of Wool, by Colour or Occasion of Maletent.

We will conclude this Reign with the following Remonstrance, wherein there are several Particulars well worth observing, and relating to the Subject in Hand.

*Grievances laid before the King, by the Archbishops, Bishops, Abbats and Priors, Earls, and Barons, and all the Commons of the Nation, of which they pray Redress.*

" In the first Place, it appears to all the Gene-
" rality of the People, that the Command laid on
" them by the King's Writ was insufficient; because
" no certain Place was express'd to which they
" were to repair; for as much as it was requisite
" to provide Money and Necessaries suitable to
                                                    " the

" the Place. And whether they were to do Service
" or not; and for as much as it is said in general,
" that our Lord designs to sail over into *Flanders,*
" all the People are of Opinion, that they are not
" to do any Service; because neither they, nor
" their Predecessors, or Progenitors ever did any
" Service in that Country. And tho' it were so,
" that they were to do Service there as elsewhere,
" yet they have not Ability to do it, in regard
" that they are overmuch opprefs'd by divers
" Tallages, Aids, taking up of Wheat, Oats,
" Malt, Wool, Leather, Oxen, Cows, and falt
" Meat, without the Payment of one Penny, which
" ought to have been their Support. They say
" therefore that they can give no Aid, by reason
" of the Poverty they are in, occasion'd by the
" aforesaid Tallages, and Seizures; for they have
" scarce enough to maintain them; and many have
" no Suftenance at all, nor wherewith to till their
" Lands. Thus all the People find themselves
" much aggriev'd, for that they are not treated
" according to the Laws and Cuftoms of the
" Land, by which their Predecessors were wont
" to be govern'd, but they are willfully put by
" them. Many also find themselves much ag-
" griev'd in this, that they were wont to be dealt
" with according to the Articles contain'd in *Magna*
" *Charta,* all which Articles are difregarded, to
" the great Hurt of all the People. Wherefore
" they pray our Lord the King, that he will please
" to redrefs thefe Things, to his own Honour, and
" the Prefervation of his People. Befides, the
" People find themselves much aggriev'd about the
" Affize of the Foreft, which is not obferv'd as
" it was wont; nor is the Charter of the Foreft
" obferv'd, but Attachments are made at Will
" out of the Affizes, otherwise than was wont to

" be

" be done.  The People in general also find them-
" selves aggriev'd on account of the Duty upon
" Wool, which is too burdensome, *viz.* 40 *s.* of every
" Sack, and of broken Wool seven Marks of each
" Sack; for the Wool of *England* amounts to almost
" the Value of half the Land, and the Duty paid out
" of it arises to the fifth Part of the Value of all
" the Land.  But in regard that the People wish
" Honour and Health to our Lord the King, as is
" their Duty, they are not of Opinion that it is
" for the King's Advantage to go over into *Flan-*
" *ders*, unless he were better assured of the *Flem-*
" *mings* for himself, and for his Nation; as also
" because of *Scotland*, which begins to rebel, whilst
" he is still in this Country; and they do con-
" clude those People will do worse, when they
" are assur'd that the King has cross'd the Sea.
" And not only for *Scotland*, but for other Parts
" also, which are not well settled.  *Tho. Walsingham.*

This Remonstrance is here inserted on account
of the Money Grievances complain'd of, which
show the Duties paid at that time, and the abso-
lute manner of imposing and collecting them, without Parliament, by the King's own Authority,
notwithstanding that Parliaments were then in Use.
It was made in the Year of our Lord 1298, which
is the 25th of this King's Reign.

It is observable, that in the last Parliament held
by this King, which was at *Carlisle*, the Members
it was compos'd of were 87 Earls and Barons, 20
Bishops, 61 Abbats, and 8 Priors; besides the
many Deans, Archdeacons, and other inferior
Clergy of the Convocation; also the Master of the
Knights *Templars* : Of every Shire two Knights,
of every City two Citizens, and of every Borough
two Burgesses.  I would have given the Names of
all the Upper House; but the same being in *Stow's*
                                                    Chronicle,

Chronicle, it may perhaps be thought fuperfluous. We therefore proceed to

# K. EDWARD II.

UPON the Death of his Father afcended the Throne in his own Right, in the Year of our Lord 1307, and paffing over into *France*, marry'd *Ifabel* the Daughter of *Philip* the Fair King of *France*, a wicked Woman, who in the end prov'd his Deftruction. He was certainly a good Prince, tho' fo unfortunate as to have fo vile a Wife, and fuch rebellious Subjects. Nor was he more fortunate in his Son, who, as much as he is cry'd up on account of his Succeffes in *France*, was unnatural in taking a Crown reeking with his murder'd Father's Blood; and, notwithftanding fome excufe him on account of his Youth, no lefs unnatural in his riper Years, when he not only omitted punifhing, but even preferr'd the very Murderers of his unhappy Parent. All the Rebellions before his Reign had been upon Pretence of the Extortions and Exactions of Subjects; in this King's Reign, of nineteen Years, there were fo few, that Malice itfelf could never mention them as a Colour for the moft inhumane Ufage he met with. His greateft Crime was that he had Favourites, and thofe who could not be fo never ceas'd to contrive his Ruin. His Queen becoming fcandalous in her Familiarity with *Mortimer* Earl of *March*, conceiv'd fuch an implacable Hatred againft him, that fhe never ceas'd till fhe had his Blood. Her Prieft of *Baal*, as Sir *Thomas de la Moor* rightly calls him, *Adam Orleton* Bifhop of *Hereford*, had been guilty of fo many Villanies, that he had no other way to fecure himfelf, than by committing a greater than any of the former, in the horrid butchering of his

Sovereign.

Sovereign. In short, this unfortunate Monarch was first rebelliously depos'd, then led about obscurely from one Castle to another, crown'd with Hay, shav'd with Ditch-water, shut up in a Room with Carrion to be poison'd by the Stench; and that failing, in the end stifled with a Feather-bed, and an hot Iron run up his Fundament into his Bowels, through a Pipe, that the Burning might not appear outwardly. Thus (says Sir *Thomas de la Moor*, who was his Servant) the World hated him, as it had before hated his Master CHRIST; and as Heaven receiv'd the Master rejected by the *Jews*, so it did his Disciple afterwards, being stript of the Kingdom of *England.*

Of his Taxes, Mr. *Madox*, in his History of the *Exchequer*, has no more, than that, in the Reign of King *Edward* II. an Aid was granted to the King in his Parliament holden at *York*, *in Subsidium* of his War in *Scotland.* And a Subsidy was also granted towards the same War, and call'd *Donum.*

All that Sir *Robert Cotton*'s own MS. says of this King is, that *Edward* II. impos'd 2 *s. ultra antiquam Consuetudinem*, over and above the ancient Custom, upon all Goods of Merchant Strangers, in his second Year. No other Exercise of royal Power falling within my Observation in his Time. The other MSS. quoted in other Reigns have nothing worth observing of him.

*Anno Dom.* 1320, *Reg.* 13, The Pope granted to the King the Tenth of Ecclesiastical Revenues for one Year, as before that Time he had likewise done. *N. Trivet.*

*Anno Dom.* 1323, *Reg.* 16, The King, besides a great Subsidy granted him by the Temporality, had 5 *d.* in the Mark of the Clergy of the Province of *Canterbury*, and 4 *d.* of those of *York*. *N. Trivet.*

*Anno. Dom.* 1315, *Reg.* 8, Provisions being grown so excessively dear, that the Commonalty could

not

not fubfift, it was ordain'd in the Parliament then affembled at *London*, that the beft fat Ox, not fed with Grain, fhould be fold for 16 *s.* but if fed with Corn, and fat, for 24 *s.* at moft; the beft fat Cow alive for 12 *s.* a fat Hog two Years old for 3 *s.* 4 *d.* a Sheep fhorn for 14 *d.* a Sheep with the Wool on for 20 *d.* a fat Goofe for 2 *d. ob.* a good Capon for 2 *d.* a good Hen for 1 *d.* four Pidgeons for 1 *d.*

Thefe muft at that Time have been accounted high Prices, becaufe fet in a Time of great Scarcity. However, that Regulation took no Effect ; for all Provifions grew afterwards dearer. And during this great Dearth, *Walfingham*, who tells us the aforefaid Prices, adds, that

Wheat, Beans, and Peas, were fold for 20 *s.* a Quarter; Malt, a Mark a Quarter; and a Quarter of Salt for 35 *s.*

In the Year 1316, the Famine was fo great, that before the Feaft of the *Affumption* of our Lady, a Quarter of Wheat was fold for 40 *s.* and a Quarter of Salt for the fame Price.

No more occurs any where as to the Value of Money and Taxes rais'd in this King's Reign.

## K. EDWARD III.

STay'd not to fucceed his Father in the Throne, but was fet upon it by the rebellious Subjects, and his bafe Mother, when he was fourteen Years of Age, which was fufficient to have known his Duty to a Parent. He began that ufurping Part of his Reign on the 25th of *January*, in the Year of our Lord 1326. The reft of his Life was fuitable to fuch a Beginning : His Reign began with the Murder of his Father, and all the reft of it was a continual Scene of Blood and Defolation.

H 4                                                    The

The Admirers of his great Atchievements in *France* can never juftify his Barbarities in that Country: The Defolation he made there was fcarce inferior to that of the *Goths* or *Vandals*. He feem'd to delight in Mifchief, deftroying thoufands of innocent defencelefs People, and, not content with the Plunder, burning down to the Ground Towns and Villages without Number, which being open Places, had never been in a Capacity to oppofe him. The Account Dr. *Barnes*, who yet endeavours to magnify all his Actions, performing rather the Part of a Panegyrift than a faithful Hiftorian, gives of him, is fo horrid, that it cannot but fhock any Man, who when he reads retains any Thoughts of Chriftianity, and does not entirely fet his Fancy upon a cruel Heathen Hero. His Son, the *Black Prince*, as he met with like Succeffes, fo he practis'd the like Inhumanities, flaughtering Men, Women, and Children, indifferently, to fatisfy his Rage, efpecially where any Place made a brave Defence, which ought to have excited a generous Soul to honour thofe that had done their Duty well. Both Father and Son were utter Strangers to that noble Practice, of which we have feen many Examples in our Time, as deprav'd as the World is thought to be grown. The Account Authors give of the King's Death, after he had liv'd to fee his Victories dwindle away, and to devote himfelf to Lewdnefs in his old Age, was mean, and, if we may believe moft Writers, fcarce Chriftian. As to the Bufinefs here peculiarly treated of, none ever rack'd his People more, or was better borne with by them, the Nation reducing itfelf to Want and Beggary for the vain Oftentation of his Grandeur.

The firft of this King's Exactions I meet with in Sir *Robert Cotton's* MS. which fays, *Edward* III.

impos'd

impos'd *Tallage* through all his Domayns in his sixth Year. *Pat. A. E. 2. m. 7.*

Of this King *Leland's* MS. much made use of above, has nothing worth taking notice of. We must therefore have recourse to others.

*Anno Dom.* 1333, *Reg. 7,* The Parliament then assembled at *London,* upon Advice receiv'd, that the *Scots* had taken several Men of Note Prisoners, the King promising that he would go against them in Person, the People granted him the fifteenth Penny, and the Tenth of Cities and Boroughs, and the Clergy one Tenth. *Tho. Walsingham.*

*Anno Dom.* 1336, *Reg. 10,* A Grant of one Twentieth, or, as others, of one Fifteenth of the Temporalities; a Tenth, or, as some, a Sixth of the Clergy; a Tenth of all Burgesses; and of *English* Merchants, for every Sack of Wool 40 *s.* but of Merchant Strangers 60 *s.* Besides this, the Clergy of their own Accord granted unto the King all the Money that had been collected and laid up in the Cathedral Churches throughout *England* towards the Holy War. This Money others affirm, and with more Probability, that the King of his own Power seiz'd, and particularly *Walsingham;* nor is it in the least to be imagin'd that the Clergy would give away to other Uses the Money deposited by Order of the Pope, they then standing too much in Awe of him to dispose of what he had levy'd for that pious War. But this is a Turn of Dr. *Barnes,* who every where palliates this King's Faults.

Also this, or the following Year, the King sent his Commission to *John* Lord *Molins,* empowering him to seize on all the Merchants of *Lombardy,* with their Goods, Jewels of Gold and Silver, and other Chattels, then in the City of *London,* and to deliver them for the King's Use to the

the Conftable of the *Tower*. He is alfo faid to have feiz'd into his Hands rich Veftments, and Veffels of Silver, and other Ornaments, out of Abbies.

In the Year 1338, being the twelfth of his Reign, the Laity granted him the one Half of their Wool throughout the whole Realm, and the Clergy nine Marks of every Sack of their beft Wool. Now what was the Amount hereof is fcarce to be made out; only this we are told, that he fent 10000 Sacks of Wool into *Brabant*, which were there fold at 40 *l.* the Sack, fo that the whole was 400,000 *l.*

Befides, the King then feiz'd on all that belong'd to the Alien *Cluniack* and *Ciftercian* Monks, to the *Lombards*, and all the triennial Tithes defign'd for the Holy War, as was faid above.

Dr. *Barnes*, in his *Edward* III. p. 125, fays, the Proportion-Wool above mention'd, for only the Counties of *Leicefter*, *Lincoln*, and *Northampton*, came to 1211 Sacks. Befides all which, he had an Aid of the Bifhops, Abbats, Priors, Reftors, Vicars, and Juftices, who went not with him to the War, of fome 100 *l.* apiece, of others 200 *l.* according to their Eftates and Abilities. And moreover, at *Michaelmas* following, a Tenth was granted of the Clergy for two Years to come.

In *Rymer's Fœdera*, Vol. 5, p. 456, and in the Second Additional Volume to *Dugdale's Monafticon Anglicanum*, it appears that the abovemention'd Grant of Wool was of half the Wool of *England*, amounting to 20000 Sacks, or Packs, as there mention'd in a Grant of Exemption from the fame to the Abbat of *Ofney*. Thus, if we allow 40 *l.* a Sack, as is before mention'd, the whole Amount of the Wool will be 800,000 *l.* an immenfe Sum in

those

thofe Days. Befides the Tenth of the Clergy, and the Aid there fpoken of.

In the Year 1339, the thirteenth of the King's Reign, the Lords in Parliament granted to the King the tenth Sheaf of all the Corn of their Demefnes, except of their bound Tenants; the tenth Fleece of Wool, and the tenth Lamb of their own Store, to be paid for two Years.

Then another Seffion following foon after, becaufe the Commons had defir'd a Refpite, to go home to confult thofe who fent them ; for then it feems they acted fo cautioufly ; the Commons, I fay, gave the King thirty thoufand Sacks of Wool, the which, computed at 40 *l. per* Sack, as has been above fhewn, the whole Amount came to one Million two hundred thoufand Pounds ; Sums, if real, never heard of before.

Befides all this, the maritime Parts were charg'd with furnifhing a Navy at their own Coft, and the inland with ferving in Perfon, or finding Men for the neceffary Defence of the Kingdom.

A Parliament held the 14th Year of his Reign, which was of CHRIST 1340, granted, towards carrying on the War againft *France,* the Ninth of all Grain, of Wool, and of Lambs, to be taken for two Years; alfo the ninth Part of all the Goods of Citizens and Burgeffes; and of foreign Merchants, and others not having Sheep or Corn, the nineteenth of their Goods to the Value. The Clergy in like manner, at the fame time, gave the King a Tenth.

In the King's fifteenth Year the Parliament confirm'd the former Grant. In this Seffion there is fome Explanation what each Sack was valu'd at. It is true, it has been faid above that the King fold 10000 Sacks of Wool in *Brabant* at 40 *l.* a Sack; but here it is exprefs'd, that every Sack of
the

the beſt Wool ſhould be anſwer'd to the King at
6 *l.* the next Sort at 5 *l.* and the worſt at four
Marks; beſides his Cuſtom of 40 *s.* for every Sack.

The eighteenth Year the Clergy granted the
King a *Deſme*, or Tenth Triennial, or for three
Years; and the Commons two Fifteenths of the
Counties, and two *Deſmes*, or Tenths of Cities
and of Towns. And after this a third Fifteenth.

*Anno Reg.* 21, *Dom.* 1347, Two Fifteenths were
again given the King ſtill for carrying on the War
againſt *France.* At the ſame time he had 40 *s.*
of every Knight's Fee, the uſual Aid upon
Knighting his Son, the Prince of *Wales.*

The Subſidy of Wool, that is, the forty Shillings upon every Sack, is, in the Parliament *Anno
Reg.* 22, *Dom.* 1348, computed at 60000 *l.* a year,
which gives us ſome farther Light into the Value
of what was then granted the King in Sacks of
Wool.

The ſame Year the Parliament granted the King
three Fifteenths, to be paid in three Years.

*Anno Reg.* 27, *Dom.* 1353, The King had granted him the Subſidy of Wool for three Years; the
which computed, as is obſerv'd above, at 60000 *l.*
a year, amounts to one hundred and eighty thouſand Pounds.

*Anno Reg.* 29, *Dom.* 1355, Granted to his Majeſty for ſix Years following the Subſidy of Wool, at
the Rate of 50 *s.* of every Sack that ſhould be exported during that Time. And whereas it was
then reckon'd that an hundred thouſand Sacks were
then exported yearly, this Duty amounted to two
hundred and fifty thouſand Pounds *per annum*; ſo
that the whole ſix Years Income was one Million
and an half, or fifteen hundred thouſand Pounds.

*Anno Reg* 36, *Dom.* 1362, The Parliament granted to the King for three Years 26 *s.* 8 *d.* of every
Sack

Sack of Wool, befides a Subfidy of Wools, Fells, and Skins.

*Anno Reg.* 42, *Dom.* 1368, The Parliament granted to the King, for two Years, of every Wool-pack 36 *s.* 8 *d.* for every twelve Score of Fells as much ; and of every Laft of Skins 4 *l.* over and above the ufual Cuftom of 6 *s.* 8 *d.* for every Wool-pack, and the fame for every twelve Score of Fells ; and of 13 *s.* 4 *d.* for every Laft of Skins.

*Anno Reg.* 43, *Dom.* 1369, For a new War with *France* there was granted, for three Years, of Denizens, for every Sack of Wool 43 *s.* 4 *d.* of every twenty Dozen of Fells 43 *s.* 4 *d.* and of every Laft of Skins 4 *l.* But of Aliens, for every Sack of Wool 53 *s.* 4 *d.* for every twelve Score Fells as much ; and for every Laft of Skins 5 *l.* 6 *s.* 8 *d.* over and above the old Cuftoms.

The Lands of religious Aliens were again feiz'd into the King's Hands.

*Anno Reg.* 45, *Dom.* 1371, The Clergy granted to the King an Aid, towards his Wars with *France,* of fifty thoufand Pounds ; and the Laity alfo granted the like Sum. This is the firft Sum we thus meet with particularly fpecify'd in Money. And it is worth obferving, that this whole great **Tax** was but one hundred thoufand Pounds towards carrying on fo great a War, and that the Clergy paid the one half of it.

*Anno Dom.* 1372, *Reg.* 46, King *Edward,* having made extraordinary great Preparations to raife the Siege of *Rochel,* then invefted by the *French,* was fo long detain'd by contrary Winds, that he was forc'd to defift, and difperfe his Fleet, and difmifs his Land Forces. In this Enterprize, *Walfingham* fays, he fpent in vain above nine hundred thoufand Pounds ; a Sum fo immenfe in thofe Days, that it feems almoft incredible, confidering the great Expences

pences he had been at before in a War of so many Years Continuance, the Amount of those Taxes that have been seen before, and the then Prices of all Things.

*Anno Reg.* 47, *Dom.* 1373, Granted for the same War two Fifteenths, to be paid in two Years; of every twenty Shillings of Merchandise coming into the Realm, or going out, six Pence, for two Years (except of Wool-Skins and Wool-Fells;) also the Subsidy of Wool for two Years.

*Anno Reg.* 50, *Dom.* 1376, The Parliament granted the same Subsidy of Wool, Skins, and Wool-Fells, as is mention'd last above, and this to endure for three Years from the Feast of *St. Michael* next ensuing.

*Anno Reg.* 51, *Dom.* 1377, The Lords and Commons granted the King a Poll-Tax, at four Pence a Head for every Man and Woman passing the Age of fourteen Years, Beggars only excepted. The Clergy at the same time granted twelve Pence of every Person benefic'd, and of all other religious Persons four Pence by the Poll, the four Orders of Friers *Mendicants* only excepted. Here it is worth observing, that the King demanding of the City of *London* to advance him 4000 *l.* upon this Poll, and the Mayor, *Adam Staple,* proving backward in performing the same, he was by the King turn'd out of that Office, and Sir *Richard Whittington* put into his Place. Circumstances are in all respects considerably alter'd since that Time.

Besides all the former Impositions there was a Loan, which, though out of Course of Time, being very particular, may well come into this Place.

*Anno Reg.* 44, *Dom.* 1369, King *Edward* III. borrow'd of the Prelates and others many great Sums of Money, saying he would bestow the same in Defence of the Church and Realm. It is to be

ob-

obferv'd, that this way of borrowing was no better than taking by Force ; for they durft not then deny to lend; and it does not appear that they were ever repaid.

For the Payment of the faid fifty thoufand Pounds given by the Clergy, Chantry Priefts were tax'd, according to the Sum they receiv'd by the Year; as alfo Benefices, which had never been tax'd before.

The fifty thoufand Pounds given by the Laity were affefs'd on all the Parifhes in *England,* at the Rate of 23 *s.* 4 *d.* every Parifh, the great Parifhes to help out the lefs ; fuppofing that there had been Parifhes enough in *England* to make up the Sum at that Rate : But upon Enquiry it appear'd that the Number of Parifhes fell too fhort by much ; whereupon it was ordain'd in a great Council, fummon'd to that Effect, that each Parifh fhould pay 5 *l.* 16*s.* the greater to help the leffer. Whereupon the Names of the Shires were fet down, with the Number of Churches in each of them, and the Sum that every Shire was to pay, being as follows :

| Shires. | Parifhes. | What every Shire did pay. | | |
|---|---|---|---|---|
| | | *l.* | *s.* | *d.* |
| 1 Kent | 397 | 2279 | 8 | 0 |
| 2 Surrey | 118 | 684 | 8 | 0 |
| 3 Suffex | 284 | 1657 | 4 | 0 |
| 4 Southampton | 230 | 1334 | 0 | 0 |
| 5 Wiltfhire | 239 | 1386 | 4 | 0 |
| 6 Somerfetfhire | 391 | 2267 | 16 | 0 |
| 7 Dorfetfhire | 237 | 1374 | 12 | 0 |
| 8 Devonfhire | 381 | 2149 | 16 | 0 |
| 9 Cornwal | 194 | 1125 | 4 | 0 |
| 10 Glocefterfhire | 254 | 1473 | 4 | 0 |
| 11 Herefordfhire | 144 | 834 | 4 | 0 |
| 12 Shropfhire | 114 | 661 | 4 | 0 |

| Shires. | Pariſhes. | What every Shire did pay. | | |
|---|---|---|---|---|
| | | *l.* | *s.* | *d.* |
| 13 Staffordſhire | 100 | 580 | 0 | 0 |
| 14 Oxfordſhire | 200 | 1160 | 0 | 0 |
| 15 Barkſhire | 156 | 904 | 16 | 0 |
| 16 Bedfordſhire | 121 | 701 | 16 | 0 |
| 17 Buckinghamſhire | 200 | 1160 | 0 | 0 |
| 18 Northamptonſhire | 303 | 1757 | 8 | 0 |
| 19 Rutlandſhire | 44 | 255 | 4 | 0 |
| 20 Warwickſhire | 183 | 1061 | 8 | 0 |
| 21 Leiceſterſhire | 209 | 1212 | 4 | 0 |
| 22 Nottinghamſhire | 164 | 951 | 4 | 0 |
| 23 Darbyſhire | 96 | 556 | 16 | 0 |
| 24 Lincolnſhire | 627 | 3636 | 16 | 0 |
| 25 Northumberland | 60 | 348 | 0 | 0 |
| 26 Weſtmorland | 32 | 185 | 12 | 0 |
| 27 Cumberland | 96 | 556 | 16 | 0 |
| 28 Lancaſhire | 58 | 336 | 8 | 0 |
| 29 Norfolk | 806 | 3674 | 16 | 0 |
| 30 Suffolk | 515 | 2926 | 0 | 0 |
| 31 Cambridgeſhire | 172 | 997 | 8 | 0 |
| 32 Huntingdonſhire | 62 | 535 | 12 | 0 |
| 33 London | 110 | 637 | 0 | 0 |
| 34 Middleſex | 63 | 365 | 8 | 0 |
| 35 Eſſex | 400 | 2259 | 18 | 0 |
| 36 Hertfordſhire | 136 | 730 | 16 | 0 |
| 37 Yorkſhire | 540 | 3071 | 12 | 0 |
| 38 Worceſterſhire | 139 | 806 | 4 | 0 |
| 39 Durham | 61 | 553 | 16 | 0 |

Sum of all the Shires in *England*, without the
City of *London* and the Biſhoprick of *Durham*, is
37. The Total of Pariſh Churches 8600, and all
the Money amounted to 50181 *l.* 8 *s.* of the which
was withdrawn 181 *l.* 8 *s.* by reaſon that ſome
Pariſhes in the County of *Suffolk* paid only 112 *s.*
7 *d. ob.* and ſome in the County of *Devonſhire* but
112 *s.*

11 *s.* 10 *d. q.* by reason of their great Poverty; and thus the King was answer'd 50000 *l.*

*Cheshire*, a County Palatine, came not to this Parliament. In the City of *Chester* are ten Parish Churches; and in the Shire, without the City, there are 87 Parish Churches, besides Chapels.

*Note,* That I have given this exactly as I find it in *Stow,* tho' the Totals do not answer to the particular Sums, as not knowing how to set it right; for, notwithstanding the Difference, it may be acceptable to the Curious, and shows the manner of raising the aforesaid Tax.

*Stat.* 1 *Edw.* III. Because before this Time, in the Time of King *Edward* Father to the King that now is, the King by evil Counsellors caus'd to be seiz'd into his Hands the Temporalities of divers Bishops, with all their Goods and Chattels therein found, without any Cause, and the same held in his Hands by a long Season, and continually thereof took the Profits, to the great Damage of the said Bishops, Wastes and Destructions of their Chattels, Manors, Parks, and Woods; the King willeth and granteth that from henceforth it shall not be done.

Thus ends the Reign of King *Edward* III, than whom *England* never had a greater Oppressor, if wasting the whole Substance of the People may be call'd Oppression, and yet scarce any found less Opposition from the Subjects. The Reason is plain; for the great ones being then the Ringleaders of all Rebellions, the greater Number of them were employ'd in the Wars in *France,* where they enrich'd themselves with Plunder and Rapine; the rest had Employments at home, where they were no less busy in pilfering from all below them. The Commonalty, having no Heads to lead them against their Sovereign, and being kept miserably

poor with perpetual heavy Impofitions, were quiet,
ſtudying rather how to get Bread than to oppoſe
their Superiors; for nothing is more certain, than
that Eafe and Plenty make Men wanton, no leſs
than other Animals; whereas a ſtrict Hand kept
over them makes them humble and peaceable. Beſides, the continual Draughts for Supplies in *France*,
where infinite Numbers periſh'd, notwithſtanding
their Succeſſes, drein'd the Country of the more
turbulent Spirits, who delighting in Confuſion,
found Work cut out for them abroad, without being left to contrive Miſchief at home. Witneſs
that great Number of Miſcreants, who, during the
ſhort Glimmerings there were of Peace between
the two Nations, ravag'd a great Part of *France*,
without any Show of legal Authority, with the
utmoſt Barbarity, under the Command of the
(by ſome) much admir'd Sir *Robert Knoles*, and
others, King *Edward*, contrary to all Humanity,
conniving at thoſe Villanies; for tho' he pretended to forbid it, he never took any effectual
means to quell it; but on the contrary, as ſoon
as Occaſion offer'd, he cheriſh'd all that Crew
of cruel Robbers. He went not out of this World
altogether unpuniſh'd for all the Crimes he had
been guilty of, ſeeing his darling Son, ſo like himſelf,
ſnatch'd away before him, meeting with mighty
Loſſes and Diſappointments in his old Age, and
dying after ſuch a manner as is much to be lamented; and after his Death the Scourge follow'd his
Family, his Grandſon and Succeſſor being depos'd
and inhumanly murder'd, as we ſhall ſee in his Life,
that elder Branch of the Family expiring in him,
and ſo making room for a long and ſucceſsful Uſurpation, which alſo ended in the Extirpation of the
elder Branch of that Line, yet put not an end to
the fatal Conſequences of Rebellion, till the two
Houſes

Houfes of *York* and *Lancafter* were united in King *Henry* VII. and his Queen.

## K. RICHARD II.

OF the Name, and the fecond unfortunate Monarch, fince the Conqueft, rebellioufly depos'd, and then inhumanely murder'd, the one the almoft neceffary Confequence of the other; for no Ufurper can think himfelf fafe, whilft the depos'd Prince lives. To put fome Glofs upon the violent thrufting of King *Richard* from the Throne, an Act of Refignation was extorted from him, when in the Hands of his Enemies, who could compel him to fubmit to what Terms they pleas'd, in hopes of finding fome Mercy among them, tho' all in vain; for when they had brought him to their Beck, they foon after deftroy'd him. It will be an hard Task to find out the Crimes this King was depos'd for; the whole Courfe of his Life appears much more innocent than thofe were who treated him in fuch cruel manner. As to his Perfon, he is allow'd to have been one of the moft beautiful and graceful Men of his Time, which might perhaps contribute to draw on him the Envy of the great Men, whofe Pride was fuch that they could not bear to be outdone by any one; for they hated all that was commendable in others; and tho' they did not vie to excel in Virtue, they grudg'd to have any furpafs them even in Vice. The greateft Fault charg'd on him was Profufenefs, being no more than a Generofity beyond moft of his Progenitors; which, if it does happen to grow to an Excefs in Princes, is no more than what may be juftly tolerated, confidering it is the Effect of Greatnefs of Mind. However, when we come to fum up the

Aids

Aids given him by his People, they will appear to
have been much inferior to what fome other Kings
had in the like Time as his Reign lafted.    But his
great Guilt confifted in being of a peaceable Temper, and delighting in a quiet Life.    His Father
and Grandfather had lavifh'd Blood enough, and
it might in reafon have been thought time to
avoid the Effufion of more ; but then his People
living at Eafe grew wanton, and fince he would
not fhed the Blood of others, they imbru'd their
Hands in his.    A wretched Generation! that could
only delight in the Deftruction of their own Kind,
either ranging abroad to devour their Neighbours,
or elfe raging againft one another at home.    Thus
began the Practice in *England* of murdering Sovereigns, in the Perfon of King *Edward* II. and fo
it was afterwards follow'd.    Let us proceed to the
Revenues during his Reign :

*Anno Dom.* 1377, *Reg.* 1, King *Richard* II.
affembled his Parliament at *London*, which continu'd from *Michaelmas* till the Feaft of *St. Andrew*
the Apoftle.    The Knights here beginning where
they had left off the foregoing Seffion, infifted for
the Banifhment of *Alice Peres* (*one of King* Edward
III.*'s Concubines, who had done more Mifchief, and
fcrap'd together more Wealth than all the reft of them*)
for that fhe, in Contempt of an Act of Parliament
pafs'd to that effect, and in Breach of the Oath fhe
had taken, had prefum'd to come into the (late)
King's Court, to perfwade, and obtain of him
whatfoever fhe defir'd.    Tho' fhe had with her
Money corrupted many of the Lords, and all the
Lawyers in *England*, who pleaded for her not only
underhand, but in a publick manner; however be-
ng, through the Induftry and Wifdom of the aforefaid Knights, convicted out of her own Mouth, fhe
was outlaw'd, and all her Eftate real and perfonal
con-

confifcated. Two Tenths were alfo now granted as an Aid to the King, to be paid within that Year; but upon Condition, that the King fhould not for the future burden the People by extorting Money of the Subjeĉts upon fuch Demands, but fhould live upon his own, and maintain his Wars, for that his own royal Patrimony (as was there alledg'd) was fufficient for him, as well to keep his Houfe, as to defray the Charge of the War, provided the faid Patrimony were manag'd by faithful Officers. *Tho. Walfing.* Now what that Revenue was, or from whence it accru'd, does not any where appear : In the next Reign there is a fhort Note of the Amount, which feems very trivial for fo great an Expence, and fhall be there taken notice of.

*Anno Dom.* 1378, *Reg.* 2, At the Feaft of *St. Luke* a Parliament was held at *Gloucefter*, where, among many other Aĉts pafs'd for the Benefit of the Subjeĉts, it was at laft accorded to give the King for that Year one Mark of every Sack of Wool, to be paid by the Merchants ; and of every Pounds worth of Wares brought from beyond the Sea and fold here, fix Pence, to be paid by the Buyers.

*Anno Dom.* 1379, *Reg.* 3, There was granted to the King a Subfidy to be levy'd of the great Men of the Land, to the end that the Commons might be fpar'd. The Dukes of *Lancafter* and *Britanny* paid twenty Marks, every Earl fix Marks, Bifhops and mitred Abbats as much, and every Monk three Shillings and four Pence ; alfo every Juftice, Sheriff, Knight, Efquire, Parfon, Vicar, and Chaplain, were charg'd after a certain Rate, but not any of the Commons that were of the Laity.

I 3

*Anno Dom.* 1380, *Reg.* 4, The Parliament then assembled at *Northampton*, to avoid the mutinous Temper of the *Londoners*, granted the King a Subsidy.

*Anno Dom.* 1381, *Reg.* 5, A Subsidy was granted, *viz.* of every Priest, whether Secular or Regular, and of each Nun, half a Mark; and of every Head of the Laity, Men or Women, marry'd or unmarry'd, *Walsingham* says, twelve Pence, others but four Pence. Upon the collecting of this Duty happen'd the Rabble Rebellion of *Wat. Tyler*, *Jack Straw*, and others; a Story too well known to need any thing being said of it here, but showing how apt the People were to run mad upon every trivial Occasion. This Tax could not be so grievous, but that the Mischiefs occasion'd by that Insurrection did more Harm than all the Amount of that Duty could arise to : And if it be said, that it was not the Greatness of the Demand which put the Multitude into that Ferment, but the Insolence of the Collector, discovering the Nakedness of *Wat. Tyler*'s Daughter, then it is granted that the People had no occasion to complain of Taxes; and as for the Insolence of the Collector, much greater was the Barbarity of the Father in cleaving his Head, for which he certainly deserv'd Death, to avoid which, he rais'd such a Commotion as had well nigh brought the whole Nation to Destruction.

This same Year was granted to the King a Duty of two Shillings, upon every Tun of Wine imported, by the Parliament assembled at *Westminster*, and proportionably for a lesser Quantity. Also six Pence in the Pound to take and receive of all manner of other Merchandizes to be brought out and coming within the Realm, as well (that is to say) of all manner of woollen Clothes, as of any other Merchandizes, except Wools, Leather, and Wool-Fells, over
the

the Cuftoms and Subfidies thereof due before this Grant, from the 21ft Day of *May* this prefent Year, till the Feaft of *St. Michael* next coming, and from the fame Feaft for two whole Years next enfuing. So always that the Money thereof coming be wholly apply'd upon the fafe keeping of the Sea, and no Part elfewhere. And at the Requeft of the Commons, the King willeth, that Sir *John Philpot* Kt. be Receiver and Keeper of the Money rifing of the faid Subfidy from the Town of *Southampton* towards the North; and that *John Polimond* and *Thomas Beaupeny* be Receivers and Keepers of the faid Subfidy in the Town of *Southampton*, and from thence towards the Weft, by the King's Letters Patents thereof to be made to the faid Perfons in due Form.

*Anno Dom.* 1382, *Reg.* 5, 6, The Merchants granted the King for a Subfidy certain Cuftoms of their Wools, which they bought and fold, call'd a *Maletot*, to endure for four Years.

*Anno Dom.* 1383, *Reg.* 6, 7, The Moiety of a Fifteenth was granted by the Temporality; and foon after the Moiety of a Tenth by the Clergy. The Northern Lords demanded a Part of that Money; becaufe they had been deputed in this Parliament to guard thofe Parts againft the Incurfions of the *Scots.* They were anfwer'd by the Lord *William* of *Wickham*, Bifhop of *Winchefter*, that whereas they were before poor, they had been therefore made rich and Lords, that they might be the better enabled to repel the *Scots*, and to the end that the King and the Lords of the Southern Parts fhould be the lefs burthen'd, whereas otherwife they muft be every Year at the Trouble of drawing together an Army, and toiling the People with marching into thofe Parts, &c. However, they were commiffion'd to raife Forces,

and

and oppoſe the *Scots*, whenſoever they ſhould happen to infeſt thoſe Parts.

*Anno Dom.* 1384, *Reg.* 7, 8, Another half Fifteenth of the Laity, and half a Tenth of the
Clergy, granted to the King. *Walſingham* mentions not the Nature of the Impoſition, but only
ſays, that this Year much Induſtry was us'd to ex-
tort Money from the Clergy and Commonalty, for
Maintenance of the Forces employ'd in the King's
Wars.

*Anno Dom.* 1385, *Reg.* 8, 9, About the Feaſt of
*St. Martin* the Parliament ſate at *London*, where the
Laity granted the King one Fifteenth and an half,
upon Condition that the Clergy ſhould give one
Tenth and an half; which Condition the Lord
*William Courtney*, Archbiſhop of *Canterbury*, ſtiffly
oppos'd, alledging it was not fit to be done, eſpecially conſidering that the Church was free, and
no way to be tax'd by Laymen; and therefore he
would rather loſe his Head, than conſent that the
holy Church of *England* ſhould be brought into ſuch
Servitude. This Anſwer rais'd ſo great a Commotion among the Commons, that the Knights of
the Shires, with ſome of the Nobility, earneſtly
preſs'd that the Temporalities of the Clergy might
be taken from them, affirming that they were
grown ſo proud, that it was neceſſary by taking
away their Temporalities to reduce them to Alms,
that ſo they might become more humble. This
they puſh'd on, and hop'd to bring to paſs, every
one laying out for himſelf ſome Part of a Monaſtery. One of them, *Walſingham* ſays he himſelf
heard ſay, he would have a thouſand Marks a year
out of the Houſe of *St. Alban's*. But the King put
a Stop to that Madneſs, ſaying, he would maintain
the Church as he had promis'd, and rather add to
than take from it. Hereupon the Archbiſhop attended

tended the King, and acquainted him, that it had been unanimoufly agreed to, by him, and the Clergy of the Kingdom, to give him a Tenth; which the King accepted fo gracioufly, that he declar'd he was better pleas'd with that voluntary free Gift, than he fhould have been with four times the Value extorted by Compulfion. Obferve here the Goodnefs of this King, and how ill rewarded it was afterwards, even by the Generality of the Clergy, and by the Archbifhop of *Canterbury,* all whom he had fav'd from Ruin.

*Anno Dom.* 1386, *Reg.* 9, 10, The Parliament utterly refus'd to grant the King any Supply; but having proceeded againft *Michael Ate Pole,* the Chancellor, and convicted him of many Frauds and Extortions, they confifcated all he was then poffefs'd of, which they alledg'd was fo great a Treafure, that it would fuffice to anfwer all the King's Demands, and fupply his Wants; but the King bore him fo much Affection, that he took no Advantage of their Judgment, and accordingly went without any Supply.

*Anno Dom.* 1387, *Reg.* 10, This Year pafs'd away in Commotions and rebellious Actions, fo that there was nothing to be had by the King.

*Anno Dom.* 1388, *Reg.* 11, In the Parliament then affembled at *Cambridge,* after the Feaft of the *Nativity* of *St. Mary,* there was granted to the King a Tenth of the Clergy, and a Fifteenth of the Laity.

*Anno Dom.* 1389, *Reg.* 12, I do not find the King had any Aid from his Subjects.

*Anno Dom.* 1390, *Reg.* 13, The Parliament met at *Weftminfter* on the *Monday* next after the Feaft of *St. Hilary,* and gave the King 40 *s.* of every Sack of Wool, 10 *s.* thereof to be immediately apply'd to the King's Ufe, and the other 30 *s.* to be depofited

fited in the Hands of Treaſurers appointed for defraying the Charge of any War that might happen.
Beſides this, there was a Subſidy of ſix Pence in the
Pound, whereof four Pence to be depoſited as is
ſaid above, and the other two Pence to be diſpos'd
of as the King thought fit.

Anno Dom. 1391, Reg. 14, In a Parliament
aſſembled at *London*, on the *Friday* next after the
Commemoration of *All Souls*, half a Tenth and
half a Fifteenth were given to defray the Charges
of the Duke of *Lancaſter*, who was to go over into
*France* to treat of Peace. However, the whole
Tenth and Fifteenth were granted conditionally, in
caſe any Expedition were that Year undertaken
againſt the *Scots*.

Anno Dom. 1392, Reg. 15, The King ſent to
borrow 1000 *l.* of the *Londoners*, which they obſtinately refus'd beyond what became them; and not
ſo ſatisfy'd, a certain *Lombard* offering to lend the
King that Sum, they abus'd, beat, and almoſt
kill'd him. The King being inform'd of it was
much provok'd, and ſummoning almoſt all the
prime Men of the Kingdom, laid before them the
Inſolence of the Citizens of *London*, complaining of
their Preſumption. They being all offended at the
Citizens on ſeveral Accounts, conſulted how Con-
tumacy might be corrected, and their Pride brought
down; for at that Time the *Londoners* were of all
People in the World the moſt haughty, moſt arro-
gant, and moſt covetous; having little Faith in
God and the ancient Traditions, Favourers of the
*Lollards*, Slanderers of religious Perſons, Defrauders
of Tithes, and Oppreſſors of the meaner Sort.
And ſo far did their Preſumption extend, that they
durſt adventure to make new Laws, to moleſt,
burden, and depreſs ſuch as came from the
neighbouring Towns or Countries, contrary to all
human

human Reafon, and even in Oppofition to God and Juftice. I pafs by their Inhumanity, their Rapacioufnefs, their Falfhood, their Malignity, which they practis'd towards all that came near them; for fhould I go about to take notice of all the Crimes they committed about this Time, I believe they would make a confiderable Volume. In fhort, their Behaviour towards the King, and the Mifchiefs they had done to others being fum'd up, and they fenfible of their own Guilt, which was too manifeft to be conceal'd, they fubmitted themfelves wholly to the King, rather than ftand Trial with him. Whereupon the Maior, Sheriffs, and fome of the greateft Offenders, were fecur'd, and fent Prifoners to feveral Places, their Charter made void, and a Warden of the City appointed by the King. In fhort, after they had been fome time thus punifh'd, putting the King to an immenfe Charge to reduce them, his good Temper prevail'd, and going to *London* to comfort thofe then dejected People, they, to gain his farther Favour, made him very rich Prefents, and befides paid him 10000 *l.* in Money to have their Liberties reftor'd. This is what *Walfingham* tells us of the Money fo rais'd on the City, his long Relation being here much abridg'd.

*Anno Dom.* 1393, *Reg.* 16, This Year again the fame Author tells us of a Parliament affembled at *Winchefter,* after *Chriftmas,* where the Clergy granted the King half a Tenth, and the Laity half a Fifteenth, for the Expences of the Dukes of *Lancafter* and *Glocefter,* who were to go into *France* to negotiate a Peace between the two Kingdoms.

*Anno Dom.* 1394, *Reg.* 17, The Parliament met at *London* on the Octave of *St. Hilary,* where it does not appear that the Laity gave any thing; but the Clergy gave a Tenth, in cafe the King went into *Ireland;*

*Ireland;* but only half of it, if he undertook not that Expedition.

It is not from our Purpose here to obferve what *Walfingham* tells us this Year, which is, that when K. *Edward* III. had appointed Judges in *Ireland,* and fettled the *Exchequer* there, he receiv'd yearly from that Crown 30000 *l.* which was a very great Addition in thofe Days to his Revenue, and fhows *Ireland* to have been much richer than fome others would reprefent it at that Time; for it has been fince then fo harafs'd and impoverifh'd that little can be faid of it now. But then again, this fame Year the fame Author tells us, that King *Richard* was at 30000 Marks a year Expence upon that Kingdom. It may eafily be fuppos'd that King *Edward* had fo cruelly oppreft thofe People, by drawing fo much from them, that Defpair made them have Recourfe to Arms in their own Defence, when they were no longer able to anfwer fo great a Draught. Be that as it will, King *Richard* not only wanted that Supply from thence, but expended fo much of his own, and yet whatfoever he had was thought too much for him.

*Anno Dom.* 1395, *Reg.* 18, King *Richard* being then in *Ireland,* after the Octave of the *Epiphany,* *Edmund* Duke of *York,* the King's Uncle, held the Parliament at *London,* as Guardian of the Kingdom in the King's Abfence. The Duke of *Glocefter* came to this Parliament out of *Ireland,* and fo effectually laid before it the great Streights the King was reduc'd to in *Ireland,* that the Clergy granted a Tenth, and the Laity a Fifteenth; firft protefting that they were not in Rigour of Right oblig'd to it, but that they did it of their Affection.

*Anno Dom.* 1396, *Reg.* 19, The King was at very great Expence in an Interview he had with the

the King of *France*; for *Walfingham* tells us, that
he then spent above three hundred thousand Marks,
besides the Value of ten thousand in Gifts and
Presents; yet does it not appear that he receiv'd
any thing above his own Revenues from the Subjects.

*Anno Dom.* 1397, *Reg.* 20, The Parliament met
at *London* after *Chriftmas*, wherein the King, notwithstanding his great Expences abovemention'd,
could obtain no more than half a Tenth of the
Clergy. But he is said to have borrow'd much
Money of the Cities, Prelates, and other Perfons.

*Anno Dom.* 1398, *Reg.* 21, No Imposition appears this Year, all things beginning to tend to the
Deftruction of the King, who the next Year,

1399, being the 22d of his Reign, is said to
have borrow'd great Sums of the chief of the
Clergy, as well as the Laity; and to have exacted much more, by way of Compofition, from feventeen Counties of the Kingdom, which had con-
spir'd against him, in supporting the Duke of
*Gloucefter*, the Earls of *Arundel*, and *Warwick*, &c.

The MS. of *Leland*'s own Hand, in the *Cotton*
Library, made use of in the foregoing Reigns, ends
with this, and has nothing to add to what has
been already said. Sir *Robert Cotton*'s own MS.
only says, he finds no Precedent of this King
*Richard* II. raifing any Money by regal Power.
Two other MSS. afford nothing; but a third,
which in the fo often quoted Collection in the
*Cotton* Library is *p.* 64, fums up the Grants made
to this King from Parliament-Rolls, thus:

*Anno* 1 *Ric.* II. Two Fifteenths and two Tenths
in Cities and Boroughs, to be employ'd on the
Wars, granted to King *Richard* II. in the firft Year.

Subfidy of Wools and Staple Ware, as formerly
in the 50th of *Edward* III, &c. and a more Increafe

creafe of the fame Subfidy, 13 *s.* 4 *d.* of every Sack of Wool; 26 *s.* 8 *d.* of every Laft of Skins; and 6 *d.* of every 20 *s.* Merchandize coming in or going out, for Maintenance of Wars, granted to him in his fecond Year.

The Lords and Commons gave to the King, the fame Year, fuch Subfidies of Wools, as in the laft Parliament, to endure for one Year longer, and a Sum of Money of every State of the Realm. *Rot. Parl.* 2 *R.* 2.

And in the third Year of this *Richard* II. a Loan of one Fifteenth and an half out of the Cities and Towns, and one Difme and a half within Cities and Towns only, to be employ'd upon the Wars. They alfo grant the Subfidy of Wools, Wool-Fells, and Skins, as was granted the laft Parliament, requefting no other Subfidies might be ask'd of the Commons. *Rot. Parl.* 3 *R.* 2.

And in the fifth Year of the fame King, the Lords and Commons, fearing left the continual granting of Subfidies of Wools and Staple Wares might grow into a cuftomary Right, were content to yield the King the like, fo it might be with an Interruption from *Chriftmas* to *Epiphany.* At which time they granted it as four Years before; provided, 1. It fhould be beftow'd upon the Wars; 2. That the King would be advis'd by his Council; 3. That the Wars ceafing Payments might determine. *Rot. Parl.* 5 *R.* 2.

The Lords and Commons grant, in the fixth of the fame King, one Fifteenth and one Tenth, to be employ'd only upon the Defence of the Realm.

And in the feventh of *Richard* II. the Moiety of a Tenth and of a Fifteenth granted by the Laity, provided that the other Moiety fhould be granted, if the Wars with *France* and *Scotland* continu'd.

And

And in the eighth of *Richard* II. two Fifteenths granted to the King conditionally, that the one Moiety of the Fifteenth granted the laſt Parliament might ceaſe.

And in the tenth of *Richard* II. half a Tenth and half a Fifteenth granted. And for Defence of the Sea, of every Tun of Wine 3 *s.* and 12 *d.* of every Pound of Merchandize. And the Subſidy of Wools and Staple Wares granted for one Year ; and another half of a Fifteenth upon Conditions.

And in the eleventh Year, for Defence of the Realm, one Subſidy of Wool-Skins and Wool-Fells ; for every Sack of Wool, above the old Cuſtom, from Deniſons 43 *s.* 4 *d.* from Strangers 46 *s.* 8 *d.* for every Laſt of Skins, above the old Cuſtoms, from Deniſons 4 *l.* 6 *s.* 8 *d.* from Strangers 4 *l.* 13 *s.* 4 *d.*

And for three Years Subſidies, granted upon Condition they be employ'd upon the Defence of the Realm, and that the Staple be removed from *Calais* into *England.*

And in the fifteenth, a Diſme and a half ; a Fifteenth and a half, conditionally granted, that if the King go not in Perſon into *France,* or *Scotland,* they may be employ'd upon other Defences of the Realm.

And the ſame Year a Subſidy granted for three Years together, with half a Diſme and half a Fifteenth. And in the twenty-firſt, the Lords and Commons grant to the King, during Life, the Subſidy of all Staple Ware, together with one Diſme and a half, and one Fifteenth and a half.

Having thus mention'd all the Grants to this unfortunate King, it may be obſerv'd, that theſe were all given by Parliament, and none extorted by Violence. It is likely that a young generous Prince might be laviſh of his Treaſure, which was no Crime to merit his being depos'd and cruelly murder'd, when we daily fee fo many extravagant Youths fquander away their Eftates, without any Punifhment inflicted on them. Befides, King *Richard* fpent moft of his Treafure among his Subjects at home, which was look'd upon perhaps as one of his Faults, in that he did not carry it all abroad to make War on *France*, as his Grandfather had done. But in reality, the greateft of his Failings was his not punifhing the worft of Traitors, among whom may be reckon'd his Uncle the Duke of *Lancafter*, who laid all the Difpofitions towards dethroning him, and left them to be put in practice by his Son, who afterwards ufurp'd the Crown, and murder'd his Sovereign. That the Duke of *Lancafter* afpir'd to the Throne, is fo vifible through all his Actions, that any one who reads the Life of King *Richard* may eafily be convinc'd of it ; but the Particulars are too long for this Place. However, it may not be improper to mention, how a *Carthufian* came purpofely out of *Ireland*, and deliver'd into the King's own Hand a Paper, containing an Account of the Confpiracy carry'd on by *John* of *Gant*, Duke of *Lancafter*, to deftroy the King, and fwearing to the fame, offering to make out all the Allegations and Charges, and advifing not to let the faid Duke efcape, left he fhould immediately raife a Rebellion. But the innocent King was foon prevail'd upon to put the Paper into the Duke's Hand, who eafily perfuading that credulous Prince, had the Frier deliver'd into the Cuftody of *John Holland*, who being fubfervient to the Duke, he and one *John Grene* that fame Night hang'd up the faid *Carthufian* by his Privy-Members, laying a Stone of a great Weight on his Belly, fo that he dy'd in moft incredible Torture ; thus deftroying the only Evidence of that horrid Treafon, and deterring all others

others from difcovering it. Thus the Duke of
*Lancafter* efcap'd the Punifhment he had deferv'd,
and Traitors were left to purfue their wicked Projects, till they took effect under that Duke's Son,
who had been bred up in thofe Practices, to the
Deftruction of the Sovereign. With the fame In-
tention did *John* of *Gant* fupport all thofe that
taught rebellious Doctrines, and infulted the Bifhops, and all others that were not Promoters of
his hellifh Defigns. Tho' it be not directly to our
Purpofe, a curious Digreffion may perhaps be acceptable to the Lovers of Hiftory, which being un-
common, and only publifh'd by Mr. *Hearn* in his
*Appendix* to the Antiquities of *Glaftenbury*, a Book
very fcarce, only a fmall Number of them having
been printed, I will add one Particular as an Inftance of that great Man's exceffive Lewdnefs, befides all his other Crimes. Mr. *Hearn* has given it us
in *Latin*, as he found it. The fame in *Englifh* is thus:

*From the Theological Dictionary of* Thomas Gafcoigne,
*Doctor of Divinity of* Oxford, *MS. Fol. in the Li-
brary of* Lincoln *College in* Oxford, *out of the fecond
Part of the faid Dictionary,* p. 74. *under the Word*
Luxuria.

" I Mafter *Thomas Gafcoigne*, though unworthy,
" Doctor of Divinity, who collected and writ thefe
" things, have known feveral Men that dy'd of the
" Putrefaction of their Privy Members, and their
" Body, the which Corruption and Putrefaction
" (as they faid) was occafion'd by the Ufe of car-
" nal Copulation with Women. Likewife, the
" great Duke in *England*, viz. *J.* of *Gant*, dy'd of
" fuch Putrefaction of his Privy Members and
" Body, occafion'd by the frequent Ufe of Wo-
" men (for he was a great Fornicator) as was re-
K " ported

" ported throughout all the Kingdom of *England*;
" and lying fo in Bed before his Death, he fhow'd
" that fame Putrefaction to *Richard* II. King of
" *England*, when the fame King vifited that Duke
" in his Sicknefs; and this was told me by one
" that is a Batchelor of Divinity of Veracity.
" *William Long* alfo, a Man of a mature and decent
" Age, dy'd at *London* of fuch a Putrefaction in his
" Genitals and Body, occafion'd by carnal Copu-
" lation with Women, as he himfelf feveral times
" confefs'd before his Death, when he diftributed
" Alms, as is known to me, in the Year of our
" Lord 1430."

But enough of that Duke; and we fhall here only remark, that this is a plain Demonftration, that
the Diftemper, now commonly call'd the Pox, was
known in the World long before the Siege of *Naples*
by the *French*, which happen'd in the Days of our
King *Henry* VII. tho' not call'd by that Name.
Yet it is now generally believ'd, and confidently
affirm'd to have had its Original at that Siege,
and to have been unknown before. The Cure of
it indeed feems to have been undifcover'd; but the
Difeafe is certainly the fame that is abovemention'd.

To return to King *Richard*: He was forcibly
depos'd when he had reign'd twenty-two Years
three Months and eight Days. He was then
fent Prifoner to *Pontefract* Caftle, and there
foon after murder'd, as is ufual in fuch Cafes.
Concerning his Prodigality above hinted at, *Har-
ding* tells us, that he kept the nobleft Family and
Houfe that ever King of *England* had done; for
he daily allow'd Meat and Drink to above 10000
Perfons; fo that there were 300 Servants belonging to his Kitchen to drefs Meat for fuch
a Mul-

a Multitude; and all the other Offices of his
Houſhold were in proportion. Above 300 Women
alſo belong'd to the Court from the higheſt to the
loweſt, that is, from the Ladies to the meaner ſort
of Laundreſſes, and the like. The inferior Servants
were richly clad; and that Cuſtom then prevail'd
through all *England.* Thus, whatſoever Extrava-
gancy he was guilty of, all went among his People,
and ſtill circulated from him as it came to him.
Now that I may not be thought to have ſaid too
much in behalf of this King, as if the Notions
were only my own, hear the Account *Holingſhed,*
who is not apt to ſpeak too favourably of Kings,
gives of him. His Words are theſe :

" If I may boldly ſay what I think; he (that is,
" King *Richard* II.) was a Prince the moſt un-
" thankfully us'd of his Subjects of any one of
" whom ye ſhall lightly read. For although (thro'
" the Frailty of Youth) he demeaned himſelf more
" diſſolutely than ſeemed convenient for his royal
" Eſtate, and made choice of ſuch Counſellors as
" were not favour'd of the People, whereby he was
" the leſs favour'd himſelf; yet in no King's Days
" were the Commons in greater Wealth, if they
" could have perceiv'd their happy State; neither
" in any other Time the Nobles and Gentlemen
" were more cheriſh'd, nor Churchmen leſs wrong'd.
" But ſuch was their Ingratitude towards their
" bountiful and loving Sovereign, that thoſe whom
" he had chiefly advanc'd were readieſt to con-
" troul him, for that they might not rule all
" things at their Will, and remove from him ſuch
" as they miſlik'd, and place in their Rooms
" whom they thought good, and that rather by
" a ſtrong Hand than by gentle and courteous
" Means; which ſtirr'd ſuch Malice betwixt him

" and

" and them, till at length it could not be affwag'd
" without Peril of Deftruction to them both."

Thus *Hollingſhed*, charging the whole Blame upon
the Wickedneſs of the People, who it is certain had
not been ſo bad but for the traiterous Practices of
the great Men, all ſtriving to be greater, and the
young Duke of *Lancaſter* aſpiring to wreſt the
Crown from him, as in the End he did.

# K. HENRY IV.

SO he is call'd, and ſo he muſt paſs, tho' he is
well known to have uſurp'd the Crown by meer
Force, the People being well diſpos'd to Rebellion,
as has been hinted before.  So little Pretence he
had to any juſt Title, that when he came to his
Coronation he knew not after what manner to make
his Claim ; for tho' King *Richard* was remov'd, and
not likely to live long to diſturb him,  yet was he
far from any Right, being the Son of *John* of *Gant*,
fourth Son to King *Edward* III. whereas *Richard*
Earl of *Cambridge*, and Duke of *York*, was deſcended
from *Lionel* Duke of *Clarence*, third Son to the ſame
King *Edward :* And from hence ſprung the bloody
Wars between the Houſes of *York* and *Lancaſter*, the
former attempting to recover their Right,  and the
latter maintaining their Uſurpation,  as they did
under the three *Henries*, this Fourth, the Fifth and
the Sixth, till *Edward* the Fourth at laſt recover'd
his Due.  But this *Henry* IV. not being next in Succeſſion to King *Richard*, devis'd an Abſurdity ;
which was to ſay, that *Edmund*, the fifth Son of
King *Edward* III. had been born before the *Black
Prince*, who was indeed the eldeſt, and put by the
Succeſſion by his Father for his Deformity.  All
which

which was entirely falfe, he being, as is already faid, but the fifth Son, and no way deform'd; which was fo prepofterous a Falfhood at that Time, when thofe things were frefh and well known, that he was oblig'd to lay it down. His next Invention was to claim by Conqueft; yet that bore no better a Face than the other; for what Right of Conqueft could a Subject claim over his Sovereign and his native Country? The laft, no better than any of the former, was that King *Richard* had adopted him his Heir; a third Falfhood, and if poffible to be true, he would not have adopted him in order to cut his Throat. However our Hiftorians of thofe Times endeavour to obfcure the Truth, it appears that this King *Henry*, perceiving he had as many Enemies as there were loyal Men in the Nation, and that Attempts were made by them to reftore their lawful Sovereign, he could not well enjoy himfelf; and therefore one Day at Table, fetching a Sigh, he lamented he had no Friend that would deliver him from the Perfon that would be his Death, and whofe Death would fecure his Life. This was not an exprefs Command to any one to commit the Murder; for that he thought would have been too bare-fac'd a Scandal; yet in effect it was the fame; it was ftirring up every bloody Villain to commit the Parricide, and fo it prov'd; for the Words were no fooner fpoken, than one Sir *Piers Exton,* with feveral others like himfelf, hafted away to King *Richard* in his Confinement, and moft inhumanly butcher'd him as he was fitting at Dinner. This was the way that King *Henry* attain'd the Crown, which, when known abroad, ftruck foreign Nations with exceeding Horror, that a King anointed fhould be depos'd; and fo much it prevail'd in *France,* that an Army was there rais'd to refcue him; but the News coming of his Murder, that

K 3 Enter-

Enterprize was difappointed. Nor had his Death and Depofition a lefs Effect upon the People of *Gafcony*, then Subjects to the Crown of *England*, who look'd upon both Actions as infamous, tho' they were not able to fhow their Refentment. Let us now proceed to the Subject Matter, King *Henry*'s Treafury, and what the People gave him to fupport his unjuft Poffeffion, which will appear no way inferior to what any of the rightful Kings had, and yet perhaps never grudg'd ; for when once the People have been debauch'd into a Rebellion, they never think they can give the Idol they have fet up too much, tho' every thing the true Lord had before feem'd infupportable. We fhall fee fomething of this Nature under this King *Henry*, and begin with the *Cotton* MS. *p. 9.*

*Henry* IV. in thirteen Years, from out of the Lands of his People, receiv'd twice Relief, once *Auxilium de Medietate Feodorum*, an Aid of the Moiety of the Fees ; and, again, a Noble of every 20 *l.* throughout all the Realm ; out of the Goods of the Commons four times a Tenth, befides one for three Years ; and the like one and a half for two ; and one for three Years out of the Staple Commodities, as Wool, Fells, &c. One Subfidy for one Year, four for two apiece, and one for three Years. A Poundage at 8 *d.* once, four times at 12 *d.* whereof the laft was for two Years. The like and Years of the Tonnage, the firft only rated at 2 *s.* the reft at 3 *s.* the Ton. Out of the Moveables of the Clergy, thrice a Tenth, and twice a Moiety ; as alfo of every Stipendiary Minifter, Frier, and fuch meaner Perfons, 6 *s.* 8 *d.* apiece. Befides all this, of all he took, *anno* 8, a Contribution, *ita gravis*, fo grievous, that it was granted upon Condition that it fhould not
be

be made a Precedent, and that the Evidences after the Accounts given in fhould be burnt.

This is all we have of this King in this MS. *Leland's* MS. goes no farther than the Reign of the laft King, *Richard* II. The MS. *fol.* 8. which is Sir *Robert Cotton's,* has nothing material of this, befides the faying as above, that he took fuch an exorbitant Tax in the eighth Year of his Reign, that the Evidences were burnt, to avoid its being ever known. The MS. at *fol. 64.* fums up this King's Exactions thus:

In the firft Year of *Henry* IV. Subfidies for Kerfies mention'd. And

In the fecond Year the Lords and Commons grant one Difme and one Fifteenth, 2 *s.* upon every Ton of Wine, and 8 *d.* upon every Pound of Merchandize. And

In the fourth, a Subfidy of Wools, Wool-Fells, and Skins, granted for three Years; 3 *s.* upon every Ton of Wine; and 12 *d.* upon every Pound of Merchandize; one Difme and one Fifteenth. And for this the Lords and Commons are requir'd all to dine with the King.

In the fixth Year, two Difmes, and two Fifteenths; the Subfidies of Wool, Wool-Fells, and Skins, for two Years; and 3 *s.* upon every Ton of Wine; and 12 *d.* upon every Pound of Merchandize; upon Condition it fhould be employ'd only upon the Wars, and for Defence of the Realm.

And in the eighth Year, one Difme, and one Fifteenth. Three Parts of the Subfidy (after the Merchants be paid the fourth Parts) to be only employ'd in Defence of the Realm.

In the ninth, one Difme and an half, the like Fifteenth, and the like Subfidy, for Staple Ware and other Merchandize, for three Years, upon Condition, and be it enacted, that for two Years following the King require no more Charge of his Subjects.

And in the eleventh Year of the fame King, the Lords and Commons granted the like Subfidies to the like Term, as in the ninth of King *Henry* IV. fo as exprefs Mention were made that the fame proceeded of their own good Wills, and not of Duty. And that every Perfon having twenty Shillings Land, above all Charges, fhall pay *6 s.* 8 *d.*   Thus that MS.

The Particulars of that heavy Tax abovemention'd, of the eighth Year of this King, it is likely, are not to be found at this Time, fince all the Evidences were then deftroy'd.   All that *Walfingham,* who liv'd in thofe Days, fays of it is as follows:

In the Year of our Lord 1404, in the Parliament, was granted to the King an unufual Tax, very grievous and oppreffive to the People.   The Manner of it I would have here inferted, had not thofe that granted, and fet it on foot, rather chofen that it fhould be unknown to Pofterity ; for it was granted upon this Condition, that it fhould not be afterwards made a Precedent, nor the Evidences of it be kept in the Royal Treafury, nor in the *Exchequer;* but that all the Writings and Memorials of it, immediately after the Accounts were given in, fhould be burnt.   Nor that there fhould be Writs iffu'd out againft the Collectors, nor Writs *de melius inquirendo* concerning this Affair.

This is all the Account he will give us, tho' he pretends he can do no more ; for he is fcarce to be credited in this Particular.   The Reafon is plain, that he was a great Favourer of that Ufurpation, as evidently appears by his Hiftory, in which he much extols the ufurping Line, and fpeaks fcandaloufly enough of King *Richard* II. whereas Sir

*Thomas*

*Thomas de la More,* who then liv'd, and several others, give a very different Character of that unhappy Prince. But it is a common Practice to cry up succefsful Wickednefs, and to blacken unfortunate Innocence. That *Walfingham* could not but have known the Particulars of that Tax cannot be doubted; for he dedicated his Hiftory to *Henry* VI. *Henry* V. reign'd not ten Years, *Henry* IV. but thirteen and an half; fo that from his eighth Year to the end of his Reign there are not fix Years, which added to the nine of his Son make only fifteen. Thus it appears that *Walfingham* muft needs have been living when the Tax was paid ; and therefore, notwithftanding the burning of the Evidences, knew what the Tax was, either of his own Knowledge, or from others, fince they that paid it wanted not other Evidences to inform them what it was than their own Experience. In fhort, he was afham'd, or afraid, to tranfmit that to Pofterity, which the Parliament that gave it would have bury'd in Oblivion. And what harden'd Wretches were thofe, who, after having fo bitterly exclaim'd againft their lawful Sovereign on account of the Money given him by Parliaments, could be fo open hearted to the Murderer of that Prince, as to beftow on him fuch a Gift at once, as they own'd not fit ever more to be heard of, as believing it infamous to themfelves the Givers, no lefs than to the Receiver ! Yet was not that greedy Prince any way fatiated with that intolerable Tax ; but, as if nothing had been granted him, that fame Year fummon'd another Parliament to meet at *Coventry* ; and left Men of Literature fhould oppofe his Practices, as if there were not as much Knavery among the Learned as ever was among the Unlearned, he directed the Sheriffs of the Counties to take care that no Members fhould be return'd who knew

any

any thing of Law; and therefore this was afterwards call'd *The Unlearned Parliament.* Having
got together that ignorant Multitude, he found
himself in worfe Plight than with thofe that under-
ftood more. The Learned had given fo much that
they were afham'd it fhould be afterwards known
to Pofterity, yet they could find the Ways and
Means to raife it: Thefe poor dull Souls would not
be outdone by the others in the Value of their
Gift, but then they knew not where to raife it.
At length, after many nonfenfical Projects, fome
wife Head among them hit upon one worthy of
that Affembly, and they all approv'd of it; which
was to feize all the Revenues of the Church at once,
take away all her Temporalities, and leave her as
naked as fhe was in the Days of the Apoftles, without the Charity of the Primitive Chriftians to fupport her; for it is certain that thofe who were for
robbing her of what fhe had receiv'd from their
Forefathers, had no Thoughts of relieving her in
Diftrefs. Had not the Archbifhop of *Canterbury,*
and all the Clergy, then ftood manfully againft the
Commons, and drawn over fome of the Lords to
their Side, all the Temporalities of the Church
had been at once fwallow'd by *Henry* IV. and
*Henry* VIII. would have loft the greateft Booty of
his whole Reign. What fort of Men thofe were,
who thus gave away what had been given to God,
is eafy to guefs by their Speaker Sir *John Cheyne,*
who, when the Archbifhop of *Canterbury* told him
that the Clergy, befides their Supplies of Money,
continually pray'd for the Profperity of the King
and Kingdom, did not ftick to anfwer, that he
valu'd not the Prayers of the Church.

Befides what is mention'd in the abovequoted
*Cotton* MS. *fol. 64,* I find

In

In the fifth Year of this Reign a Tenth of the Clergy.

The fixth Year, over and above what is before mention'd, a Subfidy of 20 *s.* of every Knight's Fee ; alfo 12 *d.* in the Pound for all Land, and 12 *d.* for every Pound that every Man was worth in Moveables. The Land-Tax not only upon Lay Fees, but alfo for fuch as belong'd to the Church ; a Tax fo grievous, that the like of it had never been heard of before ; and yet it feems that afterwards of the eighth Year was ftill more intolerable. But of that enough has been faid, only I find this Particular of it not mention'd before, *viz.*

That among all the other Extortions, there was exacted half a Mark of each Stipendiary Prieft and Frier *Mendicant* that fung Anniverfary for the Dead. So that many of thofe poor Priefts muft needs be almoft ftarv'd, their Stipends being then fo fmall that many of them fcarce got Bread. As for the *Mendicants,* it is well known that they had nothing to pay it out of, all their Subfiftence depending upon what they begg'd, on which account they had been ever exempted from all Contributions whatfoever, as all are now who receive Alms of the Parifh, thofe being then Almfmen allow'd throughout the whole Chriftian World.

The MS. *fol.* 69, has no more of this King, than that Tonnage and Poundage was impos'd the fecond Year of his Reign, and fo continu'd, with one Year's Intermiffion, unto his Death.

To draw towards a Conclufion of this ufurping Reign, it is worth every Man's Obfervation, what Relief the People found by their Rebellion, and the Murder of their Sovereign. Thofe who will pleafe to compare the two Reigns, may eafily perceive the immenfe Difference. To omit nothing that may tend to Information, and give farther Light

in

in this Affair, in the same so often abovequoted MS. Volume in the *Cotton* Library, I have found the following Note:

King *Henry* IV. the twelfth Year of his Reign. The Revenues and the Profits of the Kingdom, together with the Subsidy of Wool and of the Clergy, amounted to no more than 48000 *l*. of which 24000 Marks was allotted for the Expence of the House. *Ex Rot. originali inter Acta Concilij,* mark'd $2+$ *p.* 51.

I give this Note as I found it, yet cannot but believe there must be very gross Errors in it, if we can credit what all Authors tell us of the Subsidy of Wool long before, in the Reign of King *Edward* III. which far exceeded the whole Sum here allotted for all the Revenues of the Crown, which could not even at that Time subsist upon so trifling a Revenue. How to unravel the Difficulty I know not, and must therefore be oblig'd to leave it to such as can make farther Discoveries in that Affair. Errors of this Nature put the Curious to much Trouble, and lessen the Credit of History, which is always much impair'd by the Partiality of the Writers, who very often do not stick to deliver their own Inventions as Facts, to flatter the great Men themselves who have been guilty of the greatest Enormities, or their Posterity, as particularly may be found in relation to this Reign, which lasted thirteen Years and an half, and ended in the Year of our Lord 1413. And so we proceed to

K. HENRY

## K. HENRY V.

WHO fucceeded his Father in the Throne with as little Remorfe as the other had in taking and holding it all the Days of his Life. It is reported, that at the Hour of his Death, when the Terrors of accounting for what Wrongs he had done began to prefs upon his Soul, he ftill had fo little Grace as to tell his Son, he did not know how he came by the Crown. What Senfe had he when he utter'd fuch Words, had he not been bred a Chriftian? Could he be ignorant, that to take by Force the Right of another was a moft heinous Crime? And yet to fay he knew not how he came by the Crown, looks like the moft confummate Stupidity. He had not only forcibly depos'd, but afterwards murder'd his Sovereign Lord, to take and fecure the Crown; this looks like a Man paft all Senfe of Chriftianity. His Son, no way degenerating from fuch a Father, anfwer'd, that what way foever he came by it, he himfelf was refolv'd to keep it. A Refolution worthy an immoral Heathen, without regard to Juftice or Honefty, more becoming a Savage than a rational Man! Yet is this Prince cry'd up, not only for his Conquefts abroad, but for his imaginary Virtues. And the Reafon is, becaufe, not content with robbing the rightful Owners of the Crown at home, he beggar'd thofe who had confented to become his Subjects, to deftroy thoufands of People abroad, and to advance himfelf to another Throne, which, if ever the *Englifh* had any Title to, he ftill could have none, as being an Intruder into that of *England.*

To

To come now to his Treasury, we will begin with the *Cotton* MS. *fol. 9*, which is as follows :

Next him succeeded his Son the Fifth *Henry*, in whose nine Years Reign I find no Charge impos'd upon the Land of the Subjects. Out of the Goods of his Commons he receiv'd six times the Tenths and Fifteenths intirely, and once two Thirds only of both ; from the Merchants of Staple Wares, a Subsidy once for four Years, and after for Life ; 3 *s.* Tonnage and 12 *d.* Poundage for the like Terms as the former Subsidies. Thrice he had the Tenth of his Clergy. And in the eighth of his Reign, when the Chancellor bewail'd to him in Parliament the Feeblenefs and Poverty of the People, by reason of Wars and Scarcity of Money, he (who of as many Attempts as he undertook *totidem fecit Monumenta Victoriæ suæ*, yet) for Redrefs and Eafe of thofe Miferies (as *Livy* faith of an excellent Soldier) *Pacem voluit etiam qui vincere potuit.*

Thus the MS. wherein is to be obferv'd, that it fays he laid no Charge upon the Land ; yet all other things were fo charg'd, that he cannot but own the Parliament bewail'd the Feeblenefs and Poverty of the People by reafon of the Wars and Scarcity of Money. So that notwithftanding all thofe Actions abroad, fo much applauded by thofe who look upon fuccefsful Bloodfhed and Defolation to be the higheft Pitch of Honour, yet his own Native Country was fo entirely exhaufted and ruin'd by it, that he was compell'd to agree to a Peace, the People being totally difabled from longer carrying on the War. And this is the Moderation that Prince is commended for, *viz.* that he deftroy'd Men and Countries no longer than he was able.

Of

Of this King the *Cotton* MS. at *fol. 69*, says no more, than that he kept upTonnage and Poundage, as it had been in his Father's Time, all his Life.

*Walfingham* tells us, that the firft Year of his Reign, which was of CHRIST 1413, the King demanded and had a Subfidy granted him, without adding any more of the Rate or the Amount thereof.

In 1416, for he paffes by the Years 1414 and 1415, without mentioning any Tax impos'd, he fays, the Clergy granted two Tenths, to be paid within the Space of one Year.

*Anno* 1421, the ninth of the Reign, for fo many Years again he leaps over, he fays there was granted a Tenth by the Clergy, and a Fifteenth by the Laity. This is all I find in that Author, and very much fhort of the Truth, which he very much fmothers in all that was not for the Honour of the *Lancaftrian* Family; as he is alfo very imperfect in other Refpects.

Having mention'd what was given the firft Year, let us proceed to the fecond. This Year the Parliament being met, the Project, which had been difappointed under the Father, was now again reviv'd under the Son, *viz.* the feizing into the King's Hands all the Lands that had been given to the Church, the Value whereof was thus then computed in the grofs, *viz.* that they were fufficient to maintain fifteen Earls, fifteen hundred Knights, fix thoufand two hundred Efquires, and an hundred Alms-houfes for the Relief of poor impotent and needy Perfons, befides twenty thoufand Pounds remaining to come in yearly to the King, and many other confiderable Advantages. This was a prodigious Value, and yet no more than afterwards prov'd true, when King *Henry* VIII. ufurp'd all thofe Lands. Now it feems that the
King,

King, fo much extoll'd for his Piety, was nothing averfe to this Propofal, and the Parliament very well difpos'd to it; fo that the Archbifhop of *Canterbury*, and others, thought fit rather to truft to their own bloody Politicks to divert the impendent Storm, than to have Recourfe to God. This was done by putting into the King's Head the Notion of a Right to the Crown of *France*, and of conquering that Kingdom, which fucceeded fo well, that all Mens Thoughts being taken up with that War, the feizing of thofe Lands was then no more talk'd of. But God, whom the Clergy then abandon'd to fecure their Lands by fuch a cruel piece of human Subtilty, tho' he permitted them to efcape, aveng'd it on their Succeffors, who doubtlefs had more of the World than of him, and fuffer'd them to be ftript of all, and turn'd a begging.

The War being refolv'd on, the next thing was to raife Money to carry it on; and accordingly in this fecond Year, fince it was for Mifchief, the Spirituality and Temporality freely granted and rais'd the Sum of three hundred thoufand Marks, at that time very confiderable; for it ferv'd to raife a great Army, to hire a numerous Fleet, and to furnifh all Neceffaries for that great Expedition.

What immenfe Treafure was rak'd together by him in *France* is never to be known, that way of raifing Money by open Rapine being always a Secret; but it is certain, thofe Sums muft far exceed all that the Contributions of Subjects can amount to; becaufe thefe, when they give, ftill referve fomething for themfelves; but thofe who take commonly leave nothing.

But as thofe Extortions, or rather Rapines, do not fo directly appertain to our Subject, no more of them fhall be faid in this Place; but we will return to this fecond Year of King *Henry* V.'s Reign, when,

when, befides what has been faid above, the Project of feizing all the Lands of the Church having
fail'd, it was refolv'd not to fpare fome part of that
Patrimony, fince the Whole could not then be had.
Accordingly, all the Poffeffions of the Alien Priories were granted to the King and his Heirs for
ever, being above an hundred Houfes; fo that taking them but at low Rates, they muft all together
arife to a very great Value. The Benefit of the
Conqueft made by fuch profane and oppreffive Methods has been long fince evident; for tho' it is
boafted that this King fubdu'd a great Part of
*France*, and his Son was crown'd at •*Paris*, yet
what was the Benefit of thofe fo much celebrated
Actions, but an immenfe Effufion of Blood, and
the dreining this Nation of all its Treafure? And
as for the Conquefts themfelves, that very King,
who, as has been faid, was crown'd at *Paris*, liv'd
to lofe not only thofe foreign Acquifitions gain'd
by his Father, but alfo the *Englifh* Crown, unjuftly
tranfmitted to him by his Grandfather. Such is
the Juftice of God, which, tho' ftay'd by his
Mercy, to give Sinners fufficient time to repent,
never fails to fall heavy upon them when they grow
harden'd in their Iniquities.

The third and fourth Year of this Reign I cannot find what Taxes were rais'd; and yet it is moft
certain, that at fuch a time the Nation could not
be exempt from contributing to the great Expence
that the Maintenance of a vaft Army muft occafion; for what is taken by Violence abroad never
goes to leffen the Contribution at home. Befides,
if we look back into the Account of the MS. before quoted, it appears that he had fix times
whole Tenths and Fifteenths, and feveral Subfidies
and other Impofitions, which convince us that our
Hiftorians have been very fhort in tranfmitting to

L                                    Pofterity

Posterity the exact Accounts of what Taxes were given in those Days.

The fifth Year there were granted two Tenths of the Clergy, and one Fifteenth of the Laity. Thus it seems the Clergy were oblig'd with very grievous Supplies to purchase their Peace, that by giving a considerable Part they might prevent the seizing of the whole.

Here again there is an Interruption concerning Monies levy'd till the ninth Year of this Reign. Our Authors are so full of their Conceits and the Actions in *France*, that for the most part they forget to take notice of any thing done in *England*. They spend all their Eloquence upon extolling the warlike Exploits, leaving us almost in the dark as to other political Transactions; or, at best, give such imperfect Accounts, as afford us but weak Ideas of them. The History of our Parliaments is one of the most principal Branches we ought to have been acquainted with, and yet nothing is more lightly slurr'd over than that. Our Conquests, as has been said, are long since gone from us, Parliaments still remain, and it would be a piece of Information much more worthy our Curiosity, and better for our Instruction, to have right Notions of the Original of Parliaments, and how they advanc'd themselves from such inconsiderable Beginning to the immense Power they now possess, than to spend our Time in reading how God permitted the *English* to invade and over-run *France*, as a Punishment for the Sins of those People, and when he had sufficiently chastiz'd them, rais'd their Spirits again so as to be able to expel those bold Conquerors, and rid themselves from the Sovereignty of foreign Masters; the which Work of God serves the Readers only to puff themselves up with the empty Remembrance of
what

what their Forefathers did, and to conceit themfelves great Heroes, becaufe fuch mighty Deeds
were perform'd by their Anceftors, tho' they themfelves never look'd an Enemy in the Face.

Befides all the Sums of Money levy'd as aforefaid, it appears, that King rais'd very much by
pawning of Jewels, and even thofe of the Crown,
with other things of Value; all which, after his
Deceafe, the Parliament order'd to be redeem'd,
or left to the Poffeffors for ever, as may be feen
in the Statutes of the firft Year of King *Henry* VI.
*cap.* 5. in the following Words:

And moreover the King will, and hath
ordained of the said Assent, that all they, to
whom the said King his Father hath delivered
Gages, Jewels, and other Things, shall be before the King's Councell before the Feast of
St. John Baptift **next coming, with the same
Things and Jewels. And in case they be not
satisfied of their Dueties, or within halfe a
Peere after the same Feast; then they, after
the saide halfe Peere, shall have all the saide
Jewels and Things in Peace and without Im-
peachment of the King, paying to the King
all that the same Jewels and Things shall be
found of greater value then that wherefore
they were put in Gage,** unlesse they be ancient
Jewels of the Crowne: **And that they and their
Heires, Land-Tenants, and Executors, and
every of them, shall be of the same Jewels
and Things,** which be not ancient Jewels of the
Crowne, **quit and discharged against the King,
after the halfe Peere, for ever.**

The *Cotton* MS. *p.* 64. is very fhort as to this
King's Reign, and fums up all in a few Words

thus:

thus : King *Henry* V. in his firft Year, a Subfidy of Staple Ware ; Tonnage and Poundage for four Years, as in the 13th of King *Henry* IV. upon fundry Conditions ; and in the fecond, two Difmes, and two Fifteenths, to be levied of the Laity ; and in the fourth, the like ; and in the fifth, one Difme, and one Fifteenth ; and in the feventh, one Fifteenth, one Difme, and a Third of either ; and in the ninth, one Difme, and one Fifteenth.

Thus we fee the whole Reign was a Succeffion of Taxes and Impofitions on the Subjects to carry on the Wars in *France*, on which Account they readily fubmitted to all the Oppreffion, tho' fo great that the inferior People were entirely wafted and confum'd, all the Wealth of *France* taken by Rapine being lavifh'd abroad in Excefs and Luxury. Princes that delight in War are certainly the greateft Politicians, according to the worldly Policy, which has no regard to Religion, or any other View than temporal Intereft, the great Idol of the Generality of Mankind. That they are fo is plain, in that cafting fuch a Mift before the Eyes of the Subjects, who are led away by fpecious Pretences, tho' never fo groundlefs, they keep them in fuch a continual State of Blindnefs, as not to fee their own Ruin carry'd on under the Colour of deftroying thofe they have an Averfion to, and therefore fpend their own Subftance, and become Beggars, to fatiate their Malice againft others. In the mean time Sovereigns and their Favourites, without the leaft Oppofition, enjoy the Spoil of their own and their neighbouring Countries. If they happen to fail of Succefs abroad, the Loffes muft be made good at home, in hopes of making amends for paft Difappointments ; but if Providence fo orders it that they prove victorious, they are thereby enabled to do the more Mifchief to thofe they have made
their

their Enemies, and no lefs to their own People, who being dazzled with the Reports of great Advantages gain'd, are fo dull as never to obferve that they are putting out their Money for others to receive the Intereft, and themfelves to lofe the Principal. A peaceable Prince, who only ftudies the Eafe of his Subjects, tho' ever fo frugal, is always grudg'd the leaft Duty that is paid him; becaufe Peace and Plenty make Men wanton, and then like pamper'd Horfes they will kick and wince, not for that the Rider is heavy, for that will make them quiet, but becaufe they are too well fed; for as the infallible Word of God tells us, *Behold this was the Iniquity of thy Sifter* Sodom, *Pride, Fulnefs of Bread, and Abundance of Idlenefs,* Ezek. xvi. 49. The fame may be faid of other Nations.

## K. HENRY VI.

BY many reputed a Saint, as having been a Man of much Piety and Virtue in all his Behaviour, if we only except his holding and contending for a Crown, he could not but know he had no Right to, with the Expence of very much Blood and Treafure. How to reconcile Sanctity with fo much Slaughter and Defolation in Defence of an unjuft Title, is I believe unknown to the greater part of Mankind. I will not in the leaft go about to depreciate that religious Courfe of Life he is by all Writers allow'd to have liv'd, yet cannot but wonder that fo nice a Confcience fhould never be mov'd with the Reflection of the manifeft Wrong done to his Neighbour. His own Excufe on this Account is very frivolous: He alledg'd, that the Crown had been tranfmitted to him by his Father and Grandfather; and that it came to him when he

was

was an Infant in his Cradle, and consequently incapable of judging of any Right. It is true, the
Crown descended from his Grandfather; but had
not that Grandfather depos'd and murder'd his
rightful Sovereign to come at and maintain it? Can
such a Descent justify a palpable Injustice? Besides,
after that inhuman Slaughter of King *Richard* II.
the House of *Lancaster* was not still entitl'd to the
Throne, the House of *York* had always the Right
before it; so that here was not only a wrongful
Acquisition, but ever after an unjust Possession,
as was declar'd by the Parliament upon King
*Edward* IV.'s recovering his Right. The Statute
of *Westminster*, made in the first Year of that King,
confirming all publick Acts made under the three
*Henries*, Fourth, Fifth, and Sixth, calls them pretended Reigns of any of the said late Kings in
Deed, and not of Right. As for his being crown'd
in his Infancy, it must be allow'd that was no time
to discern between Equity and Iniquity; nay, had
he always reign'd in Peace, it might have been
urg'd, that no Claim being made he continu'd in
his Innocence; but when he was grown up, after
a Reign of many Years, and not only a Demand
made, but so much Slaughter ensuing upon it, there
was no Possibility of being ignorant of the Merits
of the Cause. The best Defence that can be made
for him is, that he was a Person of much Simplicity, and therefore might be the more easily led
away by wicked Casuists; and such are to be found
in all Ages, whose Consciences are always adapted
to their Interest, and accordingly they advise such
as consult them. Of this sort was Dr. *John
Williams*, first Bishop of *Lincoln*, and afterwards
Archbishop of *York*, who perswaded King *Charles* I.
to pass that vile Bill against the Earl of *Strafford*,
look'd upon as no better than Murder by that
Prince,

Prince, who therefore was wholly averſe to it; but this crafty Caſuiſt told him, *That he muſt conſider, that as he had a private Capacity and a publick, ſo he had a publick Conſcience as well as a private ; that tho' his private Conſcience, as a Man, would not permit him to do an Act contrary to his Underſtanding, Judgment, and Conſcience ; yet his publick Conſcience, as a King, which oblig'd him to do all things for the Good of his People, and to preſerve his Kingdom in Peace for himſelf and his Poſterity, would not only permit him to do that, but even oblige and require him·* What Heathen could have found out a more damnable Diſtinction? Yet this and the like prevail'd. No doubt but that *Henry* VI. had ſuch Caſuiſts about him, who impos'd upon his Simplicity for their own private Ends, without conſidering, that tho' they find two diſtinct Capacities in the ſame Perſon, yet the Man is but one, and has but one Soul to ſave or caſt away, and is to be try'd before a Tribunal where ſophiſtical Arguments will not avail. This was well obſerv'd by a *German* Peaſant, who, ſeeing the Biſhop and Prince of *Liege* on the Road in his Coach, follow'd by his Guards, look'd earneſtly at him, and burſt out a laughing in a very loud and extravagant manner. The Biſhop obſerving him, and perceiving no Motive of Laughter, caus'd him to be call'd, and ask'd what it was that provok'd him to ſo much Mirth, ſince nothing appear'd that was likely to move it. The ſly Peaſant anſwer'd, he could not forbear laughing to think what a Fool *St. Peter* had been. The Biſhop, ſomewhat ſcandaliz'd at the Profaneneſs of the Expreſſion, again demanded what Occaſion he had to entertain ſo irreligious a Thought of that holy Apoſtle. *Sir,* reply'd the Clown, *he was a Biſhop, and the greateſt of Biſhops, and yet he walk'd afoot, hungry, and in want of Neceſſaries, through many Parts of the World; and now*

*I ſee*

*I see you, who are a Bishop too, in your Coach, and with
your Guards, which is a much easier Life ; and therefore I
cannot but think him guilty of much Folly to live so miserably. You must consider,* rejoin'd the Prelate, *that I am
Prince, as well as Bishop of* Liege, *and for that Reason
I travel with this Pomp.*   The Peasant made a Bow,
seem'd satisfy'd, and so they parted; but before
the Coach could make much way, that poor Fellow fell into another violent Fit of Laughter;
whereupon he was again call'd, and the Question
put to him, what ridiculous Notion had set him
into that Fit.   *Sir,* said the Peasant, *I cannot forbear
laughing to think what would become of the Bishop, if the
Devil should take the Prince of* Liege.   This Tale,
tho' to some it may appear trivial, is well worth
the Observation of all those who pretend to act
in two Capacities.   If whilst they live like Saints
in the one, they still retain the Crimes of the
greatest Sinners in the other, the Person, which is
inseparable, will be at a great loss to account for
the Guilt of one Capacity, tho' it alledge the Innocence of the other.

Tho' it looks like a Digression,  this is not altogether foreign from our Subject.   Usurpations occasion Wars, and Wars, besides the immense Sums
rais'd to maintain them, devour the Substance of
the Subject in Rapine and Desolation, and infinite
Numbers shed their Blood and sacrifice their Lives
in the Service of the two contending Parties.   We
will now come to those Impositions that were laid
in the usual Form under this King, of which take
the Account given in the oft quoted *Cotton* MS.
*fol. 9,* which is as follows :

*Henry* V. dying in the ninth Year of his Reign,
left a peaceable Successor and Heir (*Henry* VI.)
*nimium felix malo suo,* as the Event prov'd; for retaining nothing *ex paterna Majestate præter Speciem
Nominis,*

*Nominis,* by Fear and Facility laid the way open to his factious, ambitious Kindred to work themselves into popular Favour, and himself into Contempt. Which was soon done, by leading the easy King by Expence into Extremity, and the People into Burdens; for besides the Resumptions he took of his own and Father's Grants, which was purposely plotted to make a Consumption of Duty and Affection towards him, he, out of the old Inheritance of his Subjects, exacted *6 d.* in the Pound, *Anno* 14, and doubled twice that Valuation, not only of all Lands purchased from the Entrance of *Edward* I. but all Freehold and Copyhold under 200 *l.* and 2 *s.* in twenty of all above. He further impos'd first *6 s.* 8 *d.* and then 20 *s.* upon every Knight's Fee. Out of the Goods of his Commons he had six Tenths, whereof one for three Years; besides three Moieties and one Third; of Fifteenths, three Halfs, one Third, and Eighth entire, of which there were two for three Years Grant. Besides these former, out of the Wools he had 37107 *l.* rais'd by a Moiety of a Tenth and Fifteenth. And again of all Goods 6 *s.* 8 *d.* in the Pound. Of the Merchant, of Subsidies, rated as in former Times, he had them by Grant once but for a Year; the like doubled for two, and trebled for three and a half. This Subsidy amounted to 33 *s.* 4 *d.* of Denisons, and 53 *s.* 4 *d.* of Aliens the Sack of Wool, was twice granted for four Years at a time; and, *Anno* 31, for Term of the King's Life. Besides once a Subsidy alone of Aliens Goods, Tonnage and Poundage improv'd to *6 s.* 8 *d.* he took in his eighteenth Year after the Rates of his Father's Time; he had it first thrice by several Grants and Years, then as often for two Years, and again by a new Grant for five Years, and in the end for Term of Life. Of the Clergy

he

he had, befides one half of Difmes, four entire
Tenths.   And by the State in general, *Anno* 31,
2000 Archers maintain'd for half a Year at the
common Charge.   By the Pole he exacted, *Anno*
18, of every Merchant Stranger, if a Houfholder,
16 *s.* apiece ; if none, *6 d.*   And, *Anno* 27, *6 s.* 8 *d.*
of every fuch Stranger, and 20 *d.* of their Clerks.
*Anno* 31, he had granted, for Term of Life, 10 *l.*
a year of all Inhabitants Merchants meer Aliens,
and a Third lefs of Denifons; and 20 *s.* of every
Stranger Merchant that came into the Land.
The firft Monopolies, I find, were granted upon
the Extremity of thefe Times ; for in the twenty-
ninth, the *Spinelloes,* Merchants of *Genoa,* had by
Grant the fole Trade of many Staple Commodities ; as the Merchants of *Southampton* had all
Allum for the like Sum.   Yet for all thefe Contributions, Taxes, and Shifts, whereby the impoverifh'd People were enforc'd to petition Redrefs,
for which a Parliament was, *Anno* 10, fummon'd
only ; the King's Coffers were fo empty, and
the yearly Revenue fo fhort, as the Lord Treafurer
was conftrain'd, *Anno* 11, to complain in Parliament of the one, and declar'd there the other to
want 35000 *l.* of the needful Expence, as the beft
Motive to work a Relief from the Commonwealth,
which was by the People in part effected.   But by
*Anno* 18, the Debts were fwoln again fo great,
that the Parliament was reinforc'd not only to fee
to them, but to fupport and victual the King's
Houfhold.   Thus was this unhappy Prince's
Reign all War and Wafte, until, as one faith of
*Lepidus, a Militibus & a Fortuna defertus,* he was
left for a while a difgraced Life *Spoliata quam tueri
non poterat Dignitate.*
   The other *Cotton* MS. at *fol.* 64, runs thus :

And

And in the firſt of *Henry* VI. a Subſidy of Staple Ware, Tonnage and Poundage; and in the third, a Subſidy of Wools for three Years, Tonnage and Poundage for one Year, upon Condition the Merchants Aliens ſhould ſtraightly be look'd to.

And in the ſixth, Tonnage and Poundage for two Years; 6 *s.* 8 *d.* for every twenty Nobles; and 6 *s.* 8 *d.* for every Perſon that holdeth by Knights Fee.

And in the eighth, one Diſme and one Fifteenth to be levied of the Laity; a Subſidy of Wools for two Years.

And in the ninth, one, and one Fifteenth, and a third Part of both; Tonnage and Poundage for two Years, with Subſidy of all Merchants Strangers Goods; and of every whole Knight's Fee 20 *s.* and according to that Rate Lands purchaſed by the Clergy ſince *Edward* I. and 20 *s.* for the Value of 20 *l.* Goods.

And in the tenth of *Henry* VI. half a Diſme, and half a Fifteenth; a Subſidy of Wools for a Year; Tonnage and Poundage for two Years were granted.

And in the fourteenth Year of his Reign, a Subſidy of 6 *d.* in the Pound, to be levied upon every Man's Oath, for every Pound of yearly Revenue of Lands and Offices above 5 *l.* and one Diſme and one Fifteenth of the Laity, whereof 4000 *l.* to go to the Relief of decay'd Towns and Villages; and a Subſidy of Wool and Staple Merchandize, with Tonnage and Poundage, for two Years granted.

In the ſeventeenth Year, a Diſme, and a Fifteenth, and a Subſidy of Wools for three Years was granted to the King.

And in the eighteenth, one Diſme, one Fifteenth and a half, a Subſidy of Wools for three Years,

Years, and 6 *s.* 8 *d.* raifed upon the Tonnage and Poundage of Merchants Goods; and of all Aliens and Denifons 16 *d.* a Man, being Houfholders, and being none 6 *d.*

And in the twenty-third Year, a Tenth and half a Fifteenth, excepting 2000 *l.* to be allow'd to certain poor Towns; and a Tenth and a Fifteenth, excepting 6000 *l.* to relieve certain Towns wafted.

And a Subfidy of Wools, 33 *s.* 4 *d.* the Sack of Denifons, and 53 *s.* 4 *d.* of Aliens, granted for four Years; and Tonnage and Poundage of Denifons, and double of Aliens.

Half a Difme and half a Fifteenth of the Laity; and 16 *d.* of every Houfholder Stranger, and 6 *d.* of every other; and of every Merchant Stranger 6 *s.* 8 *d.* and 20 *d.* apiece of their Clerks; and Subfidy of Wools as in his Reign.

And in the Year following, a Subfidy of 12 *d.* in the Pound out of all yearly Revenue of Freehold, Copyhold, Office, being under the Value of 200 *l.* for every Pound being above 200 *l.* 2 *s.* the Pound.

And in the thirty-firft of *Henry* VI. one Difme and one Fifteenth; Tonnage and Poundage during the King's Life; and for like Term Subfidy of Wools, *viz.* 43 *s.* 4 *d.* for every Sack of Denifons, and 5 *l.* of Aliens; and fo of other Staple Wares according to the Rate. And during Life of every Merchant Stranger, and no Denifon, but Houfholder, 10 *l.* a year; and for every Stranger that abideth but fix Weeks in *England* 20 *s.* and of every Merchant Alien, being Denifon, 6 *l.* 13 *s.* 4 *d.* yearly, during the King's Life.

The MS. of Sir *Robert Cotton*'s own Hand, in his Library, as above, at *fol.* 80, has only thefe Words: *Henry* VI. commanded, in his fifteenth Year, two of each Parifh to appear before Commiffioners, to ferve

in

in Perfon in his Wars, or allow in Money the Rate of two Days Expence, according to their Degree and Quality. And in the two and twentieth, he chargeth the Lords Spiritual and Temporal with a Benevolence for Defence of *Calais*, and hath it willingly according to the Proportion of his Demand that there is rated.

Thus thofe MSS. which indeed do fum up all the Taxations of the Reign, but fo briefly that nothing appears very particular ; yet they are the beft Accounts we have collected, not only from Hiftorians, but alfo from Records, which are frequently quoted. It is a great Diffatisfaction to be left fo much in the dark ; but where fhall we feek for more Light ? The firft Year of his Reign, at a Parliament held at *London*, which met on the ninth of *November*, there was granted to the King a Subfidy towards carrying on the Wars in *France*; it confifted of five Nobles of every Sack of Wool exported out of the Nation, and to continue for three Years.

However, in the third Year, a Parliament met at *Weftminfter* on the laft Day of *April*, which granted another Subfidy, ftill for the fame War, of 12 *d.* in the Pound of all forts of Commodities whatfoever, either imported or exported ; and 3 *s.* a Tun for Wine, for three Years alfo. And befides all this, it was enacted that all Strangers fhould pay 43 *s.* 4 *d.* for every Sack of Wool they exported ; whereas *Englifh* Merchants paid no more than five Nobles, as has been faid above.

In his fourth Year, on the fifteenth of *March*, the Parliament met at *Leicefter*, and was call'd the Parliament of Bats ; becaufe all that came to it brought great Staves or Bats on their Shoulders, having been forbid wearing Swords ; and when thofe Bats were alfo prohibited, they carry'd

Stones,

Stones, or leaden Plummets. This Parliament was held by the Regent Duke of *Bedford*, who still craving for the *French* War, had a great Aid and Subsidy granted, as some Authors express it, without mentioning to what Value, or of what Sort.

The fifth Year no Parliament met, and consequently there was no new Imposition. But

The sixth Year there was a Parliament at *Westminster*, wherein there was granted a Subsidy of 3 *s.* of every Tun of Wine, and 12 *d.* in the Pound upon all Merchandize, except Wool, Wool-Fells, and Cloth. Besides, of every Parish in the Kingdom, excepting those in Cities and Boroughs, where the Value of the Benefice was twelve Marks, ten of the Parishioners should pay 6 *s.* 8 *d.* and every other Parishioner 8 *d.* and where the Benefice was worth 10 *l.* ten Parishioners to pay 13 *s.* 4 *d.* and so proportionably in all others. And as for the Inhabitants of Cities and Boroughs, every Man worth 20 *s.* above his Houshold Stuff and Apparel, to pay 4 *d.* and so after the same Rate up to the richest.

The seventh Year no Parliament met; the eighth the Parliament sate at *Westminster*, the ninth again at *Westminster*, the tenth in the same Place; so the following Sessions were held still at *Westminster*, till the twenty-fifth Year, when the Session was at St. *Edmund's-bury*. Then again at *Westminster*, the twenty-seventh, twenty-eighth, twenty-ninth, thirtieth, thirty-third, and thirty-ninth, which were all the Parliaments in this Reign. During all which Years, from the sixth above spoken of, nothing can be added to what has been quoted from the several MSS. before, and we are willing to avoid Repetitions.

All the Impositions mention'd must needs amount to very great Sums for those Days, tho' there is

no

no Method of giving any Guefs at them; but it muft at the fame time be confider'd, that the Reign was long, of thirty-eight Years and an half, and the continual Wars made it expenfive: Befides which, as he is faid to have been a moft innocent Man, his Minifters impos'd upon him with the greater Eafe. The moft quick-fighted Kings cannot avoid being much cheated; how much more one who fufpected no Man? And indeed all Hiftorians do inform us, that thofe who govern'd under him, for he knew little of it himfelf, did occafion all the Difcontents among the People by their greedy raking to themfelves, by which means they were all vaftly enrich'd, and he always kept poor. A Saint-like King is fcarce fit to govern a wicked People; he is too apt to believe, and they are too forward to deceive. Reftlefs Spirits muft be govern'd with an iron Rod; and it is in vain to fay that Princes fhould gain the Love of their Subjects; if they do not fear, they will never love. A Sovereign too mild is always contemn'd; for the Generality of Mankind either have not Senfe to difcern between the Virtues and the Vices of the great ones, or elfe have too much Malice to make a good Ufe of what they comprehend. It is impoffible to pleafe all, and thofe who are difcontented will always endeavour to lead the ignorant and unwary into their own mifchievous Projects, upon wild Notions, calling the Goodnefs of a Prince Folly, his Tendernefs of Heart Pufillanimity; and fo of all other commendable Qualities. However, if we pry curioufly into the Life and Actions of this King *Henry* VI. it plainly appears that he was no way qualified for Government, but might have made a very good religious Man; yet his ill Fate fet a Crown on his Head, and he had, it feems,

Ambi-

Ambition enough to defend it as long as he could, without regard to Right or Wrong.

# K. EDWARD IV.

OF the House of *York*, at length recover'd the Right of his Family, after an Usurpation of above three-score Years, in three Descents of the House of *Lancaster*, which seem'd in that time to have rivetted itself on the Throne, but was now cast out, yet so as to return again, as shall be seen in King *Henry* VII. It was not without much Effusion of Blood that King *Edward* retriev'd what was his Due; nor could he enjoy it in Peace, being always perplex'd by his rebellious Subjects, at the Instigation of the Favourers of the *Lancastrian* Line. The Battle which gain'd him the Crown was fought in *March* 1461, and cost the Lives of near thirty-five thousand Men, and a great Number of Noblemen and Gentlemen of Note. In *June* following he was crown'd at *Westminster*; and in *November* he held a Parliament there, in which King *Henry*, who was fled into *Scotland*, and very many of his Adherents, were attainted, and some of them afterwards executed.

To come to the Taxes paid to this King by his Subjects, we do not find any better Account under him than we have before. The *Cotton* MS. *fol. 9.* is very short, having only these few Lines :

*Edward* IV. besides two Resumptions, not only of the Grants of such Kings as he accounted *de Facto* and not *de Jure* to reign, but also of those made by himself; and a Sea of Profit, that by infinite Attainders flow'd daily into his Treasury; he took notwithstanding of his Commons six Tenths, three Quarters, and the like Proportions

in

In Fifteenths. A Benevolence, in *Anno* 14, which *Fabian* calleth a new Contribution, and charged them with Wages of his Archers to a Sum of 51117 *l.* Of the Merchants he had Tonnage and Poundage for Term of Life ; besides of Strangers, as well Denisons as others, a Subsidy in the twenty-second of his Reign.

The MS. at *fol.* 64, is near as short, as follows :

To *Edward* IV. in the third Year of his Reign, an Aid of 37000 *l.* is granted to be levied out of the Counties, Cities, and Towns, according to Rate specified in Record.

And in the seventh of the same King, two Dismes and two Fifteenths from the Laity, except 12000 *l.* to be deducted to the Relief of the poorest Towns.

And in the twelfth, one Disme and one Fifteenth, except 6000 *l.* to be distributed to poor Towns.

And in the same Year, one Disme and one Fifteenth ; and 51117 *l.* for the Wages of 13000 Archers ; one Disme, and one Fifteenth, and three Quarters of either granted.

And in the twenty-second of *Edward* IV. one Disme and one Fifteenth of the Laity, except 6000 *l.* to be bestow'd upon decay'd Towns.

And a yearly Subsidy upon all Strangers, as well Denisons as others, given by Parliament.

Sir *Robert Cotton*'s own MS. is the shortest, as having only these few Words : *Edward* IV. in his first Year, hath of the Clergy a Benevolence, which in the Record is call'd a voluntary Subsidy. And in the twelfth Year, by the Advice of the three Estates in Parliament, to undertake the Recovery of his Jewels ; for which they grant him a Subsidy ; which falling short of his Occasions, he taketh of his People a Benevolence.

M

All

All the feveral Impofitions being fum'd up above, it only remains to add fomewhat more particular than what is there faid, and efpecially to the Benevolence there mention'd. King *Edward*, having receiv'd very confiderable Supplies from the Parliament in his twelfth Year, and ftill wanting Money, by reafon of his extraordinary Expences, bethought himfelf of this Method: He call'd before him moft of the wealthieft People in the Kingdom, taking every one apart, and declaring to them the great Want he was in, and what were the Occafions of it, and defiring every one of them to contribute fomething voluntarily towards his Relief, according to their Ability. They being in his Prefence, and not knowing how to deny his Requeft, readily comply'd, fome giving more, and fome lefs, as their Generofity dictated, and their Subftance would afford. This he call'd a *Benevolence*, as being a voluntary Act, and feeming to be done out of meer Affection; tho' it is certain that in fo great a Number of Contributors there were many who did it much againft their Inclinations, and rather out of Fear than Love; or indeed for Shame; becaufe their King courting them in the moft obliging manner, they had no Way to get off without appearing generous.

In the Management of this Affair there happen'd a comical Paffage, which thofe who have not heard will not be difpleas'd to find here inferted. Among the reft fummon'd by King *Edward* to appear before him was a Widow, of a confiderable Age, and much more confiderable for her Wealth. He, in a pleafant and courteous manner, ask'd her how much fhe was willing to contribute to his Relief in that Time of Want. The King being of a very graceful Prefence, when fhe had taken a full View of him, fhe anfwer'd, *By my Troth, for thy lovely*

*lovely Countenance, thou shalt have even twenty Pounds.*
The Sum was great in thofe Days, and the King,
who had not imagin'd fhe would have given fo much,
return'd Thanks, and in a moft obliging manner
kifs'd her. The old Gentlewoman was fo highly
delighted with the Favour of that Kifs, and being
before taken with his Perfon, that fhe fwore he
fhould have twenty Pounds more for it; and with
the fame Chearfulnefs that fhe promis'd fhe perform'd it. Many fuch Ladies and fuch Kiffes
might have been more advantageous to the King
than an indifferent Subfidy from the Parliament,
which fome Kings have taken as much Pains to
beg, and not always been comply'd with.

Befides what Contributions King *Edward* receiv'd from his Subjects, he, for fome Years before his Death, had 5000 Crowns a year paid him
by the King of *France* in the *Tower* of *London.* This
the *Englifh* would have to be look'd upon as a Tribute; and the *French* call'd it a Penfion; neither
Name in reality any way proper. As for the firft,
it is ridiculous to think that a King of *France* fhould
pay a Tribute for his own Crown, efpecially at that
time, when he had regain'd all that ever the
*Englifh* won, befides *Normandy*, which had been
the ancient Patrimony of King *William* the Conqueror's Family, and *Aquitain*, acquir'd by Marriages, and other Means; when the former Kings,
who had loft the one half of their Dominions,
never fubmitted to any fuch Impofition. The
other Name of a Penfion, if taken in the right Senfe,
may be more proper, that is, if only as a Confideration for Lands yielded up, or Loffes fuftain'd;
but if made ufe of to fignify the retaining of the
Perfon that receives it as fubfervient to a Superior,
as very often it is, then will it be found no lefs pre-

M 2                                                  pofterous

posterous than the other Notion of a Tribute has been shown to be.

There is one Particular more reckon'd by some as a great Addition to this King's Revenues, that is, the great Number of Estates that became forfeited to him, on account of Rebellion; for at his first coming to the Crown about 140 considerable Persons were attainted by Parliament, and their Estates of consequence fell to him; besides many more afterwards upon several Occasions. But if rightly consider'd, such Forfeitures never contribute much towards the enriching of a King, especially one under his Circumstances, who had very many to reward for their faithful Service in assisting to recover his Right. Thus it is likely, that what came to him on the one Hand, was dealt out by him with the other; so that in the end it prov'd no Addition to him; tho' it is true it might save him the Expence he must have been at out of his own, had there not been so plentiful an Harvest from others.

To conclude, besides his being a rightful and lawful King, he may justly be allow'd to have been a good Man. It does not appear that he ever delighted in distressing his Subjects, and what he drew from them was no more than a necessary Support to enable him to withstand the many Troubles rais'd against him. Nor was he ambitious of extending his Dominions to aggrandize himself and ruin his People; but on the contrary, laid hold of the first Opportunity that offer'd to conclude a Peace with *France,* and desist from all those vain Notions of making Conquests, which he found by Experience could never be preserv'd. He had plain Demonstrations of it in the so much applauded Actions of King *Edward* III. and *Henry* V. who having made *France* a Field of Blood, at the Expence of their own People; the first of them liv'd

to

to lofe part of what he had gain'd himfelf, and left
the reft to be loft by his Grandfon; and fo the latter, having made a mighty Progrefs in a very fhort
time, was himfelf cut off by Death, and his Son
was turn'd out of all he had been labouring for.
King *Edward* was of a better Difpofition, and
doubtlefs thought it enough that he had recover'd
his own, without embroiling *England,* which had
fuffer'd fo much by the Civil Wars, to wreft that
from others, which in reality he had but a poor
Claim to, and which there was no Probability he
fhould ever be Mafter of. In fhort, if we may believe *Hall,* he made fuch a Speech to thofe about
him before his Death, as fhow'd him a good
Chriftian and a good King. He departed this
Life at *Weftminfter,* on the 9th of *April* 1483, in
the forty-firft Year of his Age, when he had reign'd
twenty-two Years, one Month, and eight Days.

# K. E D W A R D  V.

SON to the Fourth of the fame Name, and
confequently rightful King, but unfortunate
as to this World. He inherited his Father's Right
at thirteen Years of Age, under the Tuition of his
wicked Uncle *Richard* Duke of *Glocefter,* who being a moft inhuman Wretch, and fupported by
others as vile as himfelf, found means to ufurp the
Crown, and hellifh Inftruments to murder the infant King and his younger Brother. The firft
Method us'd to this Intent, was the removing of
all that were loyal from about the King, which
was perform'd with the Affiftance of the Duke of
*Buckingham,* as bafe a Wretch as he that employ'd
him. When this was done, the Queen Mother

took

took Sanctuary with her Sons in *Weftminfter Abbey.* The Sons were by falfe Oaths and Proteftations drawn from thence and fecur'd in the *Tower.* Then the Protector Duke of *Glocefter* began to act more bare-fac'd, and gave out that King *Edward* IV. and his Brother the Duke of *Clarence*, were both Baftards, and himfelf the true Heir of the Crown. The better to inculcate this fcandalous Notion, he apply'd to wicked Clergymen, who, according to the known Maxim, *Corruptio optimi peffima*, the beft things when corrupted become the worft, are the fitteft Inftruments for carrying on any Mifchief. Accordingly, Dr. *Shaw*, one of thofe Hell-driving Clergymen, of which all Ages have afforded fome Examples, preach'd at *St. Paul's Crofs*, where, as he had been directed, he baftardiz'd the late King, declar'd the prefent of a Baftard Defcent; and therefore gave the Right to the Crown to the Duke of *Glocefter.* This devilifh Invention did not take with that Audience; yet it ferv'd, with the Help of other accurfed Practices like it, and the Support of feveral Traitors, who expected to raife themfelves by it, to embolden *Richard* Duke of *Glocefter* to affume the Title of King. That Title he well knew could not fubfift without the Effufion of much Blood; and therefore for the more Security he caus'd the young King and his Brother to be cruelly murder'd in the *Tower*, to cut off all Pretenfions; and not being able to deftroy the Lady *Elizabeth* their Sifter, who kept in the Sanctuary at *Weftminfter*, he poifon'd his own Wife to make room to marry that Lady, who was then the undoubted Heir to the Crown, hoping by fo much Barbarity to eftablifh himfelf and his Pofterity on the Throne; but God, who permitted him thus to rage for a Time, at length cut him off, as we fhall fee in the next Reign.

King

King *Edward* V. tho' he has a Place in the Catalogue of our Kings, as indeed is due to him, was cut off, as has been faid, fo foon, that he can fcarce be faid to have reign'd; for his whole Time did not extend to a Year, and accordingly there was no Seffion of Parliament, nor any Tax rais'd in his Name. A Character of this Prince cannot be given to any great Advantage; his tender Years could not give any Proof of his Talent. All that can be faid is, that he was of a graceful Prefence; and, as far as his Age would permit, gave promifing Hopes of making a noble fpirited Sovereign, nothing being wanted in him that could poffibly appear under his Circumftances. But God had otherwife decreed, the Nation was not yet to be made happy under a Fatherly Ruler; a Tyrant was to afcend the Throne, in order to carry on that Scourge which had lain upon the People feveral Years before the legal Line was reftor'd. As the Subject in hand is only relating to the Taxes and Impofitions, all other Matters are omitted, befides bringing down the Defcent of thofe who were really Kings, or who tyrannically ufurp'd that Honour, of which fort he that follows is a fignal Inftance.

## K. R I C H A R D III.

SO he is ftyl'd, and plac'd among our Kings, tho' with as little Reafon as ever there was for giving fo honourable a Title to the moft barbarous Tyrant. And fuch a one he was; for befides the Murders of his Sovereign and his Brother, both innocent Children, and of his own Wife, he deftroy'd many Perfons of Note, only for their adhering to their Sovereign, and others out of meer Malice; and rewarded all that imbru'd their Hands in

Blood

Blood to pleaſe his brutal Temper. His Perſon repreſented the vile Diſpoſition of his Mind; for he was of Stature ſhort, and miſ-ſhapen, his Back awry, his left Shoulder ſtarting up much above his right; his Countenance ſtern, and of a bloody Hue; and every way diſagreeable to behold. As his Body, ſo was his Soul deform'd and hideous, being malicious in the higheſt degree, violently paſſionate, envious beyond meaſure, cruel as a ſavage Beaſt. Senſe he did not want, unleſs it were for any thing that was good, but rather abounded in it for all that was miſchievous. Some have attributed to him the Virtue of Generoſity, which indeed was no other than a profuſe way of corrupting vile Men to aſſiſt him in his helliſh Projects. Courage he had, like the wild Beaſts, all tending to the Deſtruction of others, and advancing of himſelf. Pride and Ambition entirely ſway'd him. His own Secrets he was ſure to keep, as not fit to be communicated to any but his own infernal Agents. In diſſembling none could outdo him, being apt to fawn when he deſign'd to deſtroy; and, like *Judas*, would kiſs and embrace the Man whoſe Throat he did deſign to cut. Falſe to thoſe that ſerv'd him moſt, and had deſerv'd his Friendſhip. In ſhort, a Monſter of a Man, if he deſerv'd that Name, having more of the Nature of a Devil incarnate, void of all Religion and Humanity.

To come now to what relates to Taxes in his Time, God ſhorten'd his Reign for the Good of the Nation; and conſequently he had but little time to oppreſs the People that way. The oft quoted *Cotton* MS. at *fol. 9.* has only this ſhort Account of him:

*Richard* his Brother ſucceeded, *Homo ingenioſiſſime nequam & facundus malo publico*, full of Art to beguile the People; for to make a juſt Semblance of
his

his unjuft Entry, befides his Act of Parliament full of dangerous Untruths, he diffembled the Part of an excellent Prince, making the Commons believe, by a Statute to which he gave firft Form as Life, difcharging them for ever from all Exactions call'd *Benevolences*, that his Opinion was *Ditare magis effe Regium quam ditefcere*; whereas he did but truly imitate *Nero*, that took away the Law *Manlia de Vectigalibus* only *ut gratiofior effet Populis*. And fo all his fhort Reign I find recorded but once any Tax upon the People; and that was a Tenth granted by the Clergy of both Provinces.

This *Richard's* Reign, as it is call'd, or rather tyrannical Rule, lafted but two Years, two Months, and one Day; only one Parliament fate in his Time; and there do not appear to have been any more Impofitions than what has been faid. At the end of the Time juft mention'd he was flain at *Bofworth* Fight, where 4000 Men loft their Lives in Defence of his Ufurpation. His Body was ftript ftark naked, not a Rag left to cover any Part, and in that manner laid acrofs a Horfe, like the dead Carcafs of a Beaft, and fo carry'd to *Leicefter*, where it was bury'd in the Church of the *Grey Friers*, more deferving to have been left a Prey to the Birds of the Air. There let us leave him to proceed to

# K. HENRY VII.

HE obtained the Crown by the Defeat and Death of the aforefaid *Richard* III. and became a rightful King by marrying the Lady *Elizabeth*, Daughter to King *Edward* IV. to whom the Right was devolv'd by the Death of her two Brothers, murder'd, as has been faid, by her's and

their

their Uncle the Tyrant *Richard*. King *Henry* was himself the Head of the House of *Lancaster*, and taking to Wife that Lady, who was Chief of the House of *York*, they united the two Families, and put an end to those Pretensions which had cost so many thousand Lives. King *Henry* was the reverse of his Predecessor, of a graceful Person, and a more graceful Soul; for he was accounted one of the wisest Princes of his Age; politick in his Government, without all the Wickedness of a *Machiavel*; a very great Lover of Justice; naturally addicted to Temperance; of an awful Gravity, without Pride or Supercilioufness; and of such excellent Conduct, that, notwithstanding all the Practices of turbulent Spirits, he preserv'd Quiet at home and Peace abroad, being content to keep his own, without invading the Rights of others; by which means he gain'd the Esteem of all neighbouring Potentates, and was honour'd by his own Subjects.

Let us now see what the *Cotton* MSS. afford us in relation to the Matter in hand under this King; and then we will proceed to farther Particulars. The MS. at *fol. 9.* runs thus:

*Henry* VII. succeeding, resum'd, in the third Year of his Reign, most Grants of Offices made by the Usurper or his Brother, and assess'd upon the Lands only of his Subjects but one Aid in *Anno* 19; out of their Goods and Lands a tenth Penny; and of the Goods, only three times the Tenth, five Fifteenths, besides a Tenth and Fifteenth arising to 120000 *l.* He took three Subsidies, whereof the last was not above 36000 *l.* and one Benevolence, the Proportion of every Alderman being 300 *l.* and the entire Sum of the City of *London* 9688 *l.* 17 *s.* 4 *d.* Of the Clergy he had twice the Tenth, and 25000 *l.* by way of Subsidy; and of them and the Commons two Loans, the
City

City of *London* rated at 6000 *l.* the other not definite in proportion, but fo affefs'd as the Commiffioners and the Lenders could agree.

As alfo to eafe the Expence of War, as Iffue of the good Money going over to *Bullen*, he ftampt an allay'd Coin, ufually then termed *Dandeprat*, a Courfe that Neceffity afterwards enforc'd his Son and Succeffors to practife, and is an apparent Symptom of a confum'd State. But that whereby he heap'd up his Mafs of Treafure (for he left in Bullion four Millions and a half, befides his Plate, Jewels, and rich Attires of Houfe) was by Sale of Offices, Redemption of Penalties, difpenfing with Laws, and fuch like, to a Year, by Value of 120000 *l.*

The MS. *fol.* 64, has only thefe Words, and there it concludes :

To *Henry* VII. in the third Year of his Reign, an Act for two Tenths, and one Fifteenth and a Subfidy is granted.

The MS. *fol* 69, is likewife fhort, being only thus much :

To *Henry* VII. the Tonnage was advanc'd to 3 *s.* and the Poundage to 12 *d.* and continu'd the moft part of his Reign without Interruption. Thus what in its firft Nature was not invefted perpetual in the Crown, but permiffive and reftrictive, as pleas'd the Affent and Occafion of the General State, is now become no conditional Gratuity, but a prerogative Duty.

The MS. *fol.* 80.

*Henry* VII. had of all his Subjects, for a Voyage into *France*, a voluntary Gift in his feventh Year ; and to aid the Chriftians againft the Incurfions of the *Turks*, he impos'd an Aid upon his People, at the Pope's Requeft, in the feventeenth of his Reign.

The

The laſt mention'd voluntary Gift, or Benevolence, other Authors ſay, was in his ſixth Year, which Difference is not very material, the Fact being certain. This way of raiſing Money he is ſaid to have made choice of to eaſe the meaner Sort, whom he chiefly endeavour'd to oblige, being ſenſible that the richeſt were the Perſons fitteſt to ſupply his Wants, and thoſe who at all times rais'd Rebellions, as grown wanton with too much Eaſe; and the Commonalty were ready to follow their Motions, as being chiefly ſupported by them, and bearing their Proportion in all Taxes and Impoſitions. Thus, by laying no Burthen upon them, he hop'd to make two ſeparate Intereſts, that when the great ones ſhould be reſtleſs they might eaſily be reduc'd, for want of the Multitude to ſupport them. A good Policy at that Time, but like all other worldly Contrivances which tend to Perpetuity, very little to be depended on; for, as the Barons, when all their Vaſſals blindly follow'd them, were ever an Over-match for the Crown; ſo the raiſing of the Commons to a Pitch of Superiority, occaſions too much Inſolence in them; and there never want Heads to carry on miſchievous Deſigns, where there are Numbers to countenance them.

The way of Benevolence, or Free-Gift, we have ſeen practis'd before, and particularly by King *Edward* IV. the ſame, tho' it appears voluntary, always carrying ſome ſort of Compulſion with it, either thro' Fear of being ill look'd upon, and the more ſeverely treated upon any Occaſion that ſhall offer, or in Hopes of finding Favour in Pretenſions; for Fear and Hope are the two prevailing Inducements to do thoſe things, which otherwiſe we are not inclin'd to. And it has been ſince ſeen that many have been very generous in ſupplying

plying the Crown at the Expence of others, not out of any Affection, or becaufe they thought it neceffary, but becaufe they have been well paid for oppreffing their Neighbours.

Howfoever this was manag'd, it is certain that King *Henry*, by fuch means, drew to him a very great Sum of Money from the wealthier Sort, yet not without much grudging ; for there are very few that care to part with their Money : And befides, thofe who are intrufted to make fuch Collections, are very rarely fo honeft as to manage them for the Intereft of the Sovereign, without ufing fuch Methods for their own private Gain, as render them and the Prince equally odious.

Having before mention'd all Taxes given in the ufual Courfe by Parliament, it will be needlefs to repeat them ; we fhall therefore only take notice of one Way found by this King, which rais'd him immenfe Sums, and afterwards coft the Lives of the two Judges who had been his chief Inftruments in the Management thereof. A Subfidy had been granted him both of the Spirituality and Temporality in his nineteenth Year ; but he growing old, and towards his End, as is ufual with many, whofe natural Temper leads that way, at the fame time grew more covetous, and thought he could never heap Treafure enough.

Being poffefs'd with this Fondnefs of Wealth, he ftudy'd the means of acquiring the fame ; and whether of himfelf, or at the Suggeftion of others, who were acquainted with his Temper, found out a Method to fatiate himfelf in fome meafure. It appear'd that many Penal Laws, and Pecuniary Statutes, had long lain unregarded and difus'd, though ftill in the fame Force as they had ever been, and made to check unruly People, and for the Good of the Publick. When Enquiry came to be

be made into the Obfervation of fuch Laws, it appear'd there were very few confiderable Perfons
but what had fome way tranfgrefs'd againft them;
and confequently were liable to the Fines and
Mulcts impos'd by them.

When firft this Courfe was undertaken, it went on
after an eafy manner, fmall Penalties being impos'd;
which being legal, and not too heavy, made little
Noife; and the Perfons themfelves who paid them
found no Caufe to complain. Soon after the Sweet
of it appearing, thofe Offences were more narrowly look'd into, and more grievoufly fin'd. The
two principal Perfons in the Management of this
Affair were Sir *Richard Empfon* and *Edmund
Dudley*, both of them very knowing in the Laws,
and well inclin'd to ingratiate themfelves with their
Sovereign, by complying with his Inclination; fo
that they perhaps adventur'd to ftrain things to the
utmoft, believing, that as they acted according to
known Laws, tho' not fo much in Ufe, they could
not incur any Danger; but, on the contrary, might
raife themfelves and their Families.

Encouragement being given, there wanted not,
as is ufual upon all fuch Occafions, great Numbers of Informers in all Parts of the Kingdom,
who brought Abundance of People into much
Trouble; for thefe being a mercenary mean fort of
Wretches, laid hold of all Opportunities to make
their own Advantage, tho' it were to the Ruin of
their Neighbours. But fuch Guilt is not only to
be charg'd on the Dregs of the Nation; all Ages
have produc'd too many Inftances of thofe who are
call'd Great and Noble, and who yet have not he-
fitated to facrifice whole Nations to their Avarice
and Ambition.

But to ftick to the Bufinefs in hand: It is fcarce
to be doubted but that *Empfon* and *Dudley* abovemention'd

mention'd might proceed with too much Rigor, according to the dead Letter of the Law, to pleafe their Prince by raifing the greater Sums of Money; and it is an old Maxim, that *fummum Jus eft fumma Injuria,* Juftice is always to be temper'd with Mercy, and fhould be fo much more where the Offenders are fcarce fenfible of the Offence they are charg'd with, as being againft Laws little known, becaufe rarely put in Execution.

What thefe two Judges were guilty of will beft appear by what was charg'd againft them, and what they alledg'd in their own Defence. The Charge was to this Effect: That they had caus'd many Perfons to be indicted of Crimes, and committed them to Prifon, without due Procefs of Law, not allowing them to make their Defence, but confining them till they had compounded by paying great Fines: That they had falfely enter'd the Lands of many People, alledging that they were held of the King *in Capite,* whereas in reality they were not fo; and by that means oblig'd them to pay heavy Fines to the King for the faid Lands: That they had fummon'd great Numbers by their Precepts to appear before them; and, when come, had imprifon'd them upon fundry Pretences till they ranfom'd themfelves with great Sums of Money, not only to the King, but to themfelves the faid Judges. Many more Particulars of this nature, as is ufual in Indictments and Impeachments, were caft into the Scale to make their Guilt appear the more heinous; but what Proof of all this I do not find: Whatfoever it was, they were both firft attainted in Parliament; and yet, as if that very Parliament had not been well fatisfy'd with their own Act, or queftion'd the Juftice of it, they were left to be try'd by the inferior Courts. This was in the Reign of King *Henry* VIII. who facrificed

thefe

thefe two Judges to pleafe the Humour of the
People, and ingratiate himfelf with them, at the
fame time facrificing his Father's Honour to fatisfy his own Ambition. But that was one of his
leaft Faults, as we fhall fee when we come to
what relates to him. Let us now finifh what we
have in hand.

Sir *Richard Empfon* and *Edmund Dudley* Efq; being
brought before the Lords, and many grievous
Offences laid to their Charge, as above hinted at,
*Empfon*, being the elder of the two, fpoke thus:

" I know (Right Honourable) that it is not un-
" known to you how profitable and neceffary Laws
" are for the good Prefervation of Man's Life,
" without the which neither Houfe, Town, nor
" City can long continue or ftand in Safety ; which
" Laws here in *England*,through Negligence of the
" Magiftrates, were partly decay'd, and partly
" quite forgotten and worn out of ufe, the Mifchief
" whereof daily encreafing, *Henry* VII. a moft
" grave and prudent Prince, wifh'd to fupprefs ;
" and therefore appointed us to fee that fuch Laws
" as were yet in ufe might continue in their full
" Force, and fuch as were out of ufe might again
" be reviv'd and reftor'd to their former State ; and
" that alfo thofe Perfons which tranfgrefs'd the
" fame might be punifh'd according to their De-
" merits; wherein we difcharg'd our Duties in
" moft faithful, wife, and beft manner we could,
" to the great Advantage and Commodity (no
" doubt) of the whole Commonwealth. Where-
" fore we moft humbly befeech you, in refpect of
" your Honours Courtefy, Goodnefs, Humanity,
" and Juftice, not to decree any grievous Sentence
" againft us, as tho' we were worthy of Punifh-
" ment;

" ment; but rather to appoint how with thank-
" ful Recompence our Pains and Travel may be
" worthily confider'd.

The Lords knew not what to object in point of
Juftice; becaufe it did not appear that they were
really guilty of any other Crime than punifhing
Offenders by Laws, which had not, as *Empfon*
alledg'd, been lately executed, which indeed was a
Fault in their Predeceffors, who ought to have obferv'd them; or, if not fit to be obferv'd, they
fhould have been repeal'd. However, Malice prevail'd, and finifh'd their Ruin, which Equity could
not do. And yet the Parliament, as has been
faid, not liking their own Proceedings, left them
ftill to be try'd at Common Law.

Accordingly *Empfon* was try'd at *Coventry*, upon
an Indictment, for that he, when Judge, having in
that fame City try'd a Felon for robbing a Houfe
there, and being fully fatisfy'd of the Proof
brought againft him, had imprifon'd the Jury for
not finding him guilty, and oblig'd them to appear
before the King's Council, where they were fin'd
eight Pounds a Man. For this alone was *Empfon*
condemn'd, without any Mention of all the other
imaginary Crimes, of which there was perhaps no
Proof at all. Being from thence convey'd to the
*Tower* of *London*, and long detain'd there, the Malice of his Enemies gave out that he had obtain'd a
Pardon, by means of the Queen; when perhaps this
Refpite was only in Confideration of his Innocence:
However, at laft, to fatisfy the Rage of thofe who
thirfted after his Blood, he was beheaded on *Tower-
Hill*, with his unfortunate Companion *Edmund
Dudley*.

This laft was arraign'd at the *Guild-Hall* in *London*, where he was condemn'd, as *Empfon* had been

N

at

at *Coventry*, and ſo ſent back to the *Tower* till he was executed, as has been ſaid.  The greateſt Crime I find prov'd upon this Man is his great Wealth, which muſt be confeſs'd to have been a great Teſtimony of Guilt, under his Circumſtances; for it is certain, that too much Riches acquir'd without proportionable Means, is an undeniable Argument of baſe Methods having been us'd in the getting of it.  His Riſe was too great to be honeſt; and therefore it is much to be fear'd that his Hands were not ſo clean as a Judge's ought to be.  What *Empſon* was worth at the time of his Death does not appear, but only that he aſcended from a very poor Station, and was poſſeſs'd of immenſe Wealth. *Dudley* is ſaid to have left twenty thouſand Pounds when he dy'd; a very great Sum in thoſe Days, tho' little regarded now, and his Beginning very inconſiderable, his firſt Advancement being to be Under Sheriff of *London.*

Many of the Informers, and other Inſtruments made uſe of by theſe Judges, were alſo try'd and ſeverely puniſh'd, of whom it is needleſs to ſpeak in this Place; and perhaps what has been already ſaid may by ſome be thought too much, as if not pertinent to the Subject; yet can I not allow this to be any Digreſſion.  Theſe Men were the Inſtruments made uſe of to bring Money into the King's Treaſury; and the Method by them taken being altogether unuſual, and as ſuch ſo ſeverely puniſh'd, the explaining of every Particular relating to it has been abſolutely neceſſary, to ſhow what has been done in all Ages, and how every King has enlarg'd his Revenue.

To conclude with this King: He left a richer Treaſury at his Death than ever any King of *England* had done before him; and we may add, than after him; for it is certain he was a greedy Hoarder of Money, tho' he had all other

good

good Qualities that could render a Prince commendable. All that Treafure he had heap'd remain'd to be fquander'd by a profufe Son, as too frequently happens. Of him we are to fpeak in the next Place.

## K. HENRY VIII.

SUcceeded his Father, and was the very reverfe of him. The Father by all Hiftorians was allow'd to have poffefs'd all Princely Virtues, and blemifh'd with no other Fault but too much Love of Money; which perhaps might be a falfe Imputation, and what thofe Authors call Covetoufnefs, no more than a provident Frugality to lay up Treafure whilft he enjoy'd Peace and Plenty, to anfwer the unforefeen Emergencies which very often involve a State in immenfe Expences; and when no Provifion is made beforehand, they at firft fall very heavy upon the Subjects. But be that as it will, nothing can be charg'd upon him but that one Crime. On the other hand, the Son was a Collection of all Vices; and, inftead of his Father's Frugality and Covetoufnefs, was a perfect *Heliogabalus* in Prodigality. The Treafures left him by his Father, and thofe beftow'd on him by his Subjects, far exceeded all that ever the Kings of *England* had before him; and I know not whether they may not be faid to have equal'd whatfoever any one has had fince; and yet it's known that the Sums fince given have been immenfe, as will appear in the Sequel.

What feveral Duties were granted to K. *Henry* VIII. by way of Taxes upon the Subjects in general, are fum'd up as follows, in the *Cotton* MS. *fol. 9.* quoted in every Reign.

His

His Succeffor (*Henry* VII.'s) reaping the Fruits of his Father's Labour, gave Eafe of Burthen to his Subjects his firft two Years; taking, within the Compafs of his other thirty-four, three Tenths of the Commons, four Fifteenths, fix Subfidies, whereof that in *Anno* 4 amounted to 160000 *l.* and that in *Anno* 7 to 110000 *l.* Tonnage he had, and Poundage once for a Year; and after for Term of Life. Of the Clergy, four Tenths by one Grant, and three by feveral, every of them not lefs than 25084 *l.* Of Subfidies, he had one of the Province of *Canterbury*, another of both; the ftipendiary Minifters thereto tax'd according to the Rates of their Wages. In *Anno* 22, they granted a Moiety of all their Goods and Lands, payable by equal Portion in five Years, every Part arifing to 95000 *l.* And not long after he had added 150000 *l.* to the yearly Revenues of his Crown, by an inhuman Spoil of facred Monuments, and impious Ruin of holy Churches, if God's Bleffing could have accompanied fo foul an Act. And as thefe former Collections he grounded upon Law, fo did he many upon Prerogative; as Benevolences and Loans from the Clergy and Commons. Of the firft there are two remarkable, that in *Anno* 17, acted by Commiffioners, who, as themfelves were fworn to Secrecy, fo were they to fwear all thofe with whom they conferr'd or contracted, the Rates directed by Inftructions, as the Thirds of all Goods, Offices, Land above 10 *l.* and the Fourth under. And altho' the Recufants, whether from Difobedience or Difability, are threaten'd with Convention before the Council, Imprifonment, or Confifcation of Goods, yet in the Defign Original under the King's Hand, it hath fo fair a Name as an *Amiable Graunte.* The other, about *Anno* 36, exacteth of all Goods, Offices, Lands, from

from 40 *s.* to 20 *l.* 8 *d.* in the Pound ; and of all
above, 12 *d.* And amongſt the many Loans, there
is none more notorious than that of *Anno* 14, which
was 10 *l.* in the Hundred of all Goods, Jewels,
Utenſils, and Land, from 20 *l.* to 300; and 20
Marks of all above, as far as the Subjeċts Fortune,
reveal'd by the Extremity of his own Oath, would
extend. And to ſtop as well Intentions, if any
had, as Expeċtations of Repayment of any Loans,
the Parliament in *Anno* 21 acquitteth the King of
all his Privy Seals or Letters miſſive.

The other *Cotton* MS. *fol.* 80, gives a very ſhort
Account, yet has ſome Particulars wanting in the
former ; and therefore is here entire thus :

*Henry* VIII. levying an Army to invade *France,*
and aſſiſt the Duke of *Bourbcn,* demandeth of his
People a Contribution, which he calleth an annual
Grant ; which, tho' with ſome Diſtraċtion and Diſ-
taſte, was yet colleċted in his fourteenth Year. * A
Benevolence was paid in the one and twentieth into the *Exchequer,* where Priors, and Clergymen of
like Ability, are rated at forty Pounds ; Knights,
at forty Marks ; Eſquires, at ten Pounds ; and Perſons of inferior Quality, at five Marks. † He gather'd
in the thirty-ſeventh and thirty-eighth of his Reign,
for urgent Occaſions touching his Perſon and State,
(for ſuch are the Words of the Inſtruċtions) two ſeveral Grants of Free Gifts from his Subjeċts; the
laſt, being ſtil'd Devotion Money, was moſt collected in 1 *Edward* VI. *Compot. Edward Peccham Militis.*

Having done with the *Cotton* MSS. as to this
Reign, we will next give a very curious MS. never
printed, that I know of, but communicated by a
N 3 worthy

---

* Inſtr. Orig. in Lib. Ro. Cotton.     † In Recept. Scacc.
Anno 21 H. 8.

worthy Friend, which will let us into fomething
more of the immenfe Value of religious Houfes
feiz'd upon by King *Henry* VIII. than any other
Author does ; and tho' fome Part of the fame may
feem too religious for this Place, it would be un-
reafonable to difmember it, which might give occafion to fufpect it had not been fairly deliver'd, as
here it is. *Anthony Wood*, in his *Athenæ Oxonienfes*,
gives the following Account of Mr. *Udal*, the
the Author of this MS.

  *Ephraim Udal*, fays *A. Wood*, was enter'd a Stu-
dent in the Publick Library at *Oxford* in *July*
1630. He was a Man of eminent Piety, exemplary
Converfation, profound Learning, and indefatigable
Induftry : Befides, he was efteem'd a Man affable,
courteous, and peaceable ; being then a *Presbyterian* ; but afterwards, feeing their wicked Practices
againft the King, came over to the Church of
*England*, for which he and his Family were ever
after perfecuted by thofe People. *See the reft in*
A. Wood. We now proceed to his MS.

## *A brief Survey of the Clergy Lands, by the Reverend* Mr. Ephraim Udal.

  The ancient Lands and Revenues of the Church
of *England* were exceeding great, and if they
fhould be eftimated according to the improv'd
Rents of Land at this Day, they may well feem
incredible. Now becaufe of the great Enquiry
made into them at this prefent, here fhall follow a
brief Catalogue of fome Churches, Colleges, and
Hofpitals, with other fuch like Houfes, as formerly belong'd to the Clergy, with a general Valuation
of their Rents, Profits, and Revenues.

Before

Before the two famous Univerfities of this Kingdom, or of any other Kingdom in *Europe,* were furnifh'd with any Number of Colleges, Libraries, Schools, Statutes, or Orders, for Education of learned Men in that manner, as they have been within a few hundred Years paft, the Piety and Practice of our Forefathers was to build many Colleges, Houfes of Religion, Hofpitals, and fuch like Societies, in feveral Parts of the Kingdom, which doubtlefs they did out of a pious Intent to advance Religion, Learning, Hofpitality, and Charity, and the Glory of God, to their beft Underftanding. So divers learned Divines, great Adverfaries to Popery, Superftition, and Idolatry, do cenfure and judge of their Actions in this kind, as Mr. *Perkins* in the Demonftration of his Problem, *pag.* 595, faith, That the Colleges and Monafteries of Antiquity were Houfes and Societies of better Ufe and Purpofe than commonly they are taken to be; for they were Schools of Learning, Communities, Colleges, and Teachers, and Learners, in thofe Days when there were no Univerfities, or very meanly furnifh'd; nor Schools of Learning but in general; thofe being the principal Places for all learned Men and chief Divines, and not only for Prayers and private Devotion.

So *Hyperius,* a learned Divine, affirmeth the fame in his Commentary on the *Hebrews,* cap. 7. p. 303. *Quo primum tempore inftituebantur Monafteria, nihil aliud erant quam quidam bonorum & ftudioforum Conventus, & Scholæ quædam, ubi, &c.* When Monafteries were firft built and founded, they were nothing elfe but Convents of honeft Men and Students, and Schools of Learning, where the Elder did teach the Younger in the Knowledge of divine Matters, where they did write Books before the Art of Printing was invented, and exercife Difpu-

N 4 tations,

tations, and did very carefully inftruct their Infe-
riors, that from among them there might be fit
and able Men chofen for the Government of the
Church, to be Bifhops and Minifters, to teach the
People.   So *St. Auguftin* and others do teftify alfo in
their Times.   So in *Germany*, out of the Monaftery
of *Fulda*, *Herefield*, and the like, Paftors and Preachers were chofen for the Inftruction and Government of the People.

And further, our Forefathers did build a goodly
College at *Rome*, richly endow'd with Lands in
*Italy*, and alfo fupply'd yearly from *England* with
a liberal Penfion, which College was intended for
the better and moft principal fort of Scholars, to
furnifh the Kingdom, being firft began by an ancient King, *Ina*, and alfo enlarg'd by others fucceeding, for Maintenance whereof they granted the
*Peter Pence* yearly to be paid out of every Hide of
Land, for the Maintenance of the faid College;
neither was it any Rent, Penfion, or Tribute, to
acknowledge the Pope's Supremacy.   For in thofe
Days, before Univerfities in thefe Weftern Parts
were founded, Learning and all Arts being fupprefs'd by the Invafion of the Northern Nations,
who overthrew the *Roman* Empire, and fet up
many Kingdoms, and planted their own barbarous
Laws and Cuftoms, under which we fuffer at this
Day, *Rome* was then the principal Place where
any excellent Learning could be gain'd, efpecially
in Divinity, before the Pope came to that Height
and Greatnefs whereunto he was afterwards rais'd
by Degrees.   That *Englifh* College continues to this
Day, being converted to a Seminary for *Englifh*
Students; and the Revenue in Lands was fo great,
tho' the *Peter Pence* were loft, that Pope *Sixtus* V.
in Queen *Elizabeth*'s Time, took away one Half of
the Lands.   But feeing the Rent of *Peter Pence* is
taken

taken off every Man's Lands, which was a great Charge, it might well content the Subjects, especially having besides so many Church Lands divided among them.

But to let pass this foreign College at *Rome*, the Colleges and religious Houses at home did afford many singular Men for the Government of the Commonwealth, as well as of the Church ; for out of them came most of the Judges and Lawyers in ancient Times, before the Canon Law became a Science ; as *Britton* Bishop of *Hereford, Martin de Patteshull, William de Rafeghe, Robert de Lexinton, Henry de Stanton*, and many others, as Lord *Coke* shows ; as also the honourable Officers of the Realm, as Lord Chancellor, Lord Treasurer, Lord Privy Seal, Master of the Rolls, *&c.* besides many singular Men learned in all kinds, as appears by their Works, and the Catalogue of them in *Bale.*

But King *Henry* VIII. upon his Breach with the Pope, finding the Clergy not to favour his Divorce, in Opposition to the Pope, began to enquire into the State of religious Houses ; and finding them to be corrupted in great Part, at leastwise it was so pretended, he caus'd all their Faults to be ript up, especially those of Uncleanness, whereof being accus'd they lost all their Lands and Estates from themselves and their Heirs for ever ; yet if now or then the Laity were to lose their Estates for such Offences, many great Families would be undone. If any such Offences were then among the Clergy, they might have been corrected without destroying them.

Yet whatsoever their Faults were, the Revenues, Lands, and Profits, might have been employ'd in great part to the publick Benefit of the Kingdom, Advancement of Learning, Piety, Charity, and Hospitality, with many other good Works in several kinds, as Reparations of Bridges, Highways, Hospitals, and many such like publick Necessities, particularly design'd and exprefly inserted in the Act 27 *Hen.* VIII. and not, as they were, in enriching and raising particular Men. For those Societies were things of excellent Use, tho' afterwards abus'd, as Sir *Richard Baker* says truly in his late History; and they should have been bestow'd rather for the Advancement of the Church, to a better Maintenance of the labouring and deserving Ministry, to the fostering of good Arts, Relief of the Poor, and other such good Uses, as Mr. *Selden* in his *Review, Chap.* 9, 10.

But to make a brief Survey of their Numbers, Rents, and Profits, here shall follow a general Catalogue, the Particulars being more fully recited by *Cambden, Speed,* and many other Historians, and Records remaining in the *Exchequer.*

*Anno* 1536, when King *Henry* VIII. first attempted the Dissolution of them, he began first with the lesser Monasteries, under 200 *l.* Value of old Rents, which were in Number   } 376

31 *Henry* VIII. Not long after he dissolv'd the great Abbies, which were in Number   } 605

Also four-score and ten Colleges in several Shires and principal Cities of the Kingdom, besides those in the Universities, which could not in reason be accounted popish and superstitious.   } 90

Then Hospitals for Relief of the Poor of all Sorts, maim'd Soldiers and decay'd People, Orphans and Widows, whereof most were built by the Bishops and Clergy, and no Reason there was to account them superstitious.   } 110

*Lastly,*

*Lastly,* Chantries and Free Chapels, two
thousand three hundred and seventy four,
whereof some worth 500 or 600 *l.* yearly,
which then were of small Value, as Rents
were then accounted.

} 2374

The like was done in *Ireland,* where there was
an infinite Number of religious Houses and Hospitals. The like also in *Scotland,* where they pretended, at the Dissolution of religious Houses, to
give all to the Crown, by the *vile Act of Annexa-
tion,* as King *James* calleth it, *lib.* 2. *Bas. Doron* ;
but they presently convey'd them all from the
Crown to themselves, in the Infancy of King
*James* ; so that the Crown is impoverish'd in both
those Kingdoms and destitute of Revenue, which
cannot but seem very strange and wonderful, seeing
their Pretence was to augment the Revenue of the
King. But of these two Kingdoms little shall be
said now; yet it were fit to make a particular
Survey and Enquiry, that the full Truth may appear, how great a Desolation and Spoil has been
made of the publick Revenues both of King and
Church, to enrich private Men, and to raise them
up to new Honours, Dignities, and Estates, more
than can be allow'd them by any Reason of State
or Equity of Law.

All these religious Houses, Churches, Colleges,
and Hospitals, in *England,* being about three thousand and five hundred, little and great in the
whole, had very great Revenues ; and if their
Rents should be valu'd and accounted as private
Mens Lands are rated, especially in these Times,
they would arise to some Millions Sterling beyond
all Imagination.

Further, after the Monasteries were seiz'd on,
the great Estate of the Knights Hospitallers was

also

alfo confifcated. The Prior of *St. John's* was accounted the firft temporal Baron of the Kingdom, and they had anciently nineteen thoufand Manors in Chriftendom, whereof a great Part was in *England*: And they had alfo the great Eftate of the *Knights Templars* conferr'd on them, which was nine thoufand Manors, as *Cambden* relates in his *Britannia, pag.* 433. All thefe, together with their perfonal Eftates, in Plate, Money, Goods, Stocks of Cattle, Furniture of Houfes and Churches, which did amount to more than the Riches and Spoil of the Temple and *Jerufalem*, when they were robb'd and plunder'd by *Nebuchadnezzar*, who yet did not convert the holy Veffels of the Temple to his private Ufe, but put them into the Houfe of his Gods at *Babylon*, from whence they were reftor'd again to the Temple by *Cyrus*, as *Ezra* i. 7. and *Daniel*.

All thefe Houfes, Colleges, and Churches, were furvey'd, valu'd, and tax'd by Commiffioners from the King; but yet rated at very low Prices, even in thofe Times, at *Robin Hood's* Pennyworths, as *Speed* fhoweth in his Hiftory, 21 *Hen.* 8.

The true Value of all their Rents and Revenues cannot eafily be accounted; becaufe the Commiffioners did far undervalue them, hoping to get many for themfelves, as they did; and becaufe a great part of their Profits came to them in Provifion of Victuals, Corn, Cattle of all forts, Wood-Sales, Fines, and many Services, with other Perquifites, which cannot eafily be accounted; but if a View of fome Particulars be look'd on, the Total will appear the better.

1. As firft, the great Abbey of *St. Albans*, in *Hartfordfhire*, if the old Lands were united together, is worth at this Day, in all Rents, Profits, and Revenues, about two hundred thoufand Pounds yearly,

yearly, according to the improv'd Rents at this Day; out of which one Half, or a great Part, might have been added to the Crown for Augmentation of Revenue, and the reft employ'd to pious and charitable Ufes in the Commonwealth; and inftead of fome fixty Monks, there might have been an hundred Preachers richly provided to preach to the Inhabitants and Country round about; befides an Hofpital of a thoufand poor People of all forts, and fix good Schoolmafters, for Education of Gentlemens Children, and the Children of many good Men, in Religion, Learning, Mufick, Writing, and all other good Qualities, to the infinite Benefit of their Parents and the whole Kingdom. Whereas, for divers Years paft, that Town having four Churches, there is no conftant Preacher in any of them, nor any one Schoolmafter; but fhifting and changing Minifters daily, and the Schoolmafters gone, having very poor Stipends.

2. The Abbey of *Glaftonbury*, in *Somerfetfhire*, is worth at this prefent, in Rents, Profits, and Revenues, all the old Lands being reckon'd together, much above three hundred thoufand Pounds yearly. It was the moft ancient Church and College in this Kingdom, or thefe Weftern Parts of *Europe*, and once recommended by the Parliament to King *Henry* VIII. to have been fpar'd in the general Deftruction and Defolation, as having been famous in the old Times of the ancient *Britons*, and for the firft coming thither of *Jofeph* of *Arimathea* and his Affiftants for Converfion of the Inhabitants; as alfo for the Burial of King *Arthur*, and many other eminent Men and Princes, before the *Saxons* came to be Owners thereof.

3. *St. Auguftin's* Abbey, near *Canterbury*, the firft Chriftian Church and College, founded by the firft
Chriftian

Chriftian King of the old *Englifh Saxons, Ethelbert,* who beftow'd it upon *Auguftin,* whom *Gregory the Great* fent with forty Preachers for the Converfion of his Kingdom, which by God's Bleffing on their Endeavours they effected, and from hence propagated Religion to *London,* and other principal Cities and Places: So that *St. Auguftine's* was, as the Firft-Fruits of the Land, prefented unto God, and might have been therefore fav'd from the Deluge. It is worth at this prefent two hundred thoufand Pounds yearly in Rents and all Profits.

4. *St. Edmund's-Bury,* in *Suffolk,* founded by King *Canutus,* is worth at this prefent two hundred thoufand Pounds yearly.

5. *Ramfey the Rich,* in *Huntingdonfhire,* worth in old Rents feven thoufand Pounds yearly, as *Cambden* fhows; and yet *Wolfey* took two thoufand Pounds Lands from it for his two Colleges, befides other things. It is worth now three hundred thoufand Pounds yearly.

6. *Crowland Abbey,* in *Lincolnfhire,* is worth above one hundred thoufand Pounds yearly, as appears by the Charters and Donations of Lands mention'd in *Ingulphus,* the Abbat here; befides many Additions fince his Time.

7. The Abbey of *Leicefter* is worth an hundred thoufand Pounds yearly. Befides, here was a Collegiate Church, a magnificent Work, fays *Cambden,* the chiefeft Ornament of that Town, founded by *Henry* the firft Duke of *Lancafter,* confifting of a Dean and twelve Prebendaries, befides other Minifters, who might have been continu'd for Preachers to that Town and Country, without any Sufpicion of Popery, Superftition, or Idolatry.

8, 9. The Abbies of *Abingdon* and *Reading,* both in *Barkfhire,* are worth above three hundred thoufand Pounds yearly.

10. The Abbey of *Evesham*, in *Worcestershire*, is worth one hundred thousand Pounds yearly.

11. The Abbey of *Tewksbury*, in *Glocestershire*, is worth about one hundred thousand Pounds yearly.

12. There were in *Shrewsbury*, besides the great Abbey, two Collegiate Churches ; the one *St. Chad's*, with eleven Prebends ; and the other *St. Mary's*, with nine Prebends ; as *Cambden* relates, worth many Thousands yearly, out of which might have been maintain'd forty Preachers for that Town and Country, besides an Hospital of five hundred poor People of all Sorts ; and the School, consisting of four Schoolmasters, maintain'd well, without robbing and spoiling the Parsonage of *Chirburg*, as now it happens.

It is endless to reckon up all the Colleges, Churches, Houses, and Hospitals, in several Shires of the Kingdom. There are divers Catalogues of them publish'd in Print, whereby it appears what great Revenue might have been added to the Crown, and yet all the good Works of Piety and Charity still maintain'd, the Gospel powerfully advanc'd, and the Church of CHRIST set upright, and all his holy Ordinances in full Force ; that we might have had a Kingdom full of Preachers, far beyond any Kingdom in the World ; and all these maintain'd without the Charge of the Inhabitants and Tradesmen, who now, in the best Cities and Towns, are put to hard Shifts and Contributions to maintain a Lecturer by Stipends in poor manner for the most part.

If the Rents, Profits, and Revenues, of all the Lands should be accounted according to the true Valuations of these Times, it would be found to amount to so many Millions Sterling as is incredible to most Men ; yet no wise Man ought to marvel at it, more than that a Quarter of Wheat

is

is now fold for thirty or forty Shillings, which was antiently at twelve Pence the Quarter, which appears by the Statutes and Records, as is in the Affife of Bread 51 *Hen.* 3.

Now, befides the Abbies and Monafteries of feveral Sorts, Colleges, Hofpitals, and Chapels, as has been fhow'd in fome few Particulars, whereby the reft may be eftimated, the old Bifhopricks were anciently endow'd with very great Revenues by the Kings of *England*, moft part whereof are already taken away, there being very few Bifhopricks that have any confiderable Lands, but only Impropriations, fince the Statute made 1 *Eliz.* whereby the Queen was enabled to take away the goodly Lands from the Bifhops, and give Impropriations for them, *which Statute is not publifh'd.* But this Exchange was very miferable, like the Change of *Glaucus* with *Diomedes,* who gave his golden Armour for the other's brazen Armour ; or like as *Rehoboam* did, who, inftead of golden Shields that his Father *Solomon* had provided in the Temple, put in their Places Shields of Brafs, as the learned Dr. *Ridley* fhows the Mifchief of this Act, in his View of the Civil Law, *Cap.* 5. *Sect.* 2, 3.

The old Bifhopricks, before the Lands were taken away, were worth twenty hundred thoufand Pounds yearly, reckoning every Bifhoprick at one hundred thoufand Pounds yearly, according to our improv'd Rents ; but now no fuch matter, nor then neither to the Bifhops themfelves, who accepted fuch fmall Rents, that the Tenants, the Poor, and the whole Kingdom, enjoy'd all the reft that was above neceffary Expence and the Performance of fome good Works. There remains now in Lands to the Bifhopricks no fuch Abundance as fome Men imagine, which will appear fully by looking into
fome

fome Statutes, where the Lands and goodly Manors are reckon'd that are taken away.

Firft, the Archbifhoprick of *York* was regulated, from which were taken away, at one Inftant, no lefs than feventy Manors, mention'd particularly in a Statute 37 *Hen. 8. chap.* 16, *viz. Rippon, Sharrow, Stanley, Ripponholme, Colleſhakeſhil, Pennicroft, Caſtle-Dike, White-Cliffe, Thorpe, Monkton, Thornton, Weſ-terdale, &c.* in feveral Shires; befides, fays the Statute, divers other Manors, Lands, Tenements, Advowſons, Patronages, Gifts, and Nominations of Hofpitals, Prebends, Churches, Chantries, Free-Chappels, and divers Royalties, Jurifdictions, &c.

One may well doubt whether there be any Lands now left to the Archbifhoprick, fo many being gone already at the Regulation of it ; *and yet it is accounted to be three thoufand Pounds yearly in all Rents and Profits.*

" The feventy Manors taken from the Archbi-
" fhop of *York,* by the Statute 37 *Hen. 8.* as men-
" tion'd in the faid Statute, are, *Rippon, Sharow,*
" *Stanley, Ripponholme, Coleſſakeſhil, Ponicrofte, Caſtle-*
" *dike, Whitecliffe, Thorpe, Monketon, Thorneton,*
" *Netherdale, Biſhopſide, Shorborne, Milford, Biſhop-*
" *plaches, Patrington, Tharethorp, Fiſmake, Halgarth,*
" *Gloughton, Wetwang, Wilton, Wilton, Epi, Topcliff,*
" *Thirsk, Aſcenby, Griſchwait, Difford, Renton, New-*
" *by, Skipton, Catton, Northby, Whaplow, Maske,*
" *Upletheme, Alton, Dalton, Craghal, Cercheton, Hex-*
" *am, Erington, Walle, Atome, Halidon, Kepwike,*
" *Groverige, Kenelegh, Eſclawont, Cadden, Ninibinros,*
" *Weſcalland, Newland, Scroby, Raveneskeld, Lanome,*
" *Askham, Sutton, Northſoke, Churchdowne, Huekil-*
" *kote, Norton, Shuddington, Widcombe, Cherney, Comp-*
" *ton, Odington,* and *Gloceſter,* with all and fingular
" their Appurtenances, in the feveral Counties of

O                                        " *York,*

" *York, Northumberland, Glocefter,* and in the Coun-
" ty and City of *Glocefter,* and divers other Ma-
" nors, Lands, Tenements, Advowfons, Patro-
" nages, Gifts, and Nominations of Hofpitals,
" Prebends, Churches, Chantries, Free-Chapels,
" and other fpiritual Promotions, *&c.*

" *Note,* That *Wilton* is nam'd twice together
" in the Statute, as it appears above.

2. The like was done to *Canterbury,* by the fame
Statute, when that was regulated, by divers Deeds
and Conveyances, as is there fpoken of, and Refe-
rence made to them, as the Manors of *Charmies,
Laybourne, Maighfield, &c.* It is now accounted
about four thoufand Pounds yearly.

" The Manors, *&c.* taken from the Archbifhop
" of *Canterbury,* by the fame Statute, are as fol-
" lows : The Manors of *Charing* and *Layborne,* the
" Caftle of *Layborne,* View of *Frankplege* at *Colehill,*
" to be holden of Tenants and Refiants within the
" faid Manor of *Charing;* and the Advowfons and
" Patronages of the Rectories and Churches of
" *Charing, Layborne,* and *Ridley,* in the County of
" *Kent.* And the Manors of *Maighfield,* otherwife
" call'd *Maughfield,* the Parks of *Maughfield* and
" *Frankham,* the Rectories of *Maughfield* and *Wade-*
" *hurft,* the Advowfons and Patronages of the Vi-
" carage of *Maighfield* and *Wadehurft,* in the Coun-
" ty of *Suffex;* and the Manors of *Harrow, Wood-*
" *hall, Heefe, Hegefton, Sudbury,* the Park call'd
" *Pinner Park,* the Advowfon and Patronage of the
" Parfonage and Vicarage of the Parfonage and
" Rectory of the Church of *Tryng,* in the County
" of *Hertford;* the Advowfon and Patronage of
" the Parfonage and Church of *Halton,* in the
" County of *Buckingham,* with all their Rights,
" Members, Liberties, *&c.*

3. So

3. So from *London,* in the fame Statute, in the Time of Bifhop *Bonner,* as *Chelmesford* and *Crondon* in *Effex (and the Park of* Crondon) ; and afterwards, in the Time of *Edward* VI. many more, as is publifh'd, when *Ridley* was enforc'd to yield up, by his Deed dated the 12th of *January,* 4 *Edw.* VI. the Manors of *Branketry* and *Southminfter,* and the Patronage of the Church of *Cogfhal* in *Effex* ; the Manors of *Stepney* and *Hackney* in *Middlefex* ; and the Marfh of *Stepney,* with all and fingular Meffuages, Lands, and Tenements to the faid Manors belonging; and alfo the Advowfon of the Vicarage of the Parifh Church of *Cogfhal* in *Effex* aforefaid ; which Grant was confirm'd by the Dean and Chapter of *St. Paul's, Stepney,* and *Hackney,* as only belonging to them. The faid King *Edward,* by his Letters Patents, dated the 16th of *April,* in the fourth Year of his Reign, granted to Sir *Thomas Wentworth* Lord Chamberlain of the King's Houfhold, for and in Confideration of his good and faithful Service before done, a Part of the late receiv'd Gift, *viz.* the Lordfhips of *Hackney* and *Stepney,* with all the Members and Appurtenances thereunto belonging in *Stepney, Hackney, Shoreditch, Holywell-ftreet, Whitechapel, Stratford* at *Bow, Poplar, North-ftreet, Limehoufe, Ratcliff, Clere-ftreet, Brook-ftreet, Mile-end, Bleton, Hall-Green, Old-Ford, Weft-Heath, Kingfland, Stakehvell, Newington-ftreet* alias *Hackney-ftreet, Clopton, Church-ftreet, Well-ftreet, Hancunter, Green-ftreet, Gunfter-ftreet* alias *Moor-ftreet,* together with the Marfh of *Stepney, &c.* The Rents of Houfes in thefe Streets do arife to an infinite Sum in thefe Times.

And yet afterwards, in the Time of Queen *Elizabeth,* they regulated this Bifhoprick further, taking away divers Manors; fo that whether any Manors confiderable be now left remaining is doubt-

ful.

ful.   The Rents are not above 1100 *l*. yearly, beſides ſome Perquiſites.

4. From *Lincoln* all the goodly Lands, Caſtles,
and Manors, were taken away, upon the Yielding
and Reſignation of *Holbeach*, made Biſhop for that
Purpoſe, 1 *Edw*. VI.   The old Rents were under
two thouſand Pounds yearly; but now they are
above one hundred thouſand to the preſent Owners.
There is no Land left to the Biſhoprick, but only
ſome four hundred Pounds yearly, *Buckden* in *Hun-
tingdonſhire*; the reſt is in Impropriations, about
nine hundred.

5. From *Norwich* King *Henry* VIII. took all the
goodly Lands and Manors of great Value from
Biſhop *Nix*, who was old, weak, and blind; caſ-
ting him into a *Premunire* upon a Pretence.   Yet
after, he gave ſome Lands of the Abbey of *St.
Bennet*, 21 *Regni*, to ſupport the Biſhoprick from
Ruin.

6. From *Ely* were taken all the goodly Lands and
Manors in the Time of Queen *Elizabeth*, who
gave ſome Impropriations in Recompence for them.
If theſe Lands had been apply'd to Augmentation
of the Crown, which was the Pretence, or any
other publick good Uſe, it had been more ex-
cuſable; but they are long ſince ſeiz'd on by private
Men and Courtiers, regarding their own Benefit,
and no publick Good of the Church or State.

*Weſt*, a Biſhop of *Ely*, in King *Henry* VIII.'s
Time, had eleven Ovens fill'd with Bread every
Day for the Poor; and when he travell'd, or remov'd to any Place, he gave great Alms to every
poor Body, that would come to receive, upon the
tolling of a Bell, 2 *s*. 2 *d*. to each one, which is as
much as 10 *s*. in theſe Days; beſides many other
good Works of Charity and Hoſpitality.   There
are no ſuch Works of Charity perform'd ſince that
Day

Day by any Man that enjoys any Part of the Bishops Lands.

If the Works of *Wickham*, Bishop of *Winchester*, should be mention'd, they would fill a Volume: He built many Churches, Chapels, Hospitals, and other religious Houses; he mended all the Highways from *Winchester* to *London*, on both Sides the River. But above all other Works, he built and endow'd two excellent Colleges, the one call'd *New-College* in *Oxon.* the other at *Winchester*, with a Grammar School; two excellent Nurseries of Learning and excellent Men in all Faculties, to the infinite Benefit of the Church and Commonwealth. *Cambden* says truly of him, that he was the greatest Father and Patron of good Literature that ever this Kingdom afforded.

All the rest of the Bishops, in their several Places and Times, were singular Benefactors to Learning, in building Colleges and furnishing Libraries; and which is not to be forgotten, they founded all the Colleges in both the Universities, excepting very few, which yet were built by their Perswasion or Procurement, which redounds to their everlasting Honour and eternal Praise, those Societies being the most excellent Nurseries of Learning and Religion in the whole World. Never did *Israel* enjoy the like, nor any Christian Kingdom can show the like; tho' now all is deny'd, dissembled, and blasted, and most ignorantly and impudently they are branded to have been the Authors of all Mischief in the Commonwealth.

In like manner, as is related, all the rest of the Bishops have been regulated, as the Phrase is now, having lost all their goodly Houses in and near *London*, as also in the Country, with their rich Manors and Lands; so that now there remains no fuch Booty to be found as fome Men expect and gape after.

The poor Bifhoprick of *Landaff* in *Wales,* as *Goodwin* fays, who was Bifhop there, and faw the ancient Records of that Church, if it were poffefs'd of the tenth Part of the Lands that were given to it above one thoufand two hundred Years ago by the *Britifh* Kings, it might be reckon'd among the richeft Churches in the Kingdom.

And as the Bifhopricks anciently were thus very rich and great, fo were the old Rents of the Crown; for the King had in every County of *England* fifty or fixty Manors, Lordfhips, Farms, befides many other Rents in Cities and Towns, and befides alfo Caftles, Forefts, Parks, and Warrens, with many other Perquifites, as appears fully by the principal Record of the Kingdom, *Domefday Book;* but now the greateft Part of them is gone and made away, to the great Lofs and Hindrance of the King and whole Kingdom; for if the King had his old Lands, he needed not to ask a Subfidy of his People, unlefs in great Neceffity, or fome foreign Invafion, as that of eighty-eight, or the like; for the old Crown Lands are worth yearly much above a Million Sterling, if moderately improv'd.

So alfo the Lands of the greater Nobility of the Kingdom were very great; for tho' the Lords and Barons were very many for Number, when *William the Conqueror* firft created Military and Honorary Tenures, as Mr. *Selden* fhows in his Titles of Honour, 2 *part, c.* 7. and *Cambden* in his *Britannia, p.* 799, making no lefs than many thoufand Barons throughout the Kingdom; yet the principal and greateft of them, who only were call'd to the great Affemblies and Councils of the Kingdom, were fuch as had great Eftates; for every Earl was

to

to have four hundred Pounds of old Rents, which
was a great Eftate ; and as for the Barons who had
not thirteen Knights Fees, they were not call'd to
the publick Affemblies of the Kingdom. And as
Sir *Richard Baker* fays truly in his Hiftory, in
*Edward* II. the Title of Baron, which before had
been promifcuous to Men of Eftate, was firft confin'd to fuch only as by the King were call'd to
have Voice in Parliament.

The Bifhops, having great Eftates and Lands,
were enforc'd to hold them as Baronies by *William
the Conqueror*, to do him Homage and Service, to
afford him great Supplies towards his Wars and
publick Occafions. It was no Honour to them in
thofe Times to be made or call'd Barons, but a
Burden and Charge impos'd on them ; they were
then in Place and Dignity above Earls and Barons,
and admitted from the firft Chriftianity to all the
great Councils and Affemblies of the Kingdom ;
neither needed they that Title to raife them in
Efteem, as *Cambden* and other Heralds do make it
appear. The Archbifhop of *Canterbury* did find for
the King eighty Horfe, Men, and Arms ; and fo did
all the Bifhops, Abbats, and Priors, in the Kingdom, as appears upon Record ; fo that the Clergy,
out of their great Eftates, maintain'd almoft an
Army for the King, befides Relief of maim'd Soldiers, of decay'd Gentlemen, and younger Brethren
of good Families, in their Spittles, Receipts, and
Hofpitals, which they had always ready provided
for that Purpofe. So the Nobility and Gentry
do hold at this Day very good Leafes of them and
their Churches, at eafy Rents, to their great Benefit.

*John Speed*, in his Hiftory, fays, that the Bifhopricks were only par'd a little ; but he was much
miftaken to fay fo ; for they were not only par'd to

the

the quick, but fo impoverifh'd, that the leffer Sort was holden by Commendams, and other Additaments.

And as the Bifhopricks were thus regulated, fo moft of the Deans and Chapters have loft very much; neither have the Colleges in the Univerfities been fpar'd, tho' perhaps it is unknown to moft Men: Scarce any College but has loft fome good Lands; but this being done fome Years ago, Men cannot endure to hear of it, nor to believe it, tho' Particulars are eafy to be produc'd.

If the whole Return of Bifhopricks, Colleges, Churches, Monafteries, and Hofpitals, fhould be fully reckon'd, it would be found to exceed fix Millions Sterling of yearly Rents, according to the Rates of thefe Times, and in the Lands of fuch Men as have thefe Lands thus taken away in their Poffeffion.

By the Diffolution of the religious Houfes the Crown has already loft an hundred thoufand Pounds yearly, Firft-Fruits and Penfions, or rather much more, the Statute being made before the Diffolution, 26 *Henry* VIII. whereby the King was to have a great Revenue out of their Eftates yearly; their temporal Lands being fo great, that *St. Alban's* Abbey might have yielded ten thoufand Pounds yearly; *Glaftonbury, St. Edmund's-bury, St. Auguftin's, Ramfey,* and the reft of the great Monafteries, each of them many Thoufands yearly. But all this is loft and gone, as Sir *Robert Cotton* fhows; yet by the Statute it is ftill due to the King, and may juftly be recover'd.

The Crown does receive now yearly an hundred thoufand Pounds out of the Bifhops Eftates, and the reft of the Clergy, in that poor Condition as now they ftand, the greateft Part whereof will be loft, if the Lands of the Bifhops fhould be fold in

that

that manner as is attempted; so much being gone already, the Fragments, Pittances, Scraps, Relicks, and Remnants, that are left, would not be envy'd.

If any demand what Opinion the learned Men of this last Age have given of these Doings, it is easy to show out of divers, as *Calvin*, hearing of King *Henry* VIII.'s Violence and Sacrilege in *England*, he could not forbear in his Lectures to censure him, as in *Hof. cap.* 1.

*Henricus fuit Homo plane belluinus, deterior omnibus mancipiis Antichristi Romani; nam qui sub illa servitute manent, saltem retinent aliquam speciem Pietatis ; ille autem nullo pudore Hominum retentus fuit, & ostendit se prorsus vacuum fuisse omni Timore Dei.*

That is, *Henry* was a mere brutal Man, worse than all the Slaves of the *Roman* Antichrist; for those who continue under that Servitude, at least retain some Show of Piety; but he was not curb'd by any humane Shame, and show'd he was quite void of all Fear of God.

And the like he says upon *Amos*, and elsewhere.

The Words of *Luther* against him are too bitter to be recited.

*Cambden*, the publick Historian of the Kingdom, in his *Britannia*, *p.* 163, says, that when the Churches and Colleges were pull'd down, their Revenues were sold and made away, and those Goods and Riches, which the Christian Piety of the *English* Nation had consecrated unto God, since they first profess'd Christianity, were in a Moment, as it were, dispers'd, and (to the Displeasure of no Man be it spoken) profan'd.

——— *pudet hæc opprobria nobis*
*Et dici potuisse, & non potuisse refelli.*

So likewise other great learned Men do say the like, as the excellently learned *Grotius*, in his An-
notations

notations on the Bible and other Places, *ad Artic.*
16 *Caſſand.*

*Quod vero hic dicit Caſſander, Imperatorum & Regum
hoc quoque eſſe Officium, ut Leges divinas & Canones con-
ſervent, &c.* The whole Quotation being long,
it will be more proper to give the ſame in *Engliſh*,
which is as follows : " What *Caſſander* here ſays,
" that it is alſo the Duty of Emperors and of
" Kings to maintain the divine Laws and Canons,
" is moſt true ; for they are bound to ſerve CHRIST
" even as they are Kings ; but they are to take care
" that they do not give occaſion for Schiſm ; but
" they are to know they are in ſuch manner Over-
" ſeers of the Churches of their Kingdom, as to
" remember at the ſame time that they are Sons
" of the univerſal Church. But thoſe Princes moſt
" baſely fulfil this Duty, who convert to their
" own, and indeed moſt profane Uſes, thoſe things
" which have been formerly given to God, that
" is, to pious Uſes, on this Pretence, that Biſhops
" have too much. If Biſhops have too much, let
" what is over and above be given to Prieſts and
" Deacons ; let it be given to build or repair
" Churches, let it be given to the Poor of the
" Country ; and if thoſe be wanting, to Strangers ;
" as formerly Money was ſent from *Achaia* and
" *Macedonia* into *Judea* ; let the Captives that
" are among Barbarians be redeem'd, on which
" account many Biſhops have ſold the Veſſels be-
" longing to the Church, even after they had been
" conſecrated ; and ſome have deliver'd themſelves
" up as Hoſtages. I wonder that thoſe who read
" the *Old Teſtament* are not deterr'd by the Example
" of *Achan*, and thoſe who read the *New* by that
" of *Ananias.* And this is the principal Cauſe why
" Wars are ſo laſting, not ſo much becauſe both
" Sides

" Sides make War for thefe things, but becaufe
" God thus revenges his being contemn'd.

So in his Notes upon *Daniel* v. 2. " The pro-
" faning of facred things, which was formerly an
" horrid Crime, is now become the Sport of
" Princes and profane Men, and ftill we ask why
" Defolation is every where made by fuch dreadful
" Wars.

The learned and great Divine *Rivet,* in his Reply to *Grotius* upon *Caffander,* does acknowledge,
" That it is indeed excellent Advice, if it were
" put in Execution, and thofe who ought would
" confent to it.

Moft Men are ready to fay, that the Clergy in
former Times had too much. Suppofe and grant
they had too much; yet feeing they fpent and employ'd it fo well, they were free from Blame; for
they were fo bountiful to all forts of Poor, aboun-
ding in Works of Charity and Hofpitality, that
they were great Benefactors in the Commonwealth,
that there needed not then any Statutes for Maintenance of the Poor; they fupply'd the Crown
continually with many great Gifts and Penfions,
and furnifh'd a great Part of an Army to the King,
in Times of Need, and gave great Relief to maim'd
Soldiers. They were moft gentle and favourable
Landlords to their Tenants, taking but five Pounds
Rent for a Farm that was worth fifty Pounds
yearly, and now above two hundred Pounds;
whereby the Gentry, and all Farmers that held of
them, were greatly benefited; fo that they were
no Burden to the Kingdom in any refpect. It is
now demanded by moft Men, whether this and that
be *Jure divino*; and if not *Jure divino,* then prefently they think it lawful to be taken away. But this
is a very unjuft Suggeftion; for Men may lawfully
hold and retain Lands, Money, and Goods, and
Chattels,

Chattels, or any thing elfe, tho' they cannot prove it to be due *Jure divino.* It is enough that they hold it by a good Title of Gift, Defcent, or Pur-chafe, *Jure humano.* So many Clergymen enjoy Lands juftly and lawfully *Jure humano.* Neither can they be taken away without great Injuftice and Wrong.

> *Dat Galienus Opes, dat Juftinianus Honores ;*
> *Solus Ariftoteles cogitur ire pedes.*

Phyficians and Lawyers, Citizens, Tradefmen, and Grafiers, and all forts of Men, may purchafe Lands; only Clergymen are envy'd if they pur-chafe; tho' the Number of them is very few that have purchas'd any confiderable Eftates. Citizens may ride in Coaches, but Clergymen may not ; fcarce upon a good Horfe, in the Opinion of many vulgar People. *Cambden,* in his Annals, writing that Queen *Elizabeth* going to *Paul's* in fifty-five, to render publick Thanks to God for the great Deli-verance of the Kingdom, attended with her Nobi-lity and Courtiers, in very folemn manner, fhe did ride in a Coach drawn only by two Horfes. Kings and Princes did not then ride with four Horfes, as now private Men do. What would *Cambden* have added further, if he had feen the Pride of private Perfons to be fuch as it is in thefe Times, that not only Nobles and Gentry of the beft Sort, but Tradefmen and Citizens of mean Birth, and ignoble, do ride and travel abroad with Coaches and fix Horfes, going to vifit their Country Houfes and Farms in fuch pompous Equipage, as *Agrippa* and *Berenice* came down, *with much Pomp,* A&s xxv. 23. It is eafy to name, among others of the like Sort, a Pedlar's Son by Birth, and now by trading, tricking, and turning of Wares, advanc'd to

Riches,

Riches, who comes down into the Country with Coach and fix Horfes. If any Bifhop or Clergyman ride fo coach'd, then many cry out, *Oh the Pride of Antichriftian Prelacy!* Then they grin and fhow their Teeth like the Dogs of *Egypt*, when they bark at the Crocodiles in the *Nile.* *Tully* faid of old, *Mercatores funt fordidum hominum genus,* Traders are a filthy fort of Men; and the learned Herald of our Kingdom faith of Tradefmen and Citizens, that they are accounted in our Law as far inferior to our Gentry and Nobility.

*Burgenfes, dum comparandis mercibus & rei mercatoriæ operam navarent, generofæ turbæ, militiam omnino admirantis, defpectui erant, adeo ut cum illis nec Connubia jungerent, nec Martis aleam experirentur. Vide Statu. de Merton, Anno Dom.* 1235, *cap.* 7. *De Dominis qui maritaverint illos quos habent in cuftodia fua, villanis, & aliis ficut Burgenfibus, ubi difparagentur, &c.* Anciently Citizens and Tradefmen were refus'd and deny'd to marry with the Gentry; and in Trials by Duel and Battel, which was the old Fafhion before Trials by Juries of twelve Men came in ufe, they might refufe the Trial. *Vetus Lex nihil militare a Burgenfibus expetit, in Duellum igitur fe vadatis, fubterfugere licuit, & per Campionem quem vocant, i. e. Pugilem rem decernere.*

The Tradefmen of all Cities have left off their flat Caps, which they account popifh and fuperftitious, and are become in their Attire and Habit like Nobles and Princes. Their Riches and Fulnefs has exceeded *Tyre,* defcrib'd by *Ezekiel, c.* 26, 27. and to them we are beholden for the wafteful Expence of fo much Treafure, fo many Millions of Money and Mens Lives; and ftill their Riches and Fulnefs is fo great, that they are ready to purchafe all the Clergy Lands left remaining, and to divide the Spoil among themfelves.

Time

Time was, when Purple and Scarlet, Velvet and
Cloth of Gold, were referv'd only for Princes;
neither was it lawful for common Perfons, under the
Degree of a Prince and great Nobility, to wear
the fame, as may eafily be fhow'd by many Laws;
but now what mean Perfons are cloath'd with
Purple and Scarlet, Velvet and Cloth of Gold,
and other rich Apparel, is eafy to obferve without
mention of Particulars.   Only the Clergy muft
wear little better than *John* the *Baptift* did, Apparel
of Camels Hair, or fuch coarfe Stuff; and have no
more Furniture than the old Prophet *Elifha* had,
one Table, one Candleftick, one Stool, and but
only one of any neceffary Things.

The Reader is defir'd to obferve, that what has
been faid above are Mr. *Udal*'s own Words; and to
fhow how that fame King dealt with Parliaments,
a fmall Quotation fhall be here added from Sir
*Henry Spelman*'s Hiftory of Sacrilege, *p.* 182.   His
Words are thefe:
I now come off the Rivers into the Ocean of
Iniquity and Sacrilege, where whole Thoufands of
Churches and Chapels, dedicated to the Service of
God, in the fame manner that the reft are which
remain to us at this Day, together with the Monafteries and other Houfes of Religion and intended
Piety, were by King *Henry* VIII. in a Temper of
Indignation againft the Clergy of that Time,
mingled with infatiable Avarice, fack'd and raz'd
as by an Enemy.   It is true the Parliament did
give them to him, but fo unwillingly, as I have
heard, that when the Bill had ftuck long in the
Lower Houfe, and could get no Paffage, he commanded the Commons to attend him in the Afternoon in his Gallery, where he let them wait till
late in the Afternoon; and then coming out of his
Chamber,

Chamber, walking a Turn or two among them, and looking angrily on them, firſt on one Side, and then on the other, at laſt, *I hear,* faith he, *that my Bill will not paſs ; but I will have it paſs, or I will have ſome of your Heads ;* and without other Rhetorick or Perſwaſion return'd to his Chamber. Enough was ſaid, the Bill paſs'd, and all was given him as he deſir'd.

The ſame much celebrated Sir *Henry Spelman* then proceeds thus :

It is to be obſerv'd, that the Parliament did give all theſe Things to the King, yet did they not ordain them to be demoliſh'd, or employ'd to any irreligious Uſes, leaving it more to the Conſcience and Piety of the King, who, in his Speech to the Parliament, promis'd to perform the Truſt ; wherein he faith : " I cannot a little rejoice, when
" I conſider the perfeƈt Truſt and Confidence which
" you have put in me, in my good Doings and
" juſt Proceedings ; for you, without my Deſire or
" Requeſt , have committed to my Order and
" Diſpoſition all Chantries, Colleges, and Hoſ-
" pitals, and other Places ſpecified in a certain
" Aƈt, firmly truſting that I will order them to the
" Glory of God, and the Profit of the Common-
" wealth. Surely, if I, contrary to your Expeƈta-
" tion, ſhould ſuffer the Miniſters of the Churches
" to decay, or Learning (which is ſo great a
" Jewel) to be miniſhed, or the Poor and Miſe-
" rable to be unreliev'd, you might well ſay, that
" I being put in ſuch a ſpecial Truſt, as I am in
" this Caſe, were no truſty Friend to you, nor
" charitable to my Emme Chriſten ; neither a
" Lover of the publick Wealth, nor yet one that
" feared God, to whom Account muſt be render'd
" of all our Doings. Doubt not, I pray you, but
" your Expeƈtation ſhall be ſerv'd more godly and
" goodly

" goodly than you will wifh or defire, as hereafter
" you fhall plainly perceive.

But notwithſtanding the fair Promiſes and Projects, little was perform'd; for Deſolation preſently
follow'd this Diſſolution : The Axe and the Mattock
ruin'd almoſt all the chief and moſt magnificent Ornaments of the Kingdom, *viz.* three hundred ſeven-
ty-ſix of the leſſer Monaſteries, ſix hundred forty-
five of the greater, ninety Colleges, one hundred
ten religious Hoſpitals, and two thouſand three
hundred ſeventy-four Chantries and Free-Chapels.
All theſe religious Houſes, Churches, Colleges, and
Hoſpitals, being about three thouſand five hundred, little and great, in the whole, did amount
to an ineſtimable Sum, eſpecially if their Rents
be accounted as they are now improv'd in theſe
Days.    Among this Multitude it is needleſs to
ſpeak of the great Church of *St. Mary* in *Boulogn,*
which upon the taking of that Town he caus'd to
be pull'd down, and a Mount to be rais'd in the
Place thereof for planting of Ordinance to annoy
a Siege.

1. Firſt then touching the King himſelf: The
Revenue that came to him in ten Years ſpace was
more, if I miſtake not, than quadruple that of the
Crown Lands, beſides a Magazine of Treaſure
rais'd out of the Money, Plate, Jewels, Ornaments, and Implements of Churches, Monaſteries,
and Houſes, with their Goods, State, and Cattle,
Firſt-Fruits and Tenths, given by the Parliament in
the twenty-ſixth Year of his Reign, together with
a Subſidy, Tenth, and Fifteenth, from the Laity
at the ſame time.    To which I may add the in-
comparable Wealth of Cardinal *Wolſey,* a little before confiſcated, and a large Sum rais'd by Knighthood the twenty-fifth Year of his Reign.

A Man

A Man may juftly wonder how fuch an Ocean of Wealth fhould come to be exhaufted in fo fhort a time of Peace. But God's Bleffing, as it feemeth, was not upon it; for within four Years after he had receiv'd all this, and had ruin'd and fack'd three hundred feventy-fix Monafteries, and brought their Subftance to his Treafury, befides all the goodly Revenues of the Crown, he was drawn fo dry, that the Parliament in the thirty-firft was conftrain'd, by his Importunity, to fupply his Wants with the Refidue of all the Monafteries of the Kingdom, fix hundred forty-five great ones, and illuftrious, with all their Wealth and princely Poffeffions. Yet even then was not this King fo fufficiently furnifh'd for building of a few Blockhoufes for the Defence of the Coaft, but that the next Year after he muft have another Subfidy of four Fifteenths to bear out his Charges; and, left it fhould be too little, all the Houfes, Lands, and Goods, of the Knights of *St. John of Jerufalem,* both in *England* and *Ireland.*

Had not *Ireland* come thus in my way, I had forgotten it; but to increafe the Floods of this Sea, all the Monafteries of *Ireland* likewife flow'd into it, by Act of Parliament, the next Year following, being the thirty-third of his Reign.

But as the *Red Sea,* by the miraculous Hand of God, was once dry'd up, fo was this Sea of Wealth, by the wafteful Hand of this Prince, immediately fo dry'd up, as the very next Year, *viz. Regni* 34, the Parliament was drawn again to grant him a great Subfidy; for in the Statute-Book it is fo ftil'd: And this not ferving his turn, he was yet driven, not only to enhance his gold and filver Money, *anno* 36, but, againft the Honour of a Prince, to coin bafe Money; and, when all this ferv'd not his turn, in the very fame Year, to

P                 exact

exact a Benevolence of his Subjects, to their grievous Difcontent. Perceiving therefore, that nothing could fill the Gulph of Effufion, and that there was now a juft Caufe of great Expence, by reafon of his Wars at *Bologn* and in *France*, they granted him, the thirty-feventh Year, two Subfidies at once, and four Fifteenths, and for a Corollary all the Colleges, Free-Chapels, Chantries, Hofpitals, *&c.* before mention'd, in Number two thoufand three hundred feventy-four, upon Confidence that he fhould difpofe them (as he promis'd folemnly in the Parliament) to the Glory of God, who in Truth (for ought that I can hear) had little Part thereof.

The next Year was his fatal Period, otherwife it was much to be fear'd that Deans and Chapters, if not Bifhopricks (which have been long levell'd at) had been his next Defign; for he took a very good Say of them, by exchanging Lands with them, before the Diffolution, giving them rack'd Lands, and fmall things for goodly Manors and Lordfhips, and alfo Impropriations for their folid Patrimony in finable Lands; like the Exchange that *Palamedes* made with *Glaucus*, much thereby increafing his own Revenues; as he took feventy Manors from *York*, befides other Lands, Tenements, Advowfons, Patronages, *&c.* in the thirty-feventh of his Reign. He took alfo thirty and above, as I remember, in the twenty-feventh Year, from the Bifhop of *Norwich*, whom he left not (that I can learn) one Foot of the goodly Poffeffions of his Church, fave the Palace at *Norwich*; and how many I know not, in the thirty-feventh Year alfo, from the Bifhop of *London*.

Thus that great Man Sir *Henry Spelman*, of the infinite Sums given to this King, and his no lefs infinite Prodigality. The next Summary of the
Amount

Amount of the leffer Monafteries, and of the moveable Treafure taken out of the Churches, is from *Stow.*

In a Parliament begun in the Month of *February* (153⅚) were granted to the King, and his Heirs, all the religious Houfes in the Realm of *England,* of the Value of 200 *l.* and under, with all the Lands and Goods to them belonging. The Number of thefe Houfes then fuppref's'd was three hundred feventy-fix, the Value of their Lands them 32000 *l.* and more by year; the moveable Goods, as they were fold *Robin Hood's* Pennyworths, amounted to more than 100000 *l.* and the religious Perfons that were in the faid Houfes were clearly put out, fome went to other greater Houfes, fome went abroad to the World. It was a pitiful thing to hear the Lamentations the People in the Country made for them; for there was great Hofpitality kept among them; and it was thought more than ten thoufand Perfons, Mafters and Servants, had loft their Livings by the putting down of thofe Houfes that time. *Stow's Chron. p.* 572.

In 1538, St. *Auguftine's* Abbey at *Canterbury* was fuppref's'd to the King's Ufe, and the Shrine and Goods taken to the King's Ufe; as alfo the Shrine of *Thomas Becket,* in the Priory of *Chrift's Church,* was likewife taken to the King's Ufe. This Shrine was built about a Man's Height all of Stone, then upward of Timber plain, within the which was the Cheft of Iron, containing the Bones of *Thomas Becket,* Skull and all, with the Wound of his Head, and the Piece cut out of his Skull in the fame Wound. Thefe Bones, by Commandment of the Lord *Cromwell,* were then and there burnt. The Timber-work of the Shrine, on the Outfide, was cover'd with Plates of Gold, damask'd with gold Wire, which Ground of Gold was again co-

ver'd

ver'd with Jewels of Gold, as Rings, ten or twelve cramp'd with gold Wire into the Ground of Gold, many of those Rings having Stones in them; Brooches, Images, Angels, precious Stones, great Pearls, &c. The Spoil of which Shrine, in Gold and precious Stones, fill'd two great Chests, such as six or seven strong Men could no more than convey one of them out of the Church at once. *Ibid. ut supra.*

After what has been said of the endless Mass of Treasure King *Henry* engross'd to his own Use, by the Seizure of Lands and Goods devoted to the Service of God, as represented by the abovequoted Authors, Mr. *Udal,* Sir *Henry Spelman,* and *Stow,* it will be proper to make some sort of Estimate, tho' very uncertain, of what those Things have been reputed to be worth. It must be very uncertain, in regard that the Valuations given in at that time were made as the Commissioners pleas'd, who under-rated every thing to obtain Grants of the same for themselves; besides that the Lands of the Church were scarce ever let at the tenth Part of the real Value, the Proprietors being the best of Landlords, and letting the Lands on at the same Rates that they had been two, three, or five hundred Years before, notwithstanding that the Value of Lands had been continually increasing, as was that of all other Things; and since the Suppression those very Rents are so much advanc'd as scarce appears credible. To perform what is here mention'd, we insert the Totals of the Valuations given in at the Time of the Suppression of all the Monasteries and religious Houses in each County of *England* and *Wales,* because it would be too tedious to mention every House.

The

|  | *l.* | *s.* | *d.* |
|---|---|---|---|
| The total Sum of the Value of all religious Houſes in *Cornwal* | 1091 | 14 | 4¾ |
| The net Income of the ſame | 987 | 12 | 1¼ |
| Total Value of religious Houſes in *Bedfordſhire* | 2701 | 10 | 7¾ |
| The net Income of the ſame | 2261 | 19 | ½ |
| *St. Auguſtine's* at *Briſtol* Total | 767 | 15 | 3¼ |
| The net Income | 670 | 13 | 11½ |
| Total of the Biſhoprick of *Bangor* | 234 | 00 | 5½ |
| The net Value | 207 | 16 | 2 |
| Total Value in *Nottinghamſhire* | 2591 | 8 | 4 |
| The net Value | 2025 | 6 | 10¾ |
| Total Value in *Cambridgeſhire* | 2831 | 00 | 3⅓ |
| Total Value in *Lincolnſhire* | 8755 | 18 | 5¼ |
| The net Value | 7253 | 19 | 10¾ |
| Total Value in *Carlile* | 1097 | 10 | 8¾ |
| The net Value | 973 | 14 | 7½ |
| Total Value at *Newcaſtle* upon *Tine* | 1171 | 11 | 10 |
| The net Value | 977 | 14 | 3½ |
| Total Value in *Lancaſhire* | 856 | 6 | 5 |
| The net Value | 484 | 18 | 6½ |
| Total Value in the Dioceſe of *St. Aſaph* | 647 | 10 | 7 |
| The net Value | 598 | 18 | 1 |
| Total Value in the Dioceſe of *St. David* | 1128 | 6 | 7 |
| The net Value | 1055 | 9 | 6 |
| Total Value in *Suſſex* | 2897 | 14 | 7 |
| The net Sum | 2498 | 00 | 9¼ |
| Total Value in *Dorſetſhire* | 3626 | 16 | 0 |
| The net Value | 3107 | 19 | 7¾ |
| Total Value in the Biſhoprick of *Durham* | 2018 | 11 | 4¾ |
| The net Sum | 1708 | 2 | 6 |
| The Total in the County of *York* | 13278 | 9 | 2¼ |
| The net Sum | 10577 | 12 | 5¾ |

Total

|  | l. | s. | d. |
|---|---|---|---|
| Total Value in *Norfolk* | 5444 | 9 | 0 |
| The net Sum | 4588 | 12 | $6\frac{1}{2}$ |
| Total Value in *Northamptonshire* | 3631 | 10 | $3\frac{3}{4}$ |
| The net Sum | 3915 | 7 | $10\frac{3}{4}$ |
| Total Value in *London* and *Middlesex* | 10205 | 8 | $3\frac{3}{4}$ |
| The net Sum | 8542 | 6 | 8 |
| Total Value in *Essex* | 5529 | 1 | $2\frac{1}{4}$ |
| The net Sum | 4699 | 4 | $2\frac{3}{3}$ |
| Total Value in *Wiltshire* | 3915 | 15 | $11\frac{3}{4}$ |
| The net Sum | 3457 | 6 | $4\frac{1}{2}$ |
| Total Value in *Worcestershire* | 4395 | 12 | $0\frac{1}{2}$ |
| The net Sum | 4078 | 10 | $7\frac{1}{2}$ |
| Total Value in *Somersetshire* | 8152 | 11 | 7 |
| The net Sum | 7487 | 18 | $7\frac{1}{4}$ |
| Total Value in *Warwickshire* | 2759 | 1 | 0 |
| The net Sum | 2221 | 1 | 9 |
| Total Value in *Herefordshire* | 298 | 7 | $9\frac{1}{2}$ |
| The net Sum | 263 | 12 | $1\frac{1}{2}$ |
| Total Value in *Berkshire* | 4640 | 18 | $2\frac{1}{2}$ |
| The net Sum | 4211 | 18 | $0\frac{1}{2}$ |
| Total Value in *Kent* | 6801 | 6 | $7\frac{1}{2}$ |
| The net Sum | 6295 | 6 | 3 |
| The Total in *Shropshire* | 2631 | 17 | $11\frac{1}{2}$ |
| The net Sum | 2240 | 15 | $6\frac{1}{4}$ |
| The Total of *Glocestershire* | 6839 | 11 | 9 |
| The net Sum | 6672 | 19 | $2\frac{3}{4}$ |
| Total Sum of the Archdeaconry of *Richmond* | 3747 | 9 | 5 |
| The net Sum | 2877 | 8 | 10 |
| Total Value in *Hartfordshire* | 3835 | 19 | $9\frac{1}{2}$ |
| The net Sum | 2883 | 13 | 7 |
| Total Value in *Staffordshire* and *Rutlandshire* | 1648 | 19 | $1\frac{1}{2}$ |
| The neat Sum | 1471 | 14 | $0\frac{1}{2}$ |

Total

| | *l.* | *s.* | *d.* |
|---|---|---|---|
| Total Value of *Buckinghamſhire* | 1295 | 14 | 8½ |
| The net Sum | 972 | 17 | 0¾ |
| Total Value in *Devonſhire* | 4700 | 1 | 9½ |
| The net Sum | 6639 | 7 | 8¾ |
| Total Value of *Oxfordſhire* | 2716 | 1 | 11 |
| The net Sum | 2519 | 9 | 0 |
| Total Value in *Leiceſterſhire* | 2845 | 0 | 7 |
| The net Sum | 2450 | 3 | 4¾ |
| Total Value in *Derbyſhire* | 646 | 1 | 7½ |
| The net Sum | 542 | 17 | 1½ |
| Total Value in *Suſſex* | 5915 | 13 | 6½ |
| The net Sum | 5068 | 11 | 11½ |
| Total Value in *Suffolk* | 4176 | 3 | 8¾ |
| Total Value in *Landaff* Dioceſe | 868 | 10 | 1 |
| The net Sum | 765 | 10 | 10½ |
| Total Value in *Surrey* | 4108 | 16 | 4½ |
| The net Sum | 3652 | 1 | 8½ |
| Total Value in *Cheſhire* | 2333 | 14 | 11½ |
| The net Sum | 2089 | 14 | 0½ |
| Total Value in *Huntingdonſhire* | 2753 | 16 | 8 |
| The net Sum | 2349 | 2 | 9 |
| Total Value in *Weſtmerlan* | 166 | 10 | 6½ |
| The net Sum | 154 | 17 | 7½ |
| The Sum Total of the Value of all the religious Houſes in *England* and *Wales* | 152517 | 18 | 10¼ |
| The net Sum | 131607 | 6 | 4¾ |

Theſe are the Particulars of the ſeveral Counties and the Totals of the whole Nation, as then given in; ſo that we find 152517 *l.* 18 *s.* 10 *d.* ¼ the Total; an immenſe yearly Sum at that Time: But then if we compute this as the Gift of one Year, for

 the

the next we have feen the Parliament was oblig'd
to give more, we muft take it as at the intrin-
fick Value, that is, at twenty Years Purchafe,
at that Rate arifing to 3050340 *l.* an amazing
Gift then, tho' much outdone fince.    Now if
we proceed a Step farther, and allow for what
the real Value of the Lands was, that is, including
the Frauds of the Commiffioners in their Returns,
and the low Rents at which all thofe Lands of
Monafteries were really let, for the Advantage of
the Gentry and Farmers that held them, they cannot be fuppos'd to have been worth lefs than ten
times the Value here mention'd, as has been faid
before; and at that Rate the Amount will rife to
30,503,400 *l.*    This may appear ftupendious and
hyperbolical, but is certainly no more than the
bare Truth, and yet we are not come to the Ex-
tent of what thofe Lands are worth at this Day
with their improv'd Rents; for if we proceed to
that, it will exceed all Meafure; and yet it is but
looking back to the Computation made by Mr.
*Udal,* and it will appear that all that has been
hitherto faid falls very fhort of his Reckoning.
He values the only Eftate of the Abbey of *St.*
*Alban's* at 200000 *l.* a year, as thofe Lands are
now let; and many other Abbies he rates proportionably.    Now the Return of it made at
the Suppreffion was 2510 *l.* 6 *s.* 1 *d.* ¾ for the
Total; and the net Sum 2102 *l.* 7 *s.* 1 *d.* ¾ of
yearly Income; which being fuppos'd to have
been ten times as much, allowing for Frauds and
the Lownefs of Rents, ftill the whole is but
25100 *l.* a year, little more than the eighth Part
of 200000 *l.* affign'd by Mr. *Udal*; fo that the other
Advance of eight times the Value muft arife from
the Improvements upon Lands from that Time to
this.

In

In fhort, thefe Computations carry us too far, tho' too much can never be faid of the Subject. However this is only as to the Lands; for the Treafure in Gold, Silver, and precious Stones, we have already heard amounted to 100000 *l.* as thofe who made ten times as much of it to their own Profit were pleas'd to value it. We fee how the wifeft and moft prudent Kings have been impos'd upon, and what vaft Eftates have been purloin'd out of their fettled Revenues, and that very often by fuch Officers as were reputed very honeft Men and trufty Servants: What then muft we believe thofe wicked Commiffioners, and others employ'd in robbing of Churches for the Ufe of the King, conceal'd and ftole for their own Advantage? Befides that, when the People faw all going to Ruin, every one pillag'd what he could, without making the leaft Scruple of that Sacrilege, but believing they had as much Right to it as the King himfelf; and in reality they had fo.

Chantries and Chapels were alfo given to this King; but they efcap'd till the Time of his Succeffor, when they fhall be fpoken of: But that Reprieve was not owing to any Remorfe or want of good Will to proceed in that fort of Rapine; but it was ordain'd that he fhould leave thofe Remains of Sacrilege to his Son and Daughter, who finifh'd what he had fo far carry'd on; as we fhall fee in their Reigns.

To conclude with this King: When he had harafs'd his Subjects with continual Impofitions, notwithftanding the great Treafure left him by his Father; when he had overthrown fuch a vaft Number of majeftick Piles, erected for the Service of God, as has been already hinted; when he had devour'd and fquander'd thofe prodigious Revenues belonging to the aforefaid Houfes and their rightful

ful Owners; when he had turn'd out fo many Thoufands of religious Perfons to beg and live fcandaloufly abroad in the wide World, under Colour that they did not live regularly when fhut up in their own Houfes; when he had fhed large Streams of the Blood of his Subjeɛts, to fatiate his own Cruelty and Ambition; when he had indulg'd his Luft in the higheft Degree that ever Prince, who call'd himfelf a Chriftian, has been known to have done: In fhort, when he had, as his Friends fay of him, neither fpar'd Man in his Anger, nor Woman in his Luft, he was by God call'd away to anfwer for the fame. To whom we muft leave him, and proceed to

# K. E D W A R D  VI.

THE only Son of King *Henry* VIII. a weak fickly Infant, kept up the few Years of his Reign by Art, and yet pretended by fome Writers to have been poifon'd, to make good the mighty Charaɛter they give of his Vivacity and wonderful Learning and Judgment. They cry up this Child as a perfeɛt *Solomon* for Wifdom, as if it were poffible to perfwade any, but unthinking People, that the Wonders they invent of him were Truths. Such Praɛtices are a Difcredit to Hiftory, which is thus made to look more like Romance than Truth. It cannot be deny'd but that fome Children are more forward, and have better Capacities than others; but to reprefent them as exceeding the moft renowned of Princes in thofe Qualities of the Mind, which according to Nature require Age to ripen them, is to work Miracles which few will credit any more than the Perfons that pleafe themfelves

felves with impoſing ſuch Notions upon the unthinking Part of Mankind.

King *Edward* came to the Crown at nine Years
of Age, and reign'd ſix Years, five Months, and
odd Days; ſo that he was about ſixteen when he
died. Conſider what an Age and what a Reign
for ſuch Wonders to be told of him! No doubt
but his Actions, Words, and Thoughts, were ſuit-
able to his Years, and all the reſt can be look'd
upon as nothing but Fables; beſides that whoſo-
ever conſiders what then was done, may eaſily
diſcover there was nothing but Confuſion, the Government being unſteady and diſtracted by thoſe
who govern'd in his Name, and thoſe who were
continually contriving to pull down ſuch as were
in Power, that they might thruſt themſelves into
their Places.

To paſs by all other Hiſtorians who have been
guilty of this Extravagance in relation to the
Praiſes of this infant King, I will confine myſelf to
ſome Inſtances out of Mr. *Strype's Memorials Eccleſiaſtical,* where he has outdone all others in this
Particular. I will give his own Words, to avoid
all Imputation of deviating from his Meaning.
*Vol.* 2. *p.* 23. *chap.* 4. ſpeaking of this King, he ex-
preſſes himſelf thus: " But old Father *Latimer* upon
" this hath theſe Words: Have ye not a noble
" King? Was there ever King ſo noble, ſo godly,
" brought up with ſuch noble Counſellors, ſo ex-
" cellent and ſo well learn'd Schoolmaſters? I will
" tell you this, (and I ſpeak it even as I think) his
" Majeſty hath more godly Wit and Underſtanding,
" more Learning and Knowledge at this Age,
" than twenty of his Progenitors, that I could
" name, had at any time of their Life.

Let any Man judge whether more fulſome Flat-
tery could be utter'd. The King ſpoken of was
then

then about ten Years of Age, and yet had more
godly Wit and Underſtanding, more Learning and
Knowledge, than twenty of his Progenitors at any
time of their Life. What could be more ridiculous than ſuch an Aſſertion, and yet Mr. *Strype*
gives it us as a Matter of great Weight! But it is
hard to decide whether Father *Latimer* or Mr. *Strype*
were moſt to blame, the one for uttering ſuch pre-
poſterous Notions whilſt that Prince was living,
or the other for reviving them when they might
have been forgotten.

　　More of that profound Wiſdom he furniſhes us
with at *pag. 99*, when the King was eleven Years
of Age; but we muſt only take ſome ſhort Sketches,
without following him too cloſe. To inſtance in
this Child's great Knowledge, Mr. *Strype* produces
*Latin* Letters, writ by him in thoſe tender Years;
but he has not been ſo kind to him as Dr. *Burnet*
was to Queen *Elizabeth*, who, he ſays, writ learned
*Latin* and *Italian* Letters at four Years of Age: No
Wonder then that King *Edward* ſhould do ſo at
ten or eleven.

　　As for the Piety of that King, if we ſuppoſe
him endow'd with the great Wiſdom he ſpeaks of,
we ſhall have ſeveral Inſtances that relate to the
Matter in hand, that is, to Lands and Revenues
taken from others. In the firſt Place, he ſays, that
when the rich Biſhoprick of *Wincheſter* was given to
*Ponet* or *Poinet*, it was upon Condition that he
ſhould ſurrender to the King many Manors, and, in
effect, all the Temporalities of that Biſhoprick;
in lieu wereof he gave him ſeveral Rectories. Thus
did it become a Simoniacal Contract, and that Biſhoprick was ſacrilegiouſly robb'd. Yet was not
this to enrich the King, but to give to his Courtiers,
as by the following Parcels may appear.

To

To Sir *John Gates*, the Manors of *Sutton, Ropley, &c.* in *Southampton* and *Surrey*, of the yearly Value of 145 *l.* 19 *s.* 9 *d.* ⅐.

To Sir *Philip Hoby*, the Manors of *Marden, &c.* in the County of *Southampton*, the yearly Value of 87 *l.* 18 *s.* 7 *d.*

To Sir *Andrew Dudley*, the Manor of *Witney, &c.* of the yearly Value of 180 *l.* 7 *d.* ¾.

To Sir *Henry Seimour*, Lands to the yearly Value of 186 *l.* 4 *d.*

To *William Fitz-Williams*, the Manor of *High-Clere, &c.* to the yearly Value of 84 *l.* 17 *s.* 3 *d.*

To *Henry Nevil*, the Manor of *Margrave, &c.* to the yearly Value of 114 *l.* 18 *s.* 10 *d.*

Sir *Thomas Wroth* had alfo an Annuity of 100 *l.*

In *June* 1552, *Covent-Garden* and *Long-Acre* were given to the Earl of *Bedford*. They were Lands of the Church, and it is well known how great the Value of them is now.

The Bifhoprick of *Bath and Wells* was, in the Year 1552, ftript of many Poffeffions, and all given to craving Courtiers. The fame Year, Mr. *Strype* fuppofes, the King's preffing Need occafion'd fomewhat a fevere Commiffion, as he calls it, to be iffu'd forth, not only to take away out of Churches all Garments, and other Utenfils, us'd formerly in fuperftitious Worfhip; but to take for the King's Ufe all Goods belonging to Churches that could be fpar'd. This was like gleaning, the Lands and Treafure were gone before; now went the fmall Remains before neglected as of fmall Value. Yet was all this fquander'd like the reft.

All hitherto mention'd was inconfiderable in re-fpect of the Act of Parliament of this King's firft Year, which gave to him all the Colleges, Free-Chapels, Chantries, Hofpitals, Fraternities, or Guilds, which were not in the actual and real

Poffeffion

Poffeffion of King *Henry* VIII. nor of the faid King
*Edward.* The Caufes for fo doing were the diffolving of Superftition, and the founding of Schools
of Learning, and providing for the Poor.

Mr. *Strype, Vol.* 2. *p. 63.* tells us this Act was
foon after greatly abus'd, as the firft in the former
King's Reign for diffolving religious Houfes was;
for tho' the publick Good was pretended thereby,
yet private Men in truth had moft of the Benefit,
and the King and Commonwealth, the State of
Learning, and the Condition of the Poor, left as
they were before, or worfe.

This Abufe, he adds, was reprefented in publick
Sermons, without any Redrefs; and fo far from
it, that, inftead of fetting up Schools, one there
was in the North, which had of the fame Foundation, eight Scholarfhips and two Fellowfhips in
*Cambridge,* ever replenifh'd with the Scholars of
that School, was at that time fold, decay'd, and
loft; and more there were of the like fort fo
handled.

And whereas alfo another charitable End of the
Diffolution of thefe Colleges and Chantries was for
the better Succour of the Needy, it was turn'd
much to their Damage and Prejudice alfo.

When Bifhopricks had been robb'd of the Lands,
fee what Compenfation was made, as we have it
in Mr. *Strype's Ecclefiaftical Memorials, Vol.* 2.

P. 75. *May* 22, 1547. To the Dean and Chapter of *Wigorn,* in Confideration of the Lordfhips
and Rectories of *Grimley* and *Halowe,* and the Manor of *Hymwyke* and *Woodbal,* in the County of
*Wigorn,* and others; and in Performance of King
*Henry's* Will; was granted the Rectory of *Kemfey*
in the County of *Wigorn,* with the Appurtenances,
&c.

*June*

*June* 3. To *Nicholas* Bifhop of *Wigorn*, the Advowfons and Rectories of the Churches of *Grimley* and *Halowe*, &c.

The fame *June* 3, to the fame *Nicholas*, in Confideration of the Exchange of the Lordfhips of *Stoke Epifcopi* and *Hernbury*, and other Poffeffions in *Glocefter*, *Middlefex*, and *London*, the Manors of *Grimley* and *Halowe*, Parcel of the Poffeffions of the Cathedral Church of *Wigorn*, &c.

*Auguft* 20. To *Richard* Bifhop of *Coventry* and *Litchfield*, in Confideration of the Manors of *Longdon*, *Bewdefert*, *Rugeley*, *Heywood*, *Barkefwick*, and *Cannock*, and divers other Lands and Tenements in *Staffordfhire*, were granted the Advowfon of the Rectory of *Wolftaunton* in the County of *Stafford*; and the Rectory of *Belgrave* in the County of *Leicefter*; and of the Rectories of *Pightefdey*, *Buckly*, and *Towceter*, in *Northamptonfhire*; and divers other Advowfons and Prebends in the County aforefaid, and within the Bifhoprick of *Bangor*.

*Auguft* 21. To the Dean and Chapter of the Holy Trinity, *Winton*, in Confideration of the Exchange of the Manors of *Overton*, *Alton*, *Stockton*, and *Patney*, and of the Rectories of the two former in *Wilts*, were granted the Advowfon of the Rectory of *Grefford*, within the Bifhoprick of *St. Afaph*; and of the Rectory of *Crockborn* in the County of *Somerfet*; and the Advowfon of the Rectory of *Laugherne* in the County of *Cardigan*; and the Rectories and Churches of the fame.

*Auguft* 31. To *Thomas* Archbifhop of *Canterbury*, for the Exchange of the Manor and Park of *Mayfield*, &c. were granted the Rectories of *Whalley*, *Blackborn*, and *Rochdale*, &c.

*September* 27. To the Dean and Chapter of *St. Paul's*, *London*, in Confideration of the Manor of *Rowmwel* in *Effex*, and of the Manor of *Drayton*

in

in *Middlesex,* and divers other Lands, Tenements, and Rents, was granted the Advowson of the Rectory of *Charing* in *Kent,* and the Chapel of *Egerton* in the same County, &c.

*Oct.* 7. To the Dean and Canons of the King's Free-Chapel of *St. George* within the Castle of *Windsor,* for Exchange of the Manor and Rectory of *Iver,* and of the Manor of *Damary* Court, and divers other Lands and Tenements, to King *Henry* given and made over, and divers others surrender'd by the Dean and Chapter, were granted the Rectories and Churches of *Bradwynch, Northam, Iplepen, Assington,* and *South Molton,* in the County of *Devon,* &c.

The same Date. To the Dean and Chapter of the Collegiate Church of *Thornton* in *Lincolnshire,* in Consideration of the Manor of *Carleton* in the *Moor-Land,* in the County of *Lincoln,* and divers other Lands and Tenements in the same County, were granted the Advowson of the Rectory of *Flamsted* in the County of *Hertford,* and the Advowson of the Rectory of *Holme* in *Spalding,* in the County of *York.*

Thus, when the Churches had been robb'd of all their Lands, the little Reparation they had was in Churches.

Not to divide the Account Mr. *Strype* gives us of this King, as far as relates to our Subject, here shall be subjoin'd what he has of Taxes granted to him by Parliament, and then the Rates of Provisions, &c. in his Reign, for the better judging of the Value of Money at that Time.

## Money granted by Parliament to King Edward VI.

Mr. *Strype's Ecclefiaftical Memorials, Vol.* 2. *p.* 454.

In the fecond Year of King *Edward* VI. the Parliament gave the King an Aid of twelve Pence the Pound of Goods of his natural Subjeɛts, of two Shillings the Pound of Strangers. And this to continue for three Years. And by the Statute of the fecond and third of *Edward* VI. it may appear the fame Parliament did alfo give a fecond Aid as followeth, to wit; of every Ewe kept in feveral Paftures, three Pence; of every Weather kept as aforefaid, two Pence; of every Sheep kept in the Common, three half Pence. The Houfe gave the King alfo eight Pence the Pound of every woollen Cloth made for the Sale throughout *England* for three Years. In the third and fourth Year of the King, by reafon of the troublefome gathering of the Pole Money upon Sheep, and the Tax upon Cloth, this Aɛt of Subfidy was repealed, and other Relief given the King. And in the feventh Year he had a Subfidy and two Fifteenths.

*Strype's Ecclefiaftical Memorials.* In the Year 1548, and third of *Edward* VI. Wheat was 6 s. 8 d. the Quarter; Barley, Malt, and Rye, 5 s. the Quarter; Peafe and Beans, 4 s. the Quarter.

*Rates fet upon all kinds of Victuals* Anno 1549, the fecond of *King* Edward VI.

*Strype's Ecclefiaftical Memorials, Vol.* 2. *p.* 151.

### From Midfummer *to* Hallowmas.

|  | s. | d. |
|---|---|---|
| Every Ox, being primed and well ftricken, of the largeft Bone | 38 | 0 |
| Of a meaner Sort | 28 | 0 |
| An Ox fat, and of the largeft Bone | 45 | 0 |
| Of the meaner Sort, being fat | 38 | 0 |
| Steers or Runts, being primed or well ftricken, and large of Bone | 20 | 0 |
| Of a meaner Sort | 16 | 0 |
| Being fat, and of the largeft Bone | 25 | 0 |
| Being fat, of a meaner Sort | 21 | 0 |
| Heifers and Kine, being primed and well ftricken, and large of Bone | 16 | 0 |
| Of a meaner Sort | 13 | 4 |
| Being fat and large of Bone | 22 | 0 |
| Being fat, of a meaner Sort | 18 | 0 |

### From Hallowmas *to* Chriftmas.

|  | s. | d. |
|---|---|---|
| Every Ox, being fat and large of Bone | 46 | 8 |
| Being fat, of a meaner Sort | 39 | 8 |
| Steers and Runts, being fat and large of Bone | 26 | 8 |
| Being fat, of a meaner Sort | 22 | 8 |
| Heifers and Kine, being fat and large of Bone | 23 | 0 |
| Of a meaner Sort | 19 | 0 |

*From* Chriſtmas *to* Shrovetide.

|  | s. | d. |
|---|---|---|
| Every Ox, being fat and large of Bone | 48 | 4 |
| Of a meaner Sort | 41 | 4 |
| Steers and Runts, being fat and large of Bone | 28 | 4 |
| Of a meaner Sort | 24 | 4 |

*From Sheering Time to* Michaelmas.

| | | |
|---|---|---|
| Every Weather, being a Shear-Sheep, lean and large of Bone | 3 | 0 |
| Of a meaner Sort | 2 | 4 |
| Being fat and large of Bone | 4 | 0 |
| Being fat, of a meaner Sort | 3 | 0 |
| Ewes, being lean and large of Bone | 2 | 0 |
| Being lean, of a meaner Sort | 0 | 20 |
| Being fat and large of Bone | 2 | 0 |

*From* Michaelmas *to* Shrovetide.

| | | |
|---|---|---|
| Every Weather, being a Shear-Sheep, lean and large of Bone | 3 | 0 |
| Being lean, of a meaner Sort | 2 | 4 |
| Being fat and large of Bone | 4 | 4 |
| Being fat, of a meaner Sort | 3 | 4 |

*Rates*

*Rates set upon Provisions* Anno 1550, *the fourth of King* Edward VI. *in the Time of a Dearth.*

*Strype's Ecclesiastical Memorials, Vol.* 2. *p.* 223.

*From the Feast of* All Saints *next ensuing.*

|  | The Quarter. | | |
|---|---|---|---|
|  | *l.* | *s.* | *d.* |
| White Wheat of the best Sort | o | 13 | o |
| White Wheat of the second Sort, and Red Wheat of the best Sort | o | 11 | o |
| All other Wheat, as well White, Red, and Grey, of the meanest Sort, not clean or tailed | o | 8 | o |
| Malt, clean and sweet, of the best Sort | o | 10 | o |
| Malt of the second Sort | o | 8 | o |
| Rye of the best and cleanest | o | 7 | o |
| Rye of the second Sort | o | 6 | o |
| Barley of the best Sort | o | 9 | o |
| Of the second Sort | o | 7 | o |
| Beans and Pease of the best Sort | o | 5 | o |
| Of the second Sort | o | 3 | o |
| Oats of the best Sort, clean and sweet | o | 4 | o |

Accounting eight Bushels to the Quarter.

|  | The Pound. | | |
|---|---|---|---|
| A Pound of sweet Butter not above 1 *d.* | *ob.* | o | o |
| Barrelled Butter of *Essex* not to be sold to any of the King's Subjects above | *ob.* | *di.* | *q.* |
| And barrelled Butter of any other Parts | *ob.* | o | *q.* |

Cheese

Cheese of *Essex*, to be sold from Hallowmas till New-years Crop — 0 *ob.* *di.* *q.*

Cheese of other Parts not above — 0 *ob.* 0 *q.*

*Strype ut supra, p.* 341.

*September* 5, 1552, in time of Scarcity the following Rates, by Proclamation, set upon Flesh:

Beef, Mutton, and Veal, the best, for a Penny-Farthing the Pound.

Necks and Legs at three Farthings the Pound.

The best Lamb eight Pence the Quarter.

Such as refused to sell at these Rates to forfeit their Freedom for ever.

*Repository of Originals, Strype's Ecclesiastical Memorials, Vol.* 2. *p.* 143.

*A Table, making mention of certain Prices made by the King's Majesty's Justices, of all kinds of Corn, and sundry other Necessaries.*

*Cornwall.*

A Bushel of Wheat.

At { Stretton, Launceston, Saltashe } 3 s. 4 d. { Memorand. This is twelve Gallons to the Bushel.

At { Lyskerde, Lowe } 4 s. 8 d. { Sixteen Gallons to the Bushel.

At { Bodmyn, Lostuthyel, Tregony, Trerewe, St. Columbe, Penryn, Padstow } 5 s. 8 d. { Eighteen Gallons to the Bushel.

Q 3

*Helston*

At {Helston / Redruythe} 6 s. 0 d. { This is a greater Measure still.

### A Bushel of Barley.

At {Bodmyn / Lostuthiel / Tregonye / Trerewe / St. Columbe / Penryn / Padstow} 20 d.

At {Helston / Redruythe} 5 s. It should be 15 d.

At {Launceston / Saltashe / Leskyrd / Low} 16 d.

At | Strotton | 12 d.

### A Bushel of Oats.

At {Bodmyn / Padstow / Lostuthiel} 20 d.

At {Leskyrd / Low / Saltash / Launceston} 18 d.

{ *Memorand.* The Measure of Oats is great, and not at one Size, but in some Places more than in others.

Wine.　A Gallon of the best *Gascoin* 6 d.

Linen Cloth } A Yard of {Dowlas 9 d. / Lockeram 7 d.

Hides

Hides untanned

The Hide of every

Cow 4 *s.* 3 *d.* or 3 *s.* 4 *d.*
Ox 6 *s.* 8 *d.*
Stere 4 *s.* 4 *d.* or 3 *s.* 4 *d.*
Heifer 3 *s.* 4 *d.* or 2 *s.* 8 *d.*

Shop Leather well tanned { A Dyck of Leather, *viz.* two Hides at the leaft. } 3 *l.*

A Foot of clowte Leather 3 *s.*
A Pair of Man's Shoes 10 *d.* or 11 *d.*
A Pair of Woman's Shoes 6 *d.* or 7 *d.*
A Pair of Boots, the beft, 3 *s.* 4 *d.*

Thus far we have follow'd Mr. *Strype,* and, by what has been faid, may eafily difcern how far that wonderful Wifdom by him affign'd to this King extended, of which enough has been faid, and therefore we will leave that Author.

Among all the MSS. in the *Cotton* Library quoted under other Kings, we have nothing concerning this *Edward* VI. but thefe few Words: *Edward* VI. befides Tonnage and Poundage for Life, *Anno* 1, receiv'd of his Lay Subjects fix Fifteenths, and of both three Subfidies, leaving one of the Temporality ungather'd, which his Sifter Queen *Mary* remitted when fhe came to the Crown.

The Tonnage and Poundage faid above to have been given to this King for Life was thus : Of every Tun of Wine 3 *s.* of every Tun of fweet Wine 3 *s.* over and above the aforefaid 3 *s.* that is in all 6 *s.* of every Aulne of *Rhenifh* Wine 12 *d.* The Poundage was 12 *d.* in the Pound of the Value of all Goods imported or exported ; and 12 *d.* in the Pound over and above the aforefaid 12 *d.* to be paid by Merchants Aliens for all Tin and Pewter by them exported. Excepting out of this Subfidy all manner of woollen Cloth of *Englifh* Make to be exported, and all manner of Wool, Wool-Fells, and

Hides

Hides and Backs of Leather exported, and all manner of Wines, freſh Fiſh, and Cattle imported.

The Subſidy from Wool was 33 *s.* 4 *d.* of every
Sack of Wool; and of every two hundred forty
of Wool-Fells 33 *s.* 4 *d.* and for every Laſt of Hides
and Backs 3 *l.* 6 *s.* 8 *d.*   For every Sack of Wool
exported by Strangers 3 *l.* 6 *s.* 8 *d.* and for every
two hundred forty of Wool-Fells 3 *l.* 6 *s.* 8 *d.* and
for every Laſt of Hides and Backs 3 *l.* 13 *s.* 4 *d.*

The Subſidy granted by the Clergy, in the ſe-
cond Year of this King's Reign, was of 6 *s.* in the
Pound, according to the Value of every ſpiritual
Promotion.

The Relief granted by the Laity in his third
Year, to continue by the Space of three Years, was
of every Perſon worth ten Pounds or upwards, in
Money, Goods, Cattle, *&c.* 12 *d.* in the Pound.
And of every Alien worth 20 *s.* and under 10 *l.*
12 *d.* for every Pound.

Thus it appears that this King, tho' he took as
much as he could from Churches of what his Father had left, yet the Kingdom ſav'd nothing by it,
the Taxes being laid every Year of his Reign, and
for his Life: But to ſpeak the Truth, it is more
for his Honour to own he was an Infant, and acted
as ſuch, or rather did not act at all, thoſe who
govern'd for him doing all that was done, than with
other Writers to cry him up for a *Solomon*, without
the leaſt Reaſon, and by that means to render him
guilty of all the ſhameful Actions of his impotent
Reign, which were owing to wicked Miniſters
ſeeking their own Advantage, without the leaſt
Regard either to the King or his Subjects.   I
think myſelf much more this King's Friend, than
thoſe that extol him as a Prodigy in Knowledge,
and yet doing nothing that ſhow'd him capable of
governing.   Let his Miniſters bear their own Iniquities,

quities, his Innocence is much better fhown by
owning him what he was, than for crying him up
for what he was not. In fhort, from nine Years of
Age to fixteen, no great Matters can be expected
from the forwardeft Boy in the Univerfe, efpecially as to that folid Judgment which is requir'd for
the Government of a Nation. Thus we will allow him his beft Character; that his tender Years
render'd him incapable of Rule, and therefore no
way to be charg'd with any Mifcarriages that happen'd in his Time; and fo having endeavour'd to
clear his Reputation, whereas others by their Com-
mendations do only lay an Imputation upon it, we
leave him to proceed to his Sifter,

# Q. M A R Y,

ELdeft Daughter to King *Henry* VIII. and half
Sifter to King *Edward* VI. nothing like either
of them; for they both took all they could from
the Church, and fhe reftor'd to it all that was in
her Power. Our great Antiquary *Cambden* gives
this Character of her: That fhe was *a Princefs
never fufficiently to be commended of all Men, for pious
and religious Demeanor, her Commiferation towards the
Poor, and her Munificence and Liberality towards the
Nobility and Churchmen.* In his Introduction to his
Hiftory of Queen *Elizabeth.*

Dr. *White Kennet,* in his Parochial Antiquities of
*Ambrofden* and *Burcefter, p.* 439. gives an Account
of Queen *Mary's* Piety and Juftice, in reftoring all
that was in her Poffeffion to the Clergy, which the
Curious may fee there.

Our *Cotton* MSS. fcarce take any Notice of her;
only one fays, that in the firft of her Reign fhe remitted a Subfidy of the Temporality granted by
Par-

Parliament to her Brother just before his Death, so that he had not time to receive it, and she was willing to ease the People of that Burden. All that she had during her Reign is thus summ'd up in that MS. Tonnage and Poundage, *Anno primo*, for Life; a Loan, *Anno tertio*; five fifteenths of the Commons, and of them and the Clergy three Years Subsidies.

It is so rare for Princes to remit Taxes already granted them by their Subjects, that this Instance deserves to be taken notice of; and the more, because it was her own voluntary Act and Deed, being done first by Letters Patents; yet afterwards, that it might not want the greatest Solemnity, the said Letters Patents were confirm'd by Act of Parliament, which Act, as singular, is very well worth inserting in this Place, for the more Certainty of the Truth.

*Anno* 1 *Mariæ, Seffio secunda.*

*An Act for the Releafe of the laft Subfidy of the Temporality.*

" Whereas the Queen's Highness, our Sovereign
" Lady, by her Grace's Letters Patents, sealed
" with the Great Seale, bearing Date the first Day
" of *September* laft paft, reciting, whereas in the
" Parliament holden the seventh Yeere of the Reign
" of the excellent Prince, our late Sovereign Lord
" King *Edward* VI. her Highneffe Brother, there
" was granted by Act of Parliament unto the fame
" late King two Difmes and two Fifteens, and
" one Subfidy of four Shillings of the Pound, to
" be raifed and levied of the Manors, Lands, and
" Tenements; and two Shillings eight Pence of the
" Goods and Chattels of his late Subjects; which
" Grants were then due unto her Highneffe by the
" said

" said Acte; her Majesty, for the Considerations
" expressed in the said Letters Patents, of her
" meere Grace and great Clemencie, for the Re-
" liefe and Succour of her said Subjects, did freely,
" for her, her Heires and Successors, pardon and
" remit unto her said Subjects, and their Heires
" and Executors, the saide Subsidy of four Shillings
" the Pound; and two Shillings eight Pence the
" Pound, granted in the said Parliament, as by the
" said Letters Patents more at large it doth and
" may appeare. Which Letters Patents were by
" her Highnesse Commandment published and pro-
" claimed throughout this Realme·

" Our said Sovereign Lady the Queene, upon
" her further gracious Respect and especial Love
" towards her sayde Subjects, and for the avoi-
" ding of all Doubts and Questions which might
" arise or be moved of the Validity and Force of
" the said Letters Patents, set forth by Proclama-
" tion, as is aforesaid, is pleasen and contented,
" that her said gracious Remission of the said Sub-
" sidies be ratified and confirmed by Authoritie of
" Parliament· Therefore be it enacted, by the
" Assent of the Lorde Spiritual and Tem-
" poral, and the Commons in this present
" Parliament assembled, and by the Au-
" thoritie of the same, that all and every
" Person and Persons, Bodie Politike and
" Corporat, their Heires, Successors, Exe-
" cutors, and Administrators, being Late
" Subjects, which should or ought to have
" paid any Sum, or Sums of Money, for
" the said Subsidy of four Shillings the
" Pound, and two Shillings eight Pence the
" Pound, granted in the said late Parlia-
" ment; or of or for any other Rate or Rates
" of Lands, Goods, Chattels, or otherwise
                                    "touching

" touching o2 concerning the Payment of
" any Sum o2 Sums of Money, fo2 o2 by
" reason of the Grant of the said Subsidy,
" shall be thereof cleerely acquitted and dis-
" charged against the Queenes Highnesse,
" her Heires and Successo2s, Executo2s and
" Administrato2s, to all Respects and Pur-
" poses, as if the said Act of Grant of the
" said Subsidy had never beene had no2
" made.

" Provided always, that this p2esent Act shall
" not extend to discharge any Person o2
" Persons, Bodies Politike and Co2po2at,
" of o2 fo2 the Payment of any Sum o2
" Sums of Money, which is, ought, o2
" shall be due unto her Highnesse, her Heirs
" o2 Successo2s, fo2 the two Fifteens and
" Dismes g2anted to the saide late King
" by the said Acte, any thing in this Acte
" contained notwithstanding.

The firſt Grant to this Queen was in the ſame
firſt Year, wherein the Revenues of the Crown being entirely exhauſted by her Brother and her Father, it appear'd that ſhe was abſolutely unable to
maintain a Force to guard the Seas; the Parliament therefore granted her Tonnage and Poundage
of divers Merchandize for Life ; and, what is well
worth obſerving, the Act begins with theſe following Words, which Style has been ſince much alter'd.
They are thus :

*In their moſt humble wiſe, ſhewen unto your moſt ex-
cellent Majeſtie, your poore and obedient Subjects and
Commons, &c.* and ſo they go on acknowledging
that the ſame Subſidy of Tonnage and Poundage
had been enjoy'd by her Predeceſſors, the Kings
of *England,* time out of mind. Then they proceed
                                                            with

with the fame Style of *poor Commons.* The Subfidy of Tonnage was thus:

Of every Tun of Wine coming, or that fhall or is comen into this your Realme by way of Merchandize, the Sum of 3 *s.* and fo after the Rate. And of every Tun of fweet Wine, as well Malmefie as other, 3 *s.* over and above the 3 *s.* afore granted. And of every Awne of *Rhenifh* Wine 12 *d.*

The other Subfidy, call'd Poundage, was of all manner of Goods and Merchandizes of every Merchant, Denizen and Alien, carried out of the Realm or brought into the fame by way of Merchandize, of the Value of every 20 *s.* of the fame Goods and Merchandizes 12 *d.* and of every 20 *s.* in Value of Tin and Pewter Veffel, carry'd out of the Realm by any and every Merchant Alien, 12 *d.* over and above the 12 *d.* aforefaid.

Out of this Act of Subfidy is excepted all woollen Cloth made in *England,* and all Wool, Wool-Fells, and Hides and Backs of Leather, carry'd out; and all Wines, and all manner of frefh Fifh, and Beftial coming into this Realm.

And they at the fame time granted one other Subfidy of all manner of Wool, Wool-Fells, and Leather, carry'd out of the Realm, that is, of every Merchant Denizen of and for every Sack of Wool 33 *s.* 4 *d.* and for every two hundred and forty Wool-Fells 33 *s.* 4 *d.* and of and for every Laft of Hides and Backs, of every Merchant Denizen, 3 *l.* 4 *s.* 8 *d.* and alfo of every Merchant Stranger, as well thofe already made Denizens, as that fhall be made Denizens, for every Sack of Wool 3 *l.* 6 *s.* 8 *d.* and of and for every two hundred and forty Wool-Fells 3 *l.* 6 *s.* 8 *d.* and alfo for every Laft of Hides and Backs 3 *l.* 13 *s.* 4 *d.*

In cafe of attempting to defraud the Queen of thefe Dues, the Goods to be forfeited, the one
Moiety

Moiety to her Majesty, and the other Moiety to the Person or Persons seizing.

Among the rest of the pious Acts of King *Edward* VI. in his last Year having supprefs'd the most noble Bishoprick of *Durham*, and seiz'd all the Lands of the same into his own or the Hands of his Favourites; the Queen, abhorring such sacrilegious Possessions, immediately after her Accession to the Crown restor'd all to its former Condition; and that her Restitution might remain the more firm and irrevocable, had the same confirm'd by Act of Parliament, in the second Parliament of her first Year.

The Queen, to rid her Hands of all that any way belong'd to the Church, in like manner rejected all First Fruits, and Tenths of spiritual and ecclesiastical Promotions, and all Rectories and Parsonages impropriate; and to put all such things entirely out of her own Hands, caus'd all to be confirm'd by Act of Parliament of the third Year of her Reign. She certainly never thought her Conscience safe whilst any thing belonging to the Church remain'd in her Hands; and therefore her first Care upon ascending the Throne was not to defile herself with any such Treasure, and to endeavour to deprive her Successors of that Infection, by passing the Restitution into a Law. But her Successor regarded not such Niceties.

The same third Year the Clergy granted her Majesty a Subsidy, which was also confirm'd by Act of Parliament. This Subsidy was of six Shillings in the Pound, to be taken and levied of all their spiritual Promotions within the Term of three Years next ensuing. This Subsidy granted by the Clergy, in consideration of the great and ample Benefits receiv'd of her Goodness and Munificence; and payable by every Archbishop, Bi-

shop,

fhop, Dean, Archdeacon, Prebendary, Provoft, Mafter of a College, Mafter of an Hofpital, Parfon, Vicar, and every other Perfon or Perfons, of whatfoever Name or Degree he or they be, enjoying any fpiritual Promotion, or other temporal Poffeffions to the fame fpiritual Promotions annex'd, not now divided or feparated by Act of Parliament, or otherwife, from the Poffeffions of the Clergy.

For the true and certain Knowledge of the yearly Value of every fuch fpiritual Promotion, the Payment fhall be made according to the Rate, Taxation, Valuation, and Eftimation, remaining in the Courts of the Firft-Fruits and Tenths, and of the Exchequer. But the Payment of the fix Shillings in the Pound to be made in three Years, that is, two Shillings every Year.

All Perfons having Penfions out of any of the late diffolv'd Monafteries, Colleges, Free-Chapels, Chantries, Fraternities, Guilds, and Hofpitals, or of any other Dignity or Promotion diffolv'd, to pay in like manner fix Shillings in the Pound out of fuch Penfions.

*Item,* Every ftipendiary Prieft, receiving annual Stipend of eight Pounds and under, being no Perpetuity, to pay fix Shillings eight Pence yearly; every fuch Prieft receiving above eight Pounds, and not above ten Pounds, to pay ten Shillings; and every fuch Prieft receiving above ten Pounds, and not above twenty Marks, to pay thirteen Shillings four Pence yearly, during the faid three Years; and every fuch Prieft taking Stipend above twenty Marks, to pay likewife two Shillings of the Pound of every Year during the faid three Years.

Provided that every Parfon or Vicar, whofe Benefice is above the Value of five Pounds, and not above fix Pounds thirteen Shillings four Pence, after

after the Rate of the late perpetual Tenth, shall pay every Year of the said three Years only six Shillings eight Pence, as the said Stipendiaries do, and not otherwise.

And that all other Parsons and Vicars, whose Benefices be of the Valuation of five Pounds or under, after the Rate of the said perpetual Tenth, shall not be charg'd or chargeable with this Subsidy, or any Part thereof.

The Universities of *Oxford* and *Cambridge* exempted from this Subsidy.

The same Year a Subsidy was granted to the King and Queen by the Temporality, in following manner, that is, of every Person born within the Queen's Dominions, and of every Fraternity, Guild, Corporation, Mystery, Brotherhood, and Commonalty, worth five Pounds, and under ten Pounds, for every Pound, as well in Coin and the Value of every Pound, that such Person, Fraternity, *&c.* hath of their own, as also Plate, Stock of Merchandize, Corn, and Blades, Houshold-stuff, and all Moveables, excepting their just Debts, and all Apparel, eight Pence of every Pound to and for the first Payment of the said Subsidy; and other eight Pence of every Pound for the second Payment.

Every Person, Corporation, *&c.* worth ten Pounds, and under twenty Pounds, as aforesaid, to pay twelve Pence of each Pound for the first Payment, and twelve Pence for the second Payment. And every Person and Corporation, *&c.* worth, as is aforesaid, twenty Pounds, and so upwards, to pay sixteen Pence for the first Payment of the Subsidy, and sixteen Pence for the second Payment.

Every Alien to pay to this Subsidy, for every Pound to five Pounds, eight Pence at each Payment; and for every Pound from five to ten Pounds,

Pounds, for each Payment twelve Pence. And from ten to twenty Pounds, of each Pound at each Payment eighteen Pence; and for twenty, and all above, two Shillings.

And for Lands, &c. to the yearly Value of twenty Pounds *per Annum,* two Shillings in the Pound at each Payment; and each Alien three Shillings in the Pound at each Payment.

From Payment of this Subsidy the whole Counties of *Northumberland, Cumberland, Westmerland,* the Towns of *Berwick upon Tweede,* and *Newcastle upon Tine,* and the Bishoprick of *Durham,* were entirely exempted.

There were also excepted all the Inhabitants of the Counties of *Pembroke, Carmarthen, Cardigan, Glamorgan, Brecknock, Radnor, Montgomery, Denbigh, Flint, Merioneth, Anglesey, Carnarvan,* and the County Palatine of *Chester,* that were charg'd or chargeable with a Duty call'd a Mise.

The Universities of *Oxford* and *Cambridge,* and *Eaton College,* also particularly exempted.

The fourth and fifth Year another Subsidy was granted by the Clergy, and confirm'd by Act of Parliament; but it extended only throughout the Province of *Canterbury,* all that of *York* not appearing to have granted any thing. The Subsidy was of eight Shillings in the Pound, to be levy'd in four Years, that is, two Shillings every Year.

All the Particulars, as to the manner of Payment, and as to Exemptions, being exactly the same as in the last Subsidy of the Clergy, the same need not be repeated.

The same Year the Temporality granted a Subsidy and one Fifteenth, which they declare to be for carrying on the War against the *French* and the *Scots*; towards that Expence they (tho' the Title says only one Fifteenth) here grant one whole Fif-

R                                        teenth

teenth and Tenth. The same to be paid, taken, and levy'd, of the moveable Goods, Chattels, and other things, usual to such Fifteenths and Tenths, to be contributory and chargeable within the Shires, Cities, Boroughs, Towns, and other Places of the Realm, in Manner and Form aforetime used, except the Sum of six thousand Pounds thereof, fully to be deducted, in Relief, and Comfort, and Discharge, of the poor Cities, Towns, and Boroughs, of the Realm, &c.

And furthermore, they did at the same time give and grant one entire Subsidy, to be rated, tax'd, levy'd, and paid, at one whole and entire Payment, of every Person Spiritual and Temporal, according to the Tenor of this Act; that is, of every Person, Guild, Fraternity, &c. worth five Pounds, two Shillings eight Pence of every Pound. Every Alien to pay five Shillings four Pence for every Pound.

For Lands and real Effects, four Shillings to be paid of every Pound by Natives; and eight Shillings of every Pound by Aliens.

This is so very much in all Particulars like the former Act of Subsidy, that no more need be here said of it; but that, as in the other, the Counties of *Northumberland, Cumberland, Westmerland,* the Towns of *Berwick upon Tweede,* and *Newcastle upon Tine,* and the Bishoprick of *Durham,* were again wholly exempted from this Subsidy, which was certainly on account of their lying so much expos'd, and being perpetually wasted and ravag'd by the *Scots.* The same Exception as in that Act was also in this, for the Inhabitants of the Counties of *Pembroke, Carmarthen, Cardigan, Glamorgan, Brecknock, Radnor, Montgomery, Denbigh, Flint, Merioneth, Anglesey, Carnarvan,* and the County Palatine of *Chester,* which were liable to pay the Duty call'd the Mise.

This

This is as much as I can find of Taxes rais'd during this Queen's Reign. Now how to make up the five Fifteenths abovemention'd in the *Cotton* MS. as granted by the Commons, I am entirely at a Lofs, as I am apt to think the Writer of that MS. would be, had he been put to it; but Prejudice very often leads Men afide, and makes them deliver Things as Truths, which they know nothing of; nay, very often fuch as they well know to be falfe. I do not pofitively affirm the Affertion of the five Fifteenths to be falfe; however, at the fame time, after the moft diligent Enquiry I can find no fuch Number of them, and fhall therefore leave it to more knowing Perfons to make good that Affertion, if there be any Truth in it; or if not, they will do as much Juftice in not fuffering the Publick to be impos'd on by what is falfe. That Queen, tho' fhe never deferv'd it, had and has many bitter Enemies, who did and do ftill make it their Bufinefs to caft all the Dirt they can at her, in hopes that fome will ftick.

I fhall conclude what relates to this Queen, with a few Lines concerning her, taken from the moft inveterate of her Enemies, *John Fox*, who being fuch, tho' he has heap'd an immenfe Multitude of notorious Falfhoods in his Volumes, where it was to ferve his Turn, it is likely he would not do it to the Honour of a Queen, whom he ever made it his Bufinefs to flander. He tells us, that in the Month of *March*, in the fecond Year of her Reign, fhe call'd to her *William* Lord Marquefs of *Winchefter*, Lord High Treafurer of *England*; Sir *Robert Rochefter*, her Comptroller; Sir *William Petre*, Secretary; and Sir *Francis Inglefield*, Mafter of the Wards, all of them of her Privy Council, and fpoke to them as follows: " You are here of our Council,
" and we have willed you to be called to us, to

R 2 " the

" the Intent ye might hear of me my Confcience,
" and the Refolution of my Mind, concerning the
" Lands and Poffeffions, as well of the Monafte-
" ries, as other Churches whatfoever, being now
" prefently in my Poffeffion. Firft, I do confider
" that the faid Lands were taken away from the
" Churches aforefaid in time of Schifm, and
" that by unlawful Means, fuch as are contrary
" both to the Law of God and of the Church.
" For the which Caufe my Confcience doth not
" fuffer me to detain them; and therefore I here
" exprefly refufe either to claim or to retain the
" faid Lands for mine; but with all my Heart,
" freely and willingly, without all Paction or
" Condition, and before God, I do furrender and
" relinquifh the faid Lands and Poffeffions or Inhe-
" ritances whatfoever; and do renounce the fame
" with this Mind and Purpofe, that Order and
" Difpofition thereof may be taken as fhall feem
" beft liking to our moft holy Lord the Pope, or
" elfe his Legate the Lord Cardinal, to the Ho-
" nour of God and Wealth of this our Realm.

" And albeit you may object to me again, that
" confidering the State of my Kingdom, the Dig-
" nity thereof, and my Crown Imperial, cannot be
" honourably maintain'd and furnifh'd without
" the Poffeffions aforefaid; yet notwithftanding I
" fet more by the Salvation of my Soul than by
" ten Kingdoms; and therefore the faid Poffef-
" fions I utterly refufe here to hold after that Sort
" and Title, and give moft hearty Thanks to
" Almighty God, who hath given me an Husband
" likewife minded with no lefs good Affection in
" this behalf than I am myfelf. Wherefore I
" charge and command, that my Chancellor,
" (with whom I have conferr'd my Mind in this
" Matter before) and you four, tomorrow, toge-
" ther

" ther do refort to the moft Reverend Lord Legate,
" and do fignify to him the Premifes in my Name,
" and give your Attendance upon him for the
" more full Declaration of the State of my King-
" dom, and of the forefaid Poffeffions according-
" ly, as you yourfelves do underftand the Matter,
" and can inform him in the fame.

This is a fufficient Demonftration of Queen *Mary*'s heroick Chriftianity, which regarded no worldly Crowns or Intereft where Confcience ftood in the way; but many will be offended to hear her well fpoken of, and therefore we will proceed to the next.

## Q. ELIZABETH,

HALF Sifter to Queen *Mary*, but nothing like to her in Temper; *Mary* refigning what the People had given her Brother, and cafting from her, as if infected, all that both her Father and Brother had left her belonging to the Church; *Elizabeth* immediately feizing all thofe facred Spoils again, and adding many to them, wrefted from Bifhop-ricks, and other Ecclefiaftical Benefices. She had much more of her Father, fhe grafp'd at all, and never enquir'd into the manner of taking, fo it might be had; but I fhall not fay much of her any otherwife than in relation to her Treafury, that is, her Income, and the feveral Ways by which fhe had it. Among all the *Cotton* MSS. none but one, *fol. 9*, mentions her, and that fo fparingly as if the Author were afham'd to fpeak all he knew; for fuch is the Effect of Partiality, where it does not quite falfify, at leaft to fupprefs the Truth. The Words of it are thus:

Her

Her Sifter of happy Memory (*that is*, Elizabeth *Sifter to Queen* Mary) fucceeding, befides divers Loans of her People, and others in foreign Parts (as *Anno* 5, when *William Herl* was difpatch'd into *Germany*, to take up at Intereft, for fix Years, great Sums of Money); the like *Anno* 18, from the Merchants of *Cologn* and *Hamborough*, upon Bond of the City of *London*; and again of ———— and *Pallavicin*, upon the former Security, ftrengthned with the Affurance alfo of many of her chiefeft Counfellors. And by the Grant of her Subjects thirty-eight Fifteenths, twenty Subfidies of the Commons, and eighteen Tenths of the Clergy; all which together rofe to a Sum of two Millions eight hundred thoufand Pounds. *Thus that MS.*

Let us now come to Particulars, and begin where Queen *Mary* began, that is, where fhe began to reftore to the Church, and where Queen *Elizabeth* began by taking all from it again, and that particularly in the Cafe of the Firft-Fruits and Tenths, which we will now mention as briefly as may be.

The Act for revefting the Crown under Queen *Elizabeth* in the Firft Fruits and Tenths, firft recites all the Statute of *26 Hen.* VIII. which gave thofe ecclefiaftical Revenues to that King; it then goes on mentioning feveral other Acts of that King, and of his Son King *Edward* VI. for eftablifhing the fame, and for erecting Courts of Firft-Fruits and Tenths. Next it fhows Queen *Mary*'s religious Mind in rejecting all thofe Advantages, and therefore fays fhe was more zealous than politick, which muft be indeed allow'd; for humane Policy is for feizing all, whether right or wrong; whereas religious Zeal rejects all worldly Intereft, where it carries the leaft fhow of Injuftice. But to return to this Act: Having repeated all as above, it then

then proceeds to repeal that Act of Queen *Mary*, and to give Queen *Elizabeth* all the Tenths, as they had been formerly given to her Father, to that effect reviving the Statute made in Favour of him in the twenty-fixth Year of his Reign. They also give her the Advowsons, Gifts, and Patronages, of all Vicarages belonging to any of the Rectories, Parsonages impropriate, that had been in the Posfeffion of Queen *Mary*, and which she had so generoufly given away. The Particulars of this Act are too long, and needlefs in our Cafe. However, it was provided, that all Grants, Immunities, and Liberties, given to the Univerfities of *Cambridge* and *Oxford*, or to any College or Hall in either of the faid Univerfities, and to the Colleges of *Eaton* and *Winchefter*, for or touching the Releafe or Difcharge of the faid Firft Fruits and Tenths: Alfo the Dean and Canons of the Free-Chapel of *St. George the Martyr* at *Windfor*, and all their Lands, &c. fhall be exonerated from Tenths and Firft Fruits. Likewife the Revenues of Hofpitals and Schools to be exempt from any thing contain'd in this Act.

After eftablifhing of Firft Fruits and Tenths again, all the Reftitutions made by Queen *Mary* were reaffum'd; nothing was left that could turn to any Advantage. Bifhopricks were again par'd; and it is thought they were once in no fmall Danger of being quite chipt to nothing. One great Jeft was, that feveral of the rankeft Puritans, moft inveterate Enemies to the Church of *England*, were made Bifhops and Deans in that Church, occafional Conformity being as well known then as it has been fince; for thofe Saints could comply where the Argument of a confiderable Revenue prevail'd. It is true, that Practice was not then fo univerfal as it has been fince; but there are new Fafhions in

reli-

religious Affairs as well as in Habits, and the *Presbyterians* at this Time do not pretend to be fo rigidly fanctify'd as they did in thofe Days.

Thofe things fhall be left to fuch as treat upon religious Matters, this Subject being only of Revenues; they only are hinted at as they fall in by adding to or taking from fuch Revenues. We will next prefent the Reader with a fmall Paper taken out of *Weaver's Funeral Monuments,* relating to the Frauds in the Management of what was taken from the Church. It was not improper in *Weaver,* as being a religious Affair; nor can it be thought fo here, as fhowing how the Crown was defrauded.

*An Information made to Queen Elizabeth, by                  , of the feveral Abufes and Frauds done unto the State General and Crown, by the Corruption of fuch as have been employed by her Father upon the Suppreffion of the Abbeys and Continuance of the fame.*

" Part of the corrupt, deceitful, fraudulent, and
" unrighteoufe Dealinge of many Subjects of this
" Realme at and fince the Vifitation and Suppref-
" fion of Abbeyes, which, with all the reft, God
" by his Grace hath made me hate and refufe, and
" alfo detefte and refifte in others to the utmofte of
" my fmall Powere, beyng contrary to this Com-
" mandemente of the fecond Table, *Thou fhalt not
" fteale,* whereby the Poffeffions, Revenues, and
" Treafure of the Crowne have byn unmeafurably
" robbed and diminyfhed, to the great Offence of
" God and Slaunder of the Gofpel, and to the no
" fmall impoverifhynge and weakenynge of the
" imperial

" imperial Crowne, and utter undoinge of a Nom-
" ber of your Majefties pore Tenants and Sub-
" jects, and fo to the great Slaundere of your Ma-
" jeftie and withdrawinge of their Harts from you,
" whofe Acte it is told them to be; and fo to
" them it femeth, becaufe fome of your Seales be
" at all or moft parte of them, and the Confirma-
" cion of your Head Officers at the refte; and to
" the uttere fpoyling and undoynge (before God
" and good Men) of a Nomber of lerned Perfones
" and exelente Witts, who underftanding that
" many before them had byne thereby greatly en-
" riched and advaunced, and that the Gapp there-
" unto, as unto a Vertue, was made wyde open
" for all without any Punyfhment, but rather
" Commendacions, were and are ftill the eafilier
" overcom by Temptacion of the Wifdome of
" Satane, the World, and the Flefhe, to feek and
" labour to become riche by like wicked Wayes;
" of whom, as the Nomber is now of late Yeres
" increafed, fo alfo deceave they moore fubtille
" and deteftablie, and in more things than ever
" before. For redreffe whereof, and of a Nom-
" bere of other cunnynge and clerly Thefts and
" Decepts which I know, and can in time remem-
" ber and difcovere, befide the Multetude out of
" my Compaffe fayd by common Brute to be in
" other Calings: There muft be pennede (by
" fome Perfones learnede in the Lawe, that be
" knowne to hate all kynds of Unrighteoufnes)
" fome ftrong Act or Actes, (to paffe by Parlia-
" ment, and afterwards to be roundly executed)
" with great Penalties, Forfeitures, and Ponyfh-
" ments, to reche unto Lands, Goods, and Bodie,
" as the Greatnes or the Smalnes of the Cafe
" fhall require, without the which God will be
" yet more offended, the Gofpell more flaun-
" dered,

" dered, the Crowne more impoveresh'd and we-
" kened, your People more undone, your Majefty
" more flaundered, your Peoples Harts more
" drawne from you, the lerned Perfones, and exe-
" lente Witts of your People more fpoyled, and
" many other particuler Evills will grow thereby,
" befides Gods great Strokes, which at length will
" come without Repentance and Amendment.
" Whereas that Reformacion be had, God will
" be therin pleas'd, the Gofpelle commended, the
" Crowne enrich'd, your People profited, ther
" Loves towards you encreas'd; the learned and
" exelente Wittes enforced from Deceite, to feeke
" Prefermente and Welthe by godly and honefte
" meanes; and many other things will grow ther-
" by, befides Gods good Bleffing, which your
" Majeftie fhall be fure to have for it.

*Deceiptfull and unrighteoufe Dealings,* viz. *at
and upon the Vifitation and Suppreffion of Abbeyes.*

1. " When the Images of Gold and Silver, &c.
" with the coftilye Shrines, Tabernacles, Alteres
" and Rood-loftes, and the precious Jewelles, rich
" Stones and Perles, &c. belonging to the fame,
" and the Pixes, Phalaces, Patenes, Bafines, Ewers,
" Candleftickes, Crewets, Chalices, Senfors, and
" Multitudes of other riche Veffelles of Gold and
" Silver, &c. and the coftly Alter Clothes, Cur-
" tenes, Copes, Veftments, Aulbes, Tunicles, and
" other riche Ornaments, and the fine Linnen,
" Jette, Marble, precious Wood, Braffe, Iron,
" Lead, Belles, Stone, &c. and the Houfhold
" Plate, Houfeholde Stuffe, and Furniture of Houfe-
" hold, and the Leafes and Chatalles, and the
" Horfes, Oxen, Kine, Sheepe and other Cat-
" tell, and the fuperfluous Houfes and Buildings,
" and

" and Multitudes of other things that belong'd to
" Abbeyes, &c. were worth a Million of Gold.
" The Salles of the Parte whereof were fo cun-
" ningly made, and the Prefervation of the reft
" fuche, that your Majefties Father, and the Crowne
" of *England* hade in Comparifon but mean Por-
" tiones of the fame, of which muche was un-
" pay'd by ill Dealinge in many Yeres aftre. For
" the fynding out of which, and punifhyng the
" great Decept and Fraude, thear was not then,
" nether hath thear byne at any time fince, for
" the like Evilles afterwards alfo committed to
" this Day, any good Order, or diligent Labour
" taken, but let paffe, as though to fynd out and
" punifhe fuch Wickednes were no Profite to the
" Prince and Crowne, or good Service to God.
" All which have byne the eafilier let flip, becaufe
" perhaps fome of them that fhoulde have puny-
" fhed under the Prince might alfo be partly guiltie,
" and fo, *Ca mee* ; *Ca thee*.

   " 2. *Item,* where diveres of the Vifitores and
" Suppreffores had afterwards yerly Allowance of
" Fees, Annueties, Corodies, &c. graunted by the
" Abbeyes, &c. to themfelves, their Servants and
" Friends, was it likely that they came by them
" without Fraude ?

   " 3. *Item,* the moft Part of the Evedences of
" Abbeyes and Nunneries were pilfer'd away,
" fold and lofte, as herein following under the
" Title of your Majefties **Tyme** more playnlie ap-
" peareth.

   " 4. *Item,* Manores, Landes and Tenements,
" and other Hereditaments were ofte folde at
" under yerly Rents, by many fubtile Deceipts
" and Fraudes.

   " 5. *Item,* many Lands and Tenements, &c.
" were fometime folde with thapportenances at
                                        " the

" the old yerly Rents ; but where the Woods were
" unvalued (as ofte they were) the fame went
" from the Kyng without Recompence.

" 6. *Item,* Mannores, Lands and Tenements,
" &c. fold to divers, and after the Woods were
" felled and folde, and the Rents enhaunced, or
" for great Fines leafed out for many Yeres, then
" the fame Manores, Lands, &c. were retorned to the
" Kyng for other Lands that had Plenty of Woods,
" and were unenhauncede, and unleafed in all or
" in parte, or the Leafes were expyred.

" 7. *Item,* much Lands and Tenements, and
" many great Woods, and other Hereditaments
" were then folde away, wher the Money for the
" fame by deceptful Defraude was not pay in many
" Yeres after the due Dayes of Paymente.

" So likewife in the time of the Reigne of King
" *Edward* the fixth, your Majefties Brother, many
" things were done amiffe, though not fo many
" and fo great as befoor.

" Exchanges more were then in King *Henries*
" time, and almoft as badde, whereof the Rents
" of many of them mufte needs decaye in a great
" parte, when that Leafes fhall end that were
" made by the Exchangeores, or when their Bonds
" made to warrant thos Rents fhall either be loft,
" or not extended.

" Much Lands, &c. were fold at under Values
" by great Decepte of many.

" And in the fhorte tyme of the Reigne of
" Queene *Mary,* your Majefties Sifter, many great
" Gifts, Sales and Exchanges were made, wherein
" was great Deceipt and Loffe to the Prince and
" Crowne.

" In your Majefties time, and before, all or the
" greatefte parte of all the Evidences of the Lands,
" Poffeffions, and Hereditaments of all the Ab-
                                        " beyes,

" beyes, &c. have by little and little by fraudu-
" lent means been fo pilfered, and folde awaye,
" and fo drawne into many private Men's Handes,
" that there is almoft none of them left to your Ma-
" jefties Ufe; fo that your Majeftie hath nothing
" to mainteyne your Title yf neede fo requyre,
" but onely the long Poffeffion, and your owne Re-
" cords made fince the Suppreffion, whereof a
" number of them be gone.

This Informer (a Man in Authority, as appears
by the Sequel, of whofe Name I am ignorant)
proceeds further in the Rehearfal of many more
Deceipts, Frauds and Corruptions, ufed by divers
of the Officers of thofe Days, only for their own
Lucre and Advancement, which are too many
here to fet down.

This firft Year, the Parliament granted to the
Queen a Subfidy of two Shillings eight Pence the
Pound of moveable Goods, and four Shillings of
Land, to be paid at two feveral Payments, of every
Perfon Spiritual and Temporal, towards the better
furnifhing of her Majefty with Money for the neceffary Charges which fhe was prefently occafion'd to
fuftain, finding the Treafure of the Realm greatly
confum'd, and the Revenues of the Crown fore di-
minifh'd.

Much about the fame time, fhe feiz'd all that her
Sifter had reftor'd to religious Houfes, as the Priory of St. *John* of *Jerufalem* near *Smithfield* ; the
Nuns and Friers of the two Houfes of *Sion* and
*Shene*, the one *Carthufians*, and the other *Brigittines*,
parted by the River of *Thames*; the *Grey Friers* of
*Greenwich*, all whofe Lands and Revenues fhe took
to her own Ufe, befides many more of lefs Note;
but as for *Weftminfter* Abbey, fhe only took that
from the *Monks*, and gave it to Prebendaries.

This

This ſame Year the Parliament granted the Queen the Subſidy of Tonnage and Poundage for Life, as had been before granted to ſome of her Predeceſſors, which having been ſufficiently ſpoken of under them needs no other Repetition here.

There was alſo a Confirmation of a Subſidy and two Fifteenths by the Temporality.

No more Parliaments appear to have ſate from the firſt till the fifth of this Queen, when there was a Reviver of the Statute of 22 *Hen.* 8. 12. and 2 and 4 *Edw.* 6. 16. touching relieving the poor and impotent Perſons, and puniſhing of Vagabonds. The Statute cited of *Hen.* 8. makes no other Proviſion for them, than that they ſhall be allow'd to beg within a certain Precinct by Licence from the Juſtices ; and if any begg'd without ſuch Licence, or ſuch Precinct, to be whipp'd. That of the 4th of *Edw.* 6. is much to the ſame Effect ; ſo that the Poor were left to ſtarve if they had no Licence to beg, and might have no better Fate by begging within ſuch a Precinct, none being oblig'd to give. Now comes this pious Reviver ; and indeed it is very remarkable, for it ſays thus: The poor and impotent Perſons of every Pariſh ſhall be reliev'd of that which every Perſon will of their Charity give weekly. And the ſame Relief ſhall be gather'd in every Pariſh by Collectors aſſign'd, and weekly diſtributed to the Poor ; for none of them ſhall openly go or ſit begging. And if any Pariſhioner ſhall obſtinately refuſe to pay reaſonably towards the Relief of the ſaid Poor, or ſhall diſcourage others ; then the Juſtices of the Peace at the Quarter-Seſſions may tax him to a reaſonable weekly Sum, which if he refuſe to pay, they may commit him to Priſon. And if any Pariſh have in it more impotent poor Perſons than they are able to relieve, then the Juſtices of the Peace of the County may licenſe ſo many

of

of them as they fhall think good to beg in one or
more Hundreds of the fame County. And if any
Poor beg in any other Place than he is licenfed, he
fhall be punifh'd as a Vagabond.

This feems to be the firft Statute made for theRe-
lief of the Poor; for the other two, mention'd before,
only gave them leave to beg and ftarve. And this
indeed is not much better; for it firft fays, every
Parifhioner fhall give what in his Charity he will
weekly; but then it is left to the Juftices to affefs
all that will not voluntarily give. So that here is
a free Act of Charity forc'd upon the People at the
Will of the Juftices, under Pain of Imprifonment.
But then if the Juftices thought not their own Parifh fufficient to maintain all the Poor, as many as
they pleas'd might be fent to beg and perifh in fuch
Hundreds as they were pleas'd to affign them.

This charitable Tax upon the People, tho' it
went not to the Crown, had been occafion'd by it,
which having feiz'd almoft all the Revenues of the
Church, till then the whole Support of the Poor,
under Colour of eafing the Subjects of Taxes, ever
after increas'd its own Impofitions, and entail'd the
perpetual charitable Tax of relieving the Poor as
an Addition to all the reft; and perhaps, confidering
it never does or is like to ceafe, it is one of the
heavieft Duties upon the People, efpecially the mid-
dling fort, who are fure to be affefs'd to the utmoft,
whilft many of the greateft Eftates bear the leaft
part of the Burden. The Weight of which Duty
every Houfekeeper is at this time fenfible of.

This fame fifth Year the Queen had a Subfidy of
fix Shillings in the Pound granted by the Clergy, to
be paid in three Years.

The Temporality alfo granted her a Subfidy and
two Fifteenths.

From

From this fifth till the eighth Year we have no Parliament again, and then in the said eighth the Clergy granted a Subsidy of four Shillings in the Pound, to be paid in three Years.

The Temporality also granted one Subsidy, and one Fifteenth and a Tenth.

Another Chasm follows from the eighth to the thirteenth Year, when a Subsidy of six Shillings in the Pound was granted by the Clergy, to be paid in three Years.

And by the Temporality two Fifteenths and Tenths, and one Subsidy.

The fourteenth Year a Parliament was holden, but which is a very great Rarity and very remarkable, there does not appear to have been any Tax levy'd.

The next Session was the eighteenth Year, when the Spirituality granted a Subsidy of six Shillings in the Pound, to be paid in three Years.

The Temporality at the same time give three Fifteenths and Tenths, and one Subsidy.

No Session again till the 23d Year, when the Clergy granted a Subsidy of six Shillings and eight Pence in the Pound, to be paid in three Years.

And the Temporality a Subsidy and two Fifteenths.

The twenty seventh Year was the next Session, at which the Temporality granted a Subsidy of six Shillings in the Pound, to be paid in three Years.

And the Temporality one entire Subsidy, and two Fifteenths.

*Anno* 31, the Clergy granted two Subsidies of six Shillings in the Pound, to be paid yearly by two Shillings in the Pound.

And the Temporality two Subsidies and four Fifteenths.

In her 35th Year, every Parish was charg'd with a weekly Sum towards the Relief of sick, wounded,

and

and maim'd Soldiers. This was no fmall Impofition; and tho' it did not directly go to the Crown,
being to fupport thofe it ought to have fupported,
and a Burden upon the Subjects, it may properly be
taken notice of here, tho' we fhall infift no farther
upon it.

The fame Year the Clergy granted to the Queen
two Subfidies of four Shillings in the Pound, to be
paid in two Years.

The Temporality alfo granted her three Subfidies, and fix Fifteenths and Tenths. Thus there
was no Occafion for Parliaments meeting every
Year, when the Subfidies, Fifteenths and Tenths
were heap'd for feveral Years to come, and made
the lefs Appearance being thus given all at once,
than if they had been fpun out for the peculiar
Work of every Year.

The 39th Year was remarkable for that extraordinary Piece of Charity of giving People Leave by
Act of Parliament to found and erect Hofpitals for
the Relief of the Poor. All the Hofpitals in *England*,
being a hundred and ten in number, had been before
thrown down, and their Revenues fquander'd ; and
now the wretched Poor lay perifhing about, Charity
reach'd fo far as to give Leave to relieve them, which
being worth obferving, the more particular notice
fhall be taken of it ; for now pafs'd

*An Act for erecting of Hofpitals, or Abiding and
Working Houfes for the Poor.*

It is call'd an Act for erecting of Hofpitals, whereas in reality it was only for granting Leave to erect
them. In the firft Place the Act mentions that
above hinted at, for taxing of Parifhes for Relief
of maim'd and wounded Soldiers, and others, which
it feems had not Effect : For which reafon her Ma-
j-fty now granted that it fhould be enacted, and
accordingly it was enacted, that all and every Per-

son and Persons seiz'd of an Estate in Fee simple, their Heirs, Executors, or Assigns, might at their Will and Pleasure have full Power and Authority, at any time during the Space of twenty Years next ensuing, by Deed enroll'd in the High Court of Chancery, to erect, found and establish one or more Hospitals, for the finding Sustentation and Relief of the maim'd, poor, needy, or impotent People, as to set the Poor to work, to have Continuance for ever, and from time to time to place therein such Head and Members, and such number of Poor, as to him, his Heirs and Assigns shall seem convenient. And that the same Hospitals shall be incorporated, &c. and shall be call'd by such Name as the Founder shall appoint, and the same to be a Body Corporate, with Capacity to purchase, receive, &c. any Lands, Tenements, &c. and have Power to sue and be sued, and have a common Seal.

This was a notable Piece of Charity, to give the People Leave to relieve the Distress'd out of their own Estates. However, for fear lest People should grow too extravagant in their Charity, they confin'd them to the Term of twenty Years to come, that they might not after the Expiration thereof be lavish in doing Good. And still farther to prevent any such Excess of Piety, it was enacted, that no such Hospital or House should be capable of possessing above two hundred Pounds *per Annum* in Lands, Tenements, &c. so that they were likely to be notable Hospitals with such a Revenue; but the principal Care it seems was, that the Wealthy should not be undone by being over generous in founding such Houses. This look'd as if the Queen and her Parliament had been asham'd to encourage the restoring of what her own Father had destroy'd, and the Parliament in his Time had so readily given him to squander away.

A

A good Provifo was made in this Act, that no fuch Incorporation to be founded fhall at any time hereafter do, or fuffer to be done, any Act or Thing, whereby or by means whereof any of the Lands, Tenements, Hereditaments, Stock, Goods, or Chattels of fuch Incorporation, or any Eftate, Intereft, Poffeffion or Property of or in the fame, or any of them, fhall be vefted or transferr'd in or to any other whatfoever, contrary to the Meaning of this Act.

This certainly had a View to the pretended Surrenders of fuch Places to King *Henry* VIII. which if they had been really voluntary, had ftill been invalid, as was then well known, and therefore were confirm'd by Act of Parliament. So that what was here done for the Security of thefe imaginary new Hofpitals, was no lefs imaginary than the Foundations themfelves; fince all the Security they had by this Act of Parliament was liable to be made void by the next Parliament that fhould think fit fo to do.

Tho' this Act was no Impofition on the Subject, being fo remarkable for leaving them the Liberty of relieving the Poor, or fuffering them to perifh, it well deferves to be taken notice of, to fhow what wretched Provifion was thought of for fo many Thoufands as had been fent abroad to ftarve, without any Maintenance.

This puts me in Mind of a notable Order fet forth in the 14th Year of this Queen. She being inform'd, as we are told, that certain lewd Perfons, under Pretence of executing Commiffions for Inquiries to be made for Lands conceal'd, contrary to her Majefties Meaning, challenging Lands, Stocks of Money, Plate, &c. not forbearing to make Pretence to the Bells, Lead, and other fuch things belonging to Parifh Churches or Chapels; her Ma-

jefty

jefty meaning fpeedily to obviate fuch unlawful Practices, commanded that all Commiffions then extant,
for Inquifition of any manner of Concealments,
fhould be by *Superfedeas* out of the *Exchequer* revok'd, *&c.*

This was, as the common Proverb expreffes it,
fhutting the Stable Door when the Steed was ftolen.
All the Churches had been robb'd and plunder'd,
nothing left them but bare Walls, and now an Order came forth to prevent their being ftript. A
fingular Piece of Providence and Zeal, to forbid
the taking away of what there was not!

The fame 39th Year above fpoken of, there was
a farther Taxation for the Relief of Soldiers and Mariners, where fufficient was not provided by the
Statute of the 35th of *Eliz.* The greateft Rate of
every Parifh to be tax'd, to be 8 *s.* and the leaft
2 *s.* weekly; with further Provifion, if the Rate be
not fufficient for Soldiers and Mariners in *London.*
Thus by degrees came up the Taxes for the Poor,
which are now grown up to fuch immenfe Sums, as
fcarce feem credible, being as great a Burden upon
Houfekeepers as any other.

Still this fame Year the Clergy granted to the
Queen' three Subfidies of four Shillings in the
Pound, to be paid at fix feveral Days.

At the fame time the Temporality granted no
lefs than three entire Subfidies, and fix Fifteenths
and Tenths. No doubt but there was little Occafion for frequent Parliaments, when they granted
their Money fo freely, that it requir'd fome Years
to levy the fame before any more could be any
way ask'd.

In her forty-third Year an Act of Parliament
pafs'd for Confirmation of Grants made to the
Queen's Majefty, and of Letters Patents made by
her Majefty to others, fince the twenty-fifth

Year

Year of her Majesty's Reign, mentioning, that there had been convey'd to her sundry Honours, Castles, Manors, Lands, Tenements, Rents, Reversions, Services, and other Hereditaments, by and from sundry Persons and Bodies Politick, as well for the Discharge and Satisfaction of great Debts and Sums of Money, as for other good Considerations. These were the Pretences, and they were no other; for had those Lands, &c. been legally acquir'd, there had been no Occasion for an Act of Parliament to secure them; but they were, for the most part, the Gleanings of the Patrimony of the Church, which till then had escap'd either unobserv'd, or conniv'd at: But now Men in Favour found them out, had them seiz'd for the Crown, and then begg'd them for themselves, as had been the Practice in the Reigns of her Father and Brother.

The same Year follow'd another Act for the Relief of the Poor, wherein, after Order taken for Overseers, it follows that all Persons able, be set to work by the said Overseers; as also that they raise weekly, or otherwise, (by Taxation of every Inhabitant, Parson, Vicar, and other; and of every Occupier of Lands, Houses, Tithes impropriate, Propriations of Tithes, Coal-Mines, or saleable Underwoods, in the Parish, in such competent Sum and Sums of Money as they shall think fit) a convenient Stock of Flax, Hemp, Wool, Thread, Iron, and other Ware and Stuff, to set the Poor on work; and also competent Sums of Money for and towards the necessary Relief of the Lame, Impotent, Old, Blind, and such other among them being poor and not able to work; and also for putting out of Children to be Apprentices, to be gathered out of the same Parish, according to the Ability of the same Parish, &c. And

in

in cafe the Parifh is not able to levy among themfelves fufficient Sums of Money, then two Juftices
are impower'd to levy the fame out of any other
Parifh or Parifhes within the fame Hundred ; and
if the Hundred cannot do it, the Juftices at the
Quarter Seffions to levy the fame out of any other
Parifh or Parifhes within the County.

In Default of Payment of the Money affefs'd, the
fame to be levy'd by Diftrefs ; and where no Diftrefs can be had, the Perfons not paying to be committed to Prifon.

By thefe frequent Acts for Relief of the Poor,
it appears to what a Condition the Country
was reduc'd ; for no Expedients were fufficient to
fupport the Diftrefs'd, and Peoples Hearts were fo
harden'd, that the Needy could find no Support, but
what was extorted by meer Force of Law ; and
that fo mean, that many ftill perifh'd for Want.

How little all that the Parliament did in thefe
Cafes avail'd is vifible, in that the very next Act
pafs'd in the fame Seffions is again for the neceffary Relief of Soldiers and Mariners. Still ham-
mering upon this fame Point, and little or nothing
brought to effect.

This Year the Clergy granted the Queen four
Subfidies of four Shillings in the Pound.

And the Temporality four entire Subfidies, and
eight Fifteenths and Tenths.

Thus much of Taxations of all Sorts during this
Queen's Reign : And fo we will conclude with her,
laying afide all Remarks, as have been made on
moft of the Kings her Predeceffors; for as fhe was
a Woman, it is better to let her pafs fo than fay any
thing of her that may be ill thought of; and thofe
moft fulfome Encomiums, which fome Writers of
her Time have thought fit for their private Views
to beftow on her, will rather ferve to cloy any impartial

partial Reader, than to make them conceit there is
any thing of Reality in them.


## K.  J A M E S  I.

MAY in general be call'd a good King to his
Subjects, if he can be allow'd to be a good
King, who, like a too indulgent Father, is so favourable and loving to his Children as to spoil them.
So this King carry'd himself towards the Generality of his People, easy, and never guilty of oppres-
sing them; but so far from it, as even to be blam'd
for refusing to engage in unnecessary and unjust
Wars, which must have drawn those Burdens upon
the Nation that it has groan'd under during the
Reigns of others, who have readily taken part in
Quarrels that no way concern'd them, either to gratify their own Ambition, or to vent their Spleen
and Malice. Such was the Excess of Goodness
in this King, that tho' his own Reign continu'd
peaceable, yet the Seeds of Rebellion were sown
and sprouted out plentifully under his Son, to the
Loss of that Prince's Head. Tho' King *James*, as
has been said, was so good a King to his Subjects
in general, it might be carrying the Character too
far to say he was so in all other Respects. If we
look into his Treaties abroad, some whereof may
be seen in Sir —— *Winwood's Memoirs*, we shall
find many things which are far from looking fair;
but that is not to the Subject in hand, any more
than the private Acts of his Life, and which we
shall therefore pass by. How rightful and lawful a
King he was is sufficiently express'd in the Act of
Recognition, where he is declar'd and sworn to
be such, not by Virtue of the said Act, but by
Birth-right, as being *lineally, rightfully, and lawfully*

S 4                                    *descended*

*defcended of the Body of the moft excellent Lady* Margaret, *eldeft Daughter of the moft renowned King* Henry VII. *and the moft high and noble Princefs* Queen Elizabeth, *his Wife, eldeft Daughter of King* Edward IV. *the faid Lady* Margaret *being eldeft Sifter of King* Henry VIII. *&c.* Then prefently after they declare, that the imperial Crown of *England,* and of all the Kingdoms, Dominions, and Rights belonging to the fame, did by inherent Birth-right, and lawful and undoubted Succeffion, defcend and come to his Majefty, as being lineally, juftly, and lawfully, next and fole Heir of the Blood Royal of this Realm, as aforefaid. Such was this King's Right, than which none could be more undoubted; and yet as evident as it was, the World well knows how his Son was treated, and the Ufage his Grandchildren met withal. To come now to the Duties granted to this King by Parliament, the firft we find is

An Act of Subfidy of Tonnage and Poundage granted to his Majefty in the firft Year of his Reign for Term of Life, as had been before granted to King *Henry* VII. King *Henry* VIII. King *Edward* VI. Queen *Mary,* and Queen *Elizabeth.* The Tonnage, three Shillings of every Tun of Wine imported; and three Shillings more for every Tun of fweet Wines, as well Malmfey as other, imported by Aliens; and twelve Pence of every Awme of Rhenifh Wine. The Poundage, twelve Pence in the Pound of the Value of all Goods imported or exported, excepting woollen Cloth, *&c.* as may be feen in the former Reigns.

The fecond Year of King *James* there was no Parliament, and confequently no Impofition.

The third Year the Parliament had been fo pleas'd by the King, that they thought nothing too much for him; and accordingly the Clergy granted

him

him four Subfidies, of four Shillings in the Pound each, to be paid by every Archbifhop, Bifhop, Dean, Archdeacon, Provoft, Mafter of College, Prebendary, Parfon, and Vicar, and every other Perfon and Perfons having and enjoying any fpiritual Promotion, out of nine Parts of their whole Income, in Confideration that the Tenth before belong'd to the King, according to the Taxation or Valuation then remaining in the Court of *Exchequer*. The Manner of the Payment to be thus, *viz.* eighteen Pence of every Pound, as aforefaid, to be paid upon the fecond of *October* next enfuing, being the Year 1606, for the firft Payment; for the fecond Payment of eighteen Pence more, on the 26th of *March* 1607; the third Payment of eighteen Pence, on the fecond of *October* the fame Year; the fourth Payment of eighteen Pence more, on the 26th of *March* the Year following; and fo the other Payments half-yearly on the fame Days, at eighteen Pence each Day, till the whole four Subfidies were paid. None but the Archbifhops and Bifhops, or the Deans and Chapters, to be Collectors of thefe Subfidies.

The Temporality at the fame time, not to be out-done by the Clergy, granted his Majefty three entire Subfidies, and fix Fifteenths and Tenths. The Reafons alledg'd for granting this extraordinary Supply were, firft, the Powder-Plot, fo to fhow their great Love to him; the fecond, the great Bleffing of God in his Majefty's Perfon, by Addition of another Kingdom; the third and moft urgent Reafon, as they exprefs it, the exceffive Charge for the War in *Ireland*, which was finifh'd before Queen *Elizabeth*'s Death; fo that they feem'd to be at a lofs to fhow any Reafon for their Generofity; the Plot, which had fail'd, being none; the Addition of another Kingdom no better; and a

War

War ended before his Acceffion to the Crown had as little in it as could well be imagin'd. The fourth Reafon indeed, they fay, arifes from their great Contentment and Joy of the Remembrance of his Majefty's gracious Difpofition: And this indeed might have been one for all; and it had been fufficient to have faid, that as they found him a good King, they were willing to fhow themfelves good Subjects, by generoufly fupporting his Dignity with their Purfes. The fix Fifteenths and Tenths to be rais'd of the moveable Goods, Chattels, and other things ufual to fuch Fifteenths and Tenths, to be contributory and chargeable within the Shires, Cities, Boroughs, Towns, and other Places of the Realm, in Manner and Form as formerly us'd, except the Sum of thirty-fix thoufand Pounds to be deducted, that is, fix thoufand Pounds of every of the faid whole Fifteenths and Tenths, in Relief, Comfort, and Difcharge, of the poor Towns, Cities, and Boroughs, wafted, defolate, or deftroy'd, or greatly impoverifh'd. The faid fix Fifteenths and Tenths to be paid, the firft of them at one entire Payment on or before the firft Day of *Auguft* next enfuing, the fecond on or before the firft Day of *May* 1607, the third on the firft of *November* the fame Year, the fourth on the firft of *May* 1608, the fifth on the firft Day of *May* 1609, and the fixth and laft on the firft of *May* 1610.

The three Subfidies to be levy'd at fix feveral Payments of every Perfon Spiritual or Temporal, and of every Fraternity, Guild, Corporation, Myftery, Brotherhood, or Commonalty, being worth three Pounds, for every Pound, as well in Coin as the Value of every Pound, as they have of their own, as alfo Plate, Stock of Merchandize, all manner of Corn and Grain, Houfhold-ftuff, and all other Goods moveable, and of all Sums of
Money

Money owing to them, excepting such Sums of Money as they really owe, as also Jewels, Gold, Silver, Stone, and Pearl, shall pay to and for the first Subsidy, at two several Payments, two Shillings and eight Pence of every Pound, the first Payment of the said first Subsidy twenty Pence of every Pound; and to and for the second Payment of the said first Subsidy, twelve Pence of every Pound. And for the second Subsidy, two Shillings and eight Pence of every Pound; and the same for the third Subsidy. All Aliens and Strangers to pay five Shillings and four Pence in the Pound for each of the three Subsidies. All Lands held after any manner whatsoever to pay four Shillings in the Pound for each Subsidy; and all Aliens and Strangers to pay for all Lands eight Shillings in the Pound.

This indeed was a most generous Imposition, given out of stark Love and Kindness, as they say themselves, and a wonderful Instance of the good Humour they were in at that time, or of King *James*'s good Management to bring them into that sweet Temper.

The fourth Year the Parliament met, and pass'd several Acts; but it could not be expected they should add any thing, after having the Year before given so plentifully.

The fifth and sixth Years pass'd away without any Parliaments.

The seventh Year the Clergy, towards the King's extraordinary Charges in maintaining of Religion, granted his Majesty one entire Subsidy of six Shillings in the Pound of all spiritual Livings or Promotions.

The Temporality also, without alledging any empty Reasons, freely declare, that they present his Majesty, out of mere Love, with their free Gift of one entire Subsidy, and one Fifteenth and
Tenth.

Tenth. This was dealing fairly and honeftly not to pretend Expences and Charges where there were none, and Loyalty to prefent their Sovereign with fuch a Gift as they thought might be acceptable, and perhaps convenient at that Time. The Fifteenth and Tenth to be affefs'd and levy'd as ufual in thofe Cafes. The Subfidy to be at the Rate of two Shillings and eight Pence in the Pound for Natives, and five Shillings and four Pence in the Pound for Strangers and Aliens.

From the feventh to the eighteenth Year of this King's Reign there appears not to have been any Seffion of Parliament. A very long Recefs; and yet in that Parliament of the eighteenth Year the Spirituality granted three entire Subfidies, and the Temporality two entire Subfidies.

Next follows another Interval from the faid eighteenth till the one and twentieth Year, when the Spirituality granted four entire Subfidies.

The Temporality confidering that the King might be engag'd in a War, by breaking off the two Treaties with *Spain*, viz. the one of the Marriage, and the other of the Reftitution of the Palatine, freely granted his Majefty three entire Subfidies, and three Fifteenths and Tenths, whereof 18000 Pounds fhould be employ'd towards the Repair of certain decay'd Cities and Towns, and the Refidue was to be expended in the managing of the expected War. Now for the better Employment of thofe Moneys, eight Citizens of *London* were appointed to be Treafurers, and ten other felected Perfons to be of his Majefty's Council for the War; all which to make Oath, viz. the Treafurers, that none of thofe Moneys fhould iffue out of their Hands without Warrant from the faid Council of War; and the other, that they fhould make no Warrants for the Payment of any of thefe Moneys,

but

but only for the End above mention'd; and further
should be all accountable for their Doings and Proceedings in that Behalf to the Commons in Parliament, when they or any of them should be thereunto requir'd.

Here began those Proceedings which afterwards
ran so high against King *Charles* I. The Parliament, at the beginning of King *James*'s Reign,
had granted him large Supplies as free Gift, and
for a War that had been ended by his Predecessor;
now they give Money for a War he was to begin
himself, but will not trust him with the handling
or disposing of one Penny of it; the Citizens must
keep the Cash, and their Counsellors issue Warrants
for disposing of it; so that had the King enter'd
into a War, his Hands were ty'd up, and like a
Pupil he could have dispos'd of nothing but what
those his Governours should have thought fit. We
shall see to what an Height these things were advanc'd in the unfortunate Reign of his Son.

Thus have we at once run through all the Taxes
granted by Parliament, that above mention'd being
the last during this King's Reign. It remains now
to look back to see what other Ways there were of
raising Money, and some other Observations relating to this Subject.

In his second Year, in *September*, he sent Privy
Seals to the wealthiest Citizens in *London* to borrow
Money of them; but what Sum he rais'd by this
Practice, or how it was repaid, I do not find. How-
ever, in *October* the same Year, the Customs of all
Goods imported or exported were rais'd and let
out to Farm.

In his third Year, *Henry* Lord *Mordant*, being convicted in the *Star-Chamber* of several Misprisions,
was adjudg'd to pay 10000 Marks; *Edward* Lord
*Sturton*, for such like Offences, to pay 30000 Pounds;

and

and some time after Sir *John Bennet,* Judge of the Prerogative Court, was fin'd 20000 Pounds. How these Fines were levy'd, or whether ever paid, is much to be doubted, Money not being so plentiful in those Days, and those who have such heavy Fines laid upon them scarce ever discharging the same.

In his fourth Year, instead of receiving, the King paid the Citizens of *London* 40000 Pounds Queen *Elizabeth* had borrow'd of them three Years before her Death, which gain'd him much Love at that time; but all the good Acts of Kings are soon forgot.

In his seventh Year he levy'd an Aid throughout *England,* according to the ancient Custom, for making his eldest Son Prince *Henry* Knight; and this, tho' manag'd with very great Moderation, is said to have turn'd to a very good Account.

He had also a Benevolence throughout the Realm, which occasion'd much grudging; for there are few that part with their Money contentedly, and especially to their Sovereign, tho' he stands never so much in need of it, as King *James* did at that time; for tho' he had not Wars, he had many other great Expences, which drein'd him: However, the Seed of Rebellion which grew up under his Son was then sow'd, and began to sprout.

Another Method the King found to relieve his Wants in his twelfth Year, which was by instituting a new Dignity and Title of *Baronets,* whereof none could have Cause to complain; because it was at their own Choice whether they would be advanc'd to it or no, and being a voluntary Purchase of Honour, those who were not fond of it were free to leave it. The Title was to them and their Male Heirs for ever, with the following Prerogatives; to take Place of all Knights *Batchelors,* Knights of the *Bath,* and *Bannerets*; to be impleaded by the Addition *Baronet,* and their Title *Sir,* and their
Wives

Wives *Lady* ; the King not to create any Degree, under the Dignity of a Baron, to be superior or equal to them ; no more to be made but the full number of two hundred, until some of them should be extinct. However, the younger Sons of Viscounts or Barons were adjudg'd to take Place of them, and that their Male Heirs at one and twenty should be Knighted, and to bear either in a *Canton* in their Coat of Arms, or in a Scutcheon, at their own Choice, the Arms of *Ulster,* being *Argent,* a Hand *Gules;* their Place in the King's Armies to be near the Standard, for Defence thereof.

For purchasing of this Honour, each Baronet was to maintain thirty Foot Soldiers for three Years, at eight Pence a Day, in the King's Forces, for the reducing of the Province of *Ulster* in *Ireland,* the which Expence amounted to one thousand nine hundred and five Pounds each. At their own Request the Charge was afterwards compounded at a certain Rate, and the King to take the Payment of the aforesaid Soldiers upon himself; and, as it was agreed, the Composition for all the Baronets then created, being ninety three in number, amounted to no more than ninety eight thousand five hundred and fifty Pounds.

That we may the better judge of the Difference between those Times and ours, and for the Satisfaction of the Curious, it is worth observing, that in the Reign of Queen *Elizabeth,* when *Burleigh* was Lord Treasurer, the whole Revenue of the Kingdom, besides *Woods* and the Dutchy of *Lancaster,* was one hundred eighty eight thousand one hundred ninety seven Pounds *per Annum* ; and the Payments were one hundred and ten thousand six hundred and twelve Pounds *per Annum* ; of which these were constant :

The

The Houshold, forty thousand Pounds.
The Privy Purse, two thousand Pounds.
The Admiralty, thirty thousand Pounds.

This is what was left as a standing Revenue to
King *James*, whose Expences were very much increas'd since the Queen's Time, and yet no Addition made to his constant Income.   First, in regard
that Queen *Elizabeth* had only herself; whereas
King *James*, besides himself, had a Queen, the
Prince his eldest Son, and a Nursery of other Children ; then many to gratify that had serv'd him in
*Scotland*; and the Marriage of his Daughter to the
*Palsgrave*, as he was then call'd, cost him ninety
three thousand two hundred ninety four Pounds;
not to mention many other considerable Expences
out of his own Family, too many to enumerate in
this Place.   These many Issues beyond his Income
reduc'd him to great Streights, so that he was
oblig'd to retrench all possible Expences ; and all
that falling still short, he could not avoid finding
Expedients to supply the Deficiences.

This drew on the Benevolence above hinted at,
in Hopes it might have rais'd a generous Contribution among all good Subjects; but all were willing
to receive, and few or none to give; so that the
whole Sum obtain'd by this Method amounted to only fifty two thousand nine hundred and nine Pounds.
A shameful Sum from so wealthy a Kingdom, and
a People who had pretended so much Loyalty to
that very King! Many had not Hearts to part
with their Cash; and many more, to incense the Ignorant, pretended it was contrary to Law, as if it
could be any Breach of Law for Subjects voluntarily to relieve the Wants of their Sovereign.

These

Thefe being all the Sums of any Moment rais'd for the Service of King *James* I. either by Authority of Parliament, or otherwife, we fhall proceed to his Son and Succeffor, under whom all the Mifchief that had before been hatching broke out, to the Deftruction of that unfortunate Monarch.

# K. CHARLES I.

SUcceeded his Father in the Year 1625. So much has been writ in Vindication of this King, that it will be altogether needlefs to attempt the giving him any Character in this Place; for which Reafon the Subject of his Revenue, not only the ftanding, but the few Sums given him by Parliament, and what his Neceffities oblig'd him to endeavour to raife otherwife, fhall be directly enter'd upon; and firft of the Parliamentary Grants. However, it is very well worth obferving, that as foon as the King came to the Crown, the Parliament appear'd wonderful zealous in Matters of Religion, and the Liberties of the Subject, and never defifted, or left harping upon thofe Strings, till the King had loft his Head, and the Government in Church and State was reduc'd to a perfect Anarchy, skipping from one Religion to another, and fearching fo narrowly for the Liberties of the Subject, that they were entirely loft.

However, it appears that in the King's firft Year the Spirituality granted him three entire Subfidies, and the Temporality two; but double the fame from Roman Catholicks.

The third Year the Spirituality granted five Subfidies, and the Temporality five.

The Statute Book has no more Seffions till the fixteenth Year, and then a Subfidy granted to the

T King

King of Tonnage and Poundage, and other Sums
of Money payable upon Merchandize exported and
imported.    Alfo an Act for the fpeedy Provifion of
Money for disbanding the Armies, and fettling the
Peace of the two Kingdoms of *England* and *Scotland.*

The Supply abovemention'd to have been granted the firft Year, was a fmall Compliance upon
his firft coming to the Crown; but more efpecially
to involve him in the Expence of a War about the
*Palatinate,* which his Father had long oppos'd, as
thinking it unjuft, and therefore himfelf not oblig'd
to enter into it.    However, at the laft, they had
forc'd him into it; but he died before it could be
brought to bear, and therefore left it as a Legacy
to his Son, who readily embrac'd it, as he did
afterwards fome other things, which in the end
brought him into many Troubles, and to a miferable Death.    This was however a poor Supply for
what he was going to undertake; yet he accepted
of it, hoping for much greater Affiftance; but
they had other Views, and inftead of relieving his
Wants fell to teazing of him with endlefs Grievances, whereupon the Parliament was diffolv'd.

The King being now engag'd in a War, the
Charges increas'd, and nothing to fupport them to
be expected from a Parliament; whereupon it was
refolv'd to get what Money might be by way of
Loan, Letters under the Privy-Seal being fent to
that effect to the wealthieft Perfons in the Kingdom, the King promifing for himfelf and his Heirs
to repay the Money fo lent him in eighteen Months
after the Receipt thereof.

This being but an indifferent Shift, the Parliament met again on the fixth of *February* following,
when, tho' the King fhow'd them the Neceffity he
was drove to, not being able to pay his Navy and

                                                    fupply

fupply other Wants, they ran on in the Courfe they had began about Religion and Grievances; and a Member of the Commons did not ftick to fay, *it was better to die by a foreign Enemy, than to be deftroy'd at home.* His Majefty feeing no likelihood of any Money to be obtain'd, but on the contrary all flying in his Face, again diffolv'd the Parliament; and being left deftitute, by the Advice of his Council, appointed Commiffioners to receive, by way of Loan, fome Subfidies which had been voted by the Commons, but never pafs'd into an Act. Some confiderable Sums of Money were rais'd this way, but very fhort of what had been expected, many refufing to pay, for which fome of them were committed to Prifon.

On the 17th of *March* 16$\frac{27}{28}$, the Parliament met again, and the King roundly putting them in mind of their Duty, as well as his Wants, they unanimoufly voted him five Subfidies; yet they had no fooner done it than they immediately fell upon him in fuch outragious manner, among other things going about to deprive him of Tonnage and Poundage, which was the main Support of the Crown, that he was oblig'd to diffolve them with all Speed, and then rais'd the faid five Subfidies, which had not been pafs'd into a Law, by way of Loan, each Subfidy computed at 100000 *l.* fo the five amounting to 500000 *l.*

The Expences continuing, and no way appearing to fupply them by Parliament, the King was again put to his Shifts, and, by the Advice of feveral Men learned in the Law, made ufe of fuch Methods as the Law feem'd to allow of. According to which all Men that were poffefs'd of a Knight's Fee were oblig'd to take upon them the Honour of Knighthood, or to fine for avoiding it. A Knight's Fee, in the Reign of King *Edward* II.

had

had been afcertain'd at twenty Pounds *per Annum*;
but afterwards, that being too low, King *Henry* VI.
fet it at forty Pounds. This was a Law in Force,
tho' not put in Execution of late Years; fo that the
King in his Diftrefs made ufe of it, fummoning all
Perfons of full Age, and not Knights, being feiz'd
of Lands or Rents of the yearly Value of forty
Pounds, or more, to appear before the King by a
certain Day, to take upon them the Honour of
Knighthood, upon Failure whereof Procefs was
made againft them, and they were fin'd for the
fame; all which brought but about an hundred
thoufand Pounds into the *Exchequer*, a fmall Sum
for what was then wanting; whereupon his Majefty demanded four hundred thoufand Crowns of
the King of *France* for his Queen's Portion, which
was accordingly juftly paid; but this belongs not
to us, as not coming from the Subjects, nor indeed
was it fufficient to anfwer the Demand at that
Time.

We come now to the Year 1635, the ninth of
the King's Reign, remarkable for the Demand of
Ship-Money, which afterwards made fo great a
Noife, and became one of the Pretences for the
Rebellion. The King ftill labouring under his
ufual Difficulties, and no Hopes of bringing the
Parliament to any Moderation, *Noy*, the King's
Attorney-General, as able a Lawyer as any at that
Time or fince in *England*, after having examin'd
and fearch'd all Precedents, declar'd that the King
of his own Authority, without Confent of Par-
liament, might legally raife a Naval Aid for the
Defence of the Kingdom, in Time of Neceffity, of
which Neceffity he alone was the fole Judge. His
Majefty, not willing to venture upon fo nice a Matter upon only the Judgment of his Attorney-
General, writ to the Judges, who by their Oaths
                                              are

are his proper Counsellors in all difficult Points of Law, requiring their Opinion in that Case, who all unanimously to a Man return'd the following Answer:

*May it please your most excellent Majesty,*

" We have, according to your Majesty's Com-
" mand, severally and every Man by himself, and
" all of us together, taken into serious Considera-
" tion the Case and Questions sign'd by your Ma-
" jesty, and inclos'd in your Letter: And we are
" of Opinion, that when the Good and Safety of
" the Kingdom in general is concern'd, and the
" whole Kingdom in Danger, your Majesty may,
" by Writ under your Great Seal of *England,* com-
" mand all the Subjects of this your Kingdom,
" at their Charge, to provide and furnish such
" Number of Ships, with Men, Victual, Muni-
" tion, and for such Time as your Majesty shall
" think fit, for the Defence and Safeguard of the
" Kingdom from such Peril and Danger; and that
" by Law your Majesty may compel the doing
" thereof, in case of Refusal or Refractoriness.
" And we are also of Opinion, that in such Case
" your Majesty is the sole Judge, both of the
" Danger, and when and how the same is to be
" prevented and avoided.

| | |
|---|---|
| *John Bramston,* | *George Crook,* |
| *John Finch,* | *Thomas Trevor,* |
| *Humphry Davenport,* | *George Vernon,* |
| *John Denham,* | *Robert Barkley,* |
| *Richard Hutton,* | *Francis Crawly,* |
| *William Jones,* | *Richard Weston.* |

Thus

Thus did all the Judges of *England* agree that the King might lawfully raiſe that Ship-Money. It is true, that when Mr. *Hampden* had begun to ſet the Kingdom in a Flame, by refuſing to pay twenty Shillings, at which he was aſſeſs'd in this Duty, ſome of them flew back, and gave their Opinions contrary to what they had before done under their Hands; but ſtill the greater Number adher'd to their firſt Sentiments, and accordingly Judgment was given againſt *Hampden*, whoſe only Deſign in refuſing ſo ſmall a Trifle was to blow up the Coals of Rebellion, as became manifeſt, he being among the firſt that went into it, and appear'd in Arms againſt his Sovereign, paying for the ſame not only out of his Eſtate, but with his Life, being ſoon after kill'd in Defence of that infamous Cauſe.

Upon the aforeſaid Opinion of all the Judges, Writs were iſſu'd out for raiſing the ſaid Ship-Money; and the ſame was done for four Years ſucceſſively, the yearly Produce of it being computed at two hundred thouſand Pounds; and accordingly the Total of the four Years amounted to 800000 *l.*

During the long Intervals of Parliament, Money ſtill of Neceſſity grew ſcarcer, and the Rebellion breaking out in *Scotland*, more Occaſion for it than ever. This put the King upon asking Aid of the Clergy, who generally anſwer'd his Majeſty's Expectations to the beſt of their Power; for which they were ſufficiently rail'd at by all the Favourers of the Rebellion. The Roman Catholicks had it alſo ſignify'd to them, how much it would become them to expreſs their Loyalty by contributing towards the Support of his Majeſty. They accordingly exerted themſelves, raiſing a greater Sum of Money than could have been expected from ſo ſmall a Party. The Earl of *Clarendon* owns this Fact in his Hiſtory of the Rebellion, and at the
ſame

fame time inveighs againft thofe People for that
dutiful Behaviour, as if it had been a great piece
of Infolence in them to give their own to fupport
their Sovereign ; but it is not only in this Cafe
that he runs down the beft of that King's Friends,
and extols his moft inveterate Enemies. Whofoever
will read him with Attention, may perceive that
Practice to run through his whole Work.

Next, tho' it was not a Money Tax, it may
not be improper to obferve the Method the
King was oblig'd to take for raifing an Army
againft the *Scots*, for as much as the fame was at
the Coft and Expence of the People, and confequently a Charge upon them, and for the Defence
of the Nation.

*The Countries that were appointed to fet out
Horfe and Foot againft the* Scots, *were*

|  | Foot. | Horfe. |
|---|---|---|
| Kent | 1200 | 150 |
| Cornwall | 1500 | 000 |
| Somerfet | 1200 | 150 |
| Wilts | 700 | 78 |
| Bedford | 200 | 40 |
| Berks | 400 | 44 |
| Middlefex | 750 | 40 |
| Buckingham | 300 | 40 |
| Oxon | 300 | 40 |
| Cambridge | 400 | 40 |
| Suffolk | 1500 | 50 |
| Dorfet | 700 | 50 |
| Devon | 2000 | 60 |
| Effex | 1500 | 120 |
| Gloucefter | 1000 | 100 |
| Warwick | 300 | 44 |

<br>

T 4

*Hartford*

| | Foot. | Horse |
|---|---|---|
| Hartford | 500 | 40 |
| Norfolk | 1800 | 200 |
| Northampton | 700 | 150 |
| Southampton | 1000 | 85 |
| Surry | 500 | 65 |
| Sussex | 640 | 80 |
| London | 3000 | 000 |

## WALES.

| | Foot. | Horse |
|---|---|---|
| Flint | 60 | 25 |
| Anglesey | 100 | 22 |
| Brecknock | 100 | 17 |
| Cardigan | 50 | 17 |
| Carmarthen | 100 | 17 |
| Caernarvon | 500 | 12 |
| Denbigh | 250 | 25 |
| * Glamorgan | 1000 | 100 |
| Monmouth | 500 | 56 |
| Pembroke | 150 | 50 |
| Montgomery | 100 | 100 |
| Radnor | 50 | 50 |
| Hereford | 150 | 40 |
| Shropshire | 300 | 35 |
| Worcester | 300 | 35 |
| Merioneth | 150 | 23 |
| Bristol | 50 | 00 |

The total Sum of Foot      23670

Total Sum of Horse      2366

* This seems a Mistake.

*Another*

*Another Lift quite different from that above.*

|  | Pikes. | Mufqueteers. |  |
|---|---|---|---|
| Cumberland | 125 | 125 | 50 Dragoons. |
| Northumberland | 250 | 250 | 100 Dragoons. |
| Weftmerland | 125 | 125 | 50 Dragoons. |
| Newcaftle | 250 | 250 | 340 Dragoons. |
| York | 5521 | 6720 | 60 Horfe. |
| Durham | 532 | 500 | 00 |
| Lancafbire | 420 | 180 | 50 Dragoons. |
| Northumberland | 282 | 125 | 00 |
| Chefbire | 356 | 244 | 50 Car. |
| Stafford | 248 | 152 | 30 Horfe. |
| Derby | 239 | 161 | 70 Horfe. |
| Lincoln | 1080 | 720 | 230 Car. |
| Leicefter | 290 | 110 | 38 Horfe. |
| Rutland | 60 | 40 | 30 Horfe. |

*Weftmerland, Cumberland, Northumberland,* and the Town of *Newcaftle,* not to march into the Field but upon fpecial Direction.

| Total of all the Foot in the other ten Counties | 19483 |
|---|---|
| Total of all the Horfe | 1233 |

The more Southern Counties to provide Horfes and Carriages for the Artillery, Ammunition, &c.

|  | Horfes. | Carters. |
|---|---|---|
| Bedford | 50 | 17 |
| Berks | 30 | 10 |
| Buckingham | 50 | 17 |
| Cambridge | 50 | 17 |

*Derby*

|            | Horses. | Carters. |
|------------|---------|----------|
| Derby      | 60      | 20       |
| Dorset     | 20      | 7        |
| Essex      | 60      | 20       |
| Gloucester | 50      | 17       |
| Hertford   | 50      | 17       |
| Hereford   | 30      | 10       |
| Huntingdon | 50      | 17       |
| Kent       | 20      | 7        |
| Leicester  | 70      | 23       |
| Lancaster  | 50      | 17       |
| Lincoln    | 60      | 20       |
| Middlesex  | 30      | 10       |
| Norfolk    | 60      | 20       |
| Northampton| 70      | 23       |
| Nottingham | 50      | 17       |
| Oxon       | 40      | 13       |
| Rutland    | 20      | 7        |
| Salop      | 40      | 13       |
| Somerset   | 20      | 7        |
| Southampton| 50      | 17       |
| Stafford   | 50      | 17       |
| Suffolk    | 60      | 20       |
| Warwick    | 60      | 20       |
| Worcester  | 50      | 17       |
| Wilts      | 50      | 17       |

| Total of Horses | 1350 |
|-----------------|------|

The Difference between these two Lists is very great, and no way to be reconcil'd; but they are deliver'd as handed down to us. However, the first of them seems to carry much the greater Probability, as dividing the Burden more equally than the latter.

Mono-

Monopolies having now made a great Clamour, by which the King had alfo obtain'd fome fmall Supplies, and his Majefty being willing to give the People Satisfaction in all Points, he now recall'd and made void all Patents and Grants to that effect, which here follow as mention'd in his royal Proclamation for abolifhing the fame :

A Commiffion touching Cottages and Inmates.

A Commiffion touching Scriveners and Brokers.

A Commiffion for compounding with Offenders touching Tobacco.

A Commiffion for compounding with Offenders for tranfporting of Butter.

A Commiffion for compounding with Offenders in the importing or ufing of Logwood.

A Commiffion to compound with Sheriffs, and fuch as have been Sheriffs, for felling their Under-Sheriffs Places.

A Commiffion for compounding for Deftruction of Woods in iron Works.

A Commiffion for Concealments and Incroach-ments within twenty Miles of *London.*

A Licence to tranfport Sheeps Skins and Lambs Skins.

A Commiffion to take Men bound to drefs no Venifon, Pheafants, or Partridges, in Inns, Ale-houfes, Ordinaries and Taverns.

A Commiffion touching the licenfing of the Ufe of Wine-Casks.

A Commiffion for licenfing of Brewers.

A Licence for the fole tranfporting of Lamperns.

A Grant for weighing Hay and Straw in *London* and *Weftminfter,* and three Miles compafs.

An Office of Regifter to the Commiffion for Bankrupts in divers Counties of the Realm.

An Office or Grant for gauging of Red-Her-rings.

An Office or Grant for the marking of Iron made within the Realm.

An Office or Grant for fealing of Bonelace.

A Grant for marking and gauging of Butter-Casks.

A Grant of Privilege touching Kelp and Sea-Weed.

A Grant for fealing of linen Cloth.

A Grant for the gathering of Rags.

An Office or Grant of Factory for *Scottish* Merchants.

An Office or Grant for fearching and fealing of foreign Hops.

An Office and Grant for the fealing of Buttons.

All Grants of Fines, Penalties, and Forfeitures, before Judgment granted or mention'd to be granted, by Letters-Patents, Privy-Seals, Signet, Sign-Manual, or otherwife.

All Patents for new Inventions, not put in Practice within three Years next after the Date of the faid Grants.

And the feveral Grants of Incorporation made unto Hatband-makers, Gutftring-makers, Spectacle-makers, Comb-makers, Tobacco-pipe-makers, Butchers, and Horners.

By thefe, and all other Projects of fmall Note, his Majefty is reckon'd to have receiv'd to the Value of about 200000 Pounds.

*Anno* 1639, the fifteenth of his Reign, the *Scottish* Rebellion running high, the King was oblig'd again to have recourfe to Ship-Money, the feveral Counties being charg'd to furnifh Ships as follows:

*Diftri-*

*Diftribution of Ships to the feveral Counties of* England *and* Wales, *with their Tunnage and Number of Men, as the fame was order'd to ftand this prefent Year.*

|  | Ships. | Men. | Tuns. |
|---|---|---|---|
| Berks | 1 | 128 | 320 |
| Buckingham | 1 | 144 | 360 |
| Bedford | 1 | 96 | 240 |
| Briftol | 1 | 26 | 64 |
| Cornwall | 1 | 176 | 440 |
| Cambridge | 1 | 112 | 280 |
| Cumberland and Weftmorland | 1 | 45 | 112 |
| Chefter | 1 | 96 | 240 |
| Devon | 1 | 288 | 720 |
| Darby | 1 | 112 | 280 |
| Dorfet | 1 | 160 | 400 |
| Durefm | 1 | 64 | 160 |
| Effex | 1 | 256 | 640 |
| Gloucefter | 1 | 176 | 440 |
| Hampfhire | 1 | 192 | 480 |
| Hereford | 1 | 112 | 280 |
| Huntington | 1 | 64 | 160 |
| Hertford | 1 | 128 | 320 |
| Kent and Ports | 1 | 256 | 640 |
| Lancafter | 1 | 128 | 320 |
| Leicefter | 1 | 144 | 360 |
| Lincoln | 1 | 256 | 640 |
| London | 2 | 448 | 1220 |
| Middlefex | 1 | 160 | 400 |
| Monmouth | 1 | 48 | 120 |
| Northampton | 1 | 192 | 480 |
| Nottingham | 1 | 112 | 280 |
| Northumberland | 1 | 64 | 168 |

North-

|             | Ships. | Men. | Tuns. |
|-------------|--------|------|-------|
| North-Wales | 1      | 128  | 320   |
| Norfolk     | 1      | 253  | 624   |
| Oxon        | 1      | 112  | 280   |
| Rutland     | 1      | 26   | 64    |
| Somerset    | 1      | 256  | 640   |
| Surrey      | 1      | 112  | 280   |
| Sussex      | 1      | 160  | 400   |
| Suffolk     | 1      | 256  | 640   |
| Stafford    | 1      | 96   | 240   |
| South-Wales | 1      | 160  | 400   |
| Salop       | 1      | 144  | 360   |
| Warwick     | 1      | 128  | 320   |
| Worcester   | 1      | 112  | 280   |
| Wilts       | 1      | 224  | 560   |
| York        | 1      | 384  | 960   |

Every County was affefs'd for this Charge in
Proportion to the Number of Men and Tuns; and
the following Year 1640, *Reg.* 16, there was another Impofition upon the feveral Counties as follows :

*The Proportion of Soldiers that were to be
rais'd in each County to be fent by Sea into Scotland.*

| Sussex | 600 | Huntingdon | 400 |
|--------|-----|------------|-----|
| Surry | 800 | Suffolk | 600 |
| Kent | 700 | Norfolk | 750 |
| Cinque-Ports | 300 | Cambridge | 300 |
| Middlesex | 1200 | Bedford | 400 |
| Hertford | 650 | Lincoln | 200 |
| Essex | 700 | Nottingham | 300 |
| Buckingham | 500 | Derby | 400 |
| London | 1200 | | |
| | | Total | 10000 |

The

The Refidue of the Army to be rais'd in the Northern Counties, and to march by Land to *Newcaſtle upon Tine.* Thefe Soldiers to be allow'd, at the Charge of each County, eight Pence a Day to every Man, for every Day they ſhall be exercis'd, and from the tenth of *May* till the twentieth. The Charge alfo of conducting the faid Men to the general Rendezvous of the County to be borne by the County. The Carriage of the Artillery to be alfo at the Charge of the refpective County through which it fhould paſs, at the Rate of 12 *d. per Diem* for every Horfe, and 8 *d. per Diem* for every Carter.

After all this, the Parliament met in the Year 1641, and having brought the King to their Beck, obliging him againft his Confcience to cut off the Earl of *Strafford,* and to his own Deſtruction to perpetuate their Sitting, they gave, for the Payment of the Army, and other Debts of the Kingdom, a Pole-Tax, wherein every Duke was affefs'd at 100 *l.* a Marquefs at 80 *l.* Earls at 60 *l.* Vifcounts and Barons at 40 *l.* Knights of the *Bath* at 30 *l.* Knights Batchelors at 20 *l.* Efquires at 10 *l.* every Gentleman fpending 100 *l. per Annum* at 5 *l.* and all others of Ability a competent Proportion ; the meaneft throughout the whole Kingdom was not excus'd under fix Pence. Three hundred thoufand Pounds were alfo agreed to be paid to the *Scots,* 100000 *l.* thereof at *Midfummer* come twelve Months, and the other 200000 *l.* two Years after, and fecur'd to them by Act of Parliament.

What Supplies the King had afterwards to fupport his War againft the Rebels cannot poffibly be computed, or any way accounted for. Much Money there muſt be of neceffity for fuch great Expences; but the Methods of raifing it could not be regular. The main Particulars that appear
were

were Contributions from the Country, and Loans from the loyal Gentry, among whom the Earl of *Newcastle* was very remarkable, launching out all he was able to raise and maintain Forces in Defence of his Sovereign. Another of no less Rank in Generosity was the Marquess of *Worcester*, then a Roman Catholick, who, at several times, lent his Majesty an hundred thousand Pounds. Others there were who rais'd Horse and Foot, and advanc'd Money for the Service; but neither are all known, nor the Value they contributed; and it would be tedious to mention as many as could be found. The Queen's pawning her Jewels to supply her royal Consort, and other Sums which came not from the People, do not so particularly relate to the Subjects, as to require to be here mention'd. This is what can be deliver'd in relation to King *Charles* I. tho' he reign'd some Years longer, till murder'd by his Subjects in such publick Manner as never any other Monarch was. The following Taxes and Contributions must be plac'd to the Account of

## The REBELS.

AS soon as they had by their Insolences drove the King from *London*, they began to exercise their tyrannical Power, and setting their seditious Preachers to work, blew the People into such a Flame, that nothing but their own Ruin could please them. The City of *London* went foremost in all Mischief; their Money and Plate was found to carry on the Destruction of the Nation, the poorest Wenches being so eager for carrying on that good Cause, as they call'd it, as to throw in their silver Bodkins and Thimbles for want of better Jewels.

The

The Men ran headlong to Perdition, all Degrees
vying to outdo one another in Treason againſt
their Sovereign. In ſhort, the Infection ſpread
throughout the Nation; no Corner of it was free
from Rebellion; and thoſe who had grudg'd their
lawful Prince the meaneſt Supplies, now thought
not much to laviſh out their All, to ſupport an
unjuſt Power, that not only ſtript, but flea'd them.
Much has been written of thoſe Times, and this
Place requires no more than what relates to Taxes
and Impoſitions, and all ſorts of Treaſure ſcrew'd
from the People. To deſcend to all Particulars
would require a Volume as large as this: For
which Reaſon here ſhall be only ſome ſummary
Accounts inſerted, ſuch as might appear ſufficient
to deter all thinking Perſons from running into Rebellion, but that the thinking Part of the World
is much the leaſt, and we find by Experience that
no paſt Examples are of Force to reſtrain thoſe that
come after from falling into the ſame Follies they
have known others ruin'd by before. The following is a juſt Calculation of what was rais'd during
thoſe Times of Anarchy.

*The ſeveral Sums of Money rais'd in* England
*by the* Long-Parliament, Oliver Cromwel,
*and the other then uſurping Powers, from*
November 3, 1640, *to* November 5, 1659.

### The Long-Parliament's *Account.*

|  | l. | s. | d. |
|---|---|---|---|
| SUbſidies, ſix come to | 600000 | 0 | 0 |
| Aſſeſſments to disband the Scotch and Engliſh Armies | 800000 | 0 | 0 |
| Tonnage and Poundage 19 Years | 5700000 | 0 | 0 |

V                          Captives

|  | l. | s. | d. |
|---|---|---|---|
| Captives nine Years | 27000 | 0 | 0 |
| *Ditto* five Years | 75000 | 0 | 0 |
| Sale of *Irish* Lands | 1200000 | 0 | 0 |
| Second Sale | 92500 | 0 | 0 |
| Third Sale | 30000 | 0 | 0 |
| Contribution for *Irish* Proteftants | 100000 | 0 | 0 |
| Second Contribution | 50000 | 0 | 0 |
| Third Contribution | 30000 | 0 | 0 |
| Affeffments thro' *England* for the *Britifh* Army in *Ireland* for five Years | 1200000 | 0 | 0 |
| Twentieth Parts of Goods, &c. to raife an Army for the Earl of *Effex*, for the Defence of *England* | 2745055 | 0 | 0 |
| *Ditto* fecond time | 2745055 | 0 | 0 |
| Weekly Affeffments towards Payment of the faid Army, three Years | 5617583 | 8 | 0 |
| Weekly Meal to raife Auxiliaries, fix Years | 608400 | 0 | 0 |
| Monthly Affeffments towards Payment of the faid Army, two Years | 488064 | 0 | 0 |
| Sir *William Waller's* Army's weekly Affeffment, one Year | 84258 | 5 | 0 |
| The *Scots* Army's weekly Affeffment, two Years | 168000 | 0 | 0 |
| *Brown's* Army's weekly Affeffment, one Year | 38400 | 0 | 0 |
| *Fairfax's* Army's monthly Affeffment, at 36366 *l.* three Years | 1327726 | 4 | 0 |
| *Ditto* at 60000 *l. per* Month for two Years | 1440000 | 0 | 0 |
| *Ditto* at 90000 *l. per* Month for one Year, &c. | 1080000 | 0 | 0 |

Forces

*Forces rais'd on particular Counties,* &c.

|  | *l.* | *s.* | *d.* |
|---|---:|---|---|
| *Exon,* for five Years, comes to | 12000 | o | o |
| *Hertford* one Year, then affociated | 4800 | o | o |
| *Ifle of Wight* four Years | 1900 | o | o |
| *Warwick, &c.* affociated, five Years | 133650 | o | o |
| *Plymouth,* four Years | 28800 | o | o |
| *Yarmouth,* four Years | 19200 | o | o |
| *Ailsbury,* five Years | 1000 | o | o |
| *Buckingham,* four Years | 76800 | o | o |
| *Eaftern* Affociation, five Years | 1234962 | 10 | o |
| *Dorfet* and *Pool,* two Years, and then affociated | 24780 | o | o |
| *Kent, &c.* affociated, five Years | 270000 | o | o |
| *North-Wales, &c.* five Years | 38652 | o | o |
| *Northampton,* five Years | 119200 | o | o |
| *Huntington,* two Years, and then affociated | 13200 | o | o |
| *Southampton,* four Years | 115200 | o | o |
| *Newport-Pannel,* one Year, then affociated | 49000 | o | o |
| *London, &c.* five Years | 1005600 | o | o |
| *Hull,* five Years | 46600 | o | o |
| *Chefter* County and City, one Year, then affociated | 6944 | o | o |
| *Gloucefter* County and City, three Years | 163400 | o | o |
| *Pembroke, &c.* affociated, three Years | 20090 | o | o |
| *Salop,* three Years | 57000 | o | o |
| *Leicefter,* three Years | 86400 | o | o |
| *Wilts* and *Malmsbury,* one Year, then affociated | 2900 | o | o |
| *Weftern,* affociated four Years | 509160 | o | o |
| *Worcefter, &c.* three Years | 51597 | 12 | o |
| *Middlefex,* three Years | 108000 | o | o |

|  | l. | s. | d. |
|---|---|---|---|
| *London*, to set up Posts and Chains | 96000 | 0 | 0 |
| *Lincoln*, three Years | 117600 | 0 | 0 |
| *Darby*, three Years | 48000 | 0 | 0 |
| *Northern* Association, three Years | 433831 | 14 | 0 |
| *Rutland*, three Years | 29000 | 0 | 0 |
| *Surrey*, three Years | 44000 | 0 | 0 |
| *Newark* to be reduc'd, cost | 9916 | 12 | 0 |
| *Lancaster*, two Years | 72000 | 0 | 0 |
| *Newport*, two Years | 89904 | 0 | 0 |
| *London* to assess for Horses and Arms | 10000 | 0 | 0 |
| Provision for maim'd Soldiers, &c. | 18180 | 0 | 0 |
| Excise for seventeen Years | 10200000 | 0 | 0 |
| Duty on Coals, seventeen Years | 850000 | 0 | 0 |
| Duty on Currants, seventeen Years | 51000 | 0 | 0 |

## *Sequestrations of Delinquents Estates,* viz.

|  | l. | s. | d. |
|---|---|---|---|
| Bishops Lands, four Years | 884089 | 16 | 7 |
| Dean and Chapters Lands, four Years | 564740 | 18 | 6 |
| Inferior Clergy's Lands, four Years | 2077802 | 1 | 3 |
| Temporal Estates, four Years | 280000 | 0 | 0 |
| Crown Lands, four Years | 280000 | 0 | 0 |
| Composition for Court of Wards, four Years | 400000 | 0 | 0 |
| Deans Forest, four Years | 16000 | 0 | 0 |
| Fee-Farm-Rents, four Years | 1054392 | 0 | 0 |
| Tenths of the Clergy, four Years | 400080 | 0 | 8 |
| Prince of *Wales*'s Income | 80000 | 0 | 0 |
| Timber for the Navy out of Delinquents Woods | 7760 | 0 | 0 |
| Postage of Letters, fourteen Years | 301000 | 0 | 0 |
| Wine Licence, fourteen Years | 312200 | 0 | 0 |

Compo-

|  | *l.* | *s.* | *d.* |
|---|---|---|---|
| Compofitions for Court of Wards, ten Years | 1000000 | 0 | 0 |
| Income of Offices for publick Service, fifteen Years | 850000 | 0 | 0 |
| Vintners Delinquency | 4000 | 0 | 0 |
| Compounding with Delinquents for their Eftates | 1277226 | 0 | 0 |
| Disbanding the Army | 900000 | 0 | 0 |
| Militia of *England* kept up, thirteen Years | 3120000 | 0 | 0 |
| *Oliver*'s Expedition to *Ireland* | 150000 | 0 | 0 |

### Sale of Lands, viz.

|  | *l.* | *s.* | *d.* |
|---|---|---|---|
| Bifhops Lands at ten Years | 2420224 | 11 | $6\frac{1}{2}$ |
| Dean and Chapters Lands, ten Years | 1411852 | 6 | 8 |
| Rectory and Glebe Lands, twelve Years | 6203586 | 3 | 9 |
| Crown Lands, thirteen Years | 9152000 | 0 | 0 |
| Prince of *Wales*'s Lands, thirteen Years | 260000 | 0 | 0 |
| Fee-Farm-Rents, eight Years | 1908784 | 0 | 0 |
| New-River-Water, eight Years | 8000 | 0 | 0 |
| Tenths of the Clergy, eight Years | 1200240 | 2 | 0 |
| Lord *Craven* and others Eftates, at thirteen Years | 700000 | 0 | 0 |
| *Gifford* and others Eftates, at thirteen Years | 900000 | 0 | 0 |
| Sir *John Stawell* and others, five Years | 560000 | 0 | 0 |
| Foreft Lands, thirteen Years | 56000 | 0 | 0 |
| Houfes and Caftles of the King's | 600000 | 0 | 0 |

*John*

|  | *l.* | *s.* | *d.* |
|---|---|---|---|
| *John* and *William*, *Peter*, and divers others, *viz.* 171 Persons, their Estates to pay Prince Palatine of the *Rhine* 5000 *l.* in Arrear, and 8000 *l. per Annum.* | 85000 | 0 | 0 |
| *Oliver* made Captain-General of *Fairfax*'s Forces, and the Assessment for the Armies of *England*, *Scotland*, and *Ireland*, 90000 *l. per* Month for two Years | 2160000 | 0 | 0 |
| Assessments of 120000 *l. per* Month for the said Army and Navy, one Year | 1440000 | 0 | 0 |
| Drums and Colours 90000 *l. per Annum* for ten Years | 900000 | 0 | 0 |
| *Irish* Delinquents to compound for two Years Rents | 1000000 | 0 | 0 |
| *Oliver* voted Protector, and he assess'd for the Army 120000 *l.* and 90000 *l.* for three Months | 630000 | 0 | 0 |
| Agreed 60000 *l. per* Month be the Pay of the Arms for six Years | 4320000 | 0 | 0 |
| To defray the Charges of Justice 200000 *l. per Annum* six Years | 1200000 | 0 | 0 |
| Free Gifts to the Saints in Money | 679800 | 0 | 0 |
| In Places (excluding the Army and Navy) *per Annum*, seven Years | 306110 | 0 | 0 |
| In Estates *per Annum*, for eleven Years | 189365 | 0 | 0 |

Besides,

|  | l. | s. | d. |
|---|---|---|---|
| Besides, the House of Commons voted each of their Members 4 *l. per* Week, and count but 256 Members, and no more, for fourteen Years | 745472 | 0 | 0 |

| Total | 95512095 | 5 | 11½ |

*A general Abstract of Money rais'd in* England *by the Long-Parliament, from* November 3, 1640, *to* November 1659.

|  | l. | s. | d. |
|---|---|---|---|
| Subsidies | 600000 | 0 | 0 |
| The Armies | 32780721 | 13 | 0 |
| Tonnage and Poundage | 5700000 | 0 | 0 |
| Captives | 102000 | 0 | 0 |
| Sale of *Irish* Lands | 1322500 | 0 | 0 |
| Contributions for *Irish* Protestants | 180000 | 0 | 0 |
| Forces for Defence of particular Counties | 4141088 | 8 | 0 |
| Excises | 10200000 | 0 | 0 |
| Duty on Coals | 850000 | 0 | 0 |
| *Ditto* on Currants | 51000 | 0 | 0 |
| Sequestrations of Estates | 6044924 | 17 | 0 |
| Postage of Letters | 301000 | 0 | 0 |
| Wine Licences | 312200 | 0 | 0 |
| Composition for Court of Wards | 1000000 | 0 | 0 |
| Offices to Publick Service | 850000 | 0 | 0 |
| Vintners Delinquency | 4000 | 0 | 0 |
| Compositions for Estates | 1277226 | 0 | 0 |
| Sale of *English* Lands | 25380687 | 3 | 11½ |
| Settled out of Gentlemens Estates to pay P. *Palatin* | 85000 | 0 | 0 |
| Compound with *Irish* Delinquents | 1000000 | 0 | 0 |

V 4             Charge

| | *l.* | *s.* | *d.* |
|---|---|---|---|
| Charge of Juſtice, ſix Years | 1200000 | 0 | 0 |
| To the Houſe of Commons, fourteen Years, comes to | 745472 | 0 | 0 |
| Free Gifts to the Saints, *viz.* in Money | 679800 | 0 | 0 |
| in Offices | 306110 | 0 | 0 |
| in Eſtates *per Annum* | 189365 | 0 | 0 |
| Total | 95512095 | 5 | 11½ |

Mr. *Walker*, no leſs a Rebel than thoſe he rails at in his Hiſtory of Independency, having run through all the Rebellion with them, till they turn'd him off, and therefore well acquainted with their Methods of raiſing Money, and the Amount thereof, ſums up the ſame after this Manner:

Nor is it a ſmall Artifice to raiſe Money by ſo many ſeveral and confus'd Taxes, whereas one or two Ways would have done the Work; 1. Royal Subſidy of 300000 *l.* 2. Pole-Money. 3. The free Loans and Contributions upon the publick Faith amounted to a vaſt incredible Sum of Money, Plate, Horſe, Arms, *&c.* 4. *Iriſh* Adventure for Sale of Lands, the firſt and ſecond time; 5. The Weekly Meal. 6. The City Loan after the Rate of fifty Subſidies. 7. The Aſſeſſment for bringing in the *Scots*. 8. The five and twentieth Part. 9. The weekly Aſſeſſment for my Lord General's Army. 10. The weekly or monthly Aſſeſſment for Sir *Thomas Fairfax*'s Army. 11. The weekly Aſſeſſment for the *Scots* Army. 12. The weekly Aſſeſſment for the *Britiſh* Army in *Ireland*. 13. The weekly Aſſeſſment for my Lord of *Mancheſter*'s Army. 14. Free Quarter (at leaſt) conniv'd at by the State; becauſe the Soldiers having for a time Sub-

ſiſtance

fiftance that way, are the lefs craving for their Pay, whereby their Arrears growing ftale, will at laft either be fruftrated by a tedious Committee of Accounts, or forgotten ; in the mean time the Grand Committee of Accounts difcount it out of the Commanders Arrears, whereby the State faves it. 15. The King's Revenue. 16. Sequeftrations and Plunder by Committees, which, if well anfwer'd to the State, would have carry'd on the Work ; which thus I demonftrate : One half of all the Goods and Chattels, and (at leaft) one half of all the Lands, Rents, and Revenues of the Kingdom have been fequefter'd ; and who can imagine that one half of the Profits and Goods of the Land will not maintain any Forces that can be kept and fed in *England* for the Defence thereof ? 17. Excife upon all things. This alone, if well manag'd, would maintain the War ; the *Low Countries* make it almoft the only Support. 18. Fortification Money, *&c.* By thefe feveral Ways and Taxes about forty Millions in Money and Money-worth have been milk'd from the People. A vaft Treafure, and fo exceffive, as nothing but a long Peace could import, and nothing but much Fraud and many Follies could diffipate ; and we ought not to wonder if it be accounted *inter Arcana noviffimi Imperii,* to be always making, yet never finifhing an Account thereof.

It is here to be obferv'd, that the forty Millions he here fpeaks of were only to the Year 1647 ; fo that they had not been above five Years raifing and expending them. Nor is it lefs remarkable, that *Walker* had gone Hand in Hand in the Parliament with the Extorters and Confumers of all this Treafure, being himfelf as deep concern'd as any other in the Villany, and yet never faw into it, till the *In-*
*dependents*

*dependents* thruft him and his *Presbyterian* Party from having any Share in the Cheat.

*An Abftract of the vaft Rewards many of the Rebels beftow'd on themfelves for having brought the Kingdom to Ruin, which were all Ufurpations upon the Crown and the Nation.*

*William Lenthal*, Speaker of the Houfe of Commons, worth 2000 *l. per Annum*, befides Bribes; Mafter of the Rolls, worth 3000 *l. per Annum*, befides the Sale of Offices; Chamberlain of *Chefter*, Chancellor of the *Exchequer*, worth 1230 *l. per Annum*; and one of the Commiffioners of the Great-Seal, worth 1500 *l. per Annum*, befides 6000 *l.* given him at once by the Houfe of Commons.

*Bulftrode Whitlock*, Commiffioner of the Great-Seal, worth 1500 *l. per Annum*, and 2000 *l.* given him at once in Money.

*Edward Prideaux*, once Commiffioner of the Great-Seal, as above, afterwards practis'd as King's Council, worth 500 *l. per Annum*, and Poftmafter of the inland Letters, worth 100 *l. per* Week.

The Earl of *Warwick*, Poft-mafter of foreign Letters, worth 5000 *l. per Annum.*

*Roger Hill*, a petty Lawyer, 1200 *l. per Annum* out of the Bifhop of *Winchefter's* Lands.

*Francis Rous*, Provoft of *Eaton*, worth 600 *l. per Annum*, and a College Leafe worth 600 *l.* more.

*John Lifle*, Mafter of *St. Croft's*, worth 800 *l. per Annum.*

*Oliver St. John*, Attorney and Sollicitor, and paffing of Pardons and Commiffions, worth 40000 *l.*

*Thomas*

*Thomas Pury, sen.* a broken Weaver and ignorant Sollicitor, 3000 *l.* given him.

Sir *Gilbert Gerrard*, Paymaster of the Army, worth 60000 *l.*

*John Selden*, 5000 *l.* given him.

Sir *Benjamin Rudyard*, 5000 *l.* given him.

Sir *John Hipsley*, 2000 *l.* given him.

Sir *Thomas Walfingham*, the Honour of *Eltham* given him, and cut down Timber worth 4000 *l.*

*Benjamin Valentin*, 5000 *l.* given him.

Sir *Henry Heyman*, 5000 *l.* given him.

*Denzil Hollis*, 5000 *l.* given him.

*Nath. Bacon*, 3000 *l.* given him.

*John Stevens*, 1000 *l.* given him.

*Robert Reynolds*, 2000 *l.* given him, and Lands worth 400 *l. per Annum.*

Sir *John Clotworthy* charg'd with defrauding the State of 40000 *l.*

*John Ashe*, 14200 *l.* given him.

*Francis Pierpoint*, the Archbishop of *York*'s Lands lying in *Nottinghamshire* given him.

*William Pierpoint*, 7000 *l.* given him, and all the Earl of *Kingston*'s personal Estate, worth 40000 *l.*

*John Blackston*, supported in a Cheat of 6000 *l.* left by Sir *John Fenner* for charitable Uses, had 12000 *l.* given him in Money, the Bishop of *Durham's* Castle at *Durham*, and Lands of great Value.

—— *Scawine*, 2000 *l.* given him.

*Isaac Pennington*, 7000 *l.* given him, and many of the Bishops Lands.

*Samuel Vassel*, 1000 *l.* given him.

Sir *William Brereton* had *Cashiobery*, and other Lands of the Lord *Capel*'s, worth 2000 *l. per Annum*, given him, with the Archbishop's House and Lands at *Croydon.*

*John Ven*, 4000 *l.* given him.

*Cornelius*

*Cornelius Holland* had as much of the King's Land for 200 *l. per Annum* as was worth 16 or 1800.

*Philip Skippon,* 1000 *l. per Annum* Land of Inheritance given him.

*Thomas Westro,* the Bishop of *Worcester*'s Manor of *Harthero* given him.

Sir *Arthur Haslerig*, the Bishop of *Durham*'s House, Park, and Manor of *Aukland*, and 6500 *l.* in Money given him.

The Lord *Gray* of *Grooby*, the Queen's Manor-House, Park, and Lands at *Holdenby* given him.

Sir *William Constable* sold his Land to Sir *Marmaduke Langdale* for 25000 *l.* and was restor'd to it again by the Parliament.

Sir *William Purefoy,* 1500 *l.* given him.

Sir *Edward Hungerford* had the Lands of the Countess Dowager of *Rutland,* worth 1500 *l. per Annum,* given him.

*Walter Long,* 5000 *l.* given him.

*Thomas Scot,* the Bishop's House at *Lambeth* given him.

Mr. *Ashurt,* 1000 *l.* given him.

Every Member of the House of Commons allow'd 4 *l. per* Week.

This is only a Specimen of the Generosity of those Rebels to one another. Some of the Employments they had were mention'd among the first, to show that such Places of Profit were not sufficient for the Saints; for all the rest abovemention'd had also very gainful Places; but it seems needless to mention them, because it would be too tedious. If we were now to see what *Oliver Cromwell* allow'd himself, and all his Favourites, the Sum would be immense; and the same will be found to be the Practice under all Usurpations. Where there is no
Right,

Right, Bribery and Corruption is the main Support; and thofe who live and thrive upon the Spoil of their fellow Subjects, will not fail to ftand by the Injuftice for their own Intereft. We will now leave thefe Traitors to come to the Reftoration of the rightful Heir.

# K.  C H A R L E S  II.

OF whom too much has been writ by Friends and Enemies; and many are ftill living, who knew his Perfon, and his Government, which has been vilely flander'd by fcandalous Perfons, who think they can never fufficiently rail at rightful Monarchs, tho' all their Malice turns to their own eternal Infamy. I will not prefume to give a Character of this Prince, but will only in a few Words repeat what an impartial Foreigner fays of him, *viz.* That as a wife and prudent Perfon he governed his Dominions, and labour'd to fupprefs the Remains of Rebellion, which wicked Men labour'd to revive in his Dominions ; that he was the Patron of Learning, and by his wife Conduct made his Kingdom flourifh with Plenty, Trade and Peace. To come to the Point of Taxes and Impofitions, the firft we meet with was in the twelfth Year of this King's Reign, being the Year of his Reftoration, entitled,

*A Subsidy granted to the King of Tonnage and Poundage, and other Sums of Money payable upon Merchandize exported and imported (for Life) after the following Rates.*

|  | l. | s. | d. |
|---|---|---|---|
| Of every Ton of *French* Wine imported to *London*, and its Members, by the natural born Subjects of *England* | 4 | 10 | 00 |
| For every Ton of *French* Wine imported, as above, by Foreigners | 6 | 00 | 00 |
| For every Ton of *French* Wine imported into other Ports by *English* | 3 | 00 | 00 |
| The same by Aliens | 4 | 10 | 00 |
| For every But or Pipe of Muscadels, Malmseys, Cuts, Tents, Alicants, Bastards, Sacks, Canaries, Malagas, Maderas, and other Wines whatsoever, of the Growth of the *Levant*, *Spain*, *Portugal*, or any of their Dominions, brought to the Port of *London* by *English* | 2 | 5 | 00 |
| The same by Strangers | 3 | 00 | 00 |
| The same in other Ports, imported by *English* | 1 | 10 | 00 |
| By Foreigners | 2 | 05 | 00 |
| For every Awn of *Rhenish*, or other Wine of the Growth of *Germany*, imported by *English* | 1 | 00 | 00 |
| By Strangers | 1 | 05 | 00 |

For all Goods imported or exported 12 d. *per* Pound Value for the *English*; and for Strangers 2 s. *per* Pound Value.

For

|  | *l.* | *s.* | *d.* |
|---|---|---|---|
| For every Piece of broad Cloth exported by *English* | o | 03 | 04 |
| And by Strangers | o | 06 | 08 |
| And over and above the aforesaid Impositions on Wine, every Tun of Wine of the Growth of *France,* *Germany, Portugal* or *Madera,* to pay in nine Months after importing | 3 | 00 | 00 |
| And every Tun of other Wines | 4 | 00 | 00 |

The next was,

*An Act for Provision of Money to pay off the Armies and Navy,* being by way of Poll, and rated as follows. 1. Every Duke of *England, Scotland* and *Ireland,* residing in *England,* to pay 100 *l.* every Marquiss 80 *l.* every Earl 60 *l.* a Viscount 50 *l.* a Baron 40 *l.* The eldest Son of a Duke, one and twenty Years of Age, 60 *l.* of a Marquiss 50 *l.* of an Earl 40 *l.* of a Viscount 35 *l.* of a Baron 30 *l.* a Baronet 30 *l.* a Knight of the *Bath* 30 *l.* a Knight Batchelor 20 *l.* a Serjeant at Law 20 *l.* an Esquire 10 *l.* and every Widow, according to her Husband's Degree, a third Part of what her Husband was to pay.

2. Every Parson or Vicar possess'd of a Parsonage or Vicarage, or other Estate of 100 *l. per Annum,* 40 *s.* Every Doctor of the Civil or Canon Law 5 *l.* Every Advocate 5 *l.* A Judge or Commissioner in the Court of Admiralty 20 *l.* A Doctor of Physick 10 *l.*

3. The Lord Mayor of *London* 40 *l.* Every Sheriff or Alderman, or that has fin'd for Alderman, 20 *l.* Every Deputy Alderman 10 *l.* The Town Clerk of *London* 20 *l.* Every Common-Council-Man 5 *l.* Every Master of the first twelve Companies 10 *l.* Every Warden thereof 6 *l.* 13 *s.* 4 *d.* Every-Livery Man of those Companies 5 *l.* Every one who had been Master of the Companies

panies

panies of *Dyers, Brewers, Leatherſellers, Girdlers, Sta-*
*tioners, Woodmongers, Upholſterers, Apothecaries, Pew-*
*terers, Tallow-Chandlers, Armourers* or *Saddlers,* 6 *l.*
Every Warden of any of thoſe Companies 5 *l.* Every Livery-Man of them 3 *l.* Every Yeoman 1 *l.*
Every Maſter of the Company of *Barber-Surgeons,*
*White-bakers, Wax-Chandlers, Cutlers, Butchers, Car-*
*penters, Painters,Cordwainers, Coopers, Scriveners,Brown-*
*bakers, Turners,* or *Inn-holders,* 3 *l.* Every one who
had been Warden of any of thoſe Companies 2 *l.*
Every Livery-Man thereof 1 *l.* Every Perſon who
had been Maſter of the Company of *Founders, Cut-*
*lers, Maſons, Bricklayers, Joyners, Plaiſterers, Wea-*
*vers, Fruiterers, Marblers, Embroiderers, Poulterers,*
*Cooks* or *Plummers,* 1 *l.* Every Warden of thoſe Companies 15 *s.* and every one of the Livery 10 *s.* Every
Perſon that had been of the Livery of the Companies
of *Bowyers,Fletchers, Blackſmiths,Bottle-makers, Wool-*
*packers, Farriers, Paviers, Loriners, Glaziers, Clerks,*
or *Watermen,* 5 *s.* Every Freeman of any Company within the City of *London* 12 *d.* Every Keeper
of one or more Hackney Coaches,and two Horſes,
10 *s.* Every Merchant Stranger, if a Knight, 40 *l.*
if below that Degree, and trading to Sea, 10 *l.* if
trading within the Land, 5 *l.* Every Alien uſing
Trade within any City or Corporation, if a Houſekeeper, 10 *s.* Every *Engliſh* Merchant in or about
*London,* not a Freeman, 10 *l.* Every Factor in the
City 2 *l.* Every Perſon that had been an Alderman
in any City within the Kingdom, under the Degree of a Knight or Eſquire, 5 *l.*

4. The Prothonotary of the *King's-Bench* 100 *l.*
Clerk of the Crown of the ſame 20 *l.* *Cuſtos Bre-*
*vium* of the ſame 40 *l.* Marſhal of the ſame 50 *s.*
Maſter of the Rolls 60 *l.* Clerk of the Crown in
*Chancery* 40 *l.* Clerk of the Rules, and in the *King's-*
*Bench,* 10 *l.* Maſter of the *Subpœna* Office 10 *l.*

Warden

Warden of the Fleet 50 *l.* Clerk of the Hanaper
50 *l.* Clerks of the Inrollment, each 40 *l.* each of
the fix Clerks in Chancery 10 *l.* every Curfitor of
the fame 10 *l.* Ufher of the fame 10 *l.* every Clerk
of the Pettybag 5 *l.* every Examiner 10 *l.* Chief
Regifter of the fame 20 *l.* every Under-Regifter
10 *l.* every Clerk in the Office of the Six Clerks in
Chancery 8 *l.* each of the Clerks of the Chapel of
the Rolls 3 *l.* every Prothonotary of the Common-
Pleas 50 *l. Cuftos Brevium* of the fame 80 *l.* every
Filacer of the fame 10 *l.* Clerk of the Outlawries
20 *l.* Clerk of the Statutes 20 *l.* the Clerk of the
Treafury 10 *l.* Exigenter of *London* 40 *l.* every other
Exigenter 5 *l.* the King's Remembrancer of the
*Exchequer* 40 *l.* every Teller of the fame 20 *l.* the
Treafurer's Remembrancer 20 *l.* every Attorney of
the Office of the King's Remembrancer 10 *l.* every
Attorney of the Office of Pleas 10 *l.* the Remem-
brancer of the Firft-Fruits 20 *l.* Clerk of the
Eftreats 20 *l.* Clerk of the Pleas 30 *l.* the Auditor
of the Receipts in the *Exchequer* 40 *l.* Clerk of the
Pell in the Receipt 30 *l.* Ufher of the Court of
*Exchequer* 20 *l.* every Attorney of the Office of
Pleas there 10 *l.* every Auditor of the fame 10 *l.*
every Clerk of the Court of the Dutchy of *Lan-*
*cafter* 10 *l.* every Auditor of the fame 10 *l.* every
Clerk of the Privy-Seal 10 *l.* every Clerk of the
Signet 10 *l.* every Attorney in any of the Courts at
*Weftminfter,* or within the Courts of Law or Equity, or in the Counties Palatine of *Chefter, Lancafter,*
*Durham,* and the Marches of *Wales,* 3 *l.* every Perfon in any Office or Place under the King (except
his Houfhold Servants in ordinary) 10 *l.* the Lieutenant of the *Tower* of *London* 50 *l.* every one that
could fpend in Land, Leafe, Moneys, or Stock,
100 *l. per Annum,* 40 *s.* and fo for a greater or
leffer Eftate ; every fingle Perfon above the Age of

ſixteen Years 12 *d.* every Perſon not rated, nor receiving Alms, above ſixteen Years of Age, 6 *d.*

This was perhaps the greateſt Poll-Tax, and
moſt particular, that had been known ; but all the
Produce of it was for disbanding the Army, which
had for ſeveral Years ruin'd the Nation, and the
King receiv'd no Advantage by it; ſo that there
can be no Pretence to place any of it to his Account. However, this heavy Poll falling ſhort
for disbanding of the Army, the ſame Parliament
preſently after paſs'd another, entitled

*An Act for raiſing ſeven ſcore thouſand Pounds, for
the compleat disbanding of the Army.*

The next, being indeed for his Majeſty's Uſe,
was *An Act for the ſpeedy raiſing* 70000 *l. for the
preſent Supply of his Majeſty.*

The ſame Year paſs'd an Act for *A Grant of certain Impoſitions upon Beer, Ale, and other Liquors, for
the Increaſe of his Majeſty's Revenue during his Life.*
But it is to be obſerv'd, that at the ſame time the
Parliament took from the King the Court of
Wards, and Liveries, and Tenures *in Capite,* and
by Knights Service and Purveyance ; ſo that they
gave with one Hand, and cut off with the other.
The Rates then ſettled were, for every Barrel of
Beer or Ale, above ſix Shillings the Barrel, brew'd
to be ſold, 1 *s.* 3 *d.* for every Barrel of ſix Shillings
Beer, or under, brew'd for Sale, 3 *d.* for every
Hogſhead of Cyder ſold by Retail, 1 *s.* 3 *d.* for all
Metheglin and Mead ſold, for every Gallon one
Half-penny ; for every Barrel of Beer, commonly
call'd Vinegar-Beer, 6 *d.* for every Gallon of
ſtrong Water, or *Aqua-vitæ,* 1 *d.* for every Barrel
of Beer or Ale imported from beyond the Seas, 3 *s.*
for every Tun of Cyder, or Perry, imported from
beyond the Seas, 5 *s.* and ſo proportionably for a
greater or leſſer Quantity ; for every Gallon of
Spirits,

Spirits; made of any kind of Wine or Cyder imported, 2 *d.* for every Gallon of Strong Water, perfectly made, imported from beyond the Seas, 4 *d.* For every Gallon of Coffee made and fold, to be paid by the Maker thereof, 4 *d.* for every Gallon of Chocolate, Sherbet, and Tea, made and fold, to be paid by the Maker thereof, 8 *d.*

The fame Year ftill pafs'd *An Act for erecting and eftablifhing a Poft-Office,* which then brought in a Revenue of 21000 *l.* a year. It had been firft erected under *Oliver Cromwel's* Ufurpation. The Alterations made afterwards fhall be taken notice of in their Places: The Rates fettled at the Time we fpeak of were;

## *Inland Letters.*

For the Port of every Letter, not exceeding one Sheet, to or from any Place not exceeding fourfcore *Englifh* Miles diftant from the Place where fuch Letter fhall be receiv'd, 2 *d.*

For the like Port of every Letter, not exceeding two Sheets, 4 *d.*

And for the like Port of every Packet of Letters, proportionably unto the faid Rates.

And for the like Port of every Packet of Writs, Deeds, or other things, after the Rate of 8 *d.* for every Ounce Weight.

And for the Port of every Letter, not exceeding one Sheet, above the Diftance of four-fcore Miles from the Place where the fame fhall be receiv'd, 3 *d.*

And for the like Port of a Letter not exceeding two Sheets, 6 *d.* and proportionably to the fame Rates for the like Port of all Packets of Letters.

And

And for the like Port of every other Packet of Writs, Deeds, or other things, 12 *d.* for every Ounce Weight.

And for the Port of every Letter, not exceeding one Sheet, to and from *Dublin,* 6 *d.*

For two Sheets 1 *s.* and ſo proportionably; and for every Ounce 2 *s.*

For ſingle Letters carry'd forty Miles beyond *Dublin* 2 *d.* and ſo proportionably.

## *Letters to or from Places beyond the Sea.*

*Morlaix, St. Malo's, Caen, Newhaven,* and Places of the like Diſtance, Port paid to *Roan* is for ſingle 6 *d.* double 12 *d.* treble 18 *d.* Ounce 18 *d.*

*Hamburg, Cologn, Frankfort,* Port paid to *Antwerp,* ſingle 8 *d.* double 16 *d.* treble 24 *d.* Ounce 24 *d.*

*Venice, Geneva, Leghorn, Rome, Naples, Meſſina,* and all other Parts of *Italy* by way of *Venice,* frank'd for *Mantua,* ſingle 9 *d.* double 18 *d.* treble 2 *s.* 3 *d.* Ounce 2 *s.* 8 *d.*

*Marcelia, Smirna, Conſtantinople, Aleppo,* and all Parts of *Turkey,* Port paid to *Marcelia,* ſingle 1 *s.* double 2 *s.* three Quarters of an Ounce 2 *s.* 9 *d.* Ounce 3 *s.* 9 *d.*

And for Letters brought from the ſaid Places to *England,* ſingle 8 *d.* double 1 *s.* 4 *d.* treble 2 *s.* Ounce 2 *s.*

## *And for the Port Letters brought into* England *from*

*Calais, Diep, Bologn, Abbeville, Amiens, St. Omers, Montrel,* ſingle 4 *d.* double 8 *d.* treble 1 *s.* Ounce 1 *s.*

*Roan,* ſingle 6 *d.* double 1 *s.* treble 1 *s.* 6 *d.* Ounce 1 *s.* 6 *d.*

*Genoa,*

*Genoa, Leghorn, Rome,* and other Places of *Italy,* by way of *Lyons,* frank'd for *Lyons,* single 1 *s.* double 2 *s.* three Quarters of an Ounce 2 *s.* 9 *d.* Ounce 3 *s.* 9 *d.*

## And of Letters fent outwards.

To *Bourdeaux, Rochel, Nantz, Orleans, Bayon, Tours,* and Places of like Diftance, Port paid to *Paris,* single 9 *d.* double 1 *s.* 6 *d.* treble 2 *s.* 3 *d.* Ounce 2 *s.* 3 *d.*

And for Letters brought from the fame Places to *England,* single 1 *s.* double 2 *s.* three Quarters of an Ounce 3 *s.* Ounce 4 *s.*

## Alfo Letters fent outwards.

To *Norembergh, Bremen, Dantzick, Lubeck, Leip-fick,* and other Places of like Diftance, Poft paid to *Hamburgh,* single 1 *s.* double 2 *s.* three Quarters of an Ounce 3 *s.* Ounce 4 *s.*

*Paris,* single 9 *d.* double 1 *s.* 6 *d.* treble 2 *s.* 3 *d.* Ounce 2 *s.*

*Dunkirk, Oftend, Lifle, Ipres, Courtrey, Gaunt, Bruffels, Brudges, Antwerp,* and all other Parts of *Flanders,* single 8 *d.* double 1 *s.* 4 *d.* treble 2 *s.* Ounce 2 *s.*

*Sluis, Flufhing, Middleburg, Amfterdam, Rotterdam, Delf, Hague,* and from all other Parts of *Holland* and *Zealand,* single 8 *d.* double 1 *s.* 4 *d.* treble 2 *s.* Ounce 2 *s.*

The fame Year all Arrears of the Excife due fince the time of the Rebellion ; as alfo the Eftates of feveral Rebels excepted out of the Act of Oblivion.

*Anno*

*Anno* 1661, *Reg.* 13, there pass'd *An Act for granting unto the King's Majesty twelve hundred and threescore thousand Pounds, to be assess'd and levy'd by an Assessment of three-score and ten thousand Pounds per Month, for eighteen Months.*

*Anno Reg.* 13 and 14 pass'd *An Act for establishing an additional Revenue upon his Majesty, his Heirs and Successors, for the better Support of his and their Crown and Dignity.* This was generally call'd Chimney-Money, being 2 *s.* upon every Fire-Hearth yearly, which never amounted to above three hundred thousand Pounds *per Annum* clear, yet afterwards became one Ground of endless Clamours, as if it had been the most grievous Burden ever impos'd upon Subjects. Accordingly it was afterwards taken off; but what follow'd, the Reader may observe.

*Anno Dom.* 1663, *Reg.* 15, pass'd *An Act for granting to his Majesty four entire Subsidies by the Temporality,* and *An Act for confirming four Subsidies granted by the Clergy.* The Supplies granted this Session were for carrying on the War against the *Dutch.*

The 16th and 17th Years, *An Act for granting a royal Aid unto the King's Majesty of* 2477500 *l.* to be rais'd, and levy'd, and paid in three Years. For the same *Dutch* War.

*Anno Dom.* 1665, *Reg.* 17, *Act Act for granting to his Majesty the Sum of* 1250000 *l. for his present Supply.* This Parliament met at *Oxford,* the Plague then raging in *London.*

*Anno Dom.* 1666, *Reg.* 18, *An Act for raising Moneys by a Poll, and otherwise, towards the Maintenance of the present War.* This was computed at 1256347 *l.* 13 *s.*

*Anno Dom.* 1668, *Reg.* 20, *An Act for raising* 310000 *l. by an Imposition upon Wines and other Liquors.* The Rates impos'd were 4 *d.* upon every Quart
of

of *French* Wine fold by Retail, and 6 *d.* upon every Quart of *Spanish* Wine, and 12 *d.* for every Quart of Liquors diſtill'd, fold, as has been faid, by Retail. *Note,* That before this Act *French* Wine was fold in Taverns for 8 *d.* the Quart, and upon this Impoſition it was rais'd to 12 *d.* the Quart, as it continu'd for many Years; but is now, and has been long rais'd to 5 *s.* the Quart.

*Anno Dom.* 1670, *Reg.* 22, *An Act for granting to his Majeſty an Impoſition upon all Wines and Vinegar imported between the four and twentieth Day of* June 1670, *and the four and twentieth Day of* June 1678. The Rates were, for every Tun of *French* Wine and Vinegar 8 *l.* and for every Tun of *Spaniſh* or other Wine 12 *l.*

The fame Year the King fold his Fee-Farm Rents; but what they amounted to is hard to know. Thus the Crown was quite ſtript, the Tenures *in Capite, &c.* having been taken away before, and now theſe Rents, fo that nothing remain'd.

*Anno Dom.* 1671, *Reg.* 23, *An Act for granting a Subſidy to his Majeſty for Supply of his extraordinary Occaſions.* This Subſidy was laid as follows: All Bankers to pay 15 *s.* for every hundred Pounds out of the perfonal Eſtates. All Money lent to his Majeſty, for which above fix *per Cent* was owing, to pay 15 *s.* out of every hundred Pounds. All Perfonal Eſtates, in Goods, Stock, Money, *&c.* to pay 6 *s.* for every hundred Pounds Value. All Offices to pay 2 *s.* in the Pound of their yearly Profits. All Lands and Tenements to pay 12 *d.* in the Pound of their yearly Value.

X 4 The

The ſame Year paſs'd *An Act for an Additional Exciſe upon Beer, Ale, and other Liquors.* The Rates thus :

|  | *l.* | *s.* | *d.* |
|---|---|---|---|
| For every Barrel of Beer or Ale above 6 s. the Barrel | 0 | 00 | 09 |
| For every Barrel of Beer or Ale of 6 s. the Barrel or under | 0 | 00 | 03 |
| For every Hogſhead of Cyder or Perry | 0 | 01 | 03 |
| For every Gallon of Metheglin or Mead | 0 | 00 | 00½ |
| For every Barrel of Beer, commonly call'd Vinegar-Beer | 0 | 00 | 06 |
| For every Gallon of Strong Water, or *Aqua-vitæ* | 0 | 00 | 01 |
| For every Barrel of Beer or Ale imported from beyond the Seas | 0 | 03 | 00 |
| For every Tun of Cyder imported from beyond the Seas | 4 | 00 | 00 |
| For every Gallon of Low-Wines made of Liquors imported | 0 | 00 | 02 |
| For every Gallon of Coffee made and ſold | 0 | 00 | 02 |
| For every Gallon of Chocolate, Sherbet, and Tea | 0 | 00 | 08 |

The ſame Year, *An Act for laying Impoſitions on Proceedings at Law,* at the following Rates :

|  | *l.* | *s.* | *d.* |
|---|---|---|---|
| For every Charter or Grant under the Great-Seal of *England,* or County Palatine of *Lancaſter,* not exceeding one Skin of Parchment | 2 | 00 | 00 |

If

|  | l. | s. | d. |
|---|---|---|---|
| If above one Skin, for every other Skin | 1 | oo | oo |
| For every Grant of Lands, Fee, Perpetuity, Leafe for Years, &c. under the Great-Seal, Seal of the *Exchequer*, or County or Dutchy of *Lancafter*, in one Skin of Parchment | 1 | oo | oo |
| If above one Skin, for every other Skin | o | 10 | oo |
| For every Grant of any Sum of Money, or Pardon, not exceeding one Skin | 2 | oo | oo |
| If above one Skin, every other Skin | 1 | oo | oo |
| For every fpiritual Prefentation and Donation of the Value of 20 *l.* or above, in the King's Books | 2 | oo | oo |
| If the Value but 10 *l.* or above, in the King's Books | o | 10 | oo |
| For every Conveyance, Deed, &c. enroll'd | o | 05 | oo |
| For every Writ or Covenant for which under 20 *s.* is paid | o | 03 | 04 |
| For every fuch Writ for which 20 *s.* or above is paid | o | 06 | 08 |
| For every Writ of Entry in the Alienation Office | o | 06 | 08 |
| For every original Writ, *Subpœna*, Bill of *Middlefex*, *Latitat*, Writ of *Capias*, *Quo minus*, Writ of *Dedimus Poteftatem*, &c. | o | oo | 06 |
| For renewing every fuch Procefs | o | oo | 04 |
| For the Entry of every fuch Action where the Debt or Damage does not amount to 40 *s.* | o | oo | 06 |

For

|  | *l.* | *s.* | *d.* |
|---|---|---|---|
| For every Exemplification, paſſing the Seal of any Court, not exceeding one Skin | 0 | 07 | 06 |
| If above one Skin, for every other Skin | 0 | 05 | 00 |
| For every Pleading in *Chancery, Exchequer,* or Dutchy of *Lancaſter* | 0 | 01 | 00 |
| For every Copy taken out of the ſame Courts, for every Sheet | 0 | 00 | 01 |
| For every Copy in any other Court of Equity or Conſcience, for every Sheet | 0 | 00 | 01 |
| For every Order enter'd, and Report filed in the ſame Courts | 0 | 00 | 06 |
| For every Copy of ſuch Order or Report | 0 | 00 | 03 |
| For every Copy of Proceeding in the Courts at *Weſtminſter*, for which 8 *d. per* Sheet is paid, for every ſuch Sheet | 0 | 00 | 01 |
| For every Copy of Proceedings in thoſe Courts, for which 4 *d. per* Sheet is paid, for every Sheet | 0 | 00 | 01 |
| For every Copy of ſuch Proceedings, where the Debt or Damage does amount to 40 *s.* for every Sheet | 0 | 00 | 01 |
| For every Affidavit, where any Fee is due to the Officer | 0 | 00 | 06 |
| For the Copy of every ſuch Affidavit | 0 | 00 | 04 |
| For every ſpecial Bail, or Appearance taken | 0 | 00 | 06 |
| For every Rule or Order made or given | 0 | 00 | 02 |

For

|  | *l.* | *s.* | *d.* |
|---|---|---|---|
| For every Copy of fuch Rule or Order | 0 | 00 | 02 |
| For every Judgment | 0 | 01 | 00 |
| For every Decree and Difmiffion | 0 | 05 | 00 |
| For every Record of *Nifi prius* | 0 | 02 | 06 |
| For Copies of Records in the Courts of *Weftminfter* and the *Exchequer,* for every Sheet | 0 | 00 | 01 |
| For every *Poftea* return'd | 0 | 01 | 00 |
| For every Recognizance, Statute Staple, or Merchant enroll'd or enter'd | 0 | 02 | 00 |
| For every Writ of Error | 0 | 00 | 06 |
| For every Order or Rule thereupon | 0 | 01 | 00 |
| For every Citation or Monition out of any Spiritual Court | 0 | 00 | 04 |
| For every Libel, or Allegation | 0 | 01 | 00 |
| For every Depofition of Witneffes | 0 | 00 | 04 |
| For every Anfwer, Sentence, or final Decree | 0 | 00 | 06 |
| For every Commiffion iffuing out of an Ecclefiaftical Court | 0 | 02 | 00 |
| For every Inventory exhibited in an Ecclefiaftical Court, amounting to 40 *l.* and not to 100 *l.* | 0 | 01 | 00 |
| For every Inventory amounting to 100 *l.* and not to 500 *l* | 0 | 06 | 00 |
| For every Inventory amounting to 500 *l.* and not to 1000 *l.* | 0 | 12 | 00 |
| For every Inventory amounting to 1000 *l.* and above | 1 | 02 | 00 |
| For every Inftitution of any Ecclefiaftical Court | 0 | 05 | 00 |
| For every Licence that fhall pafs the Seal of any Ecclefiaftical Court, except Licences to eat Flefh in *Lent* | 0 | 01 | 00 |

For

|                                                                                                                                                 | *l.* | *s.* | *d.* |
|-------------------------------------------------------------------------------------------------------------------------------------------------|------|------|------|
| For the Copy of every Will re-gister'd, for every Sheet                                                                                         | 0    | 00   | 01   |
| For the Copy of every Inventory exhibited in any Ecclesiastical Court, shall be paid *per* Prest                                                | 0    | 00   | 02   |
| For every Appeal to the Delegates                                                                                                               | 0    | 10   | 00   |
| For every other Appeal                                                                                                                          | 0    | 03   | 04   |
| For every *Significavit pro Corporis De-liberatione*                                                                                            | 0    | 05   | 00   |
| For every Dispensation to hold two Ecclesiastical Dignities, or a Be-nefice and a Dignity                                                       | 0    | 15   | 00   |
| For every other Dispensation                                                                                                                    | 0    | 10   | 00   |
| For every Warrant, Monition, Per-sonal Decree, Libel, Allegation, Deposition, and Personal Answer, out of the Court of the High Admiral, and Courts of that Jurisdiction | 0    | 01   | 00   |
| For every Commission under the Great Seal of any of those Courts                                                                                | 0    | 05   | 00   |
| For every Sentence given in any of the said Courts                                                                                              | 0    | 05   | 00   |
| For every Attachment out of any of the said Courts                                                                                              | 0    | 03   | 04   |
| For every Relaxation of every At-tachment out of the said Courts                                                                                | 0    | 03   | 04   |

*Anno Dom.* 1673, *Reg.* 25, pass'd *An Act for raising the Sum of twelve hundred thirty eight thousand seven hundred and fifty Pounds,* on account of the *Dutch* War the Nation was then engag'd in; and to oblige the King to recall his Declaration for Liberty of Conscience; and to pass the Act for all Persons in Office to take the Test.

*Anno*

*Anno Dom,* 1677, *Reg.* 29, pafs'd *An Act for raifing five hundred eighty four thoufand nine hundred feventy eight Pounds, two Shillings and two Pence halfpenny, for the fpeedy building thirty Ships of War.* As alfo, *An Act for an additional Excife upon Beer, Ale, and other excifeable Liquors, for three Years.*

*Anno Dom.* 1678, *Reg.* 30, *An Act for raifing Money by a Poll, and otherwife, to enable his Majefty to enter into an actual War againft* the French *King, and for prohibiting* French *Commodities.*

The fame Year again, *An Act for granting a Supply to his Majefty of fix hundred nineteen thoufand three hundred and eighty Pounds, eleven Shillings and nine Pence, for difbanding the Army, and other Ufes therein mention'd.* They gave the Money juft before to raife it, and now to disband it, becaufe the King had not immediately at their Beck declar'd War with *France*; and therefore they put it out of his Power to declare it for the future, not trufting his Majefty with this Money, but putting it into private Hands to disband the faid Army. Now the Spirit of Rebellion, which had been working more privately ever fince the Reftoration, began to appear barefac'd.

*Anno Dom.* 1679, *Reg.* 31, *An Act for granting a Supply to his Majefty of two hundred and fixty thoufand four hundred fixty two Pounds, feventeen Shillings and three Pence, for paying off and disbanding the Forces raifed fince the* 29th *of* Sept. 1677. The Kindnefs of this Grant was to leave his Majefty defencelefs, as will appear by their Vote the next Year.

When after having otherwife much infulted his Majefty, by thrufting the Bill of Exclufion upon him, which he had feveral times rejected, and voted his fafteft Friends to be his Enemies, they farther refolv'd,

*That*

*That whosoever shall hereafter lend, or cause to be lent, by way of Advance, any Money upon the Branches of the King's Revenue, arising by Customs, Excise, or Hearth-money, shall be judg'd to hinder the sitting of Parliaments, and shall be responsible for the same in Parliament.*

Thus they disbanded the Forces that were the King's Security, laid a scandalous Imputation upon his best Friends, and, to conclude his Ruin, endeavour'd to deprive him of any Assistance from his Subjects, whensoever he should be in the greatest Want of Money.

Thus far concerning Taxes during the Reign of King *Charles* II. His other Actions not appertaining to us, we shall only add, That he died on the 6th of *February* 1684-5, in the 55th Year of his Age, and the 37th of his Reign, leaving the Crown to his Brother,

# K. JAMES II.

A Prince so unfortunate, as not only to lose his Crown, but to be also expos'd to the Slanders of every malicious railing Scribbler, and to have it thought a Crime to vindicate him from unjust Aspersions; therefore his Character shall be pass'd by, and we shall only refer the Readers to that which Dr. *Kennet* has given of him in his Preface to an Address of Thanks; and I hope no Man will say that Doctor is his Friend, tho' he has extoll'd him beyond the Emperor *Trajan*, and even above all Monarchs that ever were, or are like to be. To come now to the Point of what Treasure he receiv'd from his Subjects.

In the Year of our Lord 1685, being the first of his Reign, was pass'd *An Act for settling the Revenue on his Majesty for his Life, which was settled on*

*his*

*his late Majefty for his Life.* This, as has been faid before, confifted in Cuftoms, Excife, and Hearth-money, and was repeal'd upon his being remov'd from the Throne.

The next, in the fame Year, was *An Act for granting his Majefty an Impofition upon all Wines and Vinegar imported between the* 24th *of* June, 1685, *and the* 24th *of* June, 1693. This was afterwards con-tinu'd under King *William*, as we fhall there fee ; and was given for a Supply for Repairs of the Na-vy, and providing Stores for the Navy and Ord-nance, and other his Majefty's weighty and impor-tant Occafions. The Rates impos'd were thefe :

|  | *l.* | *s.* | *d.* |
|---|---|---|---|
| Upon every Tun of *French* Wine and of Vinegar imported, within the Time aforefaid, into *England*, or *Wales*, or the Town of *Berwick* upon *Tweed* | 08 | 00 | 00 |
| Upon every Tun of *Spanish* Wines fo imported, or of any other Wines | 12 | 00 | 00 |

Then follow'd, ftill the fame Year, *An Act for granting to his Majefty an Impofition upon all Tobacco and Sugar imported between the* 24th *Day of* June, 1685, *and the* 24th *Day of* June, 1693. This, as well as the former, was for a further Supply for the Re-pairs of the Navy, and providing Stores for the Na-vy and Ordnance, and Payment of the Debt due to his late Majefty's Servants and Family, and other his Majefty's weighty and important Occafions. The Rates impos'd were :

Upon

|  | l. | s. | d. |
|--|----|----|-----|

Upon every Pound-weight of Tobacco imported into *England*, or
*Wales*, or the Town of *Berwick*
upon *Tweed*, of the Growth and
Production of any of his Majeſty's Plantations, Iſlands, or
Territories in *America*, 3 *d.* above
what it then paid ............ 0  00  0¾

Upon every Pound-weight of *Spaniſh* or Foreign Tobacco, not of
the *Engliſh* Plantations , above
what it then paid ............ 0  00  06½

Upon every Pound-weight of *Muſ-
covade* Sugar, of the aforeſaid
Plantations, Iſlands, Lands, or
Territories, above what was then
paid ............ 0  00  00¼

Upon every Pound-weight of Sugar of the *Engliſh* Plantations,
made fit for common uſe or ſpend-
ing, above what it then paid ............ 0  00  00¾

Upon every Pound-weight of *Muſ-
covade* Sugar of *Brazil*, or any
other Foreign Part, not of *Engliſh* Plantations, above what was
then paid ............ 0  00  00½

Upon every Pound of *Panele* Su-
gar, above what it then paid ............ 0  00  00½

Upon every Pound-weight of Foreign white Powder Sugar, above
what was then paid ............ 0  00  01¼

Upon every Pound-weight of Foreign Sugar imported in the Loaf,
above what was paid before ............ 0  00  0¾

Then

Then follows *An Act for granting an Aid to his Majesty by an Imposition on all* French *Linens, and all* East-India *Linen, and several other Manufactures of* India ; *and on all* French *wrought Silks and Stuffs, and on all other wrought Silks ; and on all* Brandies *imported after the first Day of* July, 1685, *and before the first Day of* July, 1690, *for the King's extraordinary Occasions, and for suppressing the Duke of* Monmouth's *Rebellion.*

This last Supply we see was granted his Majesty for suppressing of Rebellion ; and therefore no more needs be said of it. The other Impositions upon Wine, Vinegar, Tobacco and Sugar, were for Repairs of the Navy, and providing Stores. How well that Design was answer'd, let us hear from those who best knew it, the Persons concern'd in the Navy, as it is deliver'd in the Book call'd *The Oeconomy of his Majesty's Navy Office,* by an Officer of the Navy, Printed in the Year 1717, when Navy Officers, or few others, were too apt to speak well of King *James.* After having taken notice in his Preface of the Condition the Navy was in under King *Charles* the II. he proceeds thus :

" His royal Brother King *James* then ascending
" the Throne, prosecuted what his Predecessor had
" begun, and was as ill serv'd as the other had
" been ; for after 90000 *l.* paid to the Navy-Of-
" ficers towards repairing of the Fleet, it was
" found to be in a worse Condition than it had
" been before the Payment of that Money. Here-
" upon his Majesty resolv'd to put that Affair into
" other Hands ; and accordingly committed the
" same to Sir *Anthony Dean,* Sir *John Berry,* Mr.
" *Hewer,* and Mr. *Michel,* assigning them 400000 *l.*
" a year for Repairs, Sea Stores, and all other
" Naval Expences. These, it is to be observ'd,
" were the new Commissioners added to the old,

Y                                        " of

" of which the Lord *Falkland* and Sir *John Narbo-*
" *rough* were to continue with them at the Board,
" the firft of thofe two continuing Treafurer.

" The firft Meeting of thefe Commiffioners was
" in *April* 1686, when they foon made known the
" Weaknefs of the Reafons alledg'd for the Decay
" of the new built Ships in fo fhort a time, which
" were, their having been too haftily built, and
" confifting of foreign Plank and Timber. For,
" as to the firft, it appear'd that the fhorteft time
" any of them had been upon the Stocks had been
" nine Months, and fome of them two or three
" Years; whereas other Men of War, built be-
" fore them, had been finifh'd in fix Months, and
" always prov'd good and found. As to the fe-
" cond Reafon it was found more prepofterous;
" becaufe of above 3500 Loads of Timber provi-
" ded for thofe Ships, not above 500 had been of
" foreign Growth. Befides, nine of the moft able
" Builders in the Kingdom gave it in under their
" Hands to the King, that the foreign Plank is
" more durable and every way better for the buil-
" ding of large Ships than the *Englifh*. This will
" ftartle many, who, being fond of their own
" Country, imagine it affords every thing better
" than any other Part of the World, and particu-
" larly the Oak, which they conceit far exceeds
" any in the World for building of Ships; where-
" as fo many knowing Men, who fpoke not upon
" Notion, but by Experience, have fo pofitively
" declar'd that the Plank brought from *Dantzick,*
" *Riga, &c.* of the Growth of *Poland, Pruffia,* and
" *Bohemia,* does far exceed any of the *Englifh*
" Growth; and this Declaration of fo many able
" Shipwrights was confirm'd unanimoufly by the
" aforefaid Commiffioners; whereupon an Order
" of Council pafs'd to authorize the Commiffioners

" of

" of the Navy to contract for foreign Plank for the
" Ufe of his Majefty's Ships. All Diligence was
" then us'd in repairing the whole Fleet, and put-
" ting it into a Condition to be ferviceable upon
" Occafion; to which effect extraordinary Quanti-
" ties of all forts of Sea Stores were bought; fo
" that the Magazines and Yards were better pro-
" vided than they had been before.

" No lefs Care was taken for the reftoring of
" Difcipline at Sea, and preventing all forts of
" Diforders; and accordingly, in *July* 1686, his
" Majefty made a Regulation to this Effect:
" 1. That no Commander of any of his Majefty's
" Ships fhould, for the future, prefume to take
" aboard, or carry from one Port to another, any
" Money, Plate, Bullion, Jewels, or other Mer-
" chandize or Goods whatfoever, upon Pain of
" being difcharg'd from their prefent Employment,
" and render'd incapable of any for the future.
" 2. That none of them fhould carry any Paffen-
" gers, except Subjects redeem'd from Slavery,
" fhipwreck'd, or taken at Sea out of foreign
" Ships. 3. That Copies of all Orders given at
" Sea fhould be tranfmitted to the Admiralty.
" 4. That all Commanders of Ships fhould fend
" Accounts of their Proceedings every time they
" put into any Port. 5. That at the End of each
" Voyage they fhould deliver in a Book, contain-
" ing a particular Journal of all the Time they
" had been abroad. Laftly, his Majefty, of his
" own Bounty, was pleas'd to augment the Allow-
" ances of the Sea Commanders, for encouraging
" of them to perform their Duty, in this Manner:
" The Commander of a Firft-Rate, his ftanding
" Allowance as before, 273 *l.* 15 *s.* and for victual-
" ling, 12 *l.* 3 *s.* 4 *d.* the Addition made by his
" Majefty was 250 *l.* a year for his Table. To

" the

" the Captain of a Second-Rate, whose Allowance
" was 219 *l.* besides 12 *l.* 3 *s.* 4 *d.* for victualling,
" the King added 200 *l.* a year. To the Captain
" of a Third-Rate, whose Allowance was 182 *l.*
" besides 12 *l.* 3 *s.* 4 *d.* for victualling, 166 *l.* 5 *s.*
" To the Captain of a Fourth-Rate, before al-
" low'd 136 *l.* 10 *s.* with the same as above for
" victualling, 124 *l.* 5 *s.* To the Captain of a
" Fifth-Rate, before allow'd 109 *l.* 10 *s.* with the
" Victualling as above, 100 *l.* And lastly, to the
" Captain of a Sixth-Rate, before allow'd 91 *l.*
" and Victualling as above, 83 *l.* This without al-
" tering any thing of what had been before allow'd
" to Flag Officers. And for the Encouragement
" of such as were employ'd against the Infidels in
" *Barbary,* the King gave them the full Benefit of
" all the Prizes they should take, Hulls, Furni-
" ture, Lading, and Slaves, to be divided be-
" tween the Commander or Commanders, and
" their Officers and Companies.

" Through the Care and Industry of the above-
" nam'd Commissioners, and his Majesty's parti-
" cular Application, the Fleet so decay'd, as has
" been said, was re-establish'd in such manner,
" that from an ordinary Summer-Guard, in less
" than two Months no less than sixty-seven Ships
" of War and Fireships were put to Sea, besides
" Tenders, Yatchs, &c. whereof twelve Third,
" twenty-eight Fourth, two Fifth, and five Sixth-
" Rates, with twenty Fire-Ships. Besides this,
" the whole Navy was fully repair'd, and a com-
" pleat Proportion of eight Months Sea Stores ac-
" tually provided, and left in distinct and proper
" Repositories for every Ship so repair'd. Besides,
" there was laid up in Magazine such a further
" Reserve, for answering the general Service of
" the Navy, as amounted, in eight only Species
" thereof,

" thereof, to above 100000 *l.* being all foreign
" Commodities, and of the higheſt Importance,
" *viz.* Hemp, Pitch, Tar, Roſin, Canvas, Iron,
" Oil, and Wood; and more Magazines erected
" for the preſerving of the ſaid Stores than had
" ever been before by all the Kings of *England*
" put together.

" Nor is it fit to omit one of the greateſt Im-
" provements then made, which was to reduce the
" future Maintenance of his Majeſty's Fleet, in
" their whole Wear and Tare, to no higher a
" Charge than that of twenty-two Shillings a Man
" *per* Month, which was then alſo made good, ſa-
" ving thereby to the Crown a vaſt Expence.

" To conclude, I ſhall only mention what Num-
" ber of Ships the whole Navy, whether at Sea
" or in Harbour, then conſiſted of, *viz.* nine Firſt-
" Rates, eleven Second-Rates, thirty-nine Third-
" Rates, forty-one Fourth-Rates, two Fifth-Rates,
" ſix Sixth-Rates, three Bomb-Veſſels, twenty-ſix
" Fire-Ships, ſix Hoys, eight Hulls, three Ketches,
" fifty-eight Smacks, and fourteen Yatchs. In
" all 173 Sail, carrying 42003 Men, and 6930
" Guns.

Here is a full View of the manner how King
*James* expended the Money given him by the Parliament for the Uſe of the Navy ; by which it will
plainly appear that he laid out much more upon it
than he receiv'd. His greateſt worldly Care was
the improving of the *Engliſh* Naval Power ; and
he underſtood that Affair very well himſelf. He
alſo endeavour'd to maintain Peace, as well knowing that to be the true Happineſs of the Nation,
which grew rich and flouriſh'd by it, tho' at the
ſame time he provided all things to be in a Readi-
neſs in caſe of an unavoidable War, well knowing
that as Peace makes People happy, that Happi-

neſs

ness is not to be depended on, unless they continue
in such a Posture as to be able to enter into a War
whensoever they shall be oblig'd to it.

As to the other Actions of this King's Reign, they
are foreign from the Subject in hand; and shall
therefore be pass'd by, as will be done under the ensuing Sovereigns. The Wars, which ensu'd after the
short Administration of King *James*, gave occasion
for greater Expences, and consequently for more
Taxes; so that there comes on a larger Field of
Matter; and the rather, for that in the latter Years
the Particulars are better exprefs'd in Acts of Parliament than they were in former Ages. The Duties have been more distinctly laid on the several
Sorts of Goods imported, and the real Value of
those Duties better known, every Age improving
by the Experience of what pass'd before, and the
Books kept discovering what had been, and accordingly pointing out what was likely to be in the
same Case. Frauds and Abuses have been also frequently discover'd, and still new Laws enacted to
prevent the like for the future. The Prospect of
Gain has always prevail'd upon Traders to endeavour to run Goods, to save the Customs, tho' with
the Hazard of losing the whole; and such Practices being discover'd, the Legislature has also con-
triv'd to disappoint them, as may be seen by many
Instances in our Acts of Parliament. But leaving
those Affairs, we will now proceed to

# K. WILLIAM III.

AND, without any Introduction to his Reign,
or making the least Digression to meddle
with those things we do not profess to write of,
shall directly enter upon the present Subject;
being the Treasure he receiv'd from the People
of

of *England*, whofe Hearts being then open, they
pour'd in to him immenfe Sums, with greater
Alacrity than they had ever been known to do to
any of their former Princes. The firft Grant we
find was in the Year 1689, of the Reign 1.

*An Act for granting a prefent Aid to their Majefties
for the extraordinary Occafions which oblige them to a
great and prefent Expence.*

*An Act for raifing Money by a Poll, and otherwife,
towards the reducing of* Ireland.

*An Act for a Grant to their Majefties of an Aid of
12 d. in the Pound for one Year, for the neceffary Defence of their Realms.*

*An Act for an additional Duty of Excife upon Beer,
Ale, and other Liquors, thus :*

|  | *l.* | *s.* | *d.* |
|---|---|---|---|
| For every Barrel of Beer or Ale above 6 s. the Barrel, over and above the Duties already payable for the fame | 0 | 0 | 9 |
| For every Barrel of Beer or Ale of 6 s. the Barrel or under, over and above the Duty already payable for the fame | 0 | 0 | 3 |
| For every Barrel of Vinegar, or Vinegar-Beer, made of *Englifh* Materials, over and above the Duties already payable | 0 | 1 | 6 |
| For every Barrel of Vinegar made of foreign Materials | 0 | 4 | 0 |
| For every Barrel of Beer, Ale, or Mum, imported, over and above the former Duties | 0 | 3 | 0 |
| For every Tun of Cyder or Perry imported, over and above the former Duties | 4 | 0 | 0 |

For

|  | *l.* | *s.* | *d.* |
|---|---|---|---|
| For every Gallon of Brandy, Spirits, or *Aqua-vitæ*, imported, over and above former Duties | 0 | 2 | 0 |
| For every Gallon of Double Brandy, imported, over and above former Duties | 0 | 4 | 0 |
| For every Hogſhead of Cyder or Perry made, over and above the former Duties | 0 | 1 | 3 |
| For all Metheglin and Mead, for every Gallon | 0 | 0 | 3 |

Next follows *An Act for appropriating certain Duties for paying the* States General *of the* United Provinces *their Charges for his Majeſty's Expedition into this Kingdom, and for other Uſes.*

Sill the ſame Year, *An Act for a Grant to their Majeſties of an Aid of two Shillings in the Pound for one Year.*

*An Act for a Grant to their Majeſties of an additional Aid of twelve Pence in the Pound for one Year.*

*An Act for the charging and collecting of the Duties upon Coffee, Tea, and Chocolate, at the Cuſtom-houſe,* at the following Rates, over and beſides what is now paid or payable for the ſame.

|  | *l.* | *s.* | *d.* |
|---|---|---|---|
| Upon every hundred Weight of Coffee imported into *England, Wales,* or the Town of *Berwick upon Tweed* | 5 | 12 | 0 |
| Upon every hundred Weight of Cacao Nuts imported | 8 | 8 | 0 |
| Upon every Pound of Tea imported | 0 | 5 | 0 |

Nutmegs, Cinnamon, Cloves, and Mace, to be imported by any Perſons whatſoever in *Engliſh* Ships, from any Parts beyond the Seas, one third at leaſt of the Seamen being *Engliſhmen,* paying double the

Sums

Sums the fame are charg'd with in the Book of Rates for the Cuftoms and Duties.

*Anno Reg.* 2. *An Act for raifing Money by a Poll, and otherwife, towards the reducing of* Ireland, *and profecuting the War againft* France.

*An Act for granting to their Majefties, for their Lives, and the Life of the Survivor of them, certain Impofitions upon Beer, Ale, and other Liquors.* The Rates fo granted are the fame as in the twelfth Year of the Reign of King *Charles* II. and by another Act made in the fifteenth Year of the faid King.

*An Act for granting to their Majefties a Subfidy of Tonnage and Poundage, and other Sums of Money, payable upon Merchandizes exported and imported,* for the Term of four Years.

The fecond Seffion the fame Year; *An Act for granting an Aid to their Majefties of fixteen hundred fifty one thoufand feven hundred and two Pounds eighteen Shillings.*

*An Act for granting to their Majefties certain Impofitions upon all* Eaft-India *Goods and Manufactures, and upon all wrought Silks, and feveral other Goods and Merchandize to be imported after the five and twentieth Day of* December 1690.

|  | *l.* | *s.* | *d.* |
|---|---|---|---|
| For all Callicoes, and other *Indian* Linen, and wrought Silks, and other Manufactures of *India* and *China* (except Indigo) imported, for every hundred Pounds Value | 20 | 0 | 0 |
| For all wrought Silks from other Places, for every hundred Pounds Value | 10 | 0 | 0 |
| For all raw Silks from *India* and *China,* Value as above | 5 | 0 | 0 |

For

|  | *l.* | *s.* | *d.* |
|---|---|---|---|

For Linen, except from the *Nether-lands*, one Moiety more than in the Book of Rates.

For Linen from the *Netherlands*, double, as in the Book of Rates.

For all Timber, Boards, &c. from all Parts, except *Ireland*, for every 100 *l.* Value — 10 . 0 . 0

For every Tun of Hempſeed-oil, Rape-oil, and other Seed-oil imported — 8 . 0 . 0

For every hundred Weight of Hops imported, above the former Duty — 1 . 0 . 0

For every hundred Weight of Pepper imported, above the former Duty — 1 . 8 . 0

For every hundred Pound Value of Grocery Wares and Drugs, except Pepper, Liquorice, Currants, Sugar, Tobacco, Mace, Cinnamon, Nutmegs and Cloves, imported — 10 . 0 . 0

For every hundred Pound Value of Currants, above the former Duty — 5 . 0 . 0

For every Tun of Iron, except Buſhel Iron, imported in foreign Ships — 1 . 13 . 0

For every Tun of Iron imported in *Engliſh* Ships, above the former Duty — 1 . 3 . 0

For every hundred Weight of Foreign Iron Wire, above the former Duty — 1 . 2 . 6

For every hundred Weight of Foreign Steel Wire — 0 . 14 . 0

For every Iron Pot and Kettle, above the former Duty — 0 . 1 . 3

For every ſmall Back for Chimneys — 0 . 1 . 2

For every large Back — 0 . 2 . 4

For

|  | l. | s. | d. |
|---|---|---|---|
| For every hundred Weight of Rod Iron | 0 | 5 | 0 |
| For every hundred Weight of Frying-Pans | 0 | 4 | 0 |
| For every hundred Weight of Steel | 0 | 5 | 6 |
| For every hundred Weight of Anvils | 0 | 9 | 3 |
| For every hundred Weight of single Plates | 0 | 4 | 4 |
| For every hundred Weight of double Plates | 0 | 8 | 8 |
| For every Harnefs Plate, or Iron double | 0 | 1 | 4 |
| For every hundred Weight of Iron lefs than three quarters of an Inch fquare, or manufactur'd | 0 | 5 | 0 |
| For every hundred Weight of Brafs, Lattin, or Copper Wire | 0 | 15 | 0 |
| For every Laft of Hemp-feed,Cole-feed and Rape-feed | 4 | 0 | 0 |
| For all Yarn of Flax or Hemp, other than Cable Yarn, as much more as is before charg'd thereupon in the Book of Rates. |  |  |  |
| For every hundred Weight of Cable Yarn | 0 | 5 | 0 |
| For all Manufactures of Glafs, except *Rhenifh* and *Mufcovy* Window Glafs, for every 20 s. Value, above the former Duty | 0 | 3 | 0 |
| For every hundred Weight of Molaffes from the *Englifh* Plantations | 0 | 8 | 0 |
| For every hundred Weight of Tallow imported | 0 | 5 | 0 |
| For every hundred Weight of Tallow Candles imported | 0 | 10 | 0 |

For

|  | *l.* | *s.* | *d.* |
|---|---|---|---|
| For every Pound of Bever Wool, except comb'd in *Ruſſia*, and imported in *Engliſh* Ships | 0 | 15 | 0 |
| For every Barrel of Pot-aſhes containing two hundred Weight | 0 | 8 | 0 |
| For every hundred Weight of Cordage ready wrought | 0 | 5 | 0 |
| For every Tun of Olive Oil | 4 | 0 | 0 |
| For every Ream of Royal Paper | 0 | 2 | 0 |
| For every Ream of blue Paper, Demy-Paper and painted Paper | 0 | 1 | 6 |
| For every Bundle of brown Paper | 0 | 0 | 2 |

For all other Paper, as much more as
was charg'd in the Book of Rates.

|  | *l.* | *s.* | *d.* |
|---|---|---|---|
| For every hundred Weight of Liquorice | 0 | 18 | 8 |
| For every hundred Weight of Liquorice Powder | 1 | 17 | 4 |
| For every Pound Weight of Juice of Liquorice | 0 | 1 | 0 |
| For every hundred Weight of Barilla, or Saphora | 0 | 2 | 6 |
| For every hundred Weight of Soap | 0 | 10 | 0 |
| For all Earthen Ware not mention'd in the Book of Rates, for every twenty Shillings Value | 0 | 2 | 6 |
| For every hundred Weight of Starch | 1 | 0 | 0 |
| For every hundred Weight of Allom | 0 | 2 | 6 |
| For every hundred Weight of Brimſtone | 0 | 4 | 8 |
| For every hundred Weight of Tin | 1 | 10 | 0 |

*Note*, That all theſe Duties are upon Goods imported from abroad, and that all the Rates are additional, or over and above the Impoſitions that

were

were upon the said Goods before, though not here mention'd in every Article.

The same Year, *An Act for Continuance of several former Acts therein mention'd, for the laying several Duties upon Wines, Vinegar and Tobacco.* The Acts continued are, that of Duties upon Wine and Vinegar, and that of Tobacco and Sugar, both 1 *Jac.* II.

*An Act for the encouraging the distilling of Brandy and Spirits from Corn ; and for laying several Duties on Low Wines, or Spirits of the first Extraction.* The Rates are,

|  | *l.* | *s.* | *d.* |
|---|---|---|---|
| For every Gallon of Low Wines of the first Extraction drawn from foreign Materials | 0 | 0 | 8 |
| For every Gallon drawn from Brewers Wash or Tilt, or other *English* Materials, except from Drink brewed from any malted Corn, or from Cyder or Perry | 0 | 1 | 0 |
| For every Gallon drawn from Drink made of any malted Corn | 0 | 0 | 1 |
| For every Gallon drawn from Cyder or Perry, or any Mixture thereof | 0 | 0 | 3 |

*An Act for granting to their Majesties several additional Duties of Excise upon Beer, Ale, and other Liquors, for four Years, from the Time that an Act for doubling the Duty of Excise upon Beer, Ale, and other Liquors, during the Space of one Year, doth expire.* The Rates.

|  | *l.* | *s.* | *d.* |
|---|---|---|---|
| For every Barrel of Ale, or Beer, above 6 *s.* over and above the former Duty | 0 | 1 | 6 |
| For every Barrel of 6 *s.* Beer | 0 | 0 | 6 |

For

|                                                      | l. | s. | d. |
|------------------------------------------------------|----|----|----|
| For every Barrel of Vinegar Beer of *English* Materials | 0 | 3 | 0 |
| For every Barrel of Vinegar run thro' Rape, or of foreign Materials | 0 | 8 | 0 |
| For every Barrel of Beer, Ale, or Mum imported | 0 | 6 | 0 |
| For every Tun of Cyder or Perry imported | 0 | 8 | 0 |
| For every Gallon of single Brandy, Spirits, or *Aqua vitæ* imported | 0 | 4 | 0 |
| For every Gallon of double Brandy, &c. | 0 | 8 | 0 |
| For every Hogshead of Cyder and Perry made in *England* | 0 | 2 | 6 |
| For every Gallon of Metheglin, or Mead | 0 | 0 | 6 |

All these Rates over and above the former Duties.

In the 3d Year of the Reign, *An Act for granting to their Majesties certain Impositions upon Beer, Ale, and other Liquors, for one Year.*

The 3d and 4th Years, *An Act for granting an Aid to their Majesties of the Sum of sixteen hundred fifty one thousand seven hundred and two Pounds eighteen Shillings, towards the carrying on a vigorous War against* France.

*An Act for raising Money by a Poll, payable Quarterly for one Year, for the carrying on a vigorous War against* France.

The 4th and 5th Years of the Reign, *An Act for granting to their Majesties an Aid of four Shillings in the Pound for one Year, for carrying on a vigorous War against* France.

*An Act for granting to their Majesties certain additional Impositions upon several Goods and Merchandize, for the prosecuting the present War against* France. The Rates:

For

| | *l.* | *s.* | *d.* |
|---|---|---|---|
| For every hundred Pounds Value of Amber Beads imported | 20 | 0 | 0 |
| For every hundred Pounds Value of rough Amber imported | 10 | 0 | 0 |
| For Oil of Amber imported, for every hundred Pounds Value | 10 | 0 | 0 |
| For Anchovies, every hundred Pounds Value | 5 | 0 | 0 |
| For Soap-afhes imported, the Laft | 0 | 6 | 0 |
| For *Barbers* Aprons and Checks imported, each Piece | 0 | 0 | 8 |
| For every hundred Weight of Battery, Bafhrones, or Kettles imported | 0 | 5 | 0 |
| For every hundred Weight of Metal prepared for Battery, imported | 0 | 5 | 0 |
| For every hundred Weight of Books unbound, imported | 0 | 4 | 0 |
| For every hundred Pounds Value of Lamp-black imported | 20 | 0 | 0 |
| For every hundred Pounds Value of boltel Reins imported | 10 | 0 | 0 |
| For every Grofs of Bracelets or Necklaces of Glafs imported | 0 | 2 | 6 |
| For every hundred Pounds Value of wrought Brafs imported | 5 | 0 | 0 |
| For every hundred Pounds Value of Buckrams imported | 5 | 0 | 0 |
| For every hundred Pounds Value of Hair Buttons imported | 10 | 0 | 0 |
| For every hundred Pounds Value of Briftles imported | 5 | 0 | 0 |
| For every Pound of Bacon imported | 0 | 0 | 4 |
| For every hundred Pounds Value of Calves Skins imported | 5 | 0 | 0 |

For

|  | l. | s. | d. |
|---|---|---|---|
| For every hundred Pounds Value of Carpets imported | 5 | 0 | 0 |
| For every Grofs of Catlings and Lute-ftrings | 0 | 1 | 0 |
| For every hundred Pounds Value of *Scotch* Coals imported | 5 | 0 | 0 |
| For every thoufand of Walking Canes | 1 | 5 | 0 |
| For every thoufand of Canes called Rattans | 0 | 5 | 0 |
| For every hundred Weight of Copper imported | 0 | 7 | 6 |
| For every hundred Weight of Copper part wrought, imported | 0 | 12 | 6 |
| For every hundred Weight of Copper fully wrought, imported | 0 | 17 | 6 |
| For every hundred Pounds Value of polifh'd Coral | 20 | 0 | 0 |
| For every hundred Pounds Value of Cotton Manufactures, except Dimitty, not brought from *Eaft-India*, or *China*, imported | 5 | 0 | 0 |
| For every hundred Pounds Value of Couries imported | 10 | 0 | 0 |
| For every hundred Pounds Value of Elephants Teeth imported | 10 | 0 | 0 |
| For every hundred Pounds Value of rough Flax imported | 5 | 0 | 0 |
| For every hundred Pounds Value of drefs'd or wrought Flax imported | 15 | 0 | 0 |
| For every hundred Pounds Value of Tow imported | 5 | 0 | 0 |
| For every Yard of Flannel imported | 0 | 0 | 2 |
| For every Yard of Frize imported | 0 | 0 | $3\frac{1}{2}$ |
| For every hundred Pounds Value of Furs imported | 5 | 0 | 0 |

For

|  | *l.* | *s.* | *d.* |
|---|---|---|---|
| For every hundred Pounds Value of Gold and Silver Thread and Wire counterfeit, imported | 5 | 0 | 0 |
| For every Pound of Goats Hair, called *Carmenia* Wool, imported | 0 | 0 | 4 |
| For every Pound of other forts of Goats Hair imported | 0 | 0 | 2 |
| For every hundred Pounds Value of Hides, except Buff and Lofh imported | 5 | 0 | 0 |
| For every Buff Hide | 0 | 2 | 6 |
| For every Lofh Hide | 0 | 1 | 0 |
| For every hundred Pounds Value of Hemp rough imported | 5 | 0 | 0 |
| For every hundred Pounds Value of Diamonds, Rubies, Emeralds, Pearls and other Jewels and precious Stones imported | 1 | 0 | 0 |
| For every Pound of Indico, not of the *Englifh* Plantations | 0 | 0 | 4 |
| For every Pound of Indico of *Englifh* Plantations | 0 | 0 | 2 |
| For all Iron and Iron Works imported from *Ireland*, the fame as is paid for the like imported from other Parts. | | | |
| For every hundred Pounds Value of Lattin and round Bottoms imported | 10 | 0 | 0 |
| For every hundred Pounds Value of Leather imported | 5 | 0 | 0 |
| For every hundred Pounds Value of Lime and Lemon Juice imported | 20 | 0 | 0 |
| For every hundred Pounds Value of *Laitmus* imported | 5 | 0 | 0 |

Z

|                                                                                                          | l. | s. | d. |
|----------------------------------------------------------------------------------------------------------|-----|----|----|
| For every Tun of *Lapis Calaminaris* imported                                                            | 1   | 0  | 0  |
| For every hundred Pounds Value of Madder imported                                                        | 5   | 0  | 0  |
| For the like Value of Orchal imported                                                                    | 5   | 0  | 0  |
| For the like Value of Pintadoes, or Callicoe Cupboard Cloths imported, but from *Eaft-India* or *China*  | 5   | 0  | 0  |
| For Pitch, not of the Dominions of *England* or *Scotland*, one Moiety mote than charg'd before          |     |    |    |
| For every hundred Pounds Value of all forts of Plate                                                     | 5   | 0  | 0  |
| For the like Value of Rice imported                                                                      | 5   | 0  | 0  |
| For the like Value of all Rozen, not the Product of the Dominions of *England* or *Scotland*             | 10  | 0  | 0  |
| For every Weigh of Salt, except what is ufed in curing of Fifh                                           | 0   | 5  | 0  |
| For every hundred Pounds Value of Silks thrown in the Gum                                                | 5   | 0  | 0  |
| For every Pound of Silk wrought, other than Alamodes and Luftrings                                       | 0   | 2  | 0  |
| For Silk Ferret or Floret, one Moiety more than in the Book of Rates                                     |     |    |    |
| For every hundred Pounds Value of all Skins imported                                                     | 5   | 0  | 0  |
| For all Tar, not of the Dominions of *England* or *Scotland*, one Moiety morethan before                 |     |    |    |
| For every hundred Pounds Value of Ticks and Tickings (except *Scotch*)                                   | 5   | 0  | 0  |
| For every dozen Pounds of Thread Oufnel                                                                  | 0   | 4  | 0  |

For

|  | *l.* | *s.* | *d.* |
|---|---|---|---|
| For every hundred Pounds Value of Tapiſtry and Dornix | 10 | 0 | 0 |
| For all unwrought Inkle one Moiety more than before | | | |
| For every thouſand of Pantiles | 0 | 8 | 0 |
| For every hundred Pounds Value of all ſorts of Dying Wood, except Red Wood from *Guinea*, Drugs, and Logwood | 5 | 0 | 0 |
| For every hundred Pounds Value of Wax | 5 | 0 | 0 |
| For every Tun of *French* Wines | 8 | 0 | 0 |
| For every hundred Pounds Value of *French* Goods, except Wine, Brandy, Salt and Vinegar | 25 | 0 | 0 |
| For every hundred Pounds Value of Alamodes and Luteſtrings | 15 | 0 | 0 |
| For every hundred Weight of Lattin, Braſs, or Copper Wire | 0 | 6 | 0 |
| Upon all Goods and Merchandize, not particularly rated in the Book of Rates, paying Duty at Value, for every hundred Pounds Value | 5 | 0 | 0 |
| For every Gallon of ſingle StrongWater, *Aqua-vitæ*, or Brandy | 0 | 2 | 0 |
| For every Gallon of the ſame, double | 0 | 4 | 0 |

All theſe additional Duties over and above thoſe before impos'd.

*An Act for continuing certain Bills therein mention'd, and for charging ſeveral Joint-ſtocks.* The Act ſo continued were, that for the Impoſitions upon Wine and Vinegar, which was to have expir'd in 1696, continu'd till 1698; The Act for the Impoſition on Tobacco and Sugar, which was to have expir'd in

1696, continued till 1698 : The Act for Imposition on *India* Goods, which expir'd in 1695, continu'd to 1697. Besides these Continuations, there was a fresh Addition of five *per Cent.* to be paid out of the whole *East-India* Stock, then valu'd at seven hundred forty four thousand Pounds; twenty Shillings out of every Share of *African* Stock, and five Pounds out of every Share of the *Hudson's Bay* Company.

An. Dom. 1693. Reg. 5 & 6. *An Act for granting to their Majesties an Aid of four Shillings in the Pound for one Year, for carrying on a vigorous War against France.*

Also, *An Act for granting to their Majesties certain Rates and Duties upon Salt and upon Beer, Ale, and other Liquors,* &c. This Act to raise ten hundred thousand Pounds. The Rates,

|  | *l.* | *s.* | *d.* |
|---|---|---|---|
| For every Gallon of Foreign Salt imported, above the former Duties | o | o | 3 |
| For every Gallon of *English* Salt, above former Duties | o | o | 1 |

The Rates upon Beer, Ale and other Liquors, were one Moiety more than had been granted by the last additional Act of Duties before; this upon Liquors now given for sixteen Years, the Duties upon Salt for three Years. The Advances of the said were to be repaid in the said sixteen Years, by way of Annuities for that time.

Next, *An Act for raising Money by a Poll, payable Quarterly for one Year, for carrying on a vigorous War against France.*

Again, *An Act for granting to their Majesties several Rates and Duties upon Tonnage and Poundage of Ships and*

*and Veſſels, and upon Beer, Ale and other Liquors, &c.
to raiſe fifteen hundred thouſand Pounds, towards carrying on the War againſt* France. The Rates,

| | *l.* | *s.* | *d.* |
|---|---|---|---|
| For every Tun of the Burthen or Contents of any Ships or Veſſel, importing Goods, Wares or Merchandizes from the *Eaſt-Indies,* or any other Parts *Southward* or *Eaſtward* of the *Cape of Good Hope.* | I | 10 | 0 |
| For every Tun Burthen in like manner, from *Italy* or *Turkey* | 0 | 15 | 0 |
| For every Tun, Burthen in like manner, from *Spain* or *Portugal* | 0 | 10 | 0 |
| For every Tun Burthen from the *Weſt-Indies* | 0 | 10 | 0 |
| For every Tun Burthen from any Part of the *Netherlands* | 0 | 3 | 0 |
| For every Tun Burthen from *Norway, Hamborough,* or the *Baltick-Sea,* any *Eaſtland* Countries, or *North-Holland* | 0 | 5 | 0 |
| For every Tun Burthen from *Ireland* or *Scotland* | 0 | 2 | 0 |
| For every Tun Burthen from any Place in the *Mediterranean* Sea, not otherwiſe charg'd in this Act | 0 | 15 | 0 |
| For every Tun Burthen from *Guinea,* or *Africa* without the *Streights* | I | 0 | 0 |
| For every Tun Burthen from *Hudſon's Bay,* or any Place within that Company's Charter | I | 0 | 0 |
| For every Tun Burthen from the *Canaries, Madera,* or any the *Weſtern* Iſlands | 0 | 10 | 0 |

For

|   | *l.* | *s.* | *d.* |
|---|---|---|---|

For every Tun Burthen from *Green-*
*land, Muscovy* or *Russia*   } 0   10   0
For every Tun Burthen of Coasters    0    0    6

The Excise upon Beer, Ale and Liquors, to be
one Moiety of the Additional Excise before granted and expiring in the Year 1697.

The same Year, *An Act for granting to their Ma-*
*jesties several Duties upon Velum, Parchment and Paper*
*for four Years, towards carrying on a War against* France.
This was for stamping Velum, Parchment and Paper : The several Stamps were, one for 40 *s.* one
for 5 *s.* one for 2 *s.* 6 *d.* one of 1 *s.* and one of 1 *d.*
every Sheet or Skin us'd to be so stamp'd and to pay.
The Particulars of all the several Writings as they
are rated, are too tedious for this Place.

*An Act for the Licensing and Regulating, Hackney*
*Coaches and Stage Coaches.* By it seven hundred Hackney Coaches to be Licens'd, and every Coach to
pay for the Licence fifty Pounds ; the said Licence
to be good for twenty one Years, and that Payment by way of Fine, every Coach paying besides
it 4 *l. per Annum,* Stage Coaches to be Licens'd
but for one Year, and to pay eight Pounds for every Licence.

An. Reg. 6. *An Act for granting to their Majesties*
*a Subsidy of Tonnage and Poundage, and other Sums of*
*Money, upon Merchandize exported and imported.* It is
the same that was granted to King *Charles* the II.
for his Life, in the twelfth Year of his Reign, now
granted for five Years.

An. Reg. 6 & 7. *An Act for granting to his Majesty*
*an Aid of four Shillings in the Pound, &c.*

*An Act for granting to his Majesty certain Rates and*
*Duties upon Marriages, Births and Burials, and upon*
*Batche-*

*Batchelors and Widows, for the Term of five Years, for carrying on the War againft* France *with Vigour.*

|  | *l.* | *s.* | *d.* |
|---|---|---|---|
| For the Burial of every Perfon whatfoever | 0 | 4 | 0 |

And, over and above the faid 4 *s.* for the Burial of a Duke or Dutchefs 50 *l.* for a Marquifs or Marchionefs 40 *l.* for an Earl or Countefs 30 *l.* for a Vifcount or Vifcountefs 25 *l.* for a Baron or Baronefs, 20 *l.* for the eldeft Son of a Duke or his Wife 30 *l.* for the younger Son of a Duke or his Wife 25 *l.* for the eldeft Son of a Marquifs or his Wife 25 *l.* for the younger Son of a Marquifs or his Wife 15 *l.* for the eldeft Son of an Earl or his Wife 20 *l.* for the younger Son of an Earl or his Wife 15 *l.* for the eldeft Son of a Vifcount or his Wife 17 *l.* 10 *s.* for the younger Son of a Vifcount or his Wife 13 *l.* 6 *s.* 8 *d.* for the eldeft Son of a Baron or his Wife 15 *l.* for the younger Son of a Baron or his Wife 12 *l.* for every unmarried Daughter of a Duke 25 *l.* for every unmarried Daughter of a Marquifs 20 *l.* for every unmarried Daughter of an Earl 15 *l.* for every unmarried Daughter of a Vifcount 13 *l.* 6 *s.* 8 *d.* for every unmarried Daughter of a Baron 12 *l.* for every Widow of a Duke 50 *l.* a Widow of a Marquifs 40 *l.* of an Earl 30 *l* of a Vifcount 25 *l.* of a Baron 20 *l.* for a Baronet or his Wife 15 *l.* a Knight of the Bath or his Wife 15 *l.* a Knight Batchelor or his Wife 10 *l.* a Serjeant at Law, being the King's Serjeant 20 *l.* a King's Serjeant's Wife 10 *l.* every other Serjeant at Law 15 *l.* fuch Serjeant's Wife 7 *l.* 10 *s.* an Efquire or his Wife 5 *l.* a Gentleman or his Wife 20 *s.* every younger Child of a Baronet, Knight of the *Bath,* Knight Batchelor, Serjeant at Law, Efquire, or Gentleman, or the Wife of fuch 20 *s.* every Widow of a Knight of the *Bath* 15 *l.*

the

the Widow of a Knight Batchelor 10 *l.* the Widow
of a King's Serjeant 10 *l.* the Widow of any other
Serjeant at Law 7 *l.* 10 *s.* the Widow of an Esquire
5 *l.* the Widow of a Gentleman 20 *s.* An Archbishop 50 *l.* an Archbishop's Wife or Widow 10 *l.*
every Bishop 20 *l.* a Bishop's Wife 5 *l.* a Dean 10 *l.*
a Dean's Wife or Widow 2 *l. s.* an Archdeacon 2 *l.*
10 *s.* an Archdeacon's Wife or Widow 20 *s.* a Canon or Prebendary 2 *l.* 10 *s.* the Wife of such a one
20 *s.* a Doctor of Divinity, Law, or Physick 5 *l.*
the Wife of any such 20 *s.* Every Son or Daughter
of an Archbishop, Bishop, Dean, Archdeacon, Canon, Prebendary, Doctor of Divinity, Law, or Physick 20 *s.* Every Person having a Real Estate of
20 *l. per Annum* or upwards, or a Personal Estate of
600 *l.* or upwards, not otherwise charg'd before,
20 *s.* The Wife, Widow, or Child of any such
10 *s.*

The Duty upon Births : Every Child whatsoever,
except those that receive Alms of the Parish 2 *s.*
Every Duke and Dutchess for every Child 30 *l.* and
so descending gradually thorough all Degrees, as in
the Burials too long for this Place.

For every Marriage 2 *s.* 6 *d.* Every Duke over
and above 50 *l.* and so descending gradually thro'
all Degrees, as in the Births and Burials.

Every Batchelor above twenty-five Years of Age,
and every Widower to pay 1 *s.* yearly ; every Duke
to pay over and above 12 *l.* 10 *s.* yearly, and so
descending gradually thro' all Degrees, as in the
others.

Next follows, *An Act for granting to his Majesty
several additional Duties upon Coffee, Tea, Chocolate and
Spices, towards Satisfaction of the Debts due for Trans-
port Service for the Reduction of* Ireland. The Rates.

|  | *l.* | *s.* | *d.* |
|---|---|---|---|
| For every hundred Weight of Coffee imported | 2 | 16 | 0 |
| For every hundred Weight of Cacao Nuts imported from *English* Plantations | 2 | 16 | 0 |
| For every hundred Weight of Cacao Nuts imported from other Places | 4 | 4 | 0 |
| For every Pound of Chocolate imported | 0 | 1 | 0 |
| For every Pound of Cacao Paste imported | 0 | 2 | 0 |
| For every Pound of Tea regularly imported | 0 | 1 | 0 |
| For every Pound imported from *Holland,* &c. | 0 | 2 | 0 |
| For all Nutmegs, Cinnamon, Clove and Mace imported, for every hundred Pounds Value | 5 | 0 | 0 |
| For all Pictures imported, for every hundred Pounds Value | 20 | 0 | 0 |

The fame Year ftill, *An Act for granting to his Majefty certain Duties upon Glafs Wares, Stone and Earthen Bottles, Coals and Culm, for carrying on the War againft* France.

An. Reg. 7 & 8, *An Act for granting to his Majefty an Aid of four Shillings in the Pound for one Year, for carrying on the War againft* France.

*An Act for continuing feveral Duties granted by former Acts upon Wine and Vinegar, and upon Tobacco and* Eaft-India *Goods, and other Merchandize imported, for carrying on the War againft* France. See it before.

*An Act for granting to his Majefty feveral Rates or Duties upon Houfes, for making good the Deficiency of the clipped Money.* This is commonly call'd the Window Tax.

Every

Every Houfe to pay 2 *s.* a Houfe having ten Windows 6 *s.* every Houfe having twenty Window 10 *s.*

*An Act for granting to his Majefty an additional Duty upon all* French *Goods an Merchandize.*

French Wines imported to pay 25 *s. per* Tun above the old Rates *:* Brandy fingle Proof 30 *l.* double Proof 60 *l.* Vinegar 15 *l.* All other *French* Goods 25 *l. per Cent. ad Valorem.*

*An Act for laying feveral Duties upon Low Wines, or Spirits of the firft Extraction,* &c.

*An Act for continuing to his Majefty certain Duties upon Salt, Glafs Wares, Stone and Earthern Wares, and for granting feveral Duties upon Tobacco-pipes, and other Earthern Wares,* &c.

An. Reg. 8 & 9, *An Act for granting to his Majefty feveral Duties upon Paper, Vellum and Parchment,* &c.

*An Act for continuing certain additional Impofitions upon feveral Goods and Merchandizes, continu'd.*

*An Act for making good the Deficiencies of feveral Funds therein mention'd,* &c.

*An Act for laying a Duty upon Leather for the Term of three Years,* &c.

*An Act for granting to his Majefty certain Duties upon Malt, Mum, Sweets, Cyder and Perry,* &c.

*An Act for granting to his Majefty a further Subfidy of Tunnage and Poundage upon Merchandizes imported, for the Term of two Years and three quarters, and an additional Land Tax for one Year, for carrying on the War againft* France. The Rates,

|  | *l.* | *s.* | *d.* |
|---|---|---|---|
| Every Tun of *French* Wine imported into the Port of *London*, by *Englifh* | 4 | 10 | 0 |
| The fame by Strangers | 6 | 0 | 0 |
| The fame Wine imported by *Englifh* into all other Ports of *England* | 3 | 0 | 0 |

The

|  | *l.* | *s.* | *d.* |
|---|---|---|---|
| The fame by Aliens | 4 | 10 | o |
| Every But or Pipe of *Levant, Spanifh,* or *Portugues* Wines imported to *London* by *Englifh* | 2 | 5 | o |
| The fame imported by Aliens | 3 | o | o |
| The fame imported by *Englifh* into others Ports of *England* | 1 | 10 | o |
| The fame imported by Strangers | 2 | 5 | o |
| For every Awm of *Rhenifh*, or *German* Wine imported by *Englifh* | 1 | o | o |
| The fame imported by Aliens | 1 | 5 | o |
| For all other Goods imported of every twenty Shillings Value | o | 1 | o |

All thefe Rates over and above what was paid before

All Drugs and Spices to pay one third more than was paid before

*An Act to licence Hawkers and Pedlers, for a further Provifion for Payment of the Intereft of the Tranfport Debt for the reducing of* Ireland.

Every Hawker, Pedlar, Petty-Chapman, or other trading Perfon going from Town to Town, or to other Men's Houfes, to pay 4*l.* and 4*l.* more for every Horfe, Afs or Mule, carrying or drawing Goods,

*An Act for granting an Aid to his Majefty, as well by a Land Tax, as by feveral Subfidies, and other Duties payable for one Year.*

An. Reg. 9 & 10, *An Act for granting to his Majefty, the Sum of one Million four hundred eighty four thoufand and fifteen Pounds, one Shilling eleven Pence three Farthings, for disbanding Forces, paying Seamen, and other Ufes therein mention'd.*

*An Act for granting to his Majefty feveral Duties upon Coals and Culm.*

Still

Still the fame Year, *An Act for granting to his Majefty a further Subfidy of Tunnage and Poundage for the Service of his Majefty's Houfhold, and other Ufes therein mention'd, during his Majefty's Life.* The Rates the fame as in the laft Act above of the fame Sorts.

*An Act for granting to his Majefty, his Heirs and Succeffors, further Duties upon Stampt Vellum, Parchment and Paper.*

*An Act for encreafing his Majefty's Duties upon Luftrings and Alamodes.*

*An Act for granting to his Majefty an Aid by a quarterly Poll.*

*An Act for raifing a Sum not exceeding two Millions, upon a Fund for Payment of Annuities, after the Rate of eight Pounds* per Cent. per Annum, *and for fettling the Trade to the* Eaft-Indies.

An. Reg. 10. *An Act for granting an Aid to his Majefty, for disbanding the Army and other neceffary Occafions.* This Act was given for 800000 *l.*

An. Reg. 10 & 11. *An Act for granting to his Majefty the Sum of one Million four hundred eighty four thoufand and fifteen Pounds, one Shilling eleven Pence three Farthings, for disbanding the Army, providing for the Navy, and for oiher neceffary Occafions.*

*An Act for laying further Duties upon Sweets, &c.* which was alfo for leffening the Duties upon Vinegar and other Goods, *&c.*

An. Reg. 11 & 12. *An Act for granting an Aid to his Majefty, by Sale of the forfeited and other Eftates and Intereft in* Ireland; *and by a Land Tax in* England, *for the feveral Purpofes therein mention'd.* The Money arifing by the Sale of Lands appropriated to pay the Arrears of Officers, the Debt for Tranfport-Service and Clothing; but I have feen an Eftimate of the faid Eftates, wherein it was particularly fet down, that a certain Lady had Lands there given her to the Value of 25000 *l. per Annum,* but whether
for

for Arrears, or Tranſport, or Clothing, was not there ſet down.

*An Act for laying further Duties upon wrought Silks, Muſlins, and ſome other Commodities of the Growth of India, &c.* The Rate 15 *l.* for every hundred Pound Value.

An. Reg. 12 & 13. *An Act for granting an Aid to his Majeſty for defraying the Expence of his Navy, Guards and Garriſons for one Year, and for other neceſſary Occaſions.*

*An Act for granting his Majeſty ſeveral Duties upon Low Wines, or Spirits of the firſt Extraction, and continuing ſeveral additional Duties upon Coffee, Tea, Chocolate, Spices and Pictures ; and certain Impoſitions upon Hawkers, Pedlars and Petty-chapmen ; and the Duty of fifty* per Cent. *upon Muſlins, and for improving the Duties upon Japann'd and Lacquer'd Goods, and for continuing the Coinage Duty, for the ſeveral Terms and Purpoſes therein mention'd.*

*An Act for appropriating three thouſand ſeven hundred Pounds Weekly, out of certain Branches of Exciſe, for publick Uſes, and for making a Proviſion for the Service of his Majeſty's Houſhold and Family, and other his neceſſary Occaſions.*

An. Reg. 19. *An Act for granting an Aid to his Majeſty, by laying Duties upon Malt, Mum, Cyder and Perry.*

Thus ended this coſtly Reign, King *William* dying on the 8th of *March,* 170$\frac{1}{2}$, when he had reigned thirteen Years and ſome Months. That it was a coſtly Reign may be collected by the great Number of Money Acts paſs'd in ſo few Years; but for a more exact View of it, a curious and knowing Perſon collected the Value of what was given, till about a Year and an half before his Death ; which was as follows.

*A Ge-*

*A general Abstract of the Receipts of the publick Revenues, Taxes and Loans granted to King William, from* November 5, 1688, *to* Michaelmas 1700.

|  | *l.* | *s.* | *d.* |
|---|---|---|---|
| Customs | 10997955 | 6 | $3\frac{1}{2}$ |
| Excise | 12105151 | 19 | 7 |
| Hearth and Letter Money, &c. | 01769653 | 1 | $4\frac{3}{4}$ |
| Land Tax | 17520100 | 14 | 5 |
| Poll Tax | 02527983 | 12 | 9 |
| Promiscuous Taxes | 07170903 | 17 | $9\frac{1}{2}$ |
| Divers Receipts | 00466999 | 1 | 4 |
| State Loans | 13348680 | 5 | $10\frac{1}{4}$ |
| Remain'd *November* 5, 1688, with which the Treasury began | 80138 | 18 | 3 |
| **Total** | 65,987,566 | 17 | 8 |

If we add to this the Impositions for the last Year and odd Months that he surviv'd, after the Account above, it will not fall any thing short, upon a modest Computation of making up Seventy Millions; a Sum so prodigious, that it might seem incredible, were it not known matter of Fact, and so fresh in Memory; and what is yet more wonderful, the greater part spent Abroad; for had it still circulated at Home, it's passing thro' many Hands, would have made it the less to be felt. To add to this, it was computed that some thousands of Ships were lost, not only by Storms and such like Accidents, but taken by the *French*, who made a better Trade of Privateering, than *England* could of all

all it's Commerce Abroad. But let all that pafs, and us proceed to,

# Queen ANNE.

WHO afcended the Throne on the 8th of *March,* 170½, and following the Example of her Predeceffor, began a new War with *France,* which was no lefs coftly than the former, as fhall be here fhewn.

The firft Grant upon this Queen's immediate Exaltation was, *An Act for the better Support of her Majefty's Houfhold, and of the Honour and Dignity of the Crown.* This was the fettling of a Revenue of feven hundred thoufand Pounds a Year on her for Life, as had been done before for King *William* and Queen *Mary* for their Lives, and commonly call'd the Civil Lift, as no way tending to Military Charges. It was to be rais'd upon the Excife of Beer, Ale and other Liquors, as the fame had been paid to King *Charles* the Second, and out of the Duties of Tunnage and Poundage; as alfo of the Poft-Office, Firft-Fruits, &c. of all which enough has been faid before.

A Bill being then brought in of Deficiencies in the feveral Sums formerly granted to King *William,* and the total Sum of the faid Deficiencies amounting to no lefs than two Millions three hundred thirty eight thoufand fix hundred twenty eight Pounds, befides the Intereft due and to grow upon the Money advanc'd on thofe Duties, there immediately paffed *An Act for making good Deficiences, and for preferving publick Credit.* The Sum was to be rais'd by continuing the Act of Tunnage and Poundage, and Impofitions upon Goods imported and exported; as alfo the Duties on Wines, Tobacco, *India* Goods

Goods, &c. there being too many Particulars to repeat here, having been all mention'd in the former
Reigns, when those Acts passed.

Next follow'd, *An Act for granting an Aid to her
Majesty by divers Subsidies, and a Land Tax.*

Still the same Year, *An Act for granting to her Majesty a Land Tax for carrying on the War against* France
*and* Spain. This Tax was given for one Million
nine hundred seventy nine thousand nine hundred
thirty one Pounds nineteen Shillings and one Penny,
the several Sums every County, City, Borough,
Town and Place in *England* and *Wales* was to pay,
being therein particularly assess'd, including the
Town of *Berwick* upon *Tweed*. All the said Particulars being too long for this Place, it will be sufficient to observe, that the Tax in general was after the Rate of 4 *s. per* Pound, which shows the
Amount of all the other Acts of the same Sort.

The same Year again, *An Act for granting a Supply to her Majesty, by several Duties impos'd upon Malt,
Mum, Cyder and Perry.* The Duties were, for Malt
6 *d. per* Bushel, Mum 10 *s. per* Barrel, Cyder and
Perry 4 *s. per* Hogshead.

*An Act for continuing the Duties upon Coals, Culm and
Cinders.* See it 9 & 10 King *William*.

*An Act for granting an Aid to her Majesty, by Sale of
several Annuities at the Exchequer, for carrying on the
War against* France *and* Spain. Given for no more
than 87630 *l.* a small Sum as Money has been given
in those Times.

*An Act for granting to her Majesty several Subsidies
for carrying on the War against* France *and* Spain. The
Rates impos'd were, for every hundred Pounds
Value of trading Peoples Stock 2 *l,* 10 *s.* All Pen-
sions and Annuities 4 *s. per* Pound. Persons having
Fee or Salary, &c. Ecclesiastical, Civil, or Military 1 *s. per* Pound. Practicers in Law, Preachers in
separate

feparate Congregations, Brokers, Factors, Practifers in Phyfick and other Profeffions 4 *s. per* Pound.

An. Dom. 1703, Reg. 2 & 3. *An Act for granting an Aid to her Majefty by a Land Tax, to be raifed in the Year* 1704. The Rate the fame as the Land Tax laft above mention'd.

*An Act for granting an Aid to her Majefty by continuing the Duties upon Malt, Mum, Cyder and Perry.* The fame as above continu'd.

*An Act for granting an Aid to her Majefty for carrying on the War, and other her Majefty's Occafions, by felling Annuities at feveral Rates, and for fuch refpective Terms, or Eftates as are therein mention'd.* This given for one Million eighteen thoufand eight hundred fixty feven Pounds eighteen Shillings and fix Pence, to be advanc'd for purchafing of Annuities payable out of the Excife.

*An Act for granting to her Majefty an additional Subfidy of Tunnage and Poundage for three Years, and for laying a further Duty upon French Wines condemn'd as lawful Price, and for afcertaining the Values of unrated Goods imported from the* Eaft-Indies.

*An. Dom.* 1704, *Reg.* 3 & 4, The Land Tax of 4 *s.* in the Pound, as above, again granted.

*An Act for raifing Monies by Sale of feveral Annuities, for carrying on the prefent War.*

*An Act for continuing the Duties upon Malt, Mum, Cyder and Perry for one Year.*

*An Act for continuing Duties upon Low Wines, and* upon *Coffee, Tea, Chocolate, Spices and Pictures; and upon Hawkers, Pedlars and Petty-Chapmen; and upon Muflins, and granting new Duties upon feveral of the faid Commodities, and alfo upon Callicoes,* China *Ware and Drugs.*

*An Act for granting to her Majefty a further Subfidy on Wines and Merchandizes imported.*

*An.*

*An. Dom.* 1705, *Reg.* 4, The Land Tax again, at 4 *s.* in the Pound, as before.

*An Act for continuing the Duties upon Malt, Mum, Cyder and Perry, for the Service of the Year* 1706.

*An Act for continuing an additional Subſidy of Tunnage and Poundage, and certain Duties upon Coals, Culm and Cinders ; and additional Duties of Exciſe, and for ſettling and eſtabliſhing a Fund thereby, and by other Ways and Means, for Payment of Annuities to be ſold for raiſing a further Supply to her Majeſty, for the Service of the Year* 1706, *and other Uſes therein mention'd.*

An Act for laying further Duties on Low Wines, *&c.*

*An. Dom.* 1706, *Reg.* 5, The Land Tax 4 *s.* in the Pound again.

An Act for continuing the Duties on Malt, *&c.* again.

*An Act for continuing the Duties upon Houſes, to ſecure a yearly Fund for circulating Exchequer Bills, whereby a Sum not exceeding fifteen hundred thouſand Pounds is intended to be rais'd, for carrying on the War and other her Majeſty's Occaſions.*

*An Act for continuing the Duties on Low Wines, and Spirits of the firſt Extraction, and the Duties payable by Hawkers, Pedlars and Petty-Chapmen ; and part of the Duties on Stampt Vellum, Parchment and Paper, and the late Duties on Sweets ; and the one third Subſidy of Tunnage and Poundage, and for ſettling and eſtabliſhing a Fund thereby, &c. for raiſing a further Supply to her Majeſty, for the Service of the Year* 1707, *&c.*

*An Act for continuing ſeveral Subſidies, Impoſitions and Duties, and for making Proviſions therein mention'd to raiſe Money by way of Loan, for the Service of the War,* &c. By this Act were continued the Duties on Wine, Vinegar, Tobacco, *India* Goods, Whale Fins, and ſo many other things as would ſwell this

Compen-

Compendium beyond Meafure, were we always to defcend to Particulars.

*Anno Dom.* 1707, *Reg.* 6. The Land Tax again at 4 *s.* in the Pound.

The Duties on Malt, Mum, *&c.* continued.

An Act for raifing a further Supply by Sale of Annuities charg'd on a Fund, not exceeding 40000 *l. per Annum.* The Sum fo to be rais'd 640000 *l.*

An Act for continuing half the Tunnage, Poundage, and other Duties on Goods imported, granted to King *Charles* II. now apply'd for raifing the Sum of 1280000 *l.* to be paid by way of Annuities at 80000 *l. per Annum.*

An Act for continuing the half Subfidies therein mention'd, that is, on Wine, Vinegar, Tobacco, *India* Goods, *&c.* The Sum propos'd to be advanc'd upon this Act, to be feven hundred twenty nine thoufand fixty feven Pounds fifteen Shillings and fix Pence three Farthings.

Again, the Duties upon Coffee, Chocolate, Spices, Pictures, Muflins, and feveral other Commodities; the Sum not afcertain'd.

*Anno Dom.* 1708, *Reg.* 7. The Land Tax continu'd at 4 *s.* in the Pound.

Duties on Malt, *&c.* again continu'd.

Impofitions on Tobacco, *India* Goods, Wine, Vinegar, *&c.* continu'd, to raife Money by way of Loan; the Sum to be borrow'd 645000 *l.*

*Anno Dom.* 1709, *Reg.* 8. The Land Tax again at 4 *s.* in the Pound.

Duties on Malt, *&c.* continu'd.

Duties on Coals, *&c.* continu'd, and new Duties on Houfes, to raife the Sum of 150000 *l.* by way of Lottery.

New Duties of Excife, and upon feveral Commodities granted, to raife 900000 *l.* by Sale of Annuities.

*An Act for laying certain Duties upon Candles, and certain Rates upon Monies to be given with Clerks and Apprentices, towards raiſing her Majeſty's Supply, for the Year* 1710.

Next ſeveral **Duties,** Impoſitions and additional Taxes were continu'd, ſtill on Wine, Vinegar, Tobacco, *India* Goods, &c.

*Anno Dom.* 1710, *Reg.* 9. The Land Tax ſtill 4 *s.* in the Pound.

Duties on Malt, &c. again continu'd.

*An Act for reviving, continuing and appropriating certain Duties upon ſeveral Commodities to be exported ; and certain Duties upon Coals to be Water-born and carry'd Coaſt-wiſe, and for granting further Duties upon Candles, for thirty-two Years, to raiſe fifteen hundred Thouſand Pounds, by way of a Lottery, for the Service of the Year* 1711 *; and for ſuppreſſing ſuch unlawful Lotteries, and ſuch Inſurance-Offices, as are therein mention'd.*

*An Act for eſtabliſhing a General Poſt-Office, for all her Majeſty's Dominions, and for ſettling a Weekly Sum out of the Revenues thereof, for the Service of the War, and other her Majeſty's Occaſions.* The Rates for which Letters were within 80 Miles, 3 *d.* a ſingle Letter, 6 *d.* the double, and 12 *d.* the Ounce. Every Letter carry'd above 80 Miles, ſingle 4 *d.* double 8 *d.* the Ounce 1 *s* 4 *d.* Single Letter to *Edenburgh* 6 *d.* double 12 *d.* Ounce 2 *s.* From *Edenburgh* 50 Miles round, ſingle Letter 2 *d.* double 4 *d.* Ounce 8 *d.* From *Edenburgh* above 50 Miles and not exceeding 80 Miles, ſingle Letter 3 *d.* double 6 *d.* Ounce 12 *d.* From *Edenburgh* above 80 Miles, ſingle Letter 4 *d.* double 8 *d.* Ounce 1 *s.* 4 *d.* To or from *Dublin,* ſingle Letter 6 *d.* double 1 *s.* Ounce 2 *s.* From *Dublin* not above 40 Miles, ſingle Letter 2 *d.* double 4 *d.* Ounce 8 *d.* Above 40 Miles from *Dublin,* ſingle Letter 4 *d.* double 8 *d.* Ounce 1 *s.* 4. *d.* For

every

every Letter fent on Board, or brought from any Ship or Veffel, 1 *d.* above the aforefaid Rates.

Foreign Letters. From any Part of *France* to *London*, fingle 10 *d.* double 20 *d.* treble 2 *s.* 6 *d.* Ounce 3 *s.* 4 *d.* To and from *Spain* and *Portugal*, through *France*, Poft paid to *Bayonne*, fingle 1 *s.* 6 *d.* double 3 *s.* treble 4 *s.* 6 *d.* Ounce 6 *s.* To and from *London*, through *France*, to *Italy*, *Sicily*,, and *Turkey*, fingle 1 *s.* 3 *d.* double 2 *s.* 6. *d.* treble 3 *s.* 9 *d.* Ounce 5 *s.* From *Spanifh Netherlands* to *London*, fingle 10 *d.* double 1 *s.* 8 *d.* treble 2 *s.* 6 *d.* Ounce 3 *s.* 4 *d.* To and from *Italy* and *Sicily*, through *Spanifh Netherlands*, Poft paid to *Antwerp*, fingle 1 *s.* double 2 *s.* treble 3 *s.* Ounce 4 *s.* To and from *Germany*, *Swifferland*, *Denmark*, *Sweden*, and all Parts of the North, through *Spanifh Netherlands*, fingle 1 *s.* double 2 *s.* treble 3 *s.* Ounce 4 *s.* To and from *Spain* and *Portugal*, through *Spanifh Netherlands*, fingle 1 *s.* 6 *d.* double 3 *s.* treble 4 *s.* 6 *d.* Ounce 6 *s.* From the *United Provinces* to *London*, fingle 10 *d.* double and treble need not be repeated fince any one can double and treble the fame, Ounce 3 *s.* 4 *d.* To and from *Italy* and *Sicily*, through the *United Provinces*, fingle 1 *s.* Ounce 4 *s.* To and from *Germany*, *Swifferland*, *Denmark*, *Sweden*, and all Parts of the North, fingle 1 *s.* Ounce 4 *s.* To and from *Spain* and *Portugal*, through the *United Provinces*, fingle 1 *s.* 6 *d.* Ounce 6 *s.* To and from *Hamburgh*, through the *Spanifh Netherlands*, or the *United Provinces*, fingle 10 *d.* Ounce 3 *s.* 4 *d.* Between *London*, *Spain*, and *Portugal*, by Packet-boats, fingle 1 *s.* Ounce 6 *s.* To and from *Jamaica*, *Barbadas*, *Antigua*, *Monferrat*, *Nieves*, and *St. Chrif-tophers*, fingle 1 *s.* 6 *d.* Ounce 6 *s.* To and from *New York*, fingle 1 *s.* Ounce 4 *s.* The reft being the Rates of Letters from one Place to another in the *Englifh* Plantations in *America*, are here omitted as of little Use to us, the Curious, or such as have occasion, may recur to the Act.

The same Year *An Act for laying certain Duties upon Hides and Skins, tann'd, taw'd, or dress'd, and upon Vellum and Parchment, for the Term of thirty-two Years*, &c.   The Rates,  Dear-skins imported dress'd 6 *d. per* Pound; Loshee, Buffalo, Elk, *&c.* Hides dress'd, 4 *d. per* Pound; Hides and Calf-skins tann'd, imported, 1 *d.* ½ *per* Pound; Horse-hides dress'd, 1 *s. per* Hide; Hides of Steers, Cows, *&c.* dress'd, 2 *s. per* Hide; Calf-skins and Kids dress'd, 1 *d.* ¼ *per* Pound; all Slink-skins dress'd with the Hair on, 1 *d. per* Pound; the same and Dog-skins without Hair ½ *per* Pound; Cordivants imported, 4 *s. per* Dozen; Goat-skins, not call'd Cordivants, dress'd, 6 *d. per* Pound; Kid-skins 1 *s. per* Dozen; Sheep-skins dress'd 1 *s.* 6 *d. per* Dozen, *&c.*

*An Act for laying a Duty upon Hops.*   The Rates, 3 *d. per* Pound imported, *British* Hops 1 *d. per* Pound.

*An Act for making good Deficiencies, and satisfying the publick Debts ; and for erecting a Corporation to carry on a Trade to the* South-Seas, *&c.*   The Debts and Deficiencies mention'd in this Act are therein computed at eight millions nine hundred seventy one thousand three hundred twenty-five Pounds.   Provision was herein made, by many Impositions, to pay this vast Debt; but how perform'd we shall see hereafter.

*An Act for Duties upon Coals for building fifty new Churches.*   This not being given for the Use of the Crown need not be plac'd to that Account; but still it was an Imposition on the Subject, and afterwards part of it diverted from what it was given for.

An Act for licensing and regulating Hackney-Coaches and Chairs; and charging new Duties on

stamp'd

ftampt Vellum, Parchment, and Paper; and on Cards and Dice; and on the Exportation of Rock-Salt for *Ireland, &c.* for raifing two Millions for carrying on the War, *&c.*

*Anno Dom.* 1711. *Reg.* 10, The Land-Tax again at 4 *s.* in the Pound.

Duties upon Malt, *&c.* again continu'd.

An Act for laying feveral Duties upon all Soap and Paper made in *Great Britain,* or imported; chequer'd and ftrip'd Linnens; Silks, Callicoes, Linnens, and Stuffs, printed, painted, or ftained; ftampt Vellum, Parchment, and Paper, printed Papers, Pamphlets, and Advertifements, for raifing the Sum of eighteen hundred thoufand Pounds by way of Lottery, *&c.*

An Act for laying additional Duties on Hides and Skins, Vellum and Parchment, and new Duties on Starch, Coffee, Tea, Drugs, Gilt and Silver Wire, and Policies of Infurance; for raifing the Sum of one Million eight hundred thoufand Pounds.

*An. Dom.* 1712. *Reg.* 11. The whole Taxes continu'd as in other Years amounted to 6656967 Pounds.

*Anno Dom.* 1713, *Reg.* 12. The Land Tax Act again.

Duties upon Malt, *&c.* again continu'd.

An Act to raife twelve hundred thoufand Pounds for publick Ufes, by circulating a further Sum in *Exchequer* Bills; and for enabling her Majefty to raife five hundred thoufand Pounds on the Revenues appointed for Ufes of her Civil Government, to be apply'd for and towards the Payment of fuch Debts and Arrears owing to her Servants, Tradefmen and others, as are therein mention'd.

*Anno Dom.* 1714, *Reg.* 13. Land Tax again.

Duties upon Malt, *&c.* continu'd.

An Act for laying additional Duties on Soap and Paper, and upon certain Linnens, Silks, Callicoes and Stuffs; and upon Starch and exported Goods, and upon ftamp'd Vellum, Parchment and Paper; for raifing one Million four hundred thoufand Pounds, by way of a Lottery, for her Majefty's Supply. The War was at an End, but the Taxes were not.

But here ended the Life of Queen *Anne*, during whofe Reign, being much about the fame Length as her Predeceffor's, the Sums of Money rais'd feem to exceed thofe granted to him; fo that during thofe two Reigns, which lafted about twenty-fix Years, there may be reckon'd to have been near an hundred and fifty Millions given to the Crown, befides the Debts left upon the Nation; and fo we will leave her.

# K. GEORGE.

OF whom it may fuffice to fay, that he was proclaimed King on the Firft of *Auguft* 1714, and fo to proceed to the Taxes and Impofitions during his Time.

Anno Dom. 1714, Reg. 1. *An Act for the better Support of his Majefty's Houfhold, and of the Honour and Dignity of the Crown of* Great Britain. This is the fame, and in the fame Manner as that of the firft Year of Queen *Anne*, for granting the Sum of 700000 *l. per Annum*, as generally call'd, for the Civil Lift, for Life.

*An Act for rectifying Miftakes in the Names of the Commiffioners for the Land Tax for the Year* 1714; *and for raifing fo much as is wanting to make up the Sum of fourteen hundred thoufand Pounds, intended to be rais'd by a Lottery, foi the publick Service in the faid Year.*

Anno Dom. 1715, Reg. 2. *An Act for granting an Aid to his Majefty, to be rais'd by a Land Tax in* Great Britain, *for the Service of the Year* 1715. This, like the Land Tax before, was fet at a certain Rate upon all Counties, Cities, Boroughs, Towns, and
Places

Places in *England* and *Wales*, including the Town of *Berwick* upon *Tweed*; but lower than that, as amounting to only 1020588 *l.* 16 *s.* 6 *d.* ½. Having there mention'd the Sums then tax'd, towards that Impofition on the Cities of *London* and *Weftminfter*, it fhall be here only obferv'd, that in this Act, the faid City of *London* was affefs'd at 61667 *l.* 1 *s.* 3 *d.* ½. It is alfo worth obferving, that the whole Sum granted by this Act, being as is faid above, 1020588 *l.* 16 *s.* 6 *d.* ½. *England* is charg'd with 996111 *l.* 15 *s.* 11 *d.* ½. of the faid Sum; and *Scotland* with only 23977 *l.* 0 *s.* 7 *d.* the feveral Affeffments for the fame upon the refpective Shires, Stewartries, Cities and Boroughs, being fet down after the fame manner as thofe for *England.*

The Duties on Malt, &c. ftill continu'd, as in the former Reign.

*An Act for enlarging the Fund of the Governour and Company of the Bank of* England, *relating to Exchequer Bills; and for fettling an additional Revenue of one hundred and twenty thoufand Pounds* per Annum, *upon his Majefty during his Life, for the Service of the Civil Government, and for eftablifhing a certain Fund of fifty four thoufand fix hundred Pounds* per Annum, *in order to raife a Sum not exceeding nine hundred and ten thoufand Pounds for the Service of the Publick, by Sale of Annuities, after the Rate of fix Pounds* per Cent. per Annum, *redeemable by Parliament; and for fatisfying an Arrear for Work and Materials at* Blenheim, *incurred whilft that Building was carried on,* &c;

*An Act for raifing nine hundred and ten thoufand Pounds for publick Services, by Sale of Annuities, after the Rate of five Pounds* per Cent. per Annum, *redeemable by Parliament,* &c.

*An Act for enlarging the Capital Stock and yearly Fund of the* South Sea *Company, and for fupplying thereby eight hundred twenty two thoufand thirty two*
Pounds,

*Pounds, four Shillings and eight Pence, to publich Uſes ; and for raiſing one hundred ſixty nine thouſand Pounds, for the like Uſes, by Sale of Annuities,* &c.

*Anno Dom.* 1715 & 1716. *Reg.* 2. The Land Tax again continu'd.

Duties on Malt, &c. again continu'd.

*An Act to continue Duties for encouraging the Coinage of Money ; and to charge the Duties on Senna as a Medicinal Drug,* &c.

*An Act for appointing Commiſſioners to enquire of the Eſtates of certain Traitors, and of Popiſh Recuſants, and of Eſtates given to Superſtitious Uſes, in order to raiſe Money out of them ſeverally for the Uſe of the Publick.* By this Act, all and every the Caſtles, Honours, Lordſhips, Manors, Meſſuages, Lands, Tenements, Rents, Reverſions, Services, Remainders, Poſſeſſions, Royalties, Franchiſes, Juriſdictions and Privileges whatſoever, and all Appurtenances to them belonging; and all Rights of Entry, Rights of Action, Titles, Conditions, Uſes, Truſts, Powers, and Authorities; and all Leaſes for Life, Lives or Years, Penſions, Annuities, Rents, Charges and Hereditaments, of all Perſons convicted for levying War, &c. are veſted in the King. The Account brought in of Eſtates thus forfeited, was as follows.

## Eſtates forfeited in *Scotland.*

|  | *l.* | *s.* | *d.* |
|---|---|---|---|
| 1. *Winton* | 3393 | 00 | 11 |
| 2. *Southesk* | 3271 | 10 | 02 |
| 3. *Linlithgow* | 1297 | 04 | 04 |
| 4. *Keir* | 907 | 19 | 01 |
| 5. *Panmure* | 3456 | 11 | 10 |
| 6. *Wedderburn* | 213 | 00 | 00 |
| 7. *Ayton* | 323 | 10 | 05 |
| 8. *Kilſyth* | 864 | 19 | 09 |

9. *Bannock-*

|     |                  | *l.* | *s.* | *d.* |
|-----|------------------|------|------|------|
| 9.  | *Bannockbourn*   | 411  | 14   | 09   |
| 10. | *East-Reston*    | 137  | 09   | 10   |
| 11. | *Marr*           | 1678 | 05   | 08   |
| 12. | *Invernitie*     | 361  | 12   | 01   |
| 13. | *Invehtinsowl*   | 347  | 06   | 05   |
| 14. | *Pow-house*      | 377  | 09   | 06   |
| 15. | *Nutthil*        | 72   | 07   | 10   |
| 16. | *Bowhill*        | 27   | 14   | 07   |
| 17. | *Lathrisk*       | 208  | 03   | 09   |
| 18. | *Glenbervy*      | 75   | 12   | 10   |
| 19. | *Preston-Hall*   | 230  | 17   | 11   |
| 20. | *Wood-End*       | 83   | 06   | 04   |
| 21. | *Fairney*        | 153  | 08   | 07   |
| 22. | *Master of Nairn*| 60   | 09   | 03   |
| 23. | *Dunborg*        | 170  | 06   | 06   |
| 24. | *Earl Marischal* | 1677 | 06   | 00   |
| 25. | *Kilconquhar*    | 287  | 08   | 09   |
| 26. | Lord *Nairn*     | 740  | 10   | 03   |
| 27. | *Finglass*       | 537  | 19   | 02   |
| 28. | *Cromlix*        | 415  | 00   | 04   |
| 29. | *Nithsdale*      | 809  | 19   | 07   |
| 30. | *Ineray*         | 281  | 11   | 01   |
| 31. | *Kenmure*        | 608  | 10   | 09   |
| 32. | *Drummond*       | 2566 | 09   | 06   |
| 33. | *Burleigh*       | 697  | 10   | 07   |
| 34. | *Scarstann*      | 110  | 05   | 03   |
| 35. | *Duntroon*       | 54   | 04   | 09   |
| 36. | *Lagg*           | 424  | 15   | 00   |
| 37. | *Carnwath*       | 864  | 08   | 11   |
| 38. | *Baldoon*        | 1495 | 12   | 10   |

Total 29694  06  08

Estates

Eſtates forfeited in *Eugland.*

|  | *l.* | *s.* | *d.* |
|---|---|---|---|
| *Francis Anderſon,* Eſq; | 1425 | 13 | 01½ |
| *Hugh Anderſon,* Eſq; | 131 | 05 | 05 |
| *John Aſhton* | 60 | 08 | 08 |
| *Richard Butler* | 382 | 08 | 07¼ |
| Lord *Bolinbrooke* | 2552 | 15 | 00 |
| *Richard Billſborough* | 19 | 10 | 00 |
| *Thomas Briers* | 91 | 18 | 00 |
| *Robert Cowper* | 20 | 00 | 00 |
| *Richard Chorley,* Eſq;. | 138 | 12 | 00½ |
| *George Clifton* | 5 | 10 | 00 |
| *George Collingwood,* Eſq; | 924 | 10 | 00 |
| *Edward Core* | 19 | 12 | 06 |
| *Robert Daniel* | 8 | 00 | 00 |
| *John Dalton,* Eſq; | 661 | 19 | 06 |
| Earl of *Derwentwater* | 6371 | 04 | 05 |
| *Roger Dicconſon* | 641 | 16 | 10 |
| *Thomas Errington* | 328 | 00 | 00 |
| *Thomas Foſter,* jun. | 530 | 00 | 00 |
| *George Gibſon* | 227 | 00 | 00 |
| *John Gregſon* | 26 | 00 | 00 |
| *John Hall* | 70 | 00 | 00 |
| *Gabriel Hesketh* | 102 | 06 | 04 |
| *Gilbert Hodgſon* | 327 | 09 | 03 |
| *Philip Hodgſon* | 238 | 00 | 00 |
| *Jordan Langdale* | 79 | 00 | 00 |
| *John Leyburne* | 275 | 16 | 05 |
| Duke of *Ormond* | 21163 | 05 | 08 |
| *Henry Oxborough* | 507 | 17 | 07 |
| *John Parkinſon* | 5 | 17 | 06 |
| *William Paul* | 42 | 14 | 00 |
| *John Pleſſington* | 39 | 15 | 06 |
| *Robert Scariſbrick* | 388 | 03 | 04 |
| *William Shaftoe* | 784 | 00 | 00 |

*Richard*

|  | *l.* | *s.* | *d.* |
|---|---|---|---|
| Richard Sherburn | 32 | 10 | 00 |
| Ralph Shuttleworth | 7 | 10 | 00 |
| Richard Shuttleworth | 78 | 00 | 00 |
| Ralph Standish | 671 | 10 | $10\frac{1}{4}$ |
| James Singleton | 40 | 10 | 00 |
| Thomas Stanley | 246 | 18 | 10 |
| Lord Seaforth | 517 | 10 | 00 |
| Edward Swinburn | 305 | 00 | 00 |
| John Sturzaker | 10 | 00 | 00 |
| John Thornton | 1585 | 17 | 04 |
| Christopher Trap | 58 | 16 | 06 |
| Joseph Wadsworth | 12 | 00 | 00 |
| Thomas Walton | 97 | 00 | 00 |
| Thomas Walmsley | 51 | 17 | 06 |
| Lord Widdrington | 5154 | 06 | 10 |
| Edward Winkley | 226 | 10 | 08 |
| Richard Wythrington | 14 | 10 | 00 |
| Total | 47626 | 18 | $05\frac{1}{3}$ |
| Add to this the Total of the Scotch Estates, being | 29694 | 06 | 08 |
| The sum total of both | 77321 | 05 | $01\frac{1}{2}$ |
| These Estates at twenty Years Purchase amount to | 1546420 | 00 | 00 |
| Besides all which, *Francis Anderson's* Reversion after the Death of the Lady *Anderson, per Annum* | 400 | 00 | 00 |
| *Roger Dicconson* after the Death of *Samuel Richardson, per Annum* | 18 | 00 | 00 |
| *Thomas Foster,* jun. after his Father's Death, *per Annum* | 600 | 00 | 00 |

William

|  | *l.* | *s.* | *d.* |
|---|---|---|---|
| *William Paul,* Clerk, after the Death of his Mother, *per Annum.* | 14 | 00 | 00 |
| Lord *Seaforth,* remainder after Payment of Debts and Legacies of *Nicholas Kennet, per Annum* | 571 | 03 | 00 |
| Total | 1603 | 03 | 00 |
| Theſe Reverſions ſold at but ten Years Purchaſe amount to | 16030 | 00 | 00 |
| Timber to all theſe Eſtates computed together | 30000 | 00 | 00 |
| Beſides perſonal Eſtates, *&c.* ſeiz'd | 60000 | 00 | 00 |
| Total of theſe laſt Sums | 106030 | 00 | 00 |
| The which added to the above Total of | 1546420 | 00 | 00 |
| Makes all theſe Forfeitures amount to the total Sum of | 1652450 | 00 | 00 |

*Anno Dom.* 1717. *Reg.* 3. The Land Tax Act again.

Duties on Malt, *&c.* continu'd again.

An Act for redeeming the Duties and Revenues which were ſettl'd to pay off Principal and Intereſt on the Orders made forth on four Lottery-Acts paſs'd the ninth and tenth Years, and for eſtabliſhing a Fund for Payment of Annuities, *&c.* The general yearly Fund by this Act, to be 724849 *l.* 6 *s.* 10 *d.*

An

An Act for redeeming several Funds of the Governour and Company of the Bank of *England, &c.* and for obliging them to advance farther Sums, not exceeding 2500000 *l.* at 6 Pounds *per Cent.* &c.

An Act for redeeming the yearly Fund of the *South-Sea* Company, *&c.* and to raise for an Annuity or Annuities, at 5 *l. per Cent. per Annum*, any Sum, not exceeding two Millions, to be employ'd in lessening the national Debts and Incumbrances, *&c.*

*Anno Dom.* 1718. *Reg.* 4. The Land Tax continu'd.

Duties on Malt, *&c.* continu'd.

*Anno. Dom.* 1719. *Reg.* 5. Land Tax continu'd.
As also Duties on Malt, *&c.*

An Act for applying certain overplus Moneys, and further Sums to be rais'd, *&c.* By this Act 520000 *l.* were rais'd by Loans.

An Act for continuing certain Duties upon Coals and Culm, for establishing certain Funds to raise Money, as well to proceed in the building of new Churches, as also to compleat the Supply granted to his Majesty, *&c.* Money taken up by this Act not to exceed 360000 *l.*

An Act for redeeming the Fund appropriated for Payment of the Lottery Tickets, which were made forth for the Service of the Year 1718, *&c.* The Sum to be rais'd by this Act, was 778750 *l.*

*Anno Dom.* 1720. *Reg.* 6. Land Tax again.

Duties on Malt, *&c.* continu'd.

An Act for enabling the *South-Sea* Company to increase their present Capital Stock and Fund, by redeeming such publick Debts and Incumbrances as are therein mention'd, and for raising Money to be apply'd for lessening several of the publick Debts and Incumbrances, *&c.* By this, an immense Sum of Money was advanc'd, secur'd upon the continuing

ing of several Duties, too long to be particularly
mention'd.

An Act for making forth new Exchequer Bills,
not exceeding one Million, at a certain Interest.
This needs no Explanation.

An Act for laying a Duty upon wrought Plate,
and for applying Money arising from the clear Produce (by the Sale of forfeited Estates,) towards answering his Majesty's Supply, and for taking off the
Drawbacks upon Hops exported for *Ireland*; and
for Payment of Annuities to be purchas'd after the
Rate of four Pounds *per Cent. per Annum,* &c. The
Sum to be so rais'd by Annuities, was 312000 *l.*
the said Annuities at four Pounds *per Cent.* to be
paid out of the Duties arising by this Act.

*Anno Dom.* 1721. *Reg.* 7. Land Tax continu'd.

An Act for continuing the Duties on Malt, *&c.*
to raise Money by way of Lottery, for the Service
of the Year 1721, *&c.* The Sum given by this
Act 700000 *l.*

An Act for raising a Sum not exceeding 500000 *l.*
by charging Annuities at the Rate of five *per Cent.
per Annum* upon the Civil List Revenues, till redeem'd by the Crown, *&c.*

*Anno Dom.* 1722. *Reg.* 8. Land Tax continu'd.

Duties on Malt continu'd.

An Act for paying off and cancelling one Million
of *Exchequer* Bills, *&c.* And for issuing a further
Sum in *New-Exchequer* Bills towards his Majesty's
Supplies, *&c.* These Bills were to amount to one
Million.

It is here worth observing, that notwithstanding
all the Acts above mention'd for paying some Parts
of the publick Debts, this very Year 1722, they
seem to have been at an incredible Height; for Mr.
*Archibald Hutchinson,* a Member of the House of
Commons in his *Abstract of all the publick Debts re-*
                                                        *maining*

*maining due at* Michaelmas, 1722, gives us this following Total.

|  | *l.* | *s.* | *d.* |
|---|---|---|---|
| " By Account of the publick<br>" Debts at *Michaelmas* 1722,<br>" deliver'd to the House of<br>" Commons, they amount to | 54272387 | 5 | 7 |

*Anno Dom.* 1723. *Reg.* 9. The Land Tax conti-nu'd.

Duties on Malt, *&c.* continu'd.

An Act for reviving and adding two Millions to the Capital Stock of the *South-Sea* Company, and for reviving a proportional Part of the yearly Fund payable at the *Exchequer,* and for dividing their whole Capital (after such Division made) into two equal Parts or Moyeties; and for converting one of the said Moyeties into certain Annuities, for the Bene-fit of the Members, and for settling the remaining Mo-yety in the said Company, and for continuing for one Year longer the Provision formerly made, *&c.*

An Act for redeeming certain Annuities now pay-able by the Cashier of the Bank of *England,* at the Rate of 5 *l. per Cent. per Annum.*

An Act for the more easy assigning or transfer-ring certain redeemable Annuities payable at the *Exchequer,* by Indorsments on the standing Orders for the same.

An Act for granting an Aid to his Majesty by laying a Tax upon Papists, and for making other Persons, as upon due Summons shall refuse, or neg-lect to take the Oaths therein mention'd, to con-tribute towards the said Tax, for reimbursing to the Publick, part of the great Expences occasion'd by the late Conspiracies; and for discharging the Estates of Papists from the two third Parts of the Rents and Profits thereof, for one Year, and all the Arrears of the same, and from such Forfeitures as are therein more particularly defcrib'd. This Impofition was given for 100000 *l.* being one full third of all the Eftates of the *Roman* Catholicks, which they were to pay over and above the double Land Tax, and all other Taxes.

An Act to continue the Duties for encouragement of the Coinage of Money, &c.

*Anno Dom.* 1724. *Reg.* 10. An Act for granting an Aid to his Majefty by a Land Tax, in *Great Britain*, to be rais'd for the Service of the Year 1724.

Enacted, That the Sum of 1019324 *l.* 18 *s.* be rais'd in the Kingdom of *Great Britain*, according to the Proportions fet down in the Act. Towards the raifing the fame, all Perfons, Bodies Politick, &c. having Eftates in ready Money, or Debts, &c. or in Goods, Wares, Merchandizes, &c. or Perfonal Eftate (except fuch Sums as they *bona fide* owe, and defperate Debts, and Stocks on Land, and Houfhold-ftuff, and Loans or Debts owing from the King) fhall pay 2 *s. per* Pound, according to the Value thereof, (*i. e.*) For every hundred Pounds worth of fuch Money, and Debts or Perfonal Eftate 10 *s.* And all Perfons having any publick Employment of Profit, (except Military Officers) and their Clerks, Agents, &c. fhall pay 2 *s.* for every 20 *s.* they receive in one Year, for Salaries, Gratuities, &c. And all Perfons, Guilds, &c. having any Annuity, Penfion, Stipend, &c. out of the Receipt of the *Exchequer*, fhall pay 2 *s.* for every 20 *s.* by the Year, for every fuch Penfion, &c. All that refufe to take the Oaths to be double, except Quakers, who were to fubfcribe the Declaration of Fidelity.

An Act for continuing the Duties on Malt, Mum, Cyder and Perry, to raife Money by way of Lottery, for the Service of the Year 1724. And touch-

ing

ing loft Bills, Tickets, Certificates, or Orders; and for giving further Time for Payment of the Duties on Money given with Apprentices; and for appropriating the Supplies granted in this Seffion of Parliament.

The Rates and Proportions affign'd by this Act are the fame as in the former Acts of the fame Nature, and the Sum to be rais'd by it 763350 *l.* This to be rais'd by way of Lottery, at 10 *l. per* Ticket.

All the Monies granted this Seffion of Parliament fhall be appropriated, *viz.* 63634 *l.* 9 *s.* 9 *d.* to make good the Deficiency of the general Fund; 734622 *l.* 15 *s.* 10 *d.* for the Navy; 80000 *l.* for the Ordnance for Land Service; 923299 *l.* 2 *s.* 4 *d.* ⅘. for the Land Forces; 57301 *l.* 11 *s.* 8 *d.* ¼. to make good the Grants for the Year 1723.

An Act for repealing certain Duties therein mention'd, payable upon Coffee, Tea, Cacao Nuts, Chocolate, and Cacao Pafte imported, and for granting certain Inland Duties in lieu thereof; and for prohibiting the Importation of Chocolate ready made, and Cacao Pafte; and for the better afcertaining the Duties payable upon Coffee, Tea, and Cacao Nuts imported; and for granting Relief to *Robert Dalzell* late Earl of *Carnwath.*

The feveral Duties granted upon Coffee and Tea by the Acts 6 *W.* 3. and 3 *A.* and 10 *A.* and afterwards continu'd, and thofe on Cacao Nuts granted 6 *W.* 3. and 3 *A.* to determine and be no longer payable. The Duties paid before thofe Acts to continue, and in lieu of the latter here repeal'd, the following Inland Duties to be paid. On Coffee to be fold 2 *s, per* Pound, over and above all Duties remaining payable on Importation. On Tea 4 *s,* over and above as aforefaid. On Chocolate 1 *s.* 6 *d. per* Pound to be paid by the Makers or Sellers.

Having

Having carried on the Taxes to the end of the laſt Year, the ſumming of them up is left to the Curious, as are all other Remarks proper for this Subject.

*F I N I S.*